MEDIEVAL PURITY AND PIETY

GARLAND MEDIEVAL CASEBOOKS
VOLUME 19
GARLAND REFERENCE LIBRARY OF THE HUMANITIES
VOLUME 2006

Garland Medieval Casebooks

Joyce E. Salisbury and Christopher Kleinhenz, *Series Editors*

Sex in the Middle Ages
A Book of Essays
edited by Joyce E. Salisbury

Margery Kempe
A Book of Essays
edited by Sandra J. McEntire

The Medieval World of Nature
A Book of Essays
edited by Joyce E. Salisbury

The Chester Mystery Cycle
A Casebook
edited by Kevin J. Harty

Medieval Numerology
A Book of Essays
edited by Robert L. Surles

Manuscript Sources of
Medieval Medicine
A Book of Essays
edited by Margaret R. Schleissner

Saint Augustine the Bishop
A Book of Essays
edited by Fannie LeMoine and
Christopher Kleinhenz

Medieval Christian
Perceptions of Islam
A Book of Essays
edited by John Victor Tolan

Sovereign Lady
*Essays on Women in
Middle English Literature*
edited by Muriel Whitaker

Food in the Middle Ages
A Book of Essays
edited by Melitta Weiss Adamson

Animals in the Middle Ages
A Book of Essays
edited by Nona C. Flores

Sanctity and Motherhood
*Essays on Holy Mothers
in the Middle Ages*
edited by Anneke B. Mulder-Bakker

Medieval Family Roles
A Book of Essays
edited by Cathy Jorgensen Itnyre

The Mabinogi
A Book of Essays
edited by C.W. Sullivan III

The Pilgrimage to Compostela
in the Middle Ages
A Book of Essays
edited by Maryjane Dunn and
Linda Kay Davidson

Medieval Liturgy
A Book of Essays
edited by Lizette Larson-Miller

Medieval Purity and Piety
*Essays on Medieval Clerical
Celibacy and Religious Reform*
edited by Michael Frassetto

Hildegard of Bingen
A Book of Essays
edited by Maud Burnett McInerney

Julian of Norwich
A Book of Essays
edited by Sandra J. McEntire

Medieval Purity and Piety
Essays on Medieval Clerical Celibacy and Religious Reform

Edited by
Michael Frassetto

Garland Publishing, Inc.
a member of the Taylor & Francis Group
New York and London
1998

Library of Congress Cataloging-in-Publication Data

Medieval purity and piety : essays on medieval clerical celibacy and religious
reform / edited by Michael Frassetto.
        p.   cm. — (Garland reference library of the humanities ; v. 2006.
Garland medieval casebooks ; v. 19.)
    Includes bibliographical references and index.
    ISBN 0-8153-2430-8 (alk. paper)
    1. Celibacy—Catholic Church—History.   2. Church history—Middle
Ages, 600–1500.   3. Catholic Church—Clergy—Sexual behavior—History.
I. Frassetto, Michael.   II. Series: Garland reference library of the
humanities ; vol. 2006.   III. Series: Garland reference library of the
humanities. Garland medieval casebooks ; vol. 19.
BV4390.M43   1998
253'.252'0902—dc21   97-32004
                                                       CIP

Printed on acid-free, 250-year-life paper
Manufactured in the United States of America

Contents

Acknowledgments

Like many such essay collections, this volume began as a discussion among scholars. Unlike many similar discussions, however, this exchange occurred electronically on the discussion list mediev-l and it is to the many participants in that original conversation that this volume owes its genesis. Despite its rather unconventional origins, the successful completion of this volume is due to the very conventional, and enthusiastic, support of many friends and colleagues, old and new. I should like first to thank my series editor, Joyce Salisbury, whose inspiration and encouragement guided this volume from its inception to its completion. Certainly this volume would not have been completed without the diligence and patience of its contributors, and I would like to thank them for their help and the many insights their efforts have provided me. I should offer a special note of thanks to one of the contributors, Daniel Callahan, who has been a long-standing source of encouragement. Also, I owe a debt of gratitude to my colleague, Steve Weaver, who has managed to find more than a few obscure articles that I have needed for my work. Special thanks too to Chris Ingersoll of Hamilton College, and to my student, Laura Dean, and to the staff of Garland Publishing, especially Chuck Bartelt, who have provided much help to me in the final editing of this volume. I am grateful, too, to the editors of *Rivista di Storia e Letteratura Religiosa* for their permission to publish Maureen Miller's essay which first appeared in their fine journal. Finally, I would be remiss if I failed to offer my deepest and most heartfelt thanks to Jill for her support in the completion of this volume and other things too numerous to mention.

Michael Frassetto

Introduction

Michael Frassetto

The Apostle Paul once wrote "It is better to marry than to burn."(1
Cor. 7:9) This simple statement provided guidance for many
Christians for centuries after the apostolic age and continues to form
part of the rationale behind the church's official sanctification of
marriage. The church's response to Paul's injunction, however, was
as ambivalent as Paul's own example was. Even though the Apostle
approved of marriage, he did so only for those who were unable to
avoid the temptations of the flesh and who could not live by the
higher standard of chastity as Paul himself did.[1] Indeed, from the
early days of the Christian church the cult of virginity was held in
high esteem by the ecclesiastical elite and was deemed the purer,
truer form of Christian life.[2] Although the church held that the
better path was that of a life of celibacy, like Paul, it continued to
approve of marriage as an acceptable way of life.

This uncertain attitude toward marriage and sexual relations
within marriage would come to cause difficulties for the church
militant as it adapted itself to a worldly mission and would cause
one of the great questions of its first millennium to emerge: should
the leaders of the faithful, the priests and bishops, be allowed to
marry? This question, so basic to the organization of the church and
its spiritual mission, would shape the history of the church
throughout its first ten centuries of existence and continues to
concern Catholic leaders in our own day. The development of the
church's teaching on clerical celibacy is, thus, one of the central
problems of church history and a question of great controversy. It is
a controversy whose origins can be found in the ambiguous
teachings of Paul and can be traced through the lives of the early

saints and leaders of the monastic movement to the commentaries of the Latin Fathers and the reforms of the Carolingian church. In many ways, however, the turning point in regard to the creation of the law of clerical celibacy may be found in the great revolution of the tenth to the twelfth centuries and especially with that era's Gregorian reform movement.[3] It was during the Gregorian reform that the centuries -long debate over clerical marriage reached its culmination.[4] The leaders of this movement sought to resolve this issue by declaring all incontinent clerics anathema, a resolution that came to be the accepted policy of the church during the twelfth century. It is the history of the medieval church's response to the issue of the propriety of clerical marriage and of the long-standing and ongoing concern with clerical celibacy that forms the central theme of this book.

The history of the issue of clerical celibacy and, indeed, the history of that history is a long and complicated one as the essays by Edward Peters and Paul Beaudette show. In his essay, Peters demonstrates that the historiographic tradition of the issue of clerical celibacy is as complex and convoluted as the very question itself and one marred by the sectarianism of Catholic and Protestant scholars alike. It is only once the religious partisanship faded away and more critical scholarly motivations replaced it that the study of the development of the practice of clerical celibacy received the kind of attention it deserves. Although not without its biases, more recent scholarship has transcended the sectarianism of an earlier time and begun to explore the history of clerical celibacy in a much less polemical way. This exploration has turned not so much to the age of Paul and the era of the composition of the Gospels but, rather, to the fourth and fifth centuries as the moment when the efforts to establish a pure and chaste clergy began in earnest.[5] As Paul Beaudette argues, the roots of eleventh- and twelfth-century conciliar action can be traced to councils at Elvira and Rome, among others, during the course of the fourth and fifth centuries and at these councils many of the fundamental concerns about the purity of the priesthood were first expressed. These concerns indicate an awareness of the boundaries separating the sacred and the profane and a desire to adapt to the new, triumphant place of the church in fourth- and fifth-century society. Although similar concerns about the need for a ritually pure priesthood would be voiced throughout the next several centuries, it would, however, await later church leaders to build on this legacy and establish, finally, a celibate clergy.

It was during the central Middle Ages that ecclesiastical leaders began to refocus their attention on the question of marriage and the clergy and began a process of reform that would culminate in the Gregorian movement of the eleventh century.[6] But well before the so-called Gregorians began their assault on nicolaitism, as the practice of clerical marriage would be known, church leaders had begun to debate questions of clerical purity and clerical marriage. Indeed, as Mayke de Jong demonstrates, the issue of clerical purity was a critical concern of the Carolingian rulers and reformers. Moreover, as she notes, although the question of clerical celibacy was one of long standing, it took on new urgency and importance to Carolingian thinkers like Theodulf of Orleans. For this Carolingian bishop and for many of his contemporaries, the bodily purity of the priest was important not only for sacrifices at the altar but also for consecration of a king.

The precedents set in the Carolingian era provide an important foundation for subsequent reform efforts.[7] The pace of this reform, however, would quicken dramatically in the course of the tenth and early eleventh centuries and it was during this period that the great questions of the Gregorian movement came to be voiced. Indeed, especially in monastic circles, the tenth and eleventh centuries witnessed the renewed stirrings of religious reform and a return to the debate over the question of clerical celibacy.[8] Monastic leaders throughout western Christendom began to introduce reform in their houses in an effort to restore the original integrity of the religious life. Important initiatives were taken in many places but the most influential efforts were made at Cluny. It was the great abbots of that house who inspired far-reaching reforms of monastic life and directly or indirectly oversaw the introduction of the Cluniac model at monasteries throughout Francia in the tenth century. The reforms of Cluny resonated throughout society and opened the way for other reform efforts by the turn of the millennium, including the Peace of God movement. In many ways, therefore, the roots of the papal revolution of the eleventh century can be traced to the monastic developments of the tenth century.

Although long overlooked, the tenth and eleventh centuries were a period of important historical change, and a time in which the concerns with clerical celibacy and religious reform were raised by a number of monastic writers. The inspiration behind this renewed attention to clerical purity varied among these several writers but the question itself was an increasingly important one for them. For Odo of Cluny, as Phyllis Jestice suggests, chastity was a traditional monastic practice worthy of little attention for a monastic audience. But, Jestice notes, Odo had an audience outside the cloister for whom an extended discussion was necessary. Consequently, he devised a model of celibacy based on notions of ritual purity inspired by a desire that the clergy not pollute the altar or the Eucharist. For Abbo of Fleury, a reform-minded monk of the late tenth century, clerical celibacy remained an important issue, although for reasons very different than those inspiring Odo. As Elizabeth Dachowski shows, his concerns were motivated by a general interest in the social order and relations between the clergy and the laity. As with the Gregorian reformers of the coming generation, the issue of clerical celibacy was associated with questions of the social hierarchy and with ecclesiastical independence for Abbo. Also, as Dachowski shows, Abbo believed that the chastity of the monks demonstrated their moral superiority over the other orders of society and provided a boundary separating the clergy from the laity.

Monastic and episcopal writers of the early eleventh century continued the discussion of clerical purity begun by their predecessors in the tenth century. These writers, including Ademar of Chabannes and Gerard of Cambrai, addressed many of the same issues as did earlier commentators but were faced with new challenges as well. Around the year 1000, questions of morality and purity were raised by orthodox clerics and by heterodox dissenters.[9] In my essay, "Heresy, Celibacy, and Reform in the Sermons of Ademar of Chabannes," I argue that concerns with the revival of religious heresy led Ademar to consider questions of ritual purity, the sacraments and the relationship of the clergy and laity. David Van Meter, after surveying the attitudes of tenth-century writers, turns his attention to Gerard of Cambrai and the dissidents of that diocese. Like Ademar, the bishop of Cambrai used the appearance of the heretics as a starting point for discussions of broader social and religious issues. According to Van Meter, Gerard asserted episcopal rights against the heretics and also against members of the lay and monastic orders. In terms strengthened by apocalyptic language, Gerard stressed the sexual purity of the priesthood and the moral integrity and ecclesiastical authority of the bishops.

In many ways, Ademar, Gerard and the heretics heralded the Gregorian reform movement, the great revolution of the eleventh century. This movement, considered in the section entitled "Gregory VII, Celibacy, and the Eleventh-Century Revolution," had a far-reaching impact and addressed not only questions of clerical morality but also broader questions concerning the place of the church in the world and the relationship of the temporal and spiritual authorities. In "Property, Marriage, and the Eleventh-Century Revolution: A Context for Early Medieval Communism," R. I. Moore demonstrates the close interconnection between the social and economic changes of the eleventh century and religious reforms of the Gregorians and other spiritual leaders of that era. In this period, new forms of land tenure, new patterns of inheritance, and new marriage customs emerged. This social revolution, Moore observes, influenced religious attitudes throughout Christendom and led to religious reforms of both an orthodox and heterodox character. Throughout it all, the debate over who may properly live a life of celibacy raged and further refined social and economic relationships, especially between the laity and the clergy. Moreover, the issue of celibacy, according to Megan McLaughlin, was an underlying concern of the orthodox reformers as they came to define the relationship of the bishops to their churches and society as a whole. Indeed, the very questions of marriage and adultery, purity and incest that shaped the general social and religious debates among reformers in the eleventh century were associated with the episcopacy and the nature of its ties to the churches. And thus the image of the bishop as bridegroom came to be an important model for the reformers even though, as McLaughlin notes, it could only imperfectly serve in the struggle to create a celibate clergy.

It was, however, Pope Gregory VII (1073-1085)—the one whose name the reform movement bears—who traditionally has been seen to have exercised the greatest influence on religious reform in the eleventh century.[10] Gregory's struggles with the emperor, Henry IV, his efforts to establish "right order in the world," and his status as a champion of reform and the rights of St. Peter are well known. Unfortunately, his position as a "reformer" is all too often taken for granted, and there is a tendency to assume that he held particular positions without demonstrating that he did.[11] The essays by Uta-Renate Blumenthal and H. E. J. Cowdrey address this problem by considering Gregory's attitudes toward clerical celibacy. Before examining Gregory's contribution, Blumenthal summarizes the conciliar decisions of the earlier Middle Ages and of the first half of the eleventh century and also the activities of reformers of the mid-eleventh century. By placing Gregory's activities in this broader context she reminds us of the debt that he owed to his predecessors, especially Popes Leo IX (1048-1054) and Nicholas II (1059-1061). Moreover, it was the precedent of these popes and the importance of obedience to papal commands that formed the core of Gregory's support for clerical celibacy. For Blumenthal, his importance in the celibacy debate was his consistent enforcement of established papal policy and not the creation of a new ideal. Although not in complete disagreement with this view, Cowdrey affords Gregory a more positive role in the promotion of the ideal of clerical celibacy. Gregory did indeed enforce the policy consistently, first in his letters and then through his legates, but he also offered a new justification for the policy not found in the works of earlier theorists. This pope, Cowdrey notes, advocated the celibate ideal on moral and spiritual grounds and not in terms of cultic purity. Indeed, for Gregory, the salvation of priests' souls and the right order of the world were rooted in the practice of chastity. Despite some differences of emphasis, it is clear that both Blumenthal and Cowdrey recognize Gregory's importance in the difficult process of the creation of a celibate priesthood.

The final section of this book examines the impact of the struggle for clerical celibacy on both medieval and modern society. Indeed, as Maureen Miller demonstrates, already in the eleventh century the effort to reform the clergy had significant consequences. As a result of the broader reform occurring in the eleventh century, clerics began to identify themselves in a new fashion. Formerly clerics identified themselves, as did all members of society, by reference to their kin groups. But, Miller notes, because the Gregorian reformers sought to separate the sacred from the profane—one of the underlying motivations for the creation of a celibate priesthood—the clerics began to identify themselves by reference to the churches to which they belonged. Thus, the celibacy movement and the new forms of clerical self-identification were designed to remove the clergy from involvement in secular society. In the coming generations, reaction to the reform movement was not limited to a clerical audience but was extended to a lay audience as well. As Francis G. Gentry observes, the ideals of the Gregorians and their hostility to corrupt clergy were repeated in the vernacular poetry of the twelfth-century writer Heinrich von Melk. Although most likely a monk himself, Heinrich nonetheless reveals lay attitudes in his poetry, written not in the learned language of the clergy but in the everyday language of the laity. His poetry repeats the condemnations of simony and clerical unchastity heard so often in the later eleventh century. Indeed, as Miller and Gentry show, the effort to create a celibate priesthood left a great mark on clerical and lay circles already in the course of the eleventh and twelfth centuries.

In their essays, Jane Tibbetts Schulenburg and Daniel F. Callahan examine the broader social and historical consequences of the reform movement and the effort to establish a celibate clergy. For Schulenburg, the reform efforts and attempts to establish clerical celibacy that occurred during the central Middle Ages, 900-1200, had a pronounced effect on gender relations. With the increase in popularity of pilgrimage and the cult of the saints during this period, women, as well as men, sought greater access to altars, saints' tombs and similar holy spaces. At the same time, however, the growing emphasis on cultic purity and clerical celibacy led religious leaders to enact ever greater proscriptions against women's access to these holy spaces because of the underlying notion of the impurity of women. Although, as Schulenburg notes, there were those who rejected these misogynistic practices, the church undertook repeated efforts to segregate women from holy spaces at the same time as it sought to create a celibate clergy. And, finally, as Callahan observes, the questions concerning the practice of clerical celibacy continue to plague the church today. Indeed, in his epilogue to this book, Callahan argues that the debate concerning clerical celibacy in the Middle Ages is a debate that continues to rage in the Catholic church. Many of the issues first raised a millennium ago continue to

receive attention and the personalities involved today seem to reflect
the attitudes and ideals of the Gregorians themselves.

As the essays in this volume demonstrate, the history of the
church's creation of a celibate priesthood is a long and complex one.
The roots of the movement can be traced to the Apostolic and
Patristic eras. But it was during the Middle Ages, beginning in the
eighth century and continuing with ever greater intensity from the
tenth to the twelfth centuries, that the attempt to create a celibate
clergy achieved its greatest success. Although the Gregorian
reformers emerged triumphant by the early twelfth century, the
debate over the clerical morality and sexual purity would remain a
central theme of the history of the church until our own day. It is
the history of that debate, particularly in its medieval incarnation,
that this volume will explore.

NOTES

1. 1 Cor. 7:7. "Volo autem omnes homines esse sicut me ipsum."

2. For the development of the church's attitude toward virginity and
the body, see Peter Brown, *The Body and Society: Men Women and Sexual
Renunciation in Early Christianity* (New York, 1988).

3. Useful introductions to the Gregorian Reform movement and to
questions of reform itself can be found in Uta-Renate Blumenthal, *The
Investiture Controversy: Church and Monarchy from the Ninth to the Twelfth
Century* (Philadelphia, 1988) and Gerd Tellenbach, *The Church in Western
Europe from the Tenth to the Early Eleventh Century*, trans. Timothy Reuter
(Cambridge, 1993).

4. For further discussion, see Anne Llewellyn Barstow, *Married Priests
and the Reforming Papacy: The Eleventh-Century Debates* (New York, 1982).

5. Of course, concerns with bodily purity and chastity were not
unknown to Paul and the primitive church but the question of celibacy and
the sacerdotal order would emerge only once the priestly order itself
became more clearly defined. On early Christian concerns with issue of the

body and purity, see Brown, *Body and Society*, pp. 33-64 and Elaine Pagels, *Adam, Eve, and the Serpent* (New York, 1989), 3-78.

6. Jeffery Burton Russell, *Dissent and Reform in the Early Middle Ages* (Berkeley, 1965) notes the existence of a reform movement stretching from the Carolingian age to the age of Gregory VII. Cautions concerning the term "reform" and the nature of eleventh-century reform are raised by Maureen Miller, *The Formation of a Medieval Church: Ecclesiastical Change in Verona, 950-1150* (Ithaca, NY, 1993), 175-77 and Tellenbach, *The Church in Western Europe*, pp. 157-62.

7. On the importance of discerning the links between the Carolingian era and the later Middle Ages, see Richard E. Sullivan, "The Carolingian Age: Reflections on Its Place in the History of the Middle Ages," *Speculum* 64 (1989): 267-306.

8. The connection of monastic reform and Gregorian reform has been noted by many scholars, including H. E. J. Cowdrey, *The Cluniacs and Gregorian Reform* (Oxford, 1970) and Augustin Fliche, *La Réforme grégorienne*, 3 vols. (Paris, 1924-37).

9. See Antoine Dondaine, "L'origine de l'hérésie médiévale," *Rivista di storia della chiesa in Italia*, 6 (1952): 47-78; Malcolm Lambert, *Medieval Heresy: Popular Movements from the Gregorian Reform to the Reformation*, 2nd ed. (Oxford, 1992), and R. I. Moore, *The Origins of European Dissent*, rev. ed. (Oxford, 1985) for useful introductions to the question of the rebirth of heresy in the early eleventh century.

10. The classic statement of this view is Fliche, *La Réforme grégorienne*, 3 vols. but see the cautions of Miller, *Formation of a Medieval Church*, pp. 9-14.

11. For general considerations of Gregory and the Reform movement, see Blumenthal, *The Investiture Controversy*; Cowdrey, *The Cluniacs and Gregorian Reform*; and idem, *The Age of Abbot Desiderius: Montecassino, the Papacy, and the Normans in the Eleventh and Early Twelfth Centuries* (Oxford, 1983) and Tellenbach, *The Church in Western Europe*, esp. 185-252.

Abbreviations

AASS		*Acta sanctorum quotquot toto orbe coluntur.* Ed. Jean Bolland et al.
Annales ESC		*Annales: Economies, Sociétés, Civilisations*
CCSL		*Corpus Christianorum, Series Latina*
Mansi		*Sacrorum conciliorum nova, et amplissima collectio*, 31 vols. Ed. Giovanni Mansi
MGH		*Monumenta Germaniae Historica*, with subseries:
	Capit	*Capitularia regum Francorum*
	Capit Ep	*Capitularia episcoporum*
	Conc	*Concilia*
	Const	*Constitutiones*
	Epp	*Epistolae*
	Poet Lat	*Poetae latini*
	SS	*Scriptores*
	SSrMerov	*Scriptores merovingicarum*
PG		*Patrologia cursus completus series Graeca*, 162 vols. Ed. J.-P. Migne
PL		*Patrologia cursus completus series Latina*, 221 vols. Ed. J.-P. Migne

History and Historiography

History, Historians, and Clerical Celibacy

Edward Peters

The first extensive debates about the problem of clerical celibacy in the Latin Christian church in the later Middle Ages took place in the exchange between Guillaume Saignet and Jean Gerson early in the fifteenth century, and the topic worked its way briefly onto the agenda of the Council of Constance.[1] But the early modern historiography of the topic began a century later in the Reformation polemics over the questions of the nature of the priesthood and the sacraments.[2] As a substantial part of Reformation polemic--both between Protestants and Catholics and within the Roman Catholic church itself--increasingly came to include competing historical views of the Latin Christian church, the history of the doctrine of clerical celibacy became part of that historical polemic, and out of it emerged most of the post-sixteenth-century literature on the subject.[3] The polemical circumstances of these debates have characterized much of the historiography of the problem down to the present.

Beginning with Luther's discussion of the sacraments in *On the Babylonian Captivity of the Church* and *To the Christian Nobility of the German Nation* in 1520 and his analysis of marriage in *On Monastic Vows* and other works shortly after, the topic of clerical celibacy (including, but not restricted to clerical marriage) emerged first in sacramental theology and then in practice. Andreas Karlstadt announced his own betrothal in 1521, and several of Luther's other followers also married, including Bartholomew Bernhardi in Saxony later in the same year. Zwingli's petition to the Bishop of Constance to permit clerical marriage in 1522 raised the problem in the Swiss Confederation, followed by Zwingli's Theses 28-30 in the Zurich debate in 1523 and his own marriage in 1522 (but not made public

until 1524). By 1525 the Reformation challenge to earlier doctrines
of clerical celibacy was launched in practice as well as theory. The
marriages of Karlstadt, Bernhardi, Zwingli, Matthew Zell, Wolfgang
Capito, Martin Bucer, Luther himself, and John Calvin placed an
emphatic Reformation seal of approval on the practice of clerical
marriage, particularly after the public marriage of Zell in Strasbourg
cathedral in 1523 and the subsequent excommunication of eight
married priests by the bishop of Strasbourg in 1524.

Clerical marriage thus quickly emerged as one of the new battle-
lines in Reformation Europe. By 1534 Lutheran-converted bishops
were married in Hungary; two years later clerical celibacy was
abolished in Sweden by the Diet of Uppsala; clerical marriage was
conceded to dissenting Christians in the Augsburg Interim in 1530;
in 1549 the English Parliament passed an act permitting clergy to
marry. Although arguments against clerical celibacy were made both
by the circle of Erasmus and later at the Council of Trent by such
orthodox rulers as Frederick of Habsburg, emperor and king of
Bohemia and Hungary as well as by other Catholic princes, they
failed spectacularly; in its penultimate session (*Sessio* XXIV, 11
November, 1563, cc. 9, 10), the Council reasserted the spiritual
superiority of the celibate life and condemned all sexual activity on
the part of clergy.[4] Although both Protestants and Roman Catholics
condemned clerical (and lay) sexual activity outside marriage, in the
case of the latter, particularly clerical concubinage, whether private
or publicly acknowledged, clerical marriage remained the focus of
the conflict. In practice and in theory the problem of clerical
celibacy--with marriage as its focus--was solved in one way by most
Protestant confessions and in the opposite way by Roman Catholics.
Both positions reached deeply into both biblical literature and
ecclesiastical history, as has most of the historiography since. The
history of that historiography is thus complex, often angry, always
fascinating, and singularly unenlightening by modern historical
standards.

The Reformation divide remained relatively unchanged through
the late sixteenth and seventeenth centuries.[5] But that divide was
easier to maintain in theory than in practice. Much of the work of
the seventeenth-century Spanish Inquisition, for example, focused on
the sexual misbehavior of the clergy, and the extensive records of the
Inquisition constitute the bulk of surviving evidence for the problem

of clerical celibacy, including solicitation in the confessional, a topic that fueled later Protestant criticisms of Roman Catholicism and produced a lurid and polemical literature on the subject.[6] Denunciations of clerical sexuality appeared regularly in France during the same period.[7] It was next troubled by Enlightenment criticism of the institution in the work of Bayle, Montesquieu, Voltaire, and Rousseau, by Diderot's article in the *Encyclopédie*, and by the attack on clerical celibacy by the French Priest Pierre Desforges in his *On the Advantages of Marriage* in 1758, based on the theory of the priesthood of all believers, Enlightenment ideas of nature, reason, and human rights, and generally critical of ecclesiastical authority, all criticisms relying heavily on both theoretical and historical arguments.[8] Desforges' work earned him a stay in the Bastille, the burning of his book, and an attack in the *Apologie du célibat chretien* by the Abbé de Villiers in 1761.[9] But it did not stop criticism of celibacy on the grounds that it contradicted church tradition, as the work by Jacques Gaudin, *Les inconvénients du célibat des prêtres*, published at Geneva in 1781, reveals. In addition, the complaints of Malabar Christians against the Latinization of their rites, including the imposition of clerical celibacy, indicate further the complexities of the late eighteenth century.[10]

The renewal of widespread discussion of the topic led Clement XIII to charge the Jesuit polemicist Francesco Antonio Zaccaria with the defence of celibacy, and Zaccaria produced the *Polemical History of Holy Celibacy* in 1774 (German translation in 1781). As Owen Chadwick has said of the work "Zaccaria was a splitter of hairs and forced bits of the history to dance to his fingers as he pulled them hither and thither. But it was a masterly defence. Every Catholic who wanted now to argue for a married priesthood had to face this collection of embattled information."[11] Zaccaria did not silence everyone. Arguments in favor of and against clerical celibacy sprung up in a number of areas of the German-speaking world in the later eighteenth century, including a Febronianist pamphlet literature in Austria in the 1780s.[12] The vast process of the secularization of priests during the French Revolution and shortly afterward in Italy and Germany and by the restoration of Catholicism in France in 1801 and the general restorations after the Congress of Vienna in 1815 raised the question yet once again. The careers and opinions of such figures as Talleyrand, on the one hand, and Giuseppe Capecelatro (1744-1836), archbishop of Taranto, on the other, suggest that Josephine Austria was not the only Roman Catholic territory in which married clergy were ecclesiastically laicized or actually preferred.[13] But, as Chadwick has pointed out, Catholics increasingly associated clerical marriage with the radical republicanism of the revolutionary era, and the discussions of the late eighteenth and early nineteenth century found few adherents inside Catholicism. They had also virtually exhausted the polemical method of historical argument.

The modern historiography of the subject began in 1828 with the publication of the *Introduction of Compulsory Celibacy* by the brothers Johan Anton (1799-1860) and Augustin (1804-1874) Theiner of the university of Breslau.[14] Johan Anton was professor of exegesis and canon law at Breslau, and Augustin, who had begun the research and became a historian in the process, later became the Vatican Archivist and the continuator of Baronius' earlier history of the church.[15] By the second quarter of the nineteenth century, the disciplines of biblical exegesis, church history, and the history of canon law had begun to develop rigorous methodologies and assume a professional as well as a confessional character, and thus they became part of the movement of scholarship away from the pure service of philosophical and confessional ideologies and toward an independent and authoritative status.[16] The work of the Theiner brothers, although it argued a political position opposed to clerical celibacy, was nevertheless argued on a scholarly level considerably higher than virtually all earlier discussion of the topic and it offered a methodology for dealing with such massive collections of source materials as that of Zaccaria. If, after Zaccaria, all writers on the subject were compelled to address an accumulation of historical data, after the Theiner brothers all writers on the subject were compelled to deal with that data as learnedly and professionally as they. But learned though it was, the Theiner's history was nevertheless also polemical, and it touched upon a matter widely discussed throughout Germany and elsewhere in Europe. With the petition on the part of twenty-three Catholic laymen to the lower house of the Baden Parliament, also in 1828, that celibacy be abolished for

Catholic priests, the linking of the theory, history, and practice of clerical celibacy in increasingly secularizing states entered the modern age.[17]

Opposition to the position of the Theiner brothers was not long in coming. In 1830 Theodor Friedrich Klitsche published his *Geschichte des Cölibats der katholischen Geistlichen, von der Zeiten der Apostel bis zum Tode Gregors VIII.* Klitsche's uncritical reliance on the work of Zaccaria as well as that of the Theiners, however, provided no real answer to the latter's work. But the two-volume study by Friedrich Wilhelm Carové, *Über das Cölibatsgesetz des römischkatholischen Klerus*, which appeared in 1832, and itself expressed a sensitive and ambiguous attitude toward the institution of celibacy, stood far closer to the scholarly level of the work of the Theiners. 1832 also saw the publication of Gregory XVI's encyclical *Mirari vos*, which essentially repeated the decisions of Trent.[18] The massive bibliography by Augustin Roskovány, bishop of Neutra, *De matrimonio in ecclesia catholica* in 1840 and Roskovány's later immense bibliographical works summed up the enormous literature of the controversy to its date.[19]

From the late eighteenth century, the cultural context of the confessional, legal, and theological polemics and scholarship were broadened by another literary genre and a new sensibility, the Gothic novel and its fascination with the mysterious and erotic power of religion, particularly (with great emphasis on the psychological consequences of mandatory clerical celibacy) Roman Catholicism.[20] Matthew Lewis's *The Monk* of 1796 argued that priestly celibacy caused priests to abuse women, and its central figure, Ambrosio, was a powerful example of the dangers of the practice and its complex relation to a sexuality transformed by celibacy into a demonic force.

Such concerns found a particular reception in the United States, where the role of Roman Catholicism became a major concern in the early decades of the nineteenth century.[21] Harriet Beecher Stowe's novel, *Agnes of Sorrento*, of 1861-1863 reflects some of this concern, as does the dispute over clerical authority and trusteeship a few decades earlier.[22] One of the centers of these concerns was Philadelphia, where the Catholic priest William Hogan led a schismatic revolt against episcopal authority in the early 1820s and later published several vitriolic attacks on Catholicism, including *A*

Synopsis of Popery as It Was and Is (Hartford, 1847) and *Auricular Confession and Popish Nunneries* (2 vols., Hartford, 1847).

In the wake of the Hogan schism, the nativist anti-Catholic riots in the city in 1844, and the growing general concern over massive Catholic immigration and its impact, real or imagined, on the United States, the young Philadelphia publisher and historian, Henry Charles Lea, turned from his earlier interest in medieval English and French history toward what he later called "the inner life" of medieval Europeans focusing first on the history of law and then on that of Latin Christianity.[23] The first fruits of Lea's new research were the essays and reviews published as *Superstition and Force* in 1866. The next result, however, was a very different and entirely unexpected book, *An Historical Sketch of Sacerdotal Celibacy in the Christian Church*, which appeared in 1867. Because Lea's work is usually considered the starting-point of more recent Anglophone historiography, it is appropriate to consider it here at some length.

Lea appears to have done the research and written the text during the years of his involvement in the publishing business of his family and his extensive work on behalf of the Union cause during the Civil War. He remarked in the Preface that,

> The following work was written several years since, simply as a historical study, and with little expectation of its publication. Recent movements in several portions of the great Christian Church seem to indicate, however, that a record of ascetic celibacy, as developed in the past, may not be without interest to those who are watching the tendencies of the present.

Acknowledging the absence of such a work in English and dismissing Continental literature as being "exclusively of a controversial character," Lea proposed simply to "state facts as I found them, without regard to their bearing on either side of the questions involved."[24]

Lea's "sketch" was 601 pages long and ranged from the primitive church to Lea's own day. It was introduced by two chapters on the "Influence of the Church on Modern Civilization," and the "Effect of Celibacy in Moulding Its Destiny." The book was the second step on Lea's long career as a historian of medieval and early modern Latin Christianity, which culminated in his vast studies of confession and indulgences and the inquisitions of medieval Europe and early modern Spain. Lea's work was generally very well received in both the United States and England. W. E. H. Lecky praised it in his *History of European Morals* of 1869, and Henry Milman, then the leading church historian in Britain, praised it in a letter to Lea. An otherwise favorable review in the *Quarterly Review* of 1869 chided Lea for having failed to acknowledge the work of his scholarly predecessors, particularly the brothers Theiner. Lea replied in a letter to the *Nation* that he did not trust works of secondary scholarship, preferring to work directly from the sources, that he did not know of the Theiner work, and that at the time he did not read German. Lea continued his work with *Studies in Church History* in 1869, but he returned to the subject of clerical celibacy in revising the *Sketch* in later years and in his *A History of Auricular Confession and Indulgences* of 1896.

Lea's historical method was original and self-taught and, he argued, objective, but he wrote about the history of the Latin church with an eye constantly on his own time. His later essays on "The Religious Reform Movement in Italy" and on other explicitly contemporary ecclesiastical themes reveal a deep concern with Roman Catholic affairs. As he wrote to Lecky in 1869,

> The more I investigate the history of the Church the less easy do I find it to preserve the proper amount of toleration for intolerance, and the warmer become my convictions of the evils which have sprung from the vast theological structure erected upon the simple and sublime primal truths of Christianity.[25]

Although Lea developed a fine sense of the complexity of medieval and even early modern church history, his concern with the role of the church in his own day was acute, and it often colored his analysis of the past.

Lea's work, treating the entire history of the western church and sweeping across all of Europe down to Lea's own day, opened the subject to both Anglophone historians and polemicists. And it did not go unnoticed on the Continent. The great historian of canon law, Johann Friedrich von Schulte, noted Lea's work in his short pamphlet, *Der Cölibatszwang und dessen Aufhebung* of 1876, which strongly opposed the practice. Friedrich Nippold, in his introduction to the 1892 reprint of the work of the Theiners, called Lea's book , "the best work on the same historical subject," since that of the Theiner brothers.

But the political and ecclesiological contexts in which both early polemics and recent histories were produced were changing rapidly in the later nineteenth century. Disputes within the Roman Catholic church preceded and followed the First Vatican Council in 1870 and its assertion of papal infallibility. Catholic reform movements in Germany, France, and Italy invoked clerical celibacy as a major component of reform, and church history again became one of the battlefields. The work of the Theiners and Lea was often pressed into service in various causes, not always historical.[26] A striking example of such uses is the appropriation of the theme of sexual solicitation in the confessional from the now-unfashionable Gothic novel by anticlerical and anti-Catholic polemicists in both pamphlet and novel. Michel Morphy's *Les mystères de la pornographie cléricale* of 1884 and the work of Léo Taxil and others, including the historians Jules Michelet and Salomon Reinach, continued the theme through the late nineteenth century, and their successors brought it into the twentieth.[27]

Not only had the Theiner brothers and Lea worked up to the highest standards of nineteenth-century historical scholarship, but they had surveyed and brought into the discussion a vast mine of source material from the early church to the nineteenth century. Lea's *Sketch* appeared a year after he had finished acquiring his own set of the Abbé Migne's *Patrologia Latina*, whose 217 volumes Lea claimed (truthfully) to have read in preparing his work. The two exhaustive works of 1828 and 1867 thus dealt with virtually all the known sources on the subject up to the time of their appearance. In the course of the nineteenth century, however, the publication of patristic and medieval sources increased at a rapid rate, especially in the publication program of the *Monumenta Germaniae Historica* (*MGH*), and later work on the subject would have to take these new sources as well as developments in the disciplines of biblical scholarship, early church history, and canon law into account if the subject were to be advanced beyond the point to which the Theiner brothers and Lea had brought it.[28]

One of the earliest steps in this process was taken by Franz Xaver Funk in a series of articles between 1879 and 1897.[29] With a powerful display of the most highly developed late nineteenth-century scholarship, Funk simply brushed away the old argument that priestly celibacy dated from the apostolic period and dated the practice to the fourth century.[30] Funk's argument found acceptance among all serious scholars on both sides of the issue, including Elphège Vacandard and Henri Leclercq in influential articles in standard reference works, Vacandard in the article on celibacy in the *Dictionnaire de théologie catholique* in 1905 and Leclercq in an article in the *Histoire des conciles* of 1908.[31] By the turn of the twentieth century, thanks in large part to the work of the Theiner brothers, Lea, and Funk, the study of the history of clerical celibacy had largely left the confessional and polemical planes for that of historical scholarship, where it has generally since remained.

The consequences of this body of work are found not only in the particular histories of doctrine and canon law but also in the greatly revised picture of the vast program of moral and political reform of the late eleventh century commonly termed the Investiture Conflict. The work of Vacandard lay behind the treatment of clerical celibacy in the first great history of the Investiture Conflict in this century, Augustin Fliche's *La réforme grégorienne*, which appeared in three volumes between 1924 and 1937.[32] The subject was further developed in the wide-ranging and subsequently classic intellectual history by Gerd Tellenbach, *Libertas: Kirche und Weltordnung im Zeitalter des Investiturstreites*, which appeared in 1936 and was translated into English by R.F. Bennett in 1940 as *Church, State, and Christian Society at the Time of the Investiture Contest*.[33] Tellenbach argued that one of the principal figures of the conflict, Gregory VII, was concerned with far more than moral reform and that clerical purity was part of his larger and governing concept of world order. Tellenbach also emphasized the wide use of a vocabulary of violent sexuality in the polemics of the conflict. Tellenbach's English translator, R.F. Bennett, criticized the exclusively moral focus of Fliche.[34] Subsequent work on the question, particularly that of James Brundage, has considerably clarified Gregory VII's stand on the issue as well as Gregory's views

on human sexuality generally.[35] The history of the doctrine of
clerical celibacy from Gregory VII to the mid-thirteenth century in
canon law has been traced by Filippo Liotta, in the case of clerical
children by Bernhard Schimmelpfennig, and in both law and
hagiography most recently by Johannes Laudage.[36] The results of this
research from Fliche and Tellenbach to Liotta and Brundage have
greatly transformed our understanding not only of the issues and
intellectual context of the Investiture Conflict but also of the history
of doctrine, law, and the nature of clerical status itself in the history
of the Church and in European society generally.

In her study of the eleventh-century debates and papal and conciliar
legislation on the subject, Anne Llewellyn Barstow distinguishes
between "clerical marriage" and "priestly marriage," emphasizing
that the former designated all clerical orders, including minor
orders, while the latter referred specifically to those ordained to
perform the sacrament of the altar.[37] Her point emphasizes the wide
range of meaning possessed in medieval Europe by such terms, the
many meanings of "marriage" at the same time, and especially the
wide range of circumstances and religious sensibilities in which such
problems as sexual purity, religious dissent, and clerical celibacy
emerged. Her--and our--early Europe is a broader, deeper, and more
complex place and time than what was reflected in most of the
scholarship and polemic discussed thus far.

  In terms of theology and canon law, the Second Vatican Council
also stirred up a new discussion of the problem but in the context of
a scholarship very different from that available to the Council of
Trent and the First Vatican Council of 1870.[38] Once again, the topic
of clerical celibacy, now understood in the contexts cited by Barstow
and others, is on both the historian's and the believer's agendas.

  Barstow's study has reviewed the eleventh-century controversy
on the basis of new source materials, and, as important, from a much
wider perspective than legislation and law alone. As Barstow notes,
this broadening of the social context effectively dates from the early
studies of Arno Borst and Christopher Brooke in 1953 and 1956.[39]
Martin Boelens' study of the topic from early Christianity to the
early twelfth century incorporates virtually all recent scholarship,
with a focus on legislation.[40] Georg Denzler's extensive textual

survey of papal legislation on clerical celibacy deals with both the medieval and the modern church.[41]

The wave of new scholarship and broader general public concern during the past half century makes this a useful time to reconsider the state of a field of study that touched--and touches--a very broad range of social and religious life. If much of the historiography surveyed in this essay has indeed been polemical, complex, angry, and fascinating, it has been so because thinkers of all sorts have taken the subject seriously and have often held to their opinions somewhat more firmly than they needed to. But the seriousness and firmly held opinions on the subject of clerical celibacy also testify to the importance that the subject has held from the later Middle Ages to the present for both canonists and historians. Important subjects are inherently worth reviewing by new scholars. The historiography represented in this volume displays nothing of the polemic, limited perspectives, and ideological premises of most of the earlier historiography, and the subject will be the better for it.

NOTES

1. I am grateful to my colleague Thomas Max Safley for his generous reading of an earlier draft of this essay and his very helpful advice.

The fifteenth-century texts are edited and discussed in Nicole Grévy-Pons, *Célibat et nature: une controverse médiévale à propos d'un traité du début du XVe siècle* (Paris, 1975). Slightly earlier arguments are briefly noted in John H. Mundy, *Europe in the High Middle Ages, 1150-1309*, 2nd ed. (London-New York, 1991), 205; John E. Lynch, "Marriage and Celibacy of the Clergy. The Discipline of the Western Church: An Historico-Canonical Synopsis," *The Jurist* 32 (1972): 14-38, 189-212, at 206-207; Carol Edington, "'To speik of Preistis be sure it is na bourds': Discussing the Priesthood in Pre-Reformation Scotland," in *The Reformation of the Parishes: The Ministry and the Reformation in Town and Country*, ed. Andrew Pettegree (Manchester-New York, 1993), 22-42 at 37-38; Peter A. Dykema and Heiko A. Oberman, eds., *Anticlericalism in Late Medieval and Early Modern Europe* (Leiden-New York-Cologne, 1993), and James A. Brundage, *Law, Sex, and Christian Society in Medieval Europe* (Chicago, 1987), 474-77. Brundage offers a brief and reliable patristic and medieval history of the topic on pp. 69-70,

110-13, 150-52, 172, 182-87, 214-23, 251-53, 314-19, 342-43, 401-405, 488, particularly valuable because it is given in the broad context of sexuality and law in the medieval Christian tradition. The best general survey is that of A.M. Stickler, "L'évolution de la discipline du célibat dans l'Église en Occident de la fin de l'âge patristique au Concile de Trent, *Sacerdoce et célibat: Études historiques et théologiques*, ed. Joseph Coppens et al. (Gembloux-Louvain, 1971): 373-442. For the central period, see Jean Gaudemet, "Le célibat ecclésiastique. Le droit et la pratique du Xe au XIIIe siècle," *Zeitschrift der Savigny Stiftung für Rechtsgeschichte, Kanonistische Abteilung* 68 (1982): 1-31, rpt. in Gaudemet, *Eglise et société en Occident au Moyen Age* (London, 1984), XV. See now Monique Vleeschouwers-Van Melkebeek, "Mandatory Celibacy and Priestly Ministry in the Diocese of Tournai at the End of the Middle Ages," in *Peasants and Townsmen in Medieval Europe: Studia in Honorem Adriaan Verhulst*, ed. Jean-Marie Duvosquel and Erik Thoen (Ghent, 1995), 681-92.

There is an immense literature on Christian marriage itself. The international scholarship of the past two decades is represented in the bibliographies by Michael M. Sheehan and K.D. Scardellato, *Family and Marriage in Medieval Europe: A Working Bibliography* (Toronto, 1976) and Jean Gaudemet, *Sociétés et mariage* (Strasbourg, 1980), and in the following collections of papers: *Il Matrimonio nella Società altomedievale*, Settimane di Studio del Centro Italiano di Studi sull'Alto Medioevo, XXIV, 2 vols. (Spoleto, 1977), esp. Vol. II, 473-554; *Famille et parenté dans l'occident médiéval*, ed. Georges Duby and Jacques Le Goff, Collection de l'École française de Rome, 38 (Rome, 1977); *Love and Marriage in the Twelfth Century*, ed., Willy Van Hoecke and Andries Welkenhuysen, Mediaevalia Lovaniensia , Series I, Studia VIII (Leuven, 1981). Most recently, see Christopher Brooke, *The Medieval Idea of Marriage* (Oxford, 1989), and Philip Lyndon Reynolds, *Marriage in the Western Church: The Christianization of Marriage during the Patristic and Early Medieval Periods* (Leiden-New York-Cologne, 1994). For a still-debated study of one form of clerical marriage, see John Boswell, *Same-Sex Unions in Premodern Europe* (New York, 1994).

On the place of celibacy in medieval social thought, see Giles Constable, *Three Studies in Medieval Social and Religious Thought* (Cambridge, 1995), 249-360. The most recent study of the question and its history is Horst Fuhrmann, "'Edle Pfarrersfrau'--arme Pfarrersfrau," in Fuhrmann, *Überall ist Mittelalter. Von der Gegenwart einer vergangenen Zeit*

(Munich, 1996), 150-71, 290-92, with extensive bibliography on the historiography that supplements the discussion in this essay.

2. A concise and accurate account is that of August Franzen, *Zölibat und Priesterehe in der Auseinandersetzung der Reformationzeit und der katholischen Reform des 16. Jahrhunderts* (Münster, 1969). In the broader context, Euan Cameron, *The European Reformation* (Oxford, 1991), 115, 148-51, 402-405. For the early stages, see Erwin Iserloh, Josef Glazik, Hubert Jedin, *Reformation Katholische Reform und Gegenreformation, Handbuch der Kirchengeschichte*, Hubert Jedin, ed., Vol. IV (Freiburg-Basel-Vienna, 1975), 86-88; Lynch, "Marriage and Celibacy," 207-10; Joseph Coppens, "Érasme et le célibat," and J.-P. Massaut, "Vers la Réforme catholique. Le célibat dans l'idéal sacerdotal de Josse Clichtove," both in Coppens et al., ed., *Sacerdoce et célibat*, 443-58 and 459-506, and Brundage, 552-61.

3. On the argument within the Roman Catholic church at the Council of Trent, see Egidio Ferasin, *Matrimonio e celibato al Concilio di Trento* (Rome, 1970); F. L. Johnson and A. J. Weideman, "The Crisis of Celibacy at the Council of Trent," in *The Law on Celibacy: Soundings from Its History* (St. Meinrad, Indiana, 1966): 45-72; and Brundage, 567-69. Some of the continuing polemical character of the topic within the Roman Catholic church is indicated in the critical review article by Alfons M. Stickler, "A New History of Papal Legislation on Celibacy," *Catholic Historical Review* 65 (1979): 76-84. Further work by Stickler is cited in Fuhrmann, "'Edle Pfarrersfrau'," 290. A recent theological meditation is that of Ghislain Lafont, "The Institution of Religious Celibacy," in *The Future of the Religious Life*, ed. Peter Huizing and William Bassett, Concilium, Vol. 97 (New York, 1974/5), 49-58.

4. Before Trent there appeared a treatise by Robert Ceneau, Bishop of Oristano, entitled *Pro tuendo sacro celibatu axioma catholicum* (Paris, 1545). The same year saw published in Strasbourg the anonymous *Concubinarii. Underricht aus Götlichen und Gaistlichen Rechten ob ein Priester ein Eheweyb oder Concubin das ist ein beyschläfferin haben mög*. Most of the works of the sixteenth through the nineteenth centuries cited here and below are in the Special Collections section of the Van Pelt Library, University of Pennsylvania.

5. Examples of the Catholic literature of the period are: Cornelius Sas, *Oecumenicum De singularitate clericorum* (Brussels, 1653), written by a canon of Ypres and dedicated to the archbishop of Mechelen; Vincenzo Luigi Gotti, *Colloquia theologico-polemica in tres classes distributa* (Bologna,1727), a collection of "colloquies" in defense of clerical celibacy, papal authority, and miscellaneous doctrines, of which the first eighteen are devoted to the question of celibacy; Théophile Raynaud, *Dissertatio de sobria alterius sexus frequentatione per sacros et religiosos homines* (Lyons, 1653).

The literature on the topic in the late sixteenth and seventeenth centuries has not been studied nearly as closely as the literature of the eighteenth and nineteenth centuries. There is a very brief summary by the Conseil de Rédaction of the volume *Sacerdoce et célibat*, "Le célibat sacerdotal dans l'Église latine de Trente à nos jours," 335-45.

6. Michèle Escamilla-Colin, *Crimes et chatiments dans l'espagne inquisitoriale*, 2 vols. (Paris, 1992), Vol. II, 155-214. See also the excellent study by Stephen Haliczer, *Sexuality in the Confessional: A Sacrament Profaned* (New York-Oxford, 1996), esp. 183-203, a book that draws heavily on both archival records and the later polemical literature.

7. For France, see E. G. Léonard, *Histoire général du Protestantisme*, Vol. II, *L'établissement* (Paris, 1961).

8. On these arguments, see Paul Picard, *Zölibatsdiskussion im katholischen Deutschland der Aufklärungszeit. Auseinandersetzung mit der kanonischen Vorschrift im Namen der Vernunft und der Menschenrechte* (Düsseldorf, 1975): for Bayle, 26-29; Montesquieu 29-35; Voltaire 45-47; Rousseau 47-56; Diderot 35-45. On Desforges, see 57-66. On Catholic responses to arguments based on the rights of man generally, see Bernard Plongeron, "Anathema or Dialogue? Christian Reactions to Declarations of the Rights of Man in the United States and Europe in the Eighteenth Century," in *The Church and the Rights of Man*, ed., Alois Müller and Norbert Greinacher, Concilium, Vol. 124 (New York, 1979), 39-48. One of the most peculiar pieces in the controversy is the treatise addressed to Julius III by the alleged Russian priest Stanislas Orichow, *Il Celibato contrario ai*

precetti di natura e della religione cristiana (Milan, 1798). An English example is the anonymous *Essay on Celibacy* (London, 1753).

9. On Desforges and de Villiers, see Picard, 57-68, 180-81, and Chadwick, cited below.

10. On the Malabar Christians, see A.D. Wright, *The Counter-Reformation: Catholic Europe and the Non-Christian World* (New York, 1982), 132.

11. On the eighteenth century in general, see Picard, *Zölibatsdiskussion,* 21-67; Owen Chadwick, *The Popes and European Revolution* (Oxford, 1981), 109-11. On Desforges and Zaccaria, ibid.,436-439. See also Michel Vovelle, *La révolution contre l'Église* (Paris, 1988), 133-39.

12. The bulk of Picard's book is a detailed study of the Germanophone literature to the appearance of the encyclical *Mirari vos* in 1832. An example of the Austrian literature is the *Neue Briefe für und wider das Mönchswesen, mit unparteilicher Feder entworfen,* by Johann Ferdinand Gaum in 1782. On Gaum and the context, see Picard, 112-36.

13. On Capecelatro, see Chadwick, *The Popes and European Revolution,* 548-49.

14. *Der Einführung der erzwungenen Ehelösigkeit bei den christlichen Geistlichen und ihre Folgen* 3 vols. (Altenburg, 1828; 2nd ed. Breslau, 1845). I have used the third edition, edited by Friedrich Nippold (Barmen, 1892). There is a critical discussion in Picard, 336-38.

15. On Augustin Theiner, see Owen Chadwick, *Catholicism and History: The Opening of the Vatican Archives* (Cambridge, 1978), 32-71; Hubert Jedin, "Augustin Theiner," *Archiv für schlesische Geschichte* 31 (1973), 135-86, separately reprinted Hildesheim, (1973): on Johan Anton, see Picard, 319-21, and Winfried Leinweber, *Der Streit um den Zölibat im 19. Jahrhundert* (Münster, 1978), 82-86. Leinweber's book is an effective continuation of the discussion in Picard.

16. There is a large literature. For a useful position argument, see Arnaldo Momigliano, "Ancient History and the Antiquarian," and "Gibbon's Contribution to Historical Method," in Momigliano, *Studies in Historiography* (New York, 1966), 1-39, 40-55; see also A.G. Dickens and John Tonkin, with Kenneth Powell, *The Reformation in Historical Thought* (Cambridge, Mass., 1985).

17. There is a brief discussion in Chadwick, *The Popes and European Revolution*, 575-78.

18. On Klitsche, Carové, and *Mirari vos*, see Picard, 341-45.

19. On Roskovány, see Leinweber, 2, n.4. He also published *Celibatus et breviarium: duo gravissima clericorum officia, e monumentis omnium seculorum demonstrata. Accessit completa literatura*, 11 vols. (Pest-Neutra, 1861-1881), and *Supplementum ad collectiones monumentorum et literaturae* (Neutra, 1888). He listed over seven thousand items in his massive bibliography.

20. I have considered the genre in terms of its depiction of inquisitors (including inquisitorial sexuality) in my *Inquisition* (Berkeley-Los Angeles, 1989), 189-221. See also Haliczer, *Sexuality in the Confessional*, 182-203. But fiction was itself fueled by widely circulating reports of actual cases, such as that of the Abbé Mingrat in France in the early 1820s. For Mingrat, see René Rémond, *L'Anticléricalisme en France de 1815 à nos jours* (Paris, 1976), 73-77.

21. There is a large literature. The best recent study is that of Jenny Franchot, *Roads to Rome: The Antebellum Protestant Encounter with Catholicism* (Berkeley-Los Angeles, 1994).

22. On Stowe's novel, see Franchot, 246-55. On the trustee problem, see Patrick W. Carey, *People, Priests, and Prelates: Ecclesiastical Democracy and the Tensions of Trusteeism* (Notre Dame, 1987).

23. The most extensive biography is still that of E. Sculley Bradley, *Henry Charles Lea; A Biography* (Philadelphia, 1931). Most recently, Edward Peters, "Henry Charles Lea (1825-1909)," in *Medieval Scholarship:*

Biographical Studies in the Formation of a Discipline, Vol. I, *History*, ed., Helen Damico and Joseph Zavadil (New York, 1995), 89-100.

24. Henry Charles Lea, *An Historical Sketch of Sacerdotal Celibacy in the Christian Church* (Philadelphia, 1867), iii. Lea produced a revised and enlarged edition, published in Boston in 1884. In the third edition (2 vols., New York, 1907), Lea dropped the word "Sketch" from the title. See the discussion in Bradley, 128-36.

25 Bradley, 138. Lea's correspondence and working drafts and notes are preserved in the Lea Library of the University of Pennsylvania. Some of the later essays on contemporary issues are included in Henry Charles Lea, *Minor Historical Writings and Other Essays*, ed. Arthur Howland (Philadelphia, 1942).

26. For Germany, see Leinweber, 139-214.

27. On Morphy, Michelet, and Taxil, see Haliczer, *Sexuality in the Confessional*, 187-95. Further on Taxil, see Henry Charles Lea, "An Anti-Masonic Mystification," in Lea, *Minor Historical Writings*, 316-28. Lea published the essay in 1900. Reinach, a very competent and interesting historical scholar, translated much of Lea's work into French and published it in pamphlet form, including this article: *Léo Taxil, Diana Vaughan, et l'Église Romaine* (Paris, 1901). See also Alec Mellor, *Histoire de l'anticléricalisme français* (Paris, 1966), 359-60.

28. There are a number of accounts of the process. See R.C. Van Caenegem, *Guide to the Sources of Medieval History* (Amsterdam-New York-Oxford, 1978), 185-216.

29. Franz Xaver Funk, "Der Zölibat keine apostolische Anordnung," *Theologische Quartalschrift* 61 (1879): 208-47; and 62 (1880): 202-21; "Cölibat und Priesterehe im christlichen Altertum," *Kirchengeschichtliche Abhandlungen und Untersuchungen* 1 (1897): 121-55.

30. On Funk, see Leinweber, 152; Lynch, "Marriage and Celibacy," 15, n.1, and Anne Llewellyn Barstow, *Married Priests and the Reforming Papacy: The Eleventh-Century Debates* (New York-Toronto, 1982), 199-200.

Barstow's Introduction (1-18) offers a brief survey of the scholarship since Lea, emphasizing that her own scholarly starting point is 1897, also the year of the publication of the third volume of the *Libelli de lite* by the *MGH*.

31. Vacandard, "Célibat ecclésiastique," *Dictionnaire de théologie catholique* 2 (1905); Leclercq, "La législation conciliaire relative au célibat ecclésiastique," *Histoire des Conciles* II (1908), 1321-48.

32. Paris, 1924-1937; rpt., Geneva, 1978; Vol. I, 31-36; Vol.II, 134-146; Vol. III, 1-48. The topic has remained central in subsequent scholarship, for which see Uta-Renate Blumenthal, *The Investiture Controversy: Church and Monarchy from the Ninth to the Twelfth Century* (Philadelphia, 1988).

33. Leipzig, 1936; Oxford, 1940.

34. Tellenbach, *Church, State, and Christian Society*, 192; on the language of violent sexuality, 131-32. Tellenbach's most recent account of the period is *The Church in Western Europe from the Tenth to the Early Twelfth Century*, Timothy Reuter, trans. (Cambridge-New York, 1993), index, s.v. celibacy, clerical.

35. James A. Brundage, "Sexuality, Marriage, and the Reform of Christian Society in the Thought of Gregory VII," *Studi Gregoriani* 14 (1991): 69-73.

36. Filippo Liotta, *La continenza dei chierici nel pensiero canonistico classico da Graziano a Gregorio IX* (Milan, 1971); Johannes Laudage, *Priesterbild und Reformpapsttum im 11. Jahrhundert* (Cologne-Vienna, 1984); idem, *Gregorianische Reform und Investiturstreit* (Darmstadt, 1993); Bernhard Schimmelpfennig, "Zölibat und Lage der 'Priestersöhne' vom 11. bis 14. Jahrhundert," *Historische Zeitschrift* 227 (1978): 2-44.

37. Barstow, *Married Priests*, 3-5, 13-15.

38. Barstow, *Married Priests*, 200-201, offers a useful bibliography of the most relevant post-Vatican II literature in English.

39. Barstow, *Married Priests*, 10-13. In addition, see Christopher Brooke, "Marriage and Society in the Central Middle Ages," in *Marriage and Society*, ed. B. Outhwaite (London, 1981), 17-34, and Brooke, *The Medieval Idea of Marriage*, esp. 61-92.

40. Martin Boelens, *Die Klerikerehe in der Gesetzgebung der Kirche* (Paderborn, 1968).

41. Georg Denzler, *Das Papsttum und der Amtzölibat*, 2 vols., *Päpste und Papsttum*, Band 5.1-2 (Stuttgart, 1973-1976), But see the review article by Stickler, above, n.3.

"In the World but not of It": Clerical Celibacy as a Symbol of the Medieval Church

Paul Beaudette

Priestly celibacy is a constitutive hallmark of Roman Catholicism. With its links to the lived example of Jesus, the liturgical life of the church, and the ecclesiastical structures of administration, it is what anthropologists call a "condensed symbol."[1] Michael Crosby has written, "In fact, the specific culture of the Catholic church in its Latin rite could be defined as a celibate culture with the cleric at the center of the community."[2] It would be safer to say that one cannot begin to understand the character of the Catholic church if one does not appreciate the multireferential meaning of clerical celibacy. This helps explain why the study of its development is both so fascinating and controversial.

For such a significant element of ecclesiastical culture, one might expect to find clear legislation. Yet curiously enough, canonists and historians differ on exactly when marriage and priesthood became mutually exclusive. There is consensus, however, that the definitive legislation of priestly celibacy took place in the first half of the twelfth century in the canons of the First and Second Lateran Councils.

Canon 5 of the First Lateran Council (1123) states: "We strictly forbid presbyters, deacons, subdeacons, and monks to have concubines or to contract matrimony; and we judge, according to the definition of the sacred canons, that marriages contracted by such persons are to be dissolved and the persons should be brought to penitence."[3]

Although some writers see this canon as the definitive formulation of the discipline of celibacy, others say that it required

further canonical legislation to bring it to completion.[4] Canon 7 of
the Second Lateran Council reads:

> But that the law of continence and purity, so
> pleasing to God, may become more general among
> persons constituted in sacred orders, we decree that
> bishops, priests, deacons, subdeacons, canons
> regular, monks, and professed clerics who,
> transgressing the holy precept, have dared to
> contract marriage, shall be separated. For a union
> of this kind which has been contracted in violation
> of the ecclesiastical law, we do not regard as
> matrimony.[5]

The decrees of the Lateran Councils, and more generally, the
endeavors of the Gregorian Reform, mark a decisive stage in the
development of clerical celibacy. To understand the motivation
behind this movement, however, we must go back more than eight
centuries, to the beginnings of "the law of continence and purity"
cited in canon 7.

The Roots of the Legislation

It was in the fourth century that the conviction of the
incompatibility of sexual intercourse and the ministry gained
widespread commerce. For the three priestly ranks: deacons, priests,
and bishops, marriage was acceptable and commonplace. But after
A.D. 200 the expectation arose that these ministers and their wives
would abstain from sexual intercourse; living married life together,
in the words of the age, " as brother and sister." The beginnings of
ecclesiastical legislation on the conjugal abstinence of ministers
coincide with the beginning of the fourth century.

Somewhere between the years 300 and 309, a church council of
bishops, priests, deacons, and laity from all parts and provinces of
the Spanish peninsula was convened at Elvira, near Granada, Spain.
Although it was just a provincial, or local, synod, the Council set a
number of significant precedents.[6] Samuel Laeuchli, in his exhaustive
study of the Synod of Elvira, sees in its decrees the beginnings of
canon law.[7]

By far the most famous of these is canon 33, which reads, "It has please (the assembly) absolutely to forbid bishops, priests, and deacons or all clerics appointed to office to refrain from having relations with their wives and to produce children; anyone who does so nonetheless is excluded from the dignity of the clergy.[8]

The double-negative in the precept (". . .to forbid bishops, priests, and deacons. . .to refrain from having relations with their wives and to produce children. . .") leaves its meaning ambiguous; some have argued that the sense of this decree is exactly the opposite from that which is usually understood and that, when taken literally, its support of the conjugal rights of the clergy places it more appropriately at the end of the century than at the beginning. Maurice Meigne claims that the received text of the Elvira canons is a composite of enactments of various councils held in the fourth and perhaps fifth centuries.[9]

It is true that, although the question of obligatory clerical continence was raised at the Council of Nicaea (A.D. 325), the debate around its legislation is much more characteristic of the late rather than the early fourth century. At that time, the bishops of Rome, intent on strengthening their power within the church,[10] issued a number of decretals, or letters dealing with various issues, exhorting the clergy to adopt marital continence. Three of them are especially significant for our purposes.

Ad Gallos Episcopos is probably the first, although the question of its authorship, which bears upon its dating, is disputed.[11] In response to a letter from some Gallic bishops seeking rulings on a number of issues, this decretal transmits decisions of a Roman synod of 384, along with arguments for clerical continence. Although it bases the command for sexual abstinence among the clergy, first of all, on the duty of pastoral example and also cites the Scriptures, particularly Paul's letters, as justification, the central argument invokes the example of the Levites in the Jewish Scripture:

> This is why we read in Scripture regarding these
> three ranks that the ministers of God are under the
> obligation to observe purity; it is obvious that this
> is always a necessity for them; they must either
> give baptism or offer the sacrifice. Would an
> impure man dare soil what is holy when holy

things are for holy people? It was thus that [the
priests of the Old Testament] who offered sacrifices
in the temple rightly stayed there without going
out the entire year they were on duty and had
nothing more to do with their homes.[12]

The example of the Old Testament priesthood proved to be
a contentious one. Around that time, Himerius, metropolitan of the
province of Tarragona, wrote to Damasus, the Bishop of Rome, to
ask his advice about various problems that had arisen, among them
matters of clerical and monastic discipline. Evidently a crisis of
continence and virginity had erupted in Spain, and the miscreant
monks, nuns and clerics were appealing to the example of the
Levitical priesthood, which allowed marital activity when the priest
was not involved in the service of the temple. In his decretal *Ad
himerium*. Damasus' successor Siricius turned the example against
them.

Those priests who have continued to beget children
are wrong, he says, when they appeal to the
example of the Old Testament priests. These latter
were permitted to have children only because the
law demanded that only descendants of Levi be
admitted to the service of God. Such is no longer
the case. Furthermore, the Old Testament priests
were strictly enjoined to have no sexual relations
with their wives during the time of their service, so
that they might present before God an acceptable
offering. Priests, therefore, who want their daily
sacrifices to be pleasing to God must remain
continually chaste.[13]

The third decretal, *Ad episcopos africae*, is found in the acts of the
African Council of Telepte or Zella, where it was read in 418. It is
an account of the proceedings of a synod of eighty bishops in Rome
for the Italian provinces in 386. The decretal was written for those
Italian bishops who were unable to attend because of age or
infirmity, and a copy of it was sent to the bishops of Africa to
inform them of the decisions taken.

The body of the letter consists of eight canons of ecclesiastical discipline from other synods or councils quoted without comment, followed by a lengthy exhortation about the observance of clerical continence.

Furthermore what is right, chaste and honorable, we urge

> that priests and Levites do not have relations with their wives, because in the ministry they are occupied with the daily duties of their ministry. Paul wrote to the Corinthians: "Abstain to be free for prayer. If abstinence is prescribed for the laics in order that their prayer may be heard, how much more ought the priest at every moment be prepared, tranquil with a purity without stain, lest he have to offer the sacrifice or baptize unwillingly. . . .That is why I exhort you, I put you on guard, I beseech you that you put an end to this scandal with which paganism itself is justified in reproaching us.[14]

It is instructive to note at this point that what was being advocated for the church's ministers was not celibacy (i.e., abstinence from marriage) but continence (i.e., abstinence from sexual intercourse within marriage). Although it seems clear that pastoral availability was not a motivation here, there were a number of influences in the third and fourth centuries that gave weight to the push for clerical continence: the rise of asceticism and monasticism, the sacralization of the Christian church, and a markedly negative shift in the church's attitudes toward sexuality and marriage. We will look briefly at each of these.

Asceticism already had a long history within the church by the fourth century, as attested to by references by Clement of Rome and Ignatius of Antioch to the practice of virginity at the end of the first century. Its institutionalization in the more structured form of religious life known as monasticism did not appear until the late third century, first in its anchoritic (solitary) and then in its cenobitic (communal) forms, and it was only in the fourth century that monasticism came into its own as a movement within the church.

The process of sacralization, beginning as early as the second century, consisted of a number of elements: the reappropriation of the priestly tradition from the Jewish Scriptures, signified in the changing (increasingly sacral) terminology by which the church's ministers were described; a greater stress on the connection between the priest and the Eucharist, and the dedication of specific buildings for worship.

The writings of the Church Fathers on sexuality, marriage, and virginity also point to a growing negativity towards even chaste marriage, and an increasing conviction that virginity or continence was the preferred (or exclusive) path to Christian holiness.

While admittedly all of these were influences, the primary reason for continence among the clergy, however (which was gradually coming to be less an individual choice than an expectation associated with priestly ministry), was the ancient notion of ritual or cultic purity: "the unsuitability of sexuality for someone who stands at the altar. . .[because] the sacred and the impure are mutually exclusive."[15] This was a motive that had its roots in pagan and Jewish tradition in the third and more visibly, the fourth century. The sacralization of the church, involving the reappropriation of the Hebrew Scriptures and Jewish cultic apparatus, contributed to an altered notion of priesthood—one that included, for the first time, ritual purity concerns.

> The general principle of ritual purity by which holiness is required of those who handle the sacred elements is connected to a fundamental tenet of Christianity, that the OT is completed and perfected in the NT and specifically that the ritual observances of the OT have not passed away but have been incorporated into Christianity in a surpassing manner. Hence the observance of absolute continence for celibacy by the ministers of the church is a realization of the occasional continence demanded of the OT priests.[16]

Although the Levitical model goes back to Origen in the early third century,[17] it was from Cyprian (d. 258) that it received its major stimulus. Redefining pastoral care as, first and foremost, a "service of the altar and sacrifices,"[18] Cyprian's ideas caused the bishop and the clergy to be seen as "subject to the demands generally imposed by proximity to the sacred,"[19] demands which came to be formulated in terms largely borrowed from the Hebrew Scriptures. From the third century onward, the example of the Levitical priesthood and its laws of periodic continence were appealed to more and more frequently as a model for the Christian priesthood.[20] This association was only strengthened by the growing importance of the Eucharist within the Christian Church.[21]

It seems clear, then, that full understanding of the roots of clerical celibacy depends on an apprehension of the meaning of ritual purity. The landmark cross-cultural work on this phenomenon is Mary Douglas's *Purity and Danger*, published in 1966. In it, she demonstrates the relationship between ideas and behaviors associated with purity and boundary questions associated with a given culture. The body is often used as a symbol of society, and when the group is threatened at its margins (e.g. through assimilation by a dominant culture), concerns about bodily purity come to the fore as a symbolic manifestation of this anxiety—and, it seems, an effective means of dealing with it. Given this analysis, it would seem that the ritual purity beliefs underlying clerical continence and celibacy would indicate boundary anxieties about the church in "the world." My contention is that it was this ongoing tension within the church, concerning its increasingly close ties to the structures of society, that is largely to account for the rise of the symbolic notion of ritual purity within Christianity and its institutional expression in clerical celibacy. This supposition seems to be well borne out when we look at the historical periods when ecclesiastical legislation on continence and celibacy and theological discourse about the ritual purity of the priesthood were most vigorous.

The Situation in the Fourth Century

We have already noted that ritual purity concerns around the church's ministers arose during the third and, more dramatically, the fourth century. It is important to mention that this development marks something of a reversal of the teaching of Jesus, who in the Gospels (see Matt. 15:10-20, Mark 7:14-23) abrogated ritual purity as a basis for morality. Indeed, L. William Countryman, using Mary Douglas's ideas on ritual purity in a study of the New Testament writings, says that this shift is characteristic of the whole of the Christian Scriptures:

> Close study of the passages dealing with sexual and other forms of purity reveals a high level of agreement on this subject among New Testament authors. With the possible exception of Jude and Revelation, all the documents that dealt with physical purity at all agreed in rejecting it as an authoritative ethic for Christians as such. . . .Even Jude and Revelation do not return to the purity code of Leviticus. Though they reveal that Christianity had the capacity to begin generating its own purity rules, the particular rules they give evidence of have not commanded lasting assent in the mainstream of Orthodox Christianity since the first century.[22]

The resurgence within Christianity of the Hebrew notion of cultic purity tied to the priesthood is well explained by Douglas's thesis. Thinking and writing about the body came to occupy a more important place within the church as it spread within society:

> After the age of the apostles, evidence concerning the sexual ethos of the early Church becomes scanty for several generations. Then, during the second and third centuries, Christian writers gradually began to elevate sexual problems to a position of greater prominence than these had possessed in the thought of either Jesus or Paul. Several leading Christian writers in this later period viewed sexual relations as the prototype of all moral offenses.[23]

Indeed, Peter Brown says that it was Christianity's sexual ethos that served as its distinguishing mark while it was becoming progressively assimilated into Greco-Roman society. "Lacking the

clear ritual boundaries provided in Judaism by circumcision and
dietary laws, Christians tended to make their exceptional sexual
discipline bear the full burden of expressing the difference between
themselves and the pagan world."[24]

The transition from sporadic persecution by the Roman
authorities to toleration by them, signified by the Edict of Milan in
313, removed another significant boundary marker for the Christian
community. "The legislation and subsequent establishment of
Christianity as the imperial religion . . . may have contributed to the
development of a new purity code, for the church would have felt
the need of new boundaries to replace the unarguable ones
martyrdom had previously drawn around it."[25] Indeed, this was one
of the precipitating factors in the growth of monasticism in the
fourth century. The significance of sexual renunciation was thus
deepened: virginity for Christ's sake came to be seen as a kind of
lifelong martyrdom.[26] Not only the meaningfulness, but also the
social viability of such a life was aided by this transition: social
obstacles which the Roman law had placed in the way of those who
remained unmarried were soon abolished by Constantine, possibly,
according to James Brundage, for the purpose of regularizing the
position of Christians who voluntarily remained married as part of
their religious discipline.[27]

What we see around the time of the Edict of Thessalonica (380),
which made Christianity the state religion of the Roman Empire, is
a significant shift in the character of those aspiring to church
leadership. Not only had martyrdom become obsolete and celibacy
publicly supported but the repetition of the part of the church's
ministers of a number of privileges and civic honors served to create
a class of "clergy" who came to be distinguished more and more
from the believers to whom they ministered. This increasing
theological and liturgical dissociation from "the laity," of whom "the
world" was becoming increasingly comprised, was in marked
contrast to the social reality of the clergy, which was becoming more
and more closely linked to the structures of the empire as time went
on.

This shows up clearly in a practical issue which arose towards
the end of the fourth century: a flood of candidates for the
priesthood who were already familiar with the ways of the world
through marriage and secular careers. In a church that, by now,

"formed" men for clerical service from childhood, the new breed of candidate was less than ideal. One can sense the reservations of Siricius concerning the acceptance of such candidates to assign the rigorous transition from secular to clerical service. Besieged by requests to ordain men who had proved themselves in military or civil service,[28] he outlined in the epistle to Himerius a carefully graduated difficult and lengthy initiation process for those who had not dedicated themselves to the service of the church from their youth.

Clearer articulation of the distinction between the church and the world, however, resided chiefly on the shoulders of sexual renunciation as a clerical discipline. In addressing the issue of aspiring clerics who were not party to a lifelong formation which instilled in them the appropriateness of virginity as the way of life associated with their vocation, the Roman synod of 384 expressed a preference for clerical candidates who were married, while allowing that someone baptized as an adult and already married might also be ordained, assuming that he had remained chaste, and only married once.[29] This preference was even more strongly felt among the ascetics. Jerome, while admitting that, at the time of his writing, married men were being admitted to the priesthood, insists that it was only because unmarried candidates were too few:[30] "When perchance an unmarried man was passed over in favour of a married candidate, it was surely because he lacks other virtues requisite for the priesthood."[31]

Peter Brown says that it was a widespread backlash against the growing power of the ascetics that prompted the church to permit these married men to receive major orders. Christian congregations found themselves caught between small and increasingly vocal groups of ostentatiously unmarried young men associated with the monasteries and older, upper-class men from the cities who had proven themselves in civil or military careers, both of whom desired to join the clergy.

> In parts of Spain, and later in Gaul, many bishops came to think that to forbid ordained clergymen to sleep with their wives would make the existing clergy an acceptable "middle party." Priests and bishops who were continent by that

strict, if narrow, definition could stand between the
shrill ascetics and the new men of power, grossly
stained by the world.[32]

What we see at the end of the fourth century, then, is an unease
on the part of the Christian church concerning its association with
the Roman Empire; an unease which expressed itself most clearly in
the symbolic language of the body and most particularly in an
aversion toward intercourse, even in its most socially legitimate
forms.

> One cannot but sense the weight that had
> come to press down upon the body as the Christian
> church struggled to find a language with which to
> express its new position in the Roman world. By
> the start of the fifth century, sexuality had been
> swept into a new debate on the limits of the human
> person. The outcome of the Pelagian controversy
> in the Latin West and the extensive writings of
> Augustine of Hippo on the fallen state of the sexual
> drive were but one night's downpour in a weather-
> front that swept from one end of the
> Mediterranean to the other.[33]

The Situation in the Middle Ages

The medieval period marks the next significant moment in the
development of priestly celibacy. Although there were myriad papal
and conciliar decrees concerning clerical continence issued during
the period between the fifth and eleventh centuries, these represent
either reiterations of previous legislation, attempts to strengthen the
same with more stringent penalties or other more positive measures,
or, still later, attempts to deal with complications arising out of the
early laws.[34] The popes after the fourth century, in continuing to
press vigorously for clerical continence, clearly intended to protect
the church from intercourse, not to denigrate marriage per se.
Separation of clerical married couples was condemned by the
Apostolic Constitutions (c. 400) which excommunicated a priest or

bishop who left his wife "under the pretext of piety"[35] and opposed by Leo the Great (440-64).[36] This policy was reversed in the following century, however, at the Councils of Gerona (517) and Toledo (589) which ruled it desirable that a cleric in major orders should not live with his wife, thus marking the logical culmination of the legislation of clerical continence.

It was in the late eleventh and twelfth century that the law of clerical continence was transformed into the law of clerical celibacy. This period, like the fourth century, marked a turning point in Western society as well as in the church; the passage from one historical era to the next. It was an age characterized, according to Gerd Tellenbach, by the official church's final rejection of its old attitude of mistrust towards the world.[37] Indeed, this almost had to happen, for the church and the world, during this period, were becoming contiguous. The Middle Ages were characterized by the identification of the church with organized society[38] and the strongly felt need for boundaries to distinguish them. Norman Cantor says that the Gregorian Reform and the Investiture Controversy constituted nothing less than a world revolution—"the emergence of a new ideology that rejects the results of several centuries of development, organized into the prevailing system, and calls for a right order of the world."[39] This new order meant not only freeing the church from state control and interference by the laity but also divesting Western kingship of the quasi-sacramental character it had been able to use since the eighth century to bolster its inadequate popular appeal. At root this understanding echoes that of the sociologist Joachim Wach, who described the Investiture Contest as part of the great struggle between the Roman Church, on the one hand, and the dominant secular power of the Western world, on the other.

> The organization of the great Christian ecclesiastical body has made new progress, culminating in the doctrine and cult of the medieval church. The figure of Gregory VII stands for the gigantic attempt to impose a unified order in Christian society, including state and church, and to establish the superiority of spiritual over secular authority.[40]

Tellenbach says that the reform of the church took place on three levels: first, the relations of clergy and laity with each other; second, the internal constitution of the church, through the imposition of papal primacy, and third, the relations of church and world.[41] The echo of Mary Douglas's sensitivity to internal and external boundaries sounds rather clearly here, and it is once again Peter Brown who articulates it. "We find a sharpening and a redistribution of roles in society, dramatically pinpointed in the sudden emergence of a new relationship between clergy and laity in the time of the Investiture Contest (a contest connected with the name of one great pope—Gregory VII [1073-1085]—but in reality a process of widespread and ineluctable as a change in the tide of western society.)"[42] The new demarcation of the roles of the clergy and the laity associated with the Investiture Controversy expressed a redrawing of the lines between the sacred and the profane in a world where by the year 1000 the sacred and the profane had become almost inextricably mixed.[43] The process of disengagement of these two spheres in the succeeding centuries, Brown goes on to say, generated a release of energy and creativity analogous to a process of nuclear fission, opening up "a whole middle distance of conflicting opportunities for the deployment of human talent compared with which the society of the early Middle Ages appears as singularly monochromatic."[44]

The boundary anxieties of the Gregorian Reformers were undoubtedly justified. The church had become increasingly secularized, and church reform represented a reaction against the involvement of church officials and ecclesiastical institutions in the affairs of feudal government and society. These feudal entanglements were basically three in nature: 1) political, 2) economic, and 3) sexual/familial.

First, the breakup of the Roman, and still later, the Carolingian empire had witnessed a large-scale weakening of the unity of vision of the various episcopates as well as the power of the Bishop of Rome. In the ensuing emergence of young states, the political and ecclesial realms were often superimposed, and the choice of the holders of ecclesiastical office became a matter of no small political import. Kings and princes came to invest bishops with their symbols of office and received an act of homage in return. It was not just the

higher clergy, moreover, who appeared beholden to the political
structures of feudal society; most priests were more closely
connected to their feudal lords than to church authorities. "The
country clergy consisted of freed bondmen who were consecrated to
perform services in the private churches of the nobility; for the most
part they were left almost (or even entirely) to their own devices and
only read mass on Sundays in the neighboring villages, without
knowing what they were doing."[45]

Second, the persistent tendency to treat the church as a branch
of secular life was expressed also in the tendency to treat the
church's property as secular property. In the feudal transition from
the Roman to the Germanic legal system, the descent and division of
property shifted from the earlier corporate notion of the local
church to that of the family. Ownership of church property was
thus transferred from the bishop in the city, where control was an
easy matter, to the name of the saint to whom the church was
dedicated, usually in rural areas, and in whose name the property
was administered by the owner of the land on which the church was
built. In time churches came to be "owned" by kings, nobles,
monasteries, or by church officials in their own name.[46]
Establishment of churches was often prompted by merely temporal
interests (larger churches were usually profitable capital
investments),[47] and all too often the clergy serving such churches,
who were approved by the bishop but picked from among the
peasants or tenants of his estates by the owner or patron were mere
functionaries. In some situations the revenues accruing from such a
position attracted those of unsuitable character.[48] In others the priest,
in order to feed his family, would be required to farm the land
attached to the church, thus minimizing the opportunity for
intellectual and spiritual development and distancing him from
church authorities.[49]

Finally, sexual and familiar involvement through marriage and
concubinage of the clergy went as deep as the political and economic
entanglements already described. The law of continence, by which
technically clerics were still allowed to be married (provided they
lived apart from their wives)[50] had become such a dead letter that
canonical legislation of the period made no distinction between *uxor*
and *concubina*.[51] It must be allowed, however, that while clerical
marriage was often painted as concubinage, "the remarks of the

lawyers make it amply plain . . . the clerical concubinage was frequently and openly practiced virtually throughout the medieval period."[52] Indeed, the distinction between the two seems to have been somewhat tenuous, even for the laity, and the church tolerated concubinage as a secondary form of marriage.[53]

The practice of clerical continence in the fourth century, which had developed into what Jo Ann McNamara has called "the anomaly of chaste marriage,"[54] in the late eleventh and early twelfth centuries, came to stand, in the minds of the reformers, for every kind of worldly entanglement. It was all too clear that the church had to be free of a married clergy so that it might be free from the social and economic restrictions placed on it by the feudal system.

The situation called for a change that was structural in nature. The reformers fastened their attention on two great evils: simony (the purchase or sale of sacramental actions or offices) and nicolaism (marriage among the clergy). Through these two efforts, "the one aimed at the independence, the other at the purity of the church,"[55] the reformers hoped to eradicate the roots of the worldliness that had become endemic to church life. In their developing understanding of priestly ministry, we can distinguish echoes of the centuries-old theme of ritual purity:

> The attack on clerical marriage was closely associated with the new sacramental theology, with its growing emphasis on the objective nature of the Real Presence, and the growing sense that the priesthood and all who stood by the altar at the mass were a race apart, "separated for the work." This sense made the reformers all the more aware that clerical marriage tended to assimilate the clergy to their lay surroundings.[56]

A new wave of ascetical vigor, similar to that of the fourth century, which was being particularly felt within the monastic communities, had an important influence on the church at large during this period. It was from these new ascetic impulses and movements of the eleventh century that the reformers drew their inspiration and leadership and against what Norman Cantor has called the early medieval equilibrium ("the cooperation and even more . . . the interpenetration and identification of the Church and the world")[57] that they applied them.

It seems significant that the Gregorian Reform period which located the church against the world for most of the next millennium also determined the future of the monastic life through the institutionalization of the vows of poverty, celibacy, and obedience. "Here people sought to follow the way of salvation through the three negations, the negation of power, of possessions and of sexuality, the three areas which determined the whole of society; in this perspective, the three promises also expressed an unmistakable criticism of society."[58]

The tendency at this time to hold up the monastic life as the ideal pattern for the clergy could hardly help but result in the legal imposition of the monastic vocation of celibacy upon the secular clergy. Cantor summarizes the Gregorian Reform as the carrying of this new ascetic tendency to an extreme but still logical conclusion, by which the reformers wished "to turn the world into a monastery with a universal abbot demanding obedience from all rulers."[59]

As we have seen, the campaign to legislate priestly celibacy and to disengage the church from the world, was largely successful. The decrees of the First and Second Lateran Councils accomplished this on each of the levels cited by Tellenbach: by centralizing papal power, emphasizing the separation of clergy and laity, and reconfiguring the relationship between the church and the world.

In terms of the papacy, the Gregorian Reform could not have taken place without a tightening of discipline and a centralization of authority in the church. Indeed, the Reform movement provides us with an interesting study in the growth of papal power. The role of the papacy in the early eleventh century had become largely ceremonial; in the words of one church historian, the pope was "the high priest of the Roman pilgrimage, the dispenser of benedictions and of privileges and anathemas."[60] By the time of Innocent III, however, he had become more effectively the head of society than any civil ruler.[61] The historian of clerical celibacy, Henry C. Lea, writes:

> It is somewhat instructive, indeed, to observe that
> in the rise of papal power to its culmination under
> Innocent III it was precisely the pontiffs most

conspicuous for their enforcement of the rule of celibacy who were likewise most prominent in their assertion of the supremacy, both temporal and spiritual, of the head of the Roman Church. Whether or not they recognised and acknowledged the connection, they laboured as though the end in view was clearly appreciated and their triumphs on the one field were sure to be followed by corresponding successes on the other.[62]

With regard to the clergy-lay distinction, the dividing line in the feudal period was not a clear one; "a whole population of 'tonsured persons,' whose status remained ill-defined, formed an indeterminate borderland on the frontiers of the two great groups."[63] It was the Gregorian period which established within the church the increasingly sharp division of Christian society into two classes, the priestly above the lay. "In this view, the Church was a spiritual hierarchy culminating in the Pope; between clergy and laity there was a great gulf fixed; the lowest clerk in the hierarchy was superior to the greatest layman and this superiority had secular as well as spiritual consequences; he belonged to a privileged order, set apart by the conferring of spiritual gifts, judging laymen in his spiritual capacity but himself immune from secular judgment."[64] In a society that was universally Christian, "the church" came to be associated with the clergy, and "the world" with the laity. "Of course, everyone knew that there was another, more ancient sense of the word which embraced the whole body of the faithful, but even when the word *ecclesia* was used in this wide sense the role of the laity began to be seen as a humble one."[65]

The consolidation of papal power and the separation of clergy and laity must be understood within the context of the Investiture Controversy, which effectively shifted the basis of western unity from common allegiance to the emperor to shared membership in the same church.

This foundation gained from the time of the reform an entirely new solidity through the supranational unification of the ecclesiastical hierarchy and the constructing of a common canon law recognized in

all Christian countries. Thus the Church became
the real bearer, and the papacy at her head became
the leader, of Western Christendom.[66]

The early medieval equilibrium, which saw the church and the
world as basically coextensive, had been replaced by an
understanding that saw the church as not only above the world but
as separate from it. This conception of the Roman church would last
for over 800 years. It would be reaffirmed at the Council of Trent
and unhesitatingly maintained until Vatican II, when it would
undergo a drastic revision. It was also at these two historical
moments when the discipline of priestly celibacy which was
maintained at the Council of Trent (when, through the
establishment of the seminary system, it can realistically be said to
have been implemented for the first time) as well as at the Second
Vatican Council would be most ardently challenged.

It seems clear that the ecclesiastical discipline of clerical
celibacy, based on the rationale of ritual purity, is intimately and
symbolically tied in with the self-understanding of the church as
separate from the world. Vatican II could perhaps be most basically
characterized as a structural rejection of this vision. Perhaps this is
why, although the celibacy law was not open to discussion at the
Vatican Council, the rationale of ritual purity, which was quite
evident until the 1950s, has virtually disappeared as a justification for
it. This may also be the reason why clerical celibacy at that point
(judging by the contemporary crisis in the priesthood) ceased to
function as an appropriate symbol for the church's relationship with
the world. For Roman Catholics, the fallout from that demise is
conspicuous in its absence.

NOTES

1. See Mary Douglas, *Natural Symbols* (New York, 1970), 29, 69; Victor
Turner, "Symbols in Ndembu Ritual," *The Forest of Symbols* (Ithaca, 1967),
27-28; Edward Sapir, *Encyclopedia of the Social Sciences*, vol. XIV, 492-93,
and Sherry Ortner, "On Key Symbols," *American Anthropologist* 75 (1973):
1342.

2. Michael N. Crosby, *Celibacy: A Means of Control or Mandate of the Heart* (Notre Dame, 1996), 56.

3. Thomas P. Murphy, "A Collection of Some of the Legislative Sources of Canon 132 (Code of 1918): Texts in Translation and Perspective," *Resonance* 3 (1966): 33-34.

4. Although a number of writers see the decree of 1123 as nullifying clerical marriage [see Christopher Brooke, "Gregorian Reform in Action: Clerical Marriage in England, 1050-1200," in *Medieval Church and Society: Collected Essays* (London, 1971), 75; David P. O'Neill, *Priestly Celibacy and Maturity* (New York, 1965), 16, and C. H. Lawrence, "Origins and Development of Clerical Celibacy," *Clergy Review* (1975): 143] others question its clarity and require the decrees of the Second Lateran Council to bring it to completion [see Edward Schillebeeckx, *Celibacy* (New York, 1968), 45; James A. Brundage, *Law, Sex, and Christian Society in Medieval Europe* (Chicago, 1987), 220; Alphonse Stickler, "The Evolution of the Discipline of Celibacy in the Western Church from the End of the Patristic Era to the Council of Trent," in *Priesthood and Celibacy*, ed. Joseph Coppens (Milan/Rome, 1972), 548, and Jo Ann McNamara, "Chaste Marriage and Clerical Celibacy," in *Sexual Practices and the Medieval Church*, ed. Vern Bullough and James A. Brundage (Buffalo, NY, 1982), 32] Charles Frazee, "The Origins of Clerical Celibacy in the Western Church," *Church History* 41 (1972): 167, says, in effect, that the Lateran Councils legislated, respectively, that priests could not be married and that married men could not be priests. Roman Cholij, "Clerical Celibacy in the Western Church: Some Clarifications," *Priest and People* 3 (1982): 306ff., says that the practice of ordaining only celibate men did not commence with Lateran II but arose only very gradually without being formally instituted by any law.

5. H. Schroeder, *Disciplinary Decrees of the General Councils*, in Bernard Verkamp, "Cultic Purity and the Law of Celibacy," *Review for Religious* 30 (1971): 208.

6. See John E. Lynch, "Marriage and Celibacy of the Clergy: The Discipline of the Western Church: A Historico-Canonical Synopsis." *Jurist* 32 (1974): 22. H. Hefele and C. Leclercq, *Histoire des Conciles* (Paris, 1970),

II, 2, 1341; Joseph Blenkinsopp, *Celibacy, Ministry, Church* (New York, 1968), 20, and Charles Frazee, "Origins of Clerical Celibacy," 154.

7. Samuel Laeuchli, *Power and Sexuality: The Emergence of Canon Law at the Synod of Elvira* (Philadelphia, 1972).

8. Conc. Elvira, c. 33: Hef. I, 238f.; *PL* 84, 305, in Peter Harcx, *The Fathers on Celibacy* (De Pere, WI, 1968), 16.

9. "Concile ou Collection d'Elvire?" *Revue d'histoire ecclésiastique* 70 (1975): 361-87.

10. Frazee, "Origins of Clerical Celibacy," 156.

11. Anonymously written, it seems to originate toward the end of the pontificate of Damasus (366-84) or the beginning of that of Siricius (385-99). If it is accepted as Siricius' says Daniel Callam, "Clerical Continence in the Fourth Century: Three Papal Decretals,: *Theological Studies* 41 (1980): 36, it must be placed later than *Ad himerium*, which was one of the first acts of his term as Bishop of Rome. Roger Gryson, "Dix ans de recherches sur les originnes du célibat ecclésiastique: Reflexions sur les publications des années 1970-1979," *Revue Théologique de Louvain* 11 (1980): 166, suggests that it may not be a letter at all but a compilation of earlier writings—this is particularly true, he says, of the chapter dealing with clerical continence.

12. Christian Cochini, *Apostolic Origins of Priestly Celibacy* (San Francisco, 1990), 14-15.

13. Verkamp, "Cultic Purity," 203.

14. Ep. 5,3 (*PL* 13, 1160A-1161A) in Lynch, "Marriage and Celibacy," 26.

15. Schillebeeckz, *Celibacy*, 58.

16. Daniel Callam, "The Origins of Clerical Celibacy" (Ph.D. dissert., Oxford University, 1977), 6.

17. See Henri Crouzel, "Celibacy and Ecclesiastical Continence in the Early Church: The Motives Involved," in *Priesthood and Celibacy*, ed. Joseph Coppens (Rome/Milan, 1972), 484.

18. See Jean-Paul Audet, *Structures of Christian Priesthood* (London, 1967), 136.

19. Audet, *Structures of Christian Priesthood*, 189.

20. Verkamp, "Cultic Purity," 200, n. p.

21. See George H. Williams, "The Ministry of the Ante-Nicene Church," in *The Ministry in Historical Perspective*, eds. R. Niebuhr and D. Williams (New York, 1956), 28.

22. L. William Countryman, *Dirt, Greed, and Sex: Sexual Ethics in the New Testament and Their Implications for Today* (Philadelphia, 1988), 138.

23. James L. Brundage, *Law, Sex, and Christian Society in Medieval Europe* (Chicago, 1987), 62.

24. Peter Brown, "Late Antiquity," in *From Rome to Byzantium*, vol. 1 of *A History of Private Life*, ed. P. Veyne (Cambridge, 1987), 263.

25. Countryman, *Dirt, Greed, and Sex*, 142.

26. See Brown, "Late Antiquity," 269-70.

27. Brundage, *Law, Sex, and Christian Society*, 110.

28. Ep. VI, 1.3, in Parvis, "Clerical Continence and the Clerical Career," 323.

29. Lynch, "Marriage and Celibacy," 25.

30. Ugalde and Jackson, "St. Jerome: Celibacy and Virginity," *Resonance* 3 (1966): 16.

31. John G. Nolan, "Jerome and Jovinian," (published abstract STD dissert., The Catholic University of America, 1956), 42, in Ugalde and Jackson, "St. Jerome," 17.

32. Brown, *Body and Society*, 358.

33. Peter Brown, "Bodies and Minds: Sexuality and Renunciation in Early Christianity," in *Before Sexuality: The Construction of Erotic Experiences in the Ancient Greek World*, eds. David H. Halperin, John J. Winkler, and Froma I. Zeitlin (Princeton, 1990), 489.

34. Verkamp, "Cultic Purity," 206.

35. Philip Delhaye, "History of Celibacy," *New Catholic Encyclopedia*, vol. 3 (New York, 1967).

36. "Hence in order that from a carnal marriage a spiritual one may result, it is fitting that they not put away their wives, but those who have them should seem to have them as though they did not have them, whereby the affection of marriage may be kept and the marriage functions cease." See Leo I to Rusticus, Bishop of Narvonne, c. 10, d.XXXI in Murphy, "Legislative Sources," 27.

37. Gerd Tellenbach, *Church, State and Christian Society at the Time of the Investiture Contest* (Oxford, 1959), 157-58.

38. R. W. Southern, *Western Society and the Church in the Middle Ages* (Grand Rapids, MI, 1970), 16.

39. Norman F. Cantor, "The Crisis of Western Monasticism, 1050-1130," *American Historical Review* 66 (1960): 55.

40. Joachim Wach, *Sociology of Religion* (Chicago, 1944), 327.

41. Tellenbach, *Church, State and Christian Society*, 162.

42. Peter Brown, "Society and the Supernatural: A Medieval Change," in *Society and the Holy in Late Antiquity* (Binghamton, NY, 1982), 303.

43. Edward Schillebeeckx, in *The Church with a Human Face* (New York, 1985), 162, says: "Down to the eleventh century, consecrated hosts were buried in fields in order to ensure a good harvest. Almost everything took on a sacral dimension and there was no clear distinction between the sacraments proper and all kinds of other sacral signs and projects. Nature and grace overlapped; people lived as in a symoblic world."

44. Brown, "Society and the Supernatural," 303.

45. Schillebeeckx, *Church with a Human Face*, 163.

46. Frazee, "Origins of Clerical Celibacy," 158.

47. Frazee, "Origins of Clerical Celibacy," 158.

48. Stickler, "The Evolution of the Discipline of Celibacy," 50ff.

49. March Bloch, *Feudal Society* (Chicago, 1961), 346.

50. Cholij, "Clerical Celibacy in the Western Church," 304.

51. Lynch, "Marriage and Celibacy," 189.

52. James A. Brundage, "Concubinage and Marriage in Medieval Canon Law," in *Sexual Practices and the Medieval Church*, eds. Vern L. Bullough and James A. Brundage (Buffalo, NY, 1982), 126.

53. Brundage, "Concubinage and Marriage," 119.

54. McNamara, "Chaste Marriage and Clerical Celibacy," 33.

55. Roland H. Bainton, "The Ministry in the Middle Ages," in *The Ministry in Historical Perspective*, eds. H. Richard Niebuhr and Daniel D. Williams (San Francisco, 1983), 90.

56. Brooke, "Gregorian Reform in Action," 72.

57. Cantor, "Crisis of Western Monasticism," 56.

58. Schillebeeckx, *Church with a Human Face*, 166.

59. Cantor, "Crisis of Western Monasticism," 65.

60. L. Duchesne, *The Beginnings of the Temporal Sovereignty of the Popes* (1908) in R. W. Southern, *The Making of the Middle Ages* (London, 1959), 271.

61. Bainton, "The Ministry in the Middle Ages," 92.

62. Henry C. Lea, *The History of Sacerdotal Celibacy in the Christian Church*, 3rd ed. (New York, 1957), 279.

63. Bloch, *Feudal Society*, 345.

64. Southern, *Making of the Middle Ages*, 137.

65. Southern, *Western Society and the Church*, 38.

66. Friedrich Kempf, *The Church in the Age of Feudalism*, vol. 3 of the *Handbook of Church History* (London, 1969), 436.

Clerical Celibacy and Reform Before the
Age of Gregory VII

Imitatio Morum. The Cloister and Clerical Purity in the Carolingian World*

Mayke de Jong

The episcopal capitulary ascribed to Bishop Theodulf of Orléans (d. 821) briefly explains why, unlike their Old Testament predecessors, the Christian clergy could not marry. Having listed the appropriate penances for clerical adultery, fornication, and sodomy, the author presents his central argument:

> For the priests of the Jews were directed by Moses to take wives in order to safeguard one lineage for succession, because there were no priests except from the tribe of Levi. Nowadays, however, men from all peoples (*gentes*) are allowed into the priesthood, as is the case with baptism. There is no need to take wives for those who succeed to the priesthood not through carnal succession but through the imitation of priestly behaviour (*imitatio morum*). The priests of the Jews themselves, who had not such a sacred sacrifice as we do, were far from home and conjugal life when they performed their religious duties, and guarded their chastity close to the temple until their spell of ministry was over. Nowadays, as priests have to minister permanently, they should likewise be constantly celibate. After all, they do not deal with sacrificial animals, but with the immaculate body and blood of the Lord. Deacons and subdeacons should observe a similar chastity, because these also approach the altar as servants administering such a great sacrament.[1]

This statement conveniently summarizes the ideal of the priesthood in the early medieval West: that of a separate caste deriving its special status from its service at the altar and its physical contact with the sacred and reproducing itself by non-sexual means. All clerics involved in Mass, from bishops down to subdeacons, should therefore observe ritual purity. Their Old Testament predecessors served as a model to be imitated but also to be exceeded, for the purity of those dealing with the blood and body of Christ should exceed the demands of the *vetus lex*. It was from sexual purity that the priesthood was believed to derive its power. As a seventh-century proverb had it: "The priest in his purity fears not the attack of a king."[2] These words evoke the fearless prophets of the Old Testament withstanding royal might, but the expression also reflects the basic notion underlying the Western ideal of priestly chastity: that holiness and impurity are opposite poles. Holiness is wholeness, perfection, and unmixed apartness; impurity means disintegration, disorder, and a scandalous mingling of qualities which should remain separate. Along with blood, human sexuality was believed to be the most powerful and dangerous polluting force: it should be regulated, ordered, and kept away from the sacred.[3] For this very reason Theodulf and other Carolingian bishops also insisted that the laity abstain from the *opus coniugalis* before approaching "the sacrosanct sacrament."[4] All the more so should those dealing with the sacred on a daily basis should have "clean hands," lest they incur or create a dangerous pollution.

These ideas were neither new nor typically "early medieval."[5] In his influential letter of 384-385 to Bishop Himerius of Tarragona, Pope Siricius had already made the comparison between Jewish and Christian priests, demanding permanent chastity from the latter in view of the daily celebration of the Eucharist[6]; seven centuries later, the belief that priests might derive power and even a certain invulnerability from their purity played an important role in the ideology of the Peace of God.[7] The long history of celibacy in the Catholic church makes it difficult to grasp the novelty of certain claims. Hindsight not only tends to obscure innovation but also yields the impression that for more than a millennium ecclesiastical leaders fought a battle lost at the outset. If the Gregorian reform needed to fight clerical marriage, this argument goes, priests in preceding ages must surely have misbehaved collectively, and if they still did so in subsequent centuries, it means that we have to wait for the Counter-Reformation for any kind of "success."

This is the history of celibacy as a teleological story of success and failure. Alternatively, this history can be written in terms of a singularly powerful ideal of differentiation, defining the separateness of those mediating between God and mankind. This principle belongs to the domain of *longue durée*, but its articulation and the strategies for its realization varied widely in different historical contexts. When Pope Siricius compared Christian priests to those of the Old Testament, he had a new type of bishop or priest in mind: married men with a background in Roman public life who upon entering the church should abstain from their wives. As Peter Brown pointed out, the novelty of this claim was that Roman public men should learn to appropriate virtues formerly associated with women.[8] By the late fourth century Christianity had become the socially and politically dominant religion, heavily recruiting its leadership from the Roman elites. Such men might very well be legitimately married. When Theodulf made the same comparison, the higher clergy no longer had legitimate wives to abstain from. In his day and age, the élite of the priesthood usually entered clerical life in childhood; they were brought up in monasteries or in communities of *clerici canonici* either as child oblates vowed "to God in the monastery" or as young secular clerics.[9] The novelty of Theodulf's claims are not so much a matter of content as of context: celibacy was still an issue, but the debate had shifted to different territory. His assertion that the Christian priesthood came from all *gentes* reproducing itself through *imitatio morum* rather than through *carnis successio* had a very specific meaning against the background of an expanding Carolingian empire with an ecclesiastical leadership drawn from many *gentes*, and an ideology of a superior Frankish New Israel which transcended competing "ethnic" identities.[10] Moreover, the words *imitatio morum* refer to an equally specific strategy of creating and institutionalizing cultic purity by educating priests in the seclusion of the cloister. This paper will explore these strategies of separation, which, to my mind, are as much part of political history as any capitulary dealing with the division of the realm or the duties of counts. The "clean hands" of priests mattered to kings. In the course of the ninth century, the anointing of the priest's hands became part of the rite of ordination.[11] Such ritual innovations signified "the reinforcement of stratification, the sharp delineation of restricted channels of access to supernatural power, the specification of those offices which guaranteed the identity and continuity of new political communities."[12] Anointment clearly marked off kings and priests from the rest of the *populus Christianus*. The contrast was between those who had direct access to the sacred and those who did not; between those who "corrected" and those who were the object of *correctio*.

In theory the ritual of ordination turned the higher clergy into one unified body, but in practice the Carolingian priesthood presented many different faces. Priests might be monks or *clerici canonici* living in the cloister, members of aristocratic episcopal or abbatial entourages, servants of counts or other secular *potentes*, or local men celebrating Mass and burying the dead in the *villae, vici,* and *pagi* where they had lived all their lives. And even within this group of local priests conditions could be very different. They might minister "in areas far away from churches and priests, in great danger of pagans" or "in the *civitas*, where there are many clerics."[13] The *Capitulare missorum generale* (802) provides as revealing a picture as any of the many guises of those mediating between God and mankind and of the moral dangers threatening these different categories. "Bishops, abbots, priests, deacons or other members of the clergy" were prone to the temptation of an aristocratic lifestyle signified by hunting with dogs and birds of prey, with priests and the lower clergy serving as the entourage of the hunting party.[14] Other priests were in the service of counts but should nonetheless obey their bishops; they would have no hope of ever acquiring their own *honor* (a priesthood with a living) unless they allowed themselves to be properly instructed in sacred discipline.[15] Priests should supervise the chastity of clerics living with them, so the latter would refrain from worldly entertainment; moreover, any priest or deacon living with women who were not canonically approved would lose their *honor et hereditas* until they were subjected to royal judgment.[16]

Many of the items on this checklist of clerical vices belong to the classical repertoire of previous and later conciliar legislation.[17] Its characteristic Carolingian feature is emphatic royal interference, along with the curious fact that the most elaborate sections concerning clerical life are about "institutionalized clergy": monks, nuns, and *clerici canonici*. By far the longest chapter of the *Capitulare missorum* is devoted to monks. They should live according to the rule and never leave their monastery unless compelled by necessity or the command of their superiors.[18] Secular gain and worldly affairs should be shunned, along with strife, controversy, and especially drunkenness and feasting, "for everyone knows that through these men are most likely to be polluted by lust."[19] Scandalous rumors of sodomy had reached imperial ears, provoking a shocked reaction, for "the greatest hope of salvation to all Christians is believed to arise from this, i.e. the life and chastity of monks."[20] The theme of forbidden "wandering" (*vagare*) pervades the chapters concerning religious communities. This goes for the ones dealing with cloistered women, where "wandering" and the preserving the boundaries of the cloister is a particularly central issue[21] as well as for clauses concerning clergy living in the episcopal residence or in a religious community who were forbidden to "wander outside." They should live "under strict guardianship" (*sub omnia custodia*), lest they became prone to an entire catalogue of sins, including that of being "sarabaites."[22]

The clergy discussed in the *Capitulare missorum generalis* falls into two categories: those living in the world and those living in the cloister, *sub custodia*. All were expected to abstain from sexuality, but in a more general sense, "celibacy" was not the issue. The demands made by this capitulary are of a more subtle and specific nature: sexual asceticism was embedded in a much more encompassing code of behaviour, and some priests were more equal than others. Secular clergy living in the world needed to be extricated from secular lifestyles and loyalties described in knowledgeable detail, varying from aristocratic hunting with "hawks, falcons or sparrow-hawks" to song and dance in the local tavern. This was the problem of priests operating in the *saeculum*, high and low, who hardly distinguished themselves from their surroundings and should learn to do so by adopting a narrowly circumscribed code of behaviour of which "celibacy" was only one aspect; no demands of purity or the avoidance of pollution were wasted upon secular clerics who had uncanonical women in their house or feasted at the local *convivium*. Conversely, those living *infra claustra* stood apart by virtue of institutionalized purity. Sexual crimes committed in the cloister were by definition extraordinary and contagious, for they polluted not only the culprits but also the sacred space of which they were part. Ultimately, it was the "Christian people" who suffered the real damage, for their greatest hope of salvation arose from the chastity of monks. Even mere rumor might have a contaminating effect. It was not sodomy itself but suspicion and talk thereof (*oppinio perniciosissima*) which was at stake in the Capitulary of 802, leading to the indignant royal demand that "never again such a report shall be brought to our ears." The wording of the Capitulary suggests that this was reaction against a very particular and local scandal, which nonetheless threatened to affect the whole of the realm:

> And let it be known that in no way whatsoever do we
> dare to consent to such evil happening anywhere, any
> more, in our realm: even less so amongst some of
> those who we hope will improve the level of chastity
> and sanctity. If anything like it will reach our ears any
> more in the future, let it be certain that our revenge–
> not only against the perpetrators but also against the
> others who condoned such evil–will be such that no
> Christian who hears of it will presume to commit
> such evil any more.[23]

This is the fear of a New Israel depending on its religious communities for cultic purity and effective prayer.[24] Clean hands were to be found in the cloister, which should be kept "stable" in two different ways: the outside world should not be allowed to penetrate sacred space, and neither should its integrity be threatened by "wandering." Monks, *clerici canonici*, and nuns straying outside their community signaled a blurring of boundaries with the outside world, a loss of control, rumors inadvertently spreading, and ultimately the dissolution of a valuable powerhouse of prayer. Within this configuration male communities were especially valuable, for unlike their female counterparts, cloistered men could not only offer monastic prayers but also celebrate votive Masses on behalf of ruler and realm.[25]

The novelty and peculiarity of this interdependence between the state and monasteries as well-defined and anxiously guarded *loci sancti* becomes clear in comparison with the very different world emerging from sixth-century conciliar legislation: the episcopal *civitates* of Gaul evoked so vividly by Gregory of Tours. In spite of often heavy-handed royal interference in the affairs of the church, the sacred was then still firmly controlled by bishops and located in episcopal cities where civic pride hinged upon the reputation of the bishop, the clergy, and the local saints.[26] Clerical purity was not so much a commodity fostered and guarded in the cloister as a matter of personal virtue, with a chorus of gossiping citizens keeping its ecclesiastical leaders on the straight and narrow. Gregory's story of Bishop Brictius of Tours, St. Martin's unworthy successor, is a case in point. After having served as bishop for

33 years, Brictius was faced with a revolt in his city, for he was suspected of having impregnated a woman vowed to God. Allegedly, the furious people of Tours refused to pollute themselves any longer by kissing his unworthy hands and unanimously decided to stone him. Even the two spectacular miracles performed by the hapless bishop were insufficient to clear his name, so he was ultimately kicked out of town. All this is presented by Gregory as due punishment for Brictius' insolence, who had once dared to insult St Martin, but it is also a tale about the redoubtable force of public opinion. Significantly, Brictius' inevitable punishment took the shape of a mob of angry citizens utterly convinced that their bishop's pious façade hid a world of sin.[27]

This must have been the stuff of sixth-century episcopal nightmares. The many contemporary *canones* dealing with the need to guard clerical reputations evoke a world in which clerical behaviour was subject to rigid scrutiny by suspicious laymen. At any moment scandal might erupt, and clerical honour might be lost as happened in the case of Brictius.[28] There is more than a hint of a real and persistent fear on the part of laymen of being dependent upon a polluted clergy. Rumor was almost as bad as actual fact, for malicious gossip (*maledicorum obloquia*)[29] was referred to in terms of a "contamination" which tainted not only the life and reputation of the clerics in question but also the efficacy of the cult itself.[30] The laity, all too eager to suspect the clergy of the type of sin they committed themselves, eagerly spread rumors about clerics, said the council of Tours (567)[31], but it was agreed that priests who were unable to correct themselves could expect no veneration.[32]

Various counter-strategies emerged, aimed at the "safeguarding of reputation" (*fama custodienda*). Bishops began to look to monasteries as welcome source of clerical potential, thus avoiding the problem of married candidates for higher orders.[33] On the other hand, the key word was "testimony." A bishop living with his wife as if she were his sister should share his living quarters (and particularly his bedchamber) with priests, deacons, and a "*clericorum turba iuniorum,*" who could testify to the outside world, said the council of Tours (567).[34] Along similar lines, a married archpriest should have a team of seven lectors, subdeacons, or laymen, who were to take turns in following him wherever he went, sharing his *cella* with him at night. Lower clergy could not muster such round-the-clock surveillance, but their wives should live in another part of the house, together with the slaves.[35]

Such measures were both complicated and difficult to enforce. The most effective way to alleviate lay suspicion was to follow the monastic model and to transform the episcopal clergy into a community with strict internal surveillance and an impeccable outside reputation. This had been one of Caesarius' aims when he turned part of the clergy of Arles into an ascetic community, but the main impact of his legacy was part of Carolingian history.[36] Queen Bathild's attempt to transform a number of senior basilicas into monastic communities, exempted from episcopal interference, was probably inspired by a similar wish to enhance the purity and prestige of these venerable institutions, which were to concentrate on prayer for king and kingdom.[37] There are also signs of secular clerics in episcopal households adopting some sort of *vita communis*: the episcopal residence mentioned by the council of Tours (567) may well have contained the wife of the bishop but also harbored a *turba iuniorum*. The first hesitant signs of secular clerics adopting a *vita communis* should be looked for in episcopal households like the ones mentioned by the council of Tours (567), which may have contained the wife of the bishop but also harbored a *turba iuniorum*. The presence of such a group of young clerics served a dual purpose. Not only did they inspect and witness episcopal behaviour, but they themselves were subject to similar supervision, thus becoming well suited for ordination if they chose to enter higher orders.[38] Such arrangements were often informal, with privileged children being raised and educated by bishops, as Gregory of Tours had been by his episcopal uncles Gallus of Clermont and Nicetius of Lyon.[39] Moreover, Frankish hagiography testifies to an increasing element of *commendatio* and patronage in the relations between bishops and the clergy they had "nourished."[40] When Bishop Desiderius of Vienne was besieged by enemies, he was surrounded by his *nutritura et familia*, who were by definition his loyal followers.[41] By the seventh century, when Frankish and Burgundian bishops educated in the *aula regis* rose to prominence, their households– including the junior members–followed royal and aristocratic rather than monastic models. This must have been the context of Boniface's celebrated outburst against Frankish deacons having four or five or even more concubines in their beds but still unashamedly reading the Gospels.[42]

Whether Boniface's complaint was justified or mere innuendo is a moot point, but what has escaped historians is the tell-tale phrase *a pueritia sua semper in stupris*. Boniface was a man who himself grew up in a monastery and who was used to "minsters" raising priests-to-be.[43] No wonder that he, raised in the sacred precinct, would be horrified by debauchery which had supposedly gone on since boyhood. It was during the reform councils of 743 and 744 orchestrated by Boniface that the issues of cultic purity and monastic and/or canonical regularity first became unequivocally harnessed to the legitimation of new political power,[44] and the seed of Carolingian *correctio* was sown in the early capitularies issued by the brand-new King Pippin III.[45] Given Alcuin's dominant role at Charlemagne's court, the impact of Anglo-Saxon reform on the Carolingian church can hardly be overstated; yet there were other important models, most of all the Visigothic legislation which was to become so influential north of the Pyrenees. The influential fourth council of Toledo (633) not only issued the first decree affirming the irrevocability of child oblation,[46] but it also demanded that those clerics who were *puberes aut adolescentes* should live in a separate part of the episcopal establishment, supervised by a senior cleric who would not only taught them but also served as the inevitable "witness to their life." Those who proved free of any blemish might proceed from this collective *atrium* to a more individual tutelage by the bishop, but boys resisting discipline should be sent off to monasteries, "so their wandering and haughty mind will be restrained by a more severe rule."[47] The second council of Toledo (527) had still offered a choice between an ecclesiastical career or marriage to those "having been mancipated to the clergy by the will of their parents,"[48] but these days were obviously over by 633. Young clerics were to live together under strict supervision in separate quarters; from this reservoir of talent the bishop might choose those completely untainted for further education and promotion. Instead of being educated in the episcopal household itself, as still envisaged in 527, young clerics were now to be brought up in their own quarters, with only the morally untainted being admitted to the episcopal presence.

Those issuing this decree respected the differences between the monastery and the episcopal household, but they also tended to blur these boundaries by organizing a collective education for young clerics along monastic lines. The fourth council of Toledo resembles later Carolingian reform councils in another important respect: its primary goal was *correctio* and liturgical unity within the limits of a recently established polity. There is a strong sense of a new "Gothic" identity subsuming older "ethnic" distinctions, with frontiers separating outsiders (Jews, foreigners) from those who truly belonged. These new frontiers

were not only drawn geographically but also in terms of "proper ritual."
The celebration of Easter, the right way to administer baptism, the
blessing of candles, the correct moment to sing *Allelujah*, the saying of
Gloria et Honor Patri after Psalms, and not merely *Honor Patri*–all these
so-called details assumed major importance.[49]

Within political communities defining their identity in terms of
"correct ritual," local uproar about lapsed clerics became connected to
much larger issues. The "variety of churches" (*varietas ecclesiarum*)[50]
created the kind of *scandalum* which represented a dangerous threat to
new-found political unity. Clerical purity was too important to be left to
bishops alone. Instead it became a matter of major concern to secular
rulers, who successfully strove for control of the powerhouses of prayer
and purity, the *monasteria*. This was what Carolingian immunity and
royal *tuitio* was all about: creating *loci sancti* which would enhance rather
than diminish royal might.[51]

There was a world of difference between the priesthood inhabiting
religious communities and their "ordinary" counterparts. It was to
monasteries and *clerici canonici* that the *Admonitio generalis* (789)
entrusted the responsibility of training young clerics in the literate skills
needed for an improved liturgy; while monks and canons were busy
"correcting the orthodox books,"[52] bishops had to make sure that
country priests knew their basic liturgical formulas and understood the
prayers of Mass.[53] Even more importantly: whereas the non-
institutionalized priesthood was likely to remain entangled in local
loyalties and family networks, the "other half" had been raised in a
spiritual family in the seclusion of the cloister. Their ritual purity was
guaranteed since childhood by an upbringing *sub custodia et disciplina*.

Many Carolingian bishops had been brought up in such
communities filled with aristocratic priest-monks or "monasticized"
secular clergy. This background informed their notion of reproducing
the priesthood through *imitatio morum* as Theodulf expressed it. The
demands they made of their rural clergy were inspired by the well-
regulated life in the cloister they had experienced from childhood
onwards. These ecclesiastical leaders were not only aristocrats with good
political connections as had long been the case, but they also were
members of an old-boy network stemming from their upbringing in
monasteria and/or the court. Their high ideals of priesthood were
informed by Old Testament models; as a priestly caste they should fight
with kings for salvation of the New Israel and the Franks.[54] In their

episcopal capitularies the bishops spoke the language of the *potentes* to those who were often in fact *pauperes*. How to stop the priestly *ordo* from splitting down the middle into two groups, with parish clergy being reduced to insignificance or even downright ridicule? This was the problem to which Theodulf and his colleagues had to address themselves. When Hincmar grumbled that he had already presented his clergy with an extensive decree against illicit familiarity with women, "but I see some of you disregard it,"[55] he did so as an old boy of St. Denis and a powerful bishop who could afford to stay away from women.[56] Those he addressed, however, lived close to female relatives and neighbours not covered by the much reiterated short list of "canonical" women: mother, sister or aunt.[57] And these women were only part of the problem: an even more pressing one was that of priests falling to the temptation of asking money for their services. Many may well have needed to do so in order to survive.[58]

No such worries troubled the institutionalized clergy. Take the career of one of the most influential members of the ecclesiastical élite, Hrabanus Maurus.[59] As the son of a well-to-do couple from Mainz, he entered the royal abbey of Fulda as a child oblate in 788, to become the community's most promising scholar. In 798-799 he was sent for further training to Charlemagne's court and to Alcuin in Tours. The latter nicknamed him "Maurus," after Benedict's most beloved pupil who had also been a child oblate. His star rose quickly: in 814 he was elevated to the priesthood; in 819 he was put in charge of Fulda's monastic school; in 822 he became its abbot. Twenty years later he suffered a temporary setback, when his staunch loyalty to the Emperor Lothar got him into King Louis the German's bad books. He lost his abbacy in 842 but was allowed to retire to a comfortable *cella* near Fulda, which finally gave him the time and leisure for his scholarly work. He remained much in demand as a biblical commentator, also with the king who had deposed him. By 847 Louis decided that Hrabanus' administrative talents were no longer to be wasted. He was made archbishop of Mainz, an office he held until his death in 856. In spite of its individual features and vicissitudes, Hrabanus followed an eminently Carolingian ecclesiastical career. The *pueri nutriti* who grew up in the cloister were destined for the priesthood; if they had the talent and the connections, they would be called to serve the ruler in responsible positions of ecclesiastical leadership.

Secular clerics being recruited from monasteries were by no means a new phenomenon, and neither were bishops striving to mould their clerics into something closely resembling a monastic community. Children entering either the secular clergy or monastic communities had also been a familiar feature for centuries; after all, it was the Rule of Benedict which provided the model for Carolingian child oblation, demanding that the boys in question were offered at the altar, as a sacrifice "to God in the monastery"[60] Yet nothing in the *Regula Benedicti* itself suggests that Benedict expected such oblates to become priests or that oblates educated to become priest-monks dominated the community he had in mind. Only in the Carolingian church did child recruitment become the accepted strategy to ensure an institutionalized *imitatio morum*, to the extent that lay adults entering monasteries and clerical communities became the exception rather than the rule. By the ninth century, the ideal of priestly purity was embodied by the *puer oblatus* who had entered religious life through a ritual of sacrifice and had been raised within the monastic confines to become a pure, and therefore efficacious, mediator between God and mankind.[61] By then, the demand for both votive Masses and priests with "clean hands" had become so great that a veritable army of prayer was needed. It was the institutionalized clergy which catered to these demands. As a schoolmaster in Fulda, Hrabanus Maurus complained in 821/822 that "the education of the little ones causes us a lot of trouble, and keeps us from our study of Scripture."[62] He was not saying too much, for between 826 and 835 Fulda accepted between 100 and 130 children.[63]

Not all of these children were child oblates in the strict sense of the word; some of them may have been young secular clerics, and even the odd lay boy was admitted to the sacred precincts if he was of sufficiently high birth. Yet their upbringing in the cloister was to infuse such "old boys" with something much more than corporate identity: it was meant to transfer their loyalty from a carnal family to a spiritual one. The epitaph Hrabanus composed for himself speaks volumes:

> In this town [i.e. Mainz] I was born, and re-born from the sacred
>   font of baptism;
> then I became acquainted with Holy Scripture in Fulda where,
>   made monk, I obeyed the orders of my superiors,
> and the Holy Rule was the guideline of my life.[64]

There were the words of a man who identified with his native town through baptism, which constituted the first re-birth; the second one was that of becoming a monk in childhood, which he remained ever afterwards, no matter what other duties life thrust upon him. A similar sentiment of primary loyalty to the monastic family pervades the letters of Hrabanus' master Alcuin. His correspondence abounds with metaphors derived from parenthood and nurturing.[65] In old age, when he remembered his own education in York's *monasterium*, he wrote a grateful letter to "the beloved and venerable brothers of the church of York":

> You tended the impressionable years of my infancy with motherly affection and upheld me in the wanton period of boyhood with holy patience, teaching me with fatherly correction and fortifying me with a religious education until I became a man.[66]

He asked his former community to remember him in their prayers, expressing a fervent wish to be buried in the place where he was raised:

> Dearest fathers and brothers in the world, remember me! I am yours, whether in life or in death. Perhaps God will pity me, so that you may bury the child you taught when he is old. And if another place is assigned to my body, yet I believe my soul will be granted peace with you by God's grace through your prayers, whatever its place is to be.[67]

In the still curiously similar world of eleventh-century St. Gall, such familiar sentiments persisted. In old age, the monk going by the name of "Ekkehard IV" spoke of St. Gall's cloister as *intima nostra* or *nidus noster*, defining the characters of his monastic chronicle in terms of the contrast between this inner world and the *saeculum* outside.[68]

Writing of his community's glorious Carolingian past, Ekkehard boasted that St. Gall's cloister had been so revered that even the most powerful secular clerics or laymen had never been allowed entrance—going on to relate many instances of carefully ritualized border-crossing, precisely by the aforesaid *potentes*.[69] The real cloister was one which primarily existed in the mind, through an upbringing "*sub custodia et disciplina*." The most elaborate program for such an education had been outlined by Hildemar, a monk from Corbie who became *magister* in Civate, in Northern Italy. In his commentary on Benedict's Rule he took infinite care over sequestering his monks within the cloister, while warding off the undue influence of the ever-present world outside.[70] Clearly, he considered children who had been brought up carefully within one's own community to be excellent material for the priesthood. In their case, he felt, the abbot could be certain that they had not committed serious—that is, sexual–sins which disqualified them for service at the altar, whereas those who had not been raised under strict *custodia*, a thorough investigation was necessary before admitting him to the *oblatio sacrificii*.[71] Sexual sins standing in the way of priesthood were obviously a pressing affair, for much is made of the distinction between graver and lesser sins. The *graviora culpa*–amongst which sexual crimes loomed large–were to be punished by a public punishment which according to canon law was manifestly incompatible with being a priest or a deacon. Hildemar therefore urged the utmost discretion before taking such a drastic measure. Priests, future and present, were apparently such an important asset that in order to preserve them for the community, he diverged in certain respects from the Rule. He was familiar enough with the moral dangers threatening all-male communities but was also afraid to lose potential priests. Sexuality and service at the altar were incompatible; hence, his solicitude was for those who might in the future touch the sacraments as deacons and priests. Hildemar's strategy of education was geared towards preserving the innocence of childhood for the purity of priesthood. Unlike those converting in adulthood, the *pueri nutriti* had never been of this world and therefore should never be removed from the community, whatever their crimes might have been.

> For it is not right that he who is raised in the
> monastery from childhood in good kind of life, should
> be exiled to a worse kind of existence, i.e. a secular life,
> as happens to him who came from the world and
> never led a good life before.[72]

Once young monks had interiorized the "good life," chastity should come naturally to them, and their inner cloister should safeguard them when they were eventually exposed to the pollution of the world outside. This ideal found a literary expression in stories of high-born guests visiting the cloister, vainly attempting to disturb the children's concentration or self-control,[73] but it also informed the corporate identity as defined by an anonymous monk reporting back home on the progress of the council of Aachen (816): "We, who have lived in this way virtually from our cradle, instructed by our elders."[74]

The councils of 816 and 817 meant to make a deep impact upon monastic life and succeeded to do so.[75] These gatherings had been convened by Emperor Louis the Pious at the royal residence at Aachen, and after much deliberation, the ultimate decisions were promulgated in two royal capitularies, to be implemented under the supervision of royal *missi*. To Carolingian kings the internal life in the cloister mattered deeply, for the stability of the realm–politically, economically and, not least of all, religiously–was bound up with the stability of its *monasteria*: the purity of prayer sustained the peace in the royal household, the fertility of royal women, and the victories of royal armies. The king was to be "a comforter of churches and holy monasteries with the greatest piety of royal munificence."[76] To a certain extent the demands their royal protectors made of monasteries were contradictory: on the one hand the cloister—be it monastic or canonical–should be "regular" and therefore inaccessible to outsiders,[77] on the other it was called upon to admit young clerics for *imitatio morum* and literate training. In his first capitulary Theodulf forbade his priests to ask money for teaching local children basic literate skills,[78] but he did grant them the privilege of sending their own young relatives to one of his five private monasteries for further education.[79] By 816/817 the presence of such boys not destined for monastic life had become sufficiently massive to provoke the cloister into a counter-offensive. After lengthy deliberation, the reform-minded party in Aachen decided that from then on monastic school would only be open to *pueri oblati*,[80] providing new instructions for the proper ritual of child oblation.[81] There is no evidence that such attempts at closing off the *claustrum* carried much weight.[82] Despite efforts to keep "the world" at bay, monasteries continued to host outsiders, ranging from illustrious visitors and political prisoners to extramural pupils. It was from this alternation between openness and withdrawal that monasticism derived its tremendous influence.

It was this cycle of redrawing of the boundaries of the cloister, inevitably followed by a relaxation of the norm and yet another wave of "reform," that monasticism derived its tremendous influence. The confines of "*intima nostra*" needed to be kept well in sight, but on the other hand, the perfect realization of the ideal of seclusion would have quickly led to the total extinction of the *monasteria*. These communities attracted gifts and projected a powerful model of ritual purity precisely because they had a reputation of sanctity transmitted to the world outside by those who had been allowed a glimpse inside. It was imperfect claustrality which made monastic models of regularity and stability spill over into the world outside the cloister. The model for reproducing a pure priesthood through *imitatio morum* was equally shaped by monastic tradition. For the formation of new élite of literate and chaste priests, Theodulf still looked to his own monasteries, but his third successor Walter had different ideas:

> Let every priest have his own cleric, making sure to educate him in a religious fashion; if he has the opportunity, he should not neglect to have a *scola* in his parish, so he may bring up his trainees in an environment of sincerity and chastity.[83]

The expression *scola* has nothing to do with modern notions of schools, and everything with the *scola dominici servitii* of Benedict's Rule: the "school" Bishop Walter had in mind was that of the communal and regular life lived in monasteries, after which local priests, if they had the wherewithal, might model their own small-scale strategies of *imitatio morum*.

The tenacious survival of the ideal of clerical purity through the ages is much more surprising than the fact that many priests fell short of the norm. In this survival the cloister played a crucial role. By the ninth century, ascetic communities had come to embody the ideal of a pure priesthood. Their social and religious power, along with their tremendous wealth and their capacity for isolation turned early medieval monks and canonical clerics into powerhouses of prayer too important to be left to mere ecclesiastical authority. Instead of withstanding the might of the king, the purity of the institutionalized priesthood sustained the stability of his realm, radiating into a world of *villae, vici, parrochiani* and *vicini* which was much harder to control. This was the context in which Theodulf explained to his priests why they, unlike their Old Testament predecessors, were not allowed to marry.

NOTES

*I am grateful to Julia M. H. Smith for her helpful comments on an earlier version of this paper.

1. Theodulf, *Capitulare II* 8.4, *MGH Capit Ep* 1:170: "Nam sacerdotes Iudeorum ideo iussi sunt per Moisen ducere uxores, quia de nulla tribu nisi de Levi fiebant sacerdotes, ut progenies una custodirent per successionem. Nunc autem de omnibus gentibus, sicut ad baptismum, sic ad sacerdotium permittuntur accedere. Nullaque est necessitas uxores ducere, qui non per carnis successionem, sed per morum imitationem in sacerdotio subrogantur. Ipsi tamen Iudaeorum sacerdotes non habentes tam sanctum sacrificium, sicut et nos habemus, tempore vicis suae longe erant a domo sua et a coniugali opere et remoti iuxta templum in continentia castitatis excubabant donec tempus ministerii sui explerent. Nunc autem sicut semper ministrare debent, ita semper continentes esse oportet sacerdotes. Tractant enim non victimas pecudum, sed ipsum immaculatum corpus et sanguinem domini. Eiusdem continentiae et diaconi et subdiaconi sunt ideo, quia ipsi in tractatione tanti sacramenti ministeri accedunt altaris." See on Theodulf's episcopal capitularies, above all Peter Brommer, "Die bischöfliche Gesetzgebung Theodulfs von Orléans," *Zeitschrift der Savigny-Stiftung für Rechtsgeschichte* 91, *Kanonistische Abteilung* 60: 1-120, who sticks to the traditional dating of "around 800" for the first capitulary and "between 800 and 813" for the second (ibid., pp. 23-24). Theodulf's authorship of the second text has been a matter of debate; whereas Brommer (ibid., pp. 20-22) is convinced it was Theodulf's work, there may be good reasons to review the question of authorship once more. The two capitularies are very different in structure and contents; compared to the first capitulary, which was very influential and widely diffused, the second one had only limited impact. Martina Stratmann and Rudolf Pokorny are in the process of editing the other episcopal capitularies (*MGH Capit Ep* 2 and 3 appeared in 1995). I will reserve judgment, however, until the editors present their final volume and indices.

2. *Passio Praeiecti* c. 24, *MGH SSrerMerov* 5:239: ". . . sed verum proverbium dicitur: *integritas sacerdotum non timet impetum regis*. . ."; I

follow the translation (and interpretation) of Paul Fouracre and Richard
Gerberding, *Late Merovingian France. History and Hagiography, 640-720*
(Manchester/New York, 1996), 289. For a slightly different version of the
proverb, see *Passio Leudegarii,* c. 8, *MGH SSreMerov* 5:290. Which of the
two hagiographers was the first to use the expression must remain a moot
point; cf. Fouracre and Gerberding, *Late Merovingian France,* p. 225, n. 118.

3. The best guide into this territory remains Mary Douglas's classical
Purity and Danger. An Analysis of the Concepts of Pollution and Taboo
(London, 1966). Her insights have inspired a number of early medievalists:
see especially Albert Demyttenaere, "The Cleric, Women and the Stain.
Some Beliefs and Ritual Practices Concerning Women in the Early Middle
Ages," in *Frauen im Spätantike und Frühmittelalter. Lebensbedingunen--
Lebensnormen--Lebensformen,* ed. Werner Affeldt (Sigmaringen, 1990), 141-
165; Rob Meens, "A Background to Augustine's Mission to Anglo-Saxon
England," *Anglo-Saxon England* 23 (1994), 5-17; idem, "Pollution in the
Early Middle Ages: the Case of Food Regulations in the Penitentials," *Early
Medieval Europe* 4 (1995): 3-19; Mayke de Jong, "Pollution, Penance and
Sanctity. Ekkehard's *Life* of Iso of St Gall," in *The Community, the Family
and the Saints: Patterns of Power in Early Medieval Europe,* ed. Joyce Hill and
Mary Swann (Turnhout, forthcoming). Much light on the transformation
of attitudes toward the sacred between 300 and 1000 is shed by two
masterpieces: Robert Markus, *The End of Ancient Christianity* (Cambridge,
1990), and Peter Brown, *The Rise of Western Christendom* (Cambridge,
Mass./Oxford, 1996). Both authors have been a constant source of
inspiration.

4. Theodulf, *Capitulare I* 36-43, *MGH Capit Ep* 1: 133-140; Radulf of
Bourges, *Capitula* c. 29, *MGH Capit Ep* 1:256. See Peter Browe, *Beiträge zur
Sexualethik des Mittelaters,* Breslauer Studien zur historixchen Theologie 23
(Breslau, 1932), 37-79; above all, Pierre J. Payer, *Sex and the Penitentials: The
Development of a Sexual Code* (Toronto, 1984).

5. Dorothea Wendebourg, "Die alttestamentische Reinheitsgesetze in
der frühen Kirche," *Zeitschrift für Kirchengeschichte* 95 (1984): 149-170, and,
above all, Arnold Angenendt "Mit reinen Händen. Das Motiv der
kultischen Reinheit in der abendländischen Askese," in *Herrschaft, Kirche,*

Kultur. Beiträge zur Geschichte des Mittelalters. Festschrift für Friedrich Prinz zu seinem 65. Geburtstag, ed. Georg Jenal and Stephanie Haarländer (Stuttgart 1993), 297-316.

6. Siricius, *Epistolae et decreta* 1, 7, 8-11, *PL* 13: 1138B-1141A. The comparison of Old Testament and Christian priests is also made by Pope Innocent I (401-17) in his equally influential letter to Victricius of Rouen: Innocentius, *Epistolae et decreta* 2.9, *PL* 20: 476A/B. About the early papal pronouncements on celibacy: Roger Gryson, *Les origines du célibat ecclésiastique du pemier au septième siècle*, Recherches et synthèses, section d'histoire 2 (Gembloux, 1970), 127-77; also Martin Boelens, *Die Klerikerehe in der Gesetzgebung der Kirche unter besonderer Berücksichtigung der Strafe. Eine rechtsgeschichtliche Untersuchung von den Anfängen der Kirche bis zum Jahre 1139* (Paderborn, 1968), 25-29; Alphons M. Stickler, "L'évolution de la discipline du célibat dans l'Eglise en Occident de la fin de l'âge patristique au Concile de Trente," in *Sacerdoce et célibat. Etudes historiques et théologiques*, Bibliotheca ephemeridum theologicarum Lovaniensium 28 (Louvain, 1971), 385.

7. As the Council of Gerona (1068) expressed it: "Those clerics who renounce their wives and weapons shall be untroubled and in safety and have no fear. No one shall seize their possessions, nor do them any harm; but they and their property shall be in the peace and the truce of the Lord forever." Cited in Amy G. Remensnyder, "Pollution, Purity and Peace: An Aspect of Social Reform Between the Late Tenth Century and 1076," in *The Peace of God. Social Violence and Religious Response in France Around the Year 1000*, ed. Thomas Head and Richard Landes (Ithaca/London, 1996), 280.

8. Peter Brown, *The Body and Society. Men, Women and Sexual Renunciation in Early Christianity* (New York, 1988), 358: "In parts of Spain, and later in Gaul, many bishops came to think that to forbid ordained clergymen to sleep with their wives would make the existing clergy into an acceptable 'middle party.' Priests and bishops who were continent by that strict, if narrow, definition could stand between the shrill ascetics and the new men of power, grossly stained by the world." An excellent recent study on the development of asceticism in Late Antiquity is

Susanna Elm's *Virgins of God. The Making of Asceticism in Late Antiquity* (Oxford, 1994). About chastity in marriage: Dyan Elliot, *Spiritual Marriage. Sexual Abstinence in Medieval Wedlock* (Princeton, 1993).

9. Mayke de Jong, *In Samuel's Image. Child Oblation in the Early Medieval West* (New York/Leiden/Cologne, 1996), passim.

10. About "ethnogenesis," see Walter Pohl, "Tradition, Ethnogenese und literarische Gestaltung: eine Zwischenbilanz," *Ethnogenese und Überlieferung. Angewandte Methoden der Frühmittelalterforschung* ed. Karl Brunner and Brigitte Merta (Wien/München, 1994), 9-26, with extensive references to previous literature.

11. Janet L. Nelson, "Kingship, Law and Liturgy in the Political Thought of Hincmar of Rheims," in eadem, *Politics and Ritual in Early Medieval Europe* (London/Ronceverte, 1968), 133-71 (originally in *English Historical Review* 92 (1977), 241-79; Angenendt, "'Mit reinen Händen,'" 309-10.

12. Janet L. Nelson, "Symbols in Context: Rulers' Inauguration Rituals in Byzantium and the West in the Early Middle Ages," in eadem, *Politics and Ritual in Early Medieval Europe*, 279-80 (originally in *Studies in Church History* 13 (1976), 97-119).

13. Commenting on the difficulties of observing the two canonical times for baptism, Harabanus Maurus wrote: "Quod si fuissent pariter in civitate, ubi clericorum frequentia est, legitima tempora possent facile observare, sed qui in pagis longius ab ecclesiis ac presbyteris constituti sub maximo periculo gentilium versantur, melius puto, ut extra pascha et pentecosten baptizetur. . . ." *Epistolarum Fuldensium fragmenta* 18, *MGH Epp* 5: 522.

14. *Capitulare missorum generale* 19, *MGH Capit* I: 95. The edition presents the chapters 10-24 as a separate section, presumably because these sections deal with ecclesiastical matters; for the same reason this section has been omitted in an otherwise useful anthology of medieval sources, which thus perpetuates the traditional but erroneous view that "the duties and

conduct of clergy, monks etc." were of limited relevance to early medieval politics. Cf. Patrick J. Geary (ed.), *Readings in Medieval History* (Peterborough/Lewiston, 1991), 333.

15. *Capitulare missorum generale* 21, MGH *Capit* 1: 95.

16. *Capitulare missorum generale* 22, MGH *Capit* 1: 95-96.

17. For a brief survey of the relevant conciliar legislation, see Odette Pontal, *Die Synoden im Merowinggerreich* (Paderborn/München/Wien/ Zürich, 1986), 232-40; Wilfrid Hartmann, *Die Synoden der Karolingerzeit im Frankenreich und in Italien* (Paderborn/München/ Wien/Zürich, 1989), 418-22.

18. *Capitulare missorum generale* 17, MGH *Capit* 1: 94: "Foris monasterium nequaquam progediendi licentiam habeant, nisi maxima cogente necessitatem: quod tamen episcopus, in cuius diocese erunt, omnino praecuret, ne foris monasterio vagandi usum habeant. Sed si necessitas sit ad alium obhedientiam aliquis foris pergere, et hoc cum consilio et consensum episcopi fiat, et tales personae cum testimonium foris mittantur in quibus nulla sit suspitio mala vel a quibus nulla oppinio mala oriatur." Note the emphasis on episcopal control; this is in keeping with the general tenor of this capitulary, but it also indicates that the category of the "monachi" might comprise religious communities led by bishops rather than by abbots.

19. *Capitulare missorum generale* 17, MGH *Capit* 1: 94: "Ebrietatem et commessationem omnino fugiant, quia inde libidine maxime polluari omnibus notum est."

20. *Capitulare missorum generale* 17, MGH *Capit* 1: 94-95: "Maxime contristat et conturbat, quod sine errore magno dici potest, ut unde maxima spe omnibus christianis orriri crederent, id est de vita et castitate monachorum, inde detrimentum, ut aliquis ex monachus sodomitas esse auditum."

21. Both chapters about religious women open with "wandering":

Capitulare missorum generale 17, *MGH Capit* 18: 95: "Monasteria puellarum firmiter observata sint, et nequaquam vagare sinantur. . ."; ibid. 20: 45: "Ut abbatissae una cum santimonialibus suis se unanimiter aut diligenter infra claustra se custodiant et nullatenus foris claustra ire praesumant."

22. *Capitulare missorum generale* 17, *MGH Capit* 22: 95-96: "Canonici autem pleniter vitam obserbent canonicam, et domo episcopali vel etiam monasteria cum omnem diligentiam secundam canonica disciplina erudiantur. Nequaquam foris vagari sinantur, sed sub omni custodia vibant, non turpis lucris dediti, non fornicarii, non homicides, non fures, non raptores, non litigiosi, non iracundi, non elati, non ebriosi, sed casti corde et corpore, humiles, modesti, sobrii, mansueti, pacifici, ut filii Dei digni sint ad sacro ordine promovere; non per vicos neque per villas ad ecclesiam vicinas vel terminantes sine magisterio vel disciplina, qui sarabaiti dicuntur, luxoriando vel fornicando vel etiam caetera iniqua operando, quae consentiri absordum est." This text reveals the impact of monasticism on all forms of communal religious lifes: together with the *gyrovagi*, the *sarabaiti* belong to St. Benedict's two categories of undisciplined and therefore false monks; *Regula Benedicti* 1.6, ed. A. De Vogüé and J. Neufville, *La Règle de Saint Benoît*, Sources Chrétiennes 181 (Paris, 1972), 438. They are also mentioned in *Duplex legationis edictum* (789) *MGH Capit*. 1:63.

23. *Capitulare missorum generale* 17, *MGH Capit* 1: 95: "Et omnibus notum sit, quia nullatenus in ista mala in nulla loco amplius in toto regno nostro consentire audeamus: quanto minus quidem inter eos qui castitatis et sanctimoniae emendatores esse cupimus. Certe si amplius quid tale ad aures nostras pervenerit, non solum in eos, sed etiam in ceteris, qui in talia consentiant, talem ultionem facimus, ut nullus christianus qui hoc audierit, nullatenus tale quid perpetrare amplius presumerit." The repetitive expression "non amplius" indicates both a local scandal and the fear of pollution spreading.

24. Mayke de Jong, "Carolingian Monasticism: The Power of Prayer," in *The New Cambridge Medieval History* 2, ed. Rosamond McKitterick (Cambridge, 1995), 622-53; see also eadem, *In Samuel's Image*, 245-66.

25. About female prayer in Merovingian society, see Gisela Muschiol,

Famula Dei. Zur Liturgie in merowingischen Frauenklöstern, Beiträge zur Geschichte des alten Mönchtums und des Benediktinertums 42 (Münster, 1994). The importance of female prayer was to be partly eclipsed by priest-monks able to celebrate Mass. About the relation between monasticism and priesthood: Otto Nußbaum, *Kloster, Priestermönch und Privatmesse. Ihr Verhältnis im Westen von den Anfängen bis zum hohen Mittelalter*, Theophaneia, Beiträge zur Religions-und Kirchengeschichte des Altertums 14, (Bonn, 1961); Angelus Häussling, *Mönchskonvent und Eucharistiefeier. Eine Studie über die Messe in der abendländischen Klosterliturgie des frühen Mittelalters und zur Geschichte der Messhäufigkeit*, Liturgiehistorische Quellen und Forschungen 8 (Münster, 1973); Arnold Angenendt, "Missa specialis. Zugleich ein Beitrag zur Entstehung der Privatmessen," *Frühmittelalterliche Studien* 17 (1983): 153-221; Dorothee König, *Amt und Askese. Priesteramt und Mönchtum bei den lateinischen Kirchenvätern in vorbenediktinischer Zeit*, Regulae Benedicti Studia, Supplementa 12 (St. Ottilien, 1985).

26. Raymond Van Dam, *Leadership and Community in Late Antique Gaul* (Berkeley/Los Angeles/Oxford, 1985), esp. 230-55; Ian Wood, "The Ecclesiastical Politics of Merovingian Clermont," in *Ideal and Reality in Frankish and Anglo-Saxon Society. Studies presented to J.M. Wallace Hadrill*, ed. Patrick Wormald with Donald Bullough and Roger Collins (Oxford, 1983), pp. 32-57.

27. Gregory of Tours, *Libri decem historiarum* 2.1, MGH SSrMerov 1/1, 37-38. One of the miracles involved the newborn infant revealing that Brictius was *not* his father; for a baby making the opposite statement (about Bishop Rusticus of Trier), see the *Vita Goaris 7*, MGH SSrMerov 4, 417-19.

28. For "suspicion" of clerical behavior and possible loss of reputation, see the following councils: Epaon (517) 16, *Concilia Galliae a. 511-a. 695*, ed. C. de Clercq, CCSL 148A (Turnhout, 1963), p. 109; Orléans (538) 2, ibid., p. 115; Orléans (541) 10, ibid., p. 17; Orléans (549) 3, ibid., p. 149; Tours (567) 13, 15, 20 ibid., pp. 180-184; Mâcon (581-583) 1, ibid., p. 223.

29. Clermont (535) 16, *Concilia Galliae*, p. 109.

30. Orléans (549), 3, *Concilia Galliae*, p. 149; Orléans (541) 17, ibid., p.

136.

31. Tours 567, 15 (14), *Concilia Galliae*, p. 181: "Et ne occasio famam laceret honestatis, quia aliqui laici, dum diversa perpetrant adulteria, hoc, quod de se sciunt, in aliis suspiciatur, sicut ait Seneca: *Pessimum in eum vitium esse, qui in id, quod insanit, ceteris putat furere. . . .*"

32. Tours (567) 20 (19), *Concilia Galliae*, p. 184.

33. For the early developments, see Dorothee König, *Amt und Askese*, 210-23.

34. Tours (567) 13 (12), *Concilia Galliae*, pp. 180-81.

35. Tours (567) 20 (19), *Concilia Galliae*, pp. 183-84.

36 William E. Klingshirn, *Caesarius of Arles. The Making of a Christian Community in Late Antique Gaul* (Cambridge, 1994), 91-93; Dorothee König, *Amt und Askese*, 213-22. About Caesarius's impact on Carolingian reform: Klingshirn, *Caesarius of Arles*, 273-86.

37. Ian Wood, *The Merovingian Kingdoms, 450-751* (London/New York, 1994), 200.

38. Council of Tours (567) 13 (12), *Concilia Galliae*, pp. 180-81: ". . .ut nec hi, qui ad spem recuperandam clericorum servitute nuntriantur, famularum propinqua contagione polluantur. . . ."

39. Gregory of Tours, *Vitae patrum* 2.2, *MGH SSrMerov* 1/2, p. 220; *ibid.* 8.2, p. 242.

40. De Jong, *In Samuel's Image*, 198-204.

41. *Vita altera Desiderii* 7, *MGH SSrMerov* 3, p. 640.

42. Boniface to Pope Zachary (742) *Epistolae* 50, *MGH Epp* sel 1, 82: "Si intervenero illos inter diaconos, qui nominant, qui a pueritia sua sempra in

stupris, semper in adulteribus et in omnibus semper spurcitiis vitam ducentes, sub tali testimonio venerunt ad diaconatum, et modo in diaconatu concubinas quattuor vel quinque, vel plures noctu in lectu habentes, Evangelium tamen legere, et diaconos se nominare nec erubescunt nec metuunt: et in talibus incestis ad ordinem presbiteratus venientes et hisdem peccatis perdurantes, et peccata peccatis adicientes, presbiteratus officio funguentes, dicent se pro populo posse intercedere et sacras oblationes offerre, novissime, quod peius est, sub talibus testimoniis per gradus singulos ascendentes ordinantur et nominantur episcopi. . . ."

43. On Boniface and other Ango-Saxon child oblates, see de Jong, *In Samuel's Image*, 46-55. About "minsters": Sarah Foot, "Anglo-Saxon minsters: A Review of Terminology," (eds.), *Pastoral Care Before the Parish*, ed. John Blair and Richard Sharpe (Leicester, 1992), 212-25. But see now Catherine Cubitt, *Anglo-Saxon Church Councils c. 650-c. 850* (London/New York, 1995), 116-20.

44. See, for example, *Concilium Germanicum* (742) 6, *MGH Conc* 2/1:4, which punished fornicating *servi Dei* and *ancillae Christi* by a penance of bread and water *in carcere*; if a priest was involved he had to remain locked up for two years after having been whipped; a monk or cleric had to be incarcerated for a year after having been whipped thrice (presumably after the third offense). Not only the harshness of this punishment was new but the fact that conciliar decisions were subsequently issued as a capitulary. About the synods under Boniface, see Hartmann, *Die Synoden der Karolingerzeit*, 47-63, and for an excellent discussion of the importance of the reform council of Clofesho and Boniface's influence on its decrees, see Cubitt, *Anglo-Saxon Church Councils*, 102-10.

45. Especially the capitulary issued from the council in the royal *palatium* of Ver (755) emphasized royal control of monastic communities. Council of Ver (755) 5, *MGH Capit* 1: 34: "Ut monasteria, tam virorum quam puellarum, secundum ordinem regulariter vivant; et si hoc facere contempserint, episcopus in cuius parrochia esse videtur hoc emendare debeat. Quod si non potuerit, hoc quem metropolitanum constituimus innotescat, et ipse hoc emendare faciat. Quod si hoc nec ipse emendare potuerit, ad sinodum publicum exinde veniant, et ibidem canonicam

sententiam accipiat. Et si publicum sinodem contempserint, aut honorem suum perdat aut excommunicetur ab omnibus episcopis, et talis in eius locum in ipso sinodo constituatur per verbum et voluntatem domno rege vel consensu servorum Dei, qui secundum sanctam ipsam gregem regat." Cf. de Jong, *In Samuel's Image*, 249-51. About Carolingian reform, see especially Rosamond McKitterick, *The Frankish Church and the Carolingian Reforms 789-985* (London, 1977), and two excellent recent surveys: Giles Brown, "Introduction: The Carolingian Renaissance", in *Carolingian Culture: Emulation and Innovation* (Cambridge, 1994) ed. Rosamond McKitterick, pp. 1-51; John J. Contreni, "The Carolingian Renaissance: Education and Literary Culture," in *The New Cambridge Medieval History*, 2 ed., Rosamond McKitterick (Cambridge, 1995), pp. 709-57.

46. Fourth council of Toledo (633) 49, ed. José Vivez, *Concilios Visigóticos e Hispano-Romanos* (Madrid, 1963), 208; de Jong, *In Samuel's Image*, 40-46.

47. Ibid. 24, pp. 201-202: "Prona est omnis aetas ab adolescentia in malum, nicil enim incertius quam vita adolescentium; ob hoc constituendum oportuit, ut si qui in clero puberes aut adulescentes existunt, omnes in uno conclavi atrii conmorentur, ut lubricae aetatis annos non in luxuria sed in disciplinis ecclesiasticis agant deputari probatissimo seniori, quem et magistrum doctrinae et testem vitae habeant. Quod si aliqui ex his pupilli existunt sacerdotali tutela foveantur, ut et vita eorum a criminibus intacta sit, et res ab iniuria improborum. Qui autem his praeceptis resultaverint, monasteriis deputentur, ut vagantes animi et superbi severiori regula distringantur."

48. Second council of Toledo (527) 1, *Concilios Visigóticos*, pp. 42-43. Compare the almost contemporary council of Vaison (529) 1, *Concilia Galliae*, p. 78, which urged priests to take unmarried *lectores* into their households for instruction, "according to the custom we know to be successful in the whole of Italy;" this would earn them not only worthy successors but eternal remuneration. Once their charges had grown up, they should be given a choice between marriage and the clerical state.

49. Chapters 1-19 of the fourth council of Toledo dealt with liturgical

unification, chapters 52-53 with "wandering" monks and clerics, chapters 57-66 with relations with Jews. Significantly, chapter 2 spoke of the "scandal" of liturgical diversity in *Spania et Gallia* (ibid. p. 188); in chapter 6 on baptism (ibid., pp. 191-192) Pope Gregory the Great's liberal attitude in liturgical matters is discarded "propter vitandum autem schismaticis scandalum vel heretici dogmatis." On liturgical diversity, see Yitzak Hen, "Unity in Diversity: the Liturgy of Frankish Gaul before the Carolingians," in *Unity and Diversity in the Church*, ed. R. N. Swanson, Studies in Church History 32 (Oxford, 1996), pp. 19-30.

50. Fourth Council of Toledo c. 2, p. 188.

51. For new views on the concept of immunity, cf. *Property and Power in the Early Middle Ages* ed. Wendy Davies and Paul Fouracre (Cambridge, 1995); about royal *tuitio* of monasteries: Joseph Semmler, "Episcopi potestas und Karolingische Klosterpolitik" in *Mönchtum, Episkopat und Adel zur Gründungszeit des Klosters Reichenau*, ed. Arno Borst, Vorträge und Forschungen 20 (Sigmaringen, 1974) pp. 305-395; idem, "Pippin III. und die fränkischen Klöster", in *Francia* 3 (1975), 88-146; de Jong, *Carolingian monasticism*, 623-29.

52. *Admonitio generalis 72, MGH Capit* 1: 59-60.

53. Ibid. 70: 59.

54. On these attitudes, see Thomas F. X. Noble, "Tradition and Learning in Search of Ideology: The *Libri Carolini*," in *The Gentle Voices of Teachers. Aspects of Learning in the Carolingian Age*, ed. Richard E. Sullivan (Columbus, 1995), 227-60.

55. Hincmar, *Capitulare IV* (874) 3, *MGH Capit Ep* 2: 83: "Iam vobis capitulum ex sanctis scripturis et catholicorum dictis donavi de inconvenienti accensu et indebita familiaritate ad feminas, sed video quosdam vestrum illud parvipendere." Hincmar referred to his extensive *Capitulare II*, 21, *MGH Capit Ep* 2: 52-59, which gathers most of the traditional canonical repertoire on celibacy, including Pope Siricius' letter to Himerius of Tarragona and other papal letters.

56. Flodoard, *Historia Remensis Ecclesiae* 3.1, *MGH SS* 13: 475: "Is siquidem Hincmar a pueritia in monasterio sancti Dionysii sub Hilduino abbate monasteriali religione nutritus et studiis litterarum imbutus indeque pro sui tam generis quam sensus nobilitate in palatium Ludowici imperatoris deductus et familiarem ipsiam noticiam adeptus fuerat. . . ." For Hincmar's biography, see Jean Devisse, *Hincmar, Archevêque de Reims (845-882)* (Geneva. 1976), 1089-97; also Rudolf Schieffer, "Hinkmar von Reims," in *Theologische Realenzyklopedie* 15 (1986), 355-60.

57. A brief and fairly representative rendering of the canonical "exceptions" of Nicaea (325) c. 3 is provided by the *Capitula Corbeiensia* 6 *MGH Capit Ep* 3:12: "Ut nullus sacerdos feminam secum habitare permittat excepto matere et sorore et amita." This capitulary was issued in 803-805, possibly by Magnus of Sens. Pokorny's new edition gives a convenient survey of the many decrees in the episcopal capitularies concerning priests and "extraneous women," which will therefore not be repeated here: ibid., p. 12, n. 11. Note, however, that Theodulf (*Capitulare I* 12. *MGH Capit Ep* 1:111) took a stricter view of these matters, for the presence of close female relatives might bring more dangerous women visitors: "Nulla femina cum presbitero in una domo habitet. Quamvis enim canones matrem et sororem et huiuscemodi personas, in quibus nulla sit suspicio, cum illo habitare concedant, hoc nos omnibus idcirco amputamus, quia in obsequio sive occasione illarum veniunt aliae feminae, quae non sunt ei affinitate coniunctae et eum ad peccandum illiciant."

58. Janet L. Nelson, "Making Ends Meet: Wealth and Poverty in the Carolingian Church," *Studies in Church History* 24 (1987): 25-36 (repr. in eadem, *The Frankish World 750-900* (London/Rio Grande, 1996), 145-53). About lay society and Christian practice in the Carolingian age, see Julia M. H. Smith, "Religion and Lay Society," in *The New Cambridge Medieval History* 2, ed. Rosamond McKitterick (Cambridge, 1995), 654-78.

59. For the main data of Hrabanus's biography, see Raymond Kottje, "Hrabanus Maurus," *Die deutsche Literatur des Mittelalters. Verfasserlexikon* 4 (1983), 166-96; his oblation is discussed in de Jong, *Samuel's Image*, 73-77; about his role as biblical commentator for kings, Mayke de Jong, "Old Law

and New-found Power. Hrabanus Maurus and the Old Testament," in *Centres of Learning. Learning and Location in Pre-Modern Europe and the Near East*, ed. Jan-Willem Drijvers and Alisdair A. McDonald (Leiden/New York/Cologne, 1995), 161-74.

60. *Regula Benedicti* 59, ed. Adalbert de Vogüé and Jean Neufville, *La Règle de Saint Benoît* 2, pp. 632-34; cf. de Jong, *In Samuel's Image*, 23-30.

61. De Jong, *In Samuel's Image*, 132-44.

62. Hrabanus Maurus, *Epistolae* 5, *MGH Epp*. 5: 389: ". . .nutrimentum parvulorum, quod non parvam nobis ingerit molestiam et lectionis facit iniuriam." Brun Candidus characterized Hraban Maur as a "presbyter et monachus, multorum iure magister": *Vita metrica Eigilis* 2.17, v. 99, ed. *MGH Poet. lat.* 2: 111.

63. De Jong, *In Samuel's Image*, pp. 242-45.

64. Hrabanus Maurus, *Carmina* 97, *MGH Poet. lat.* 2: 243-4: "Urbe quidem hac genitus sum ac sacro fonte renatus,/in Fulda post haec dogma sacrum didici./Quo monachus factus seniorum iussa sequabar, /norma mihi vitae regula sancta fuit."

65. About Alcuin's monastic youth: Donald A. Bullough, "Alcuin and the Kingdom of Heaven: Liturgy, Theology and the Carolingian Age," in idem, *Carolingian Renewal. Sources and Heritage* (Manchester/New York, 1991), 161-240; idem, "Alcuino e la tradizione culturale insulare," in *I problemi dell'occidente nel secolo VIII*, Settimane di studio 20 (Spoleto, 1973), 571-600; idem, "What Has Ingeld to Do with Lindisfarne?", *Anglo-Saxon England* 22 (1993): 93-125. Mary D. Garrison, *Alcuin's world through his letters and verse* (Cambridge, 1996; PhD thesis); Mayke de Jong, "From scolastici to scioli: Alcuin and the Formation of an Intellectual Elite," in *Germania Latina* 3, ed. Alasdair McDonald and Tette Hofstra (forthcoming, Groningen, 1997).

66. Alcuin, *Epistolae, MGH Epp* 4: 85-86: "Vos fragiles infantiae meae annos materno fovistis affectu; et lascivium puericiae tempus sustinuistis

patientia et paternae castigationis disciplinis ad perfectam viri edocuistis
aetatem et sacrareum eruditione disciplinarum roborastis." Trans. Stephen
Allott, *Alcuin of York, c. A.D. 732 to 804. His Life and Letters* (York, 1974),
p. 2. Cf. his letter to his pupil Dodo, Alcuin, *Epistolae* 65, *MGH Ep* 4: 107:
"Carissimo filiolo meo, quem et sero genui et cito dimisi, nec bene
ablactatus raptus est ab uberibus meis. Inimitiorque noverca tam tenerum
de paterno gremio per libidinum vortices caro rapuit."

67. Alcuin, *Epistolae* 42:86: "O omnium dilectissimi patres et fratres,
memories mei estote. Ego vester ero, sive in vita, sive in morte. Et forte
miserebitur mei Deus, ut, cuius infantiam aluistis, eius senectutem sepelietis.
Et si alter corpori locus deputabitur, tamen animae--qualemcumque
habitura erit--per vestras sanctas, Deo donante, intercessiones, requies
vobiscum, credo, donabitur." Trans. Allott, *Alcuin of York*, p. 3.

68. Ekkehard, *Casus sancti Galli* 5, 56, ed. Hans F. Haefele, *Ekkehardi
IV Casus sancti Galli*, Ausgewählte Quellen zur deutschen Geschichte des
Mittelalters 10 (Darmstadt, 1980) 24, 156. Ekkehard's year of birth and
death are not certain, but he had already entered St. Gall by the year 1000
and lived long enough to refer in a gloss to the death of Pope Victor (1057).
Cf. Hans F. Haefele, "Ekkehard IV von St Gallen," in: *Die deutsche Literatur
des Mittelalters. Verfasserlexikon* 2 (1980), 455-465, with references to older
literature. Also: Mayke de Jong, "The Cloister as Frontier: the case of
Ekkehard's *Casus sancti Galli*," in *Grenzen und Differenz im früheren
Mittelalter*, ed. Walter Pohl and Helmut Reimitz (forthcoming).

69. Ekkehard, *Casus sancti Galli* 136, p. 264: "Claustrum autem sancti
Galli . . . ab antiqua patrum memoria tantae venerationi semper est
habitum, ut nemini vel potentissiorum seculi canonicorum vel laicorum
introitus vel etiam introspectus eius licuerit."

70. Mayke de Jong, "Growing up in a Carolingian Monastery: Magister
Hildemar and His Oblates,"*Journal of Medieval History* 9 (1983), 99-128;
eadem, *In Samuel's Image*, pp. 145-145, with references to further literature
about Hildemar.

71. Hildemar, *Expositio regulae S. Benedicti* 62, ed. R. Mittermüller,

Expositio regulae ab Hildemaro tradita et nunc primum typis mandata (Regensburg etc., 1880), pp. 570-71.

72. Hildemar, *Expositio* 28, p. 368: "Nam non est rectum, ut ita expellatur ille, qui in monasterio fuit nutritus ab infantia in bona vita, et eat ad pejorem, id est ad saecularem vitam, sicuti expellatur ille, qui de saeculo veniens et in bona vita ante non vixit." See also ibid. 2: 109 and 71: 637.

73. De Jong, *In Samuel's Image*, 152-53.

74. *Statuta Murbacensia* c. 30, ed. Joseph Semmler, *Legislatio Aquisgranensis*, *Corpus consuetudinum monasticarum* 1 (Siegburg, 1963) p. 442: "Nos vero qui ab ipsis pene cunabulis a maioribus nostris eruditi in eadem dispositione viximus. . . ." The author refers to the impending substitution of the Roman Office by that of Benedict's Rule, an innovation which led to a major crisis of identity in many Carolingian monasteries.

75. Joseph Semmler "Die Beschlüsse des Aachener Konzils im Jahre 816," *Zeitschrift für Kirchengeschichte* 74 (1963): 15-82; idem, "Benedictus II: Una regula/una consuetudo," in *Benedictine Culture, 750-1050*, ed. Willem Lourdaux and Dirk Verhelst, Mediaevalia Lovaniensia, Ser. 1, Studia 11 (Louvain, 1983), 1-49.

76. This is how the royal blessing-prayer *"Prospice"* formulated the king's position vis-à-vis the church: ". . .consolator ecclesiarum atque coenobiorum sanctorum maxima cum pietate regalis munificentiae. . ."; Janet L. Nelson, "Kingship and Empire in the Carolingian World," in *Carolingian Culture*, ed. Rosamond McKitterick (Cambridge, 1994), 58. The prayer was probably composed during the reign of Charlemagne and incorporated into the rite of royal consecration.

77. Guarding the cloister and sheltering young charges from the outside world was not only an issue in monasteries, but also in canonical communities: see the council of Aachen (816), cc. 135 and 144, *MGH Conc* II/2, pp. 413 and 418.

78. Theodulf, *Capitulare I* 20, *MGH Capit Ep* 1: 116: "Presbyteri per

villas et vicos scolas habeant. Et si quilibet fidelium suos parvulos ad discendas litteras eis commendare vult, eos suscipere et docere non rennuant, sed cum summa caritate eos doceant attendentes illud, quod scriptum est: *Qui autem docti fuerint, fulgebunt quasi splendor firmamenti. Et quia iustitiam erudiunt multi, fulgebunt quasi stellae in perpetuas aeternitates* (Dan. 12,3). Cum ergo eos docent, nihil ab eis pretii pro hac re exigant nec aliquid ab eis accipiant except, quod eis parentes caritatis studio sua voluntate obtulerint."

79. Theodulf, *Capitulare I* 19, *MGH Capit Ep* 1: 115-16: "Si quis ex presbyteris voluerit nepotem suum aut aliquem consanguineum ad scolam mittere, in ecclesia sanctae Crucis aut in monasterio Sancti Aniani aut in sancti Benedicti aut sancti Lifardi aut in ceteris de his coenobiis, quae nobis ad regendum concessa sunt, ei licentiam id faciendi concedimus."

80. Council of Aachen (817) 5, ed. Joseph Semmler, *Corpus consuetudinem monasticarum* 1: 474.

81. Ibid. 17: 477. Cf. de Jong, *In Samuel's Image*, 60-68.

82. De Jong, *In Samuel's Image*, 232-45.

83. Walter of Orléans, *Capitulare 6*, *MGH Capit* 1, p. 189: "Ut unusquisque presbiter suum habeat clericum, quem religiose educare procuret et, si possibilitas illi est, scolam in ecclesia sua habere non negligat sollerterque caveat, ut, quos ad erudiendum suscepit, caste sinceriter nutriat." This capitulary was issued c. 869-70.

Why Celibacy? Odo of Cluny and the Development of a New Sexual Morality

Phyllis G. Jestice

For at least a millennium, the stand of the Roman Catholic church has been that its clergy should be celibate. Indeed, people often assume that this was always the case. Paul's wish that all were celibate as he was is remembered and frequently quoted (I Cor. 7.7-8). On the other hand, though, it usually astonishes students in my History of Christianity course if I refer to the apostle Peter's wife (Matt. 8:14, Luke 4:38). The questions of this volume are, of course, when, where, and why clerical celibacy became one of the reformed church's prominent goals. In this paper, I would like to present a model for how clerical celibacy might have become an important reforming issue. To do this, I believe it is necessary to examine the teachings of the first firmly self-motivated reforming group in the medieval church: the reformed monks of the early tenth century. Through the writings of monastic reformers, I believe it is possible to uncover strands of doctrine that eventually joined together to impose a new sexual morality not just on secular clerics but on all Christians. The evidence suggests that, far from being a monocausal development, celibacy became a potent force only through a combination of monastic spirituality, a strong emphasis on ritual purity, and the beginnings of a real effort to convince Christians that they could hope to emulate Christ.

While many have assigned some role, more or less important, to reformed monks in the larger reform of the church and Christian society, my goal is more modest. The sources simply do not exist to postulate an official position on clerical celibacy in the tenth century. We cannot even do much more than guess about the views of a single reforming center. The most we can do is uncover hints at what one or two individuals thought and construct their theology from their often sparse words and what they imply about their values. For the issue of celibacy and how it gained a new level of importance in ecclesiastical circles, we are particularly fortunate, though, in having the works of Abbot Odo of Cluny (926-44). Through his writings, one can reconstruct an extended model of how the question of celibacy became a pressing one not just for monks but for secular clergy and, indeed, all Christians. We cannot know if Odo's ideas were a reflection of the thought of his time, a catalyst, or maybe even a largely ignored annoyance among his targeted audience. Still, they exist as evidence of ideas that existed within reformed monasticism in the early tenth century. Therefore, through an examination primarily of Odo of Cluny's works, I would like to present a model of how celibacy might well have become an issue important to ecclesiastical reformers.

Because of Abbot Odo, this study must focus almost exclusively on Cluny, the reformed monastery founded in Burgundy in 909. Of course, Cluny was not the only monastic reform center of the tenth century. Other reform loci, most notably Gorze and Brogne, were often of equal if not greater influence than were the Cluniacs upon many aspects of monastic and more general Christian life. However, for the case of celibacy, the historian must rely almost exclusively on Cluniac material to understand the thoughts and ideals of reformers. We know an enormous amount about the spiritual views of early Cluny by comparison to those of other centers, or to be more accurate, we know the views of Cluny's second abbot, St. Odo. Besides a hagiographical work about Odo by his disciple John of Salerno, there are the abbot's own *vita* of St. Gerald of Aurillac and several sermons. Odo also penned two longer contemplative reflections on the world and God's plan of salvation. These densely packed theological works, a long poetical meditation on sacred history known as the *Occupatio mentis*, and an even longer treatise in three books, the *Collationes*, give a unique insight into the beliefs and practices of an early tenth-century monk. By comparison with other sources where they exist, these works can give a sense not just of distinctly "Cluniac" spirituality but of how Odo's beliefs fit into the spectrum of tenth-century religion. Therefore, we can not only see how monks might have felt about issues related to celibacy and whether they tried to apply their "angelic" life to a broader sector of the population, we can also gain some sense of whether these ideas influenced others.

In order to understand Odo's teachings on chastity and fornication, one must realize that the abbot was not just a monk writing for other monks. A highly intelligent and well-read man, he had been a canon of St. Martin of Tours before making his monastic profession to Berno of Baume, Cluny's founding abbot. Thus Odo himself had been a member of the wealthy and privileged secular clergy. While his works display deep familiarity with monastic classics, this background perhaps made him more willing to look beyond such works than a typical monk would have been. That helps explain why Odo's *Collationes*, which gives by far the best picture of sexual views available from the first half of the century, was not simply an expression of monastic piety on the subject. Instead it gives invaluable insight into how a reworked notion of Christian celibacy could have taken root in non-monastic circles. Odo addressed this work, an extended treatise that ranges widely over issues of sin and the struggle between good and evil, to a bishop.[1] And certainly he did not intend the *Collationes* as an instruction book on the monastic life for a bishop of particularly pious inclinations. The context of the work makes it clear that Odo's aims extended beyond repeating traditional monastic piety. Many issues he addresses are more appropriate to the secular clergy than to monks, and he frequently harks back to his own experience as a canon at St. Martin of Tours for pertinent examples. Especially the third book of the treatise makes his secular bias plain. Much of it is an extended exhortation to preachers, which would have been very odd in a work on monastic spirituality. The *Collationes* appears to fit into the same tenth-century literary niche as the Irish *Dialogus de statu sanctae ecclesiae*, which, Heinz Löwe argues, comes from the intellectual world and influence of Odo of Cluny. Certainly the starting point of both works is a conviction that ecclesiastical censures have proven powerless to correct the failings of the church. Therefore, the authors consider it necessary to undertake the task of clerical reform themselves by means of moral persuasion.[2]

Hartmut Hoffmann uses the *Collationes* as his earliest witness that Cluniacs were interested in the reform of the secular clergy, instead of just monasteries.[3] Certainly Odo of Cluny could have reached a wide audience, including not just the monks of his congregation but clergy and laity he impressed with his personal charisma. As John of Salerno speaks of him, probably with little exaggeration, "He [Odo] became known to kings, was familiar to bishops. Beloved of the secular lords. For any monasteries that were built in their territories they handed over to his rule. . . ." Some bishops even left their sees and joined Odo's band of monks.[4] In such circumstances, it is not surprising that Cluny's role in the spiritual life of its era has received such extensive attention. I believe that the picture that emerges of Odo is of a man, a monk to be sure, who was able to see beyond the problems of his own order of society. Indeed, especially the *Collationes* reveal at times a breadth of thought comparable to Odo's model, the monk-pope Gregory the Great.[5]

First, it is very important to note that the main monastic collection of spiritual reasons to protect celibacy has a relatively small place in Odo's work. This is one of its most outstanding points of difference from other spiritual works coming from a monastic circle, seldom paralleled except by such rare studies as Gregory the Great's *Pastoral Rule*. Still, a long monastic tradition provides a framework of assumptions and an arsenal of arguments for Odo's treatise.

Medieval monks devoted considerable space in their literature to issues of human sexuality. To be more precise, Christian monks from very early times believed that one of the most important ingredients of a successful religious life is a commitment to unwavering chastity. This ingredient of wholesome religion was so standard in the early and central Middle Ages that few felt it necessary to belabor the point. Just to give one famous example, the vows taken by a Benedictine monk are not, as many think, a commitment to "poverty, chastity, and obedience." Instead, the Benedictine Rule enjoins the monk to "obedience, conversion of life, and stability."[6] Benedict, like other monastic legislators, assumed chastity to be such a standard element of religious life that it barely merits a passing mention in the Rule. John Cassian's extended and rather explicit descriptive statements, taking up an entire chapter and assorted other sections of his *Conferences*, made it certain that monks fully understood the dangers of rampant sexuality. It is difficult to imagine that a monk would not have been aware that sexual renunciation was a vital part of his life.[7] Penitentials urged much harsher punishments for sexual sins committed by monks than by others.[8] Indeed, by the time of the monastic renaissance in the early ninth century, the issue of chastity, as far as monks were concerned, was a dead letter. Maybe all monks did not lead a celibate life, but there was no room for discussion on whether fornicating monks had sinned or not. Thus Smaragdus in his *Diadema monachorum* addressed the issue of weakness of the flesh as a lamentable fall from proper monastic observance, but he did not question that unchastity in particular was a grave sin.[9]

One should note, though, that more than earlier authors, monastic writers of the ninth century emphasized that chastity was a sign of saintly, heroic virtue. Few appeared to believe that everyone or even many people could possibly live up to such high ideals, although of course the better Christian should try to do so. As Alcuin (died 806) pointed out in his treatise *On the Virtues and Vices*, chastity is equivalent to the angelic life.[10] This work, addressed to a count, makes it quite plain that chastity is a predominantly monastic virtue. Normal men could not hope to be angels any more than they could be saints. Thus, Alcuin did not urge sexual renunciation upon his patron. Instead, the scholar simply reminds Count Guido that legitimately married couples should engage in intercourse only at the proper times not that they should abstain completely.[11] The tenor of Alcuin's discussion is that while chastity is angelic, fornication is demonic. Still, he does not really draw out the implications of his theme.[12] Similarly, Smaragdus of St. Mihiel claims that virgins will enjoy greater happiness in the life to come than others and, like Alcuin, equates virgins and angels.[13] Again, the comparison is not one calculated to make people believe that emulation is very possible.

Comparing Odo's works to those of other authors of the ninth and tenth centuries, one would expect a greater emphasis on the precarious nature of a sinless life, especially when such matters as celibacy are concerned. Especially common from the ninth at least through the eleventh century is the depiction of a monastery as a safe haven from the storms of temptation that rock the world outside its walls. Only a monastery can offer a reasonable chance of safety. Thus in the early ninth century, the monk Candidus reported a speech supposedly by Emperor Louis the Pious to the monks of Fulda. In it, the emperor especially warned the monks to beware of seduction. He reminded the members of the community that they were all living in great peril on a shallow beach and that a tempest (temptation) could sweep them out to sea at any time.[14]

An even more telling statement of the ninth-century belief that only monks could hope to resist the more attractive temptations of the world outside of the cloister is Hrabanus Maurus' extended defense of child oblation as a permanent commitment to the monastic state. This treatise, written in c. 820, lays out one of the fullest medieval justifications of the monastic life. Hrabanus' nemesis, Gottschalk of Orbai, had tried to escape the monastery to which his parents had given him. The ensuing struggles with his abbot, Hrabanus himself, and several church councils, led to a major debate on the monastic state. Gottschalk's views amounted to a surprisingly positive valuation of life in the world, and in the process anticipated John Milton's argument that virtue has little value if protected all the time by high walls. Hrabanus, in one of the few glimpses we have of him as an individual rather than an encyclopedist, responded that there would be no hope of salvation at all if it were not for the restrictions of the cloister. His opponent may mock him for fleeing temptation, but Hrabanus responds candidly that he flees lest he be conquered by forces that are too strong for him. "For there is no security," he says, "sleeping next to a serpent."[15] Clearly only monks were responsible for avoiding certain vices because of the plain impossibility of avoiding them when "out in the world."

Such a monastically-oriented assessment of human sexuality is present in Odo's works. For example, he points out in passing that having both God and libido in the heart at the same time is impossible.[16] Similarly, he expresses concern with the spiritual state of mind of monks that has no part in his main discussion. Thus he approvingly cites a story from Jerome about how the saint would not allow monks to partake of communion if they had had lustful thoughts during the night before.[17] He assumes that the monastic vows are a permanent commitment and that this commitment should include chastity. Thus, for example, he tells of two nuns who abandoned their convent. One died soon of a tumor on her arm. The other, who receives much more attention, married soon after she reentered the world. The result was a monstrous birth, obviously God's punishment for this abuse by a nun who had been consecrated to his service.[18] Monks, or nuns, were to be chaste or could expect divine retribution. This sense that chastity was a particularly monastic virtue did not die out as soon as Odo set pen to parchment. Other tenth-century authors placed more of a stress on continence as a sign of the "angelic life" that only monks could hope to attain. Thus, Rather of Verona (d. 974) inverted Odo's warning that pride could lead to unchastity, stating, on the contrary, that the chaste should beware of pride in their superior spiritual state. These spiritual adepts, clearly monks from the context, should constantly be aware of "earthly fragility." A person can count on no earthly state as permanent. Rather concludes his peroration with the blanket statement that for a person successfully to live a chaste life is to lead an angelic life on earth.[19]

Thus the religious view of celibacy at least to the tenth century put most of its energy into a very monastically-oriented teaching on sexual vice. These essentially monastic lessons were highly spiritualized. Certainly, one should avoid the physical act of intercourse. Since monasticism was the ideal life, the situation was at least superficially simple. Everyone with any pretense to holiness ought to be chaste. In this way monastic authors oriented celibacy toward an improved spiritual state and eventual salvation rather than a particular purpose on earth that abstinence could establish. As John Cassian said, the goal of chastity was to make it possible to reach the heights of love of God.[20] The struggle for chastity is part of the ongoing war between flesh and spirit that is the lot of fallen humanity. Since vices and passions turn the eyes away from a state of purity, the would-be holy man should fight them with all his strength.[21] Chastity kept the mind turned toward God, made meditation possible, and kept the Christian's mind focused on eternal verity rather than transitory pleasures of the world.[22]

This attitude was directed mostly toward monks, carefully shut away from the temptations of daily life in the world and dedicated at least theoretically to striving for perfection. The authors of these views of celibacy showed only a passing interest in non-monks, unless their examples were intended to turn someone toward the monastic life. These authors implicitly recognized the rest of the clergy, and the rest of Christendom, as lesser animals, who were less able to fight their bestial natures because of their contact with the polluting elements of secular society. Some regulations state that bishops should remain celibate; sometimes this even extended to other highly placed members of the secular clergy. Thus a married bishop should no longer cohabit with his wife in the early centuries, and by the ninth century bishops were expected to be unwed. A particularly pious bishop might have "taken up the cross" of full monastic life as an extraordinary act of renunciation. It is likely that entire abstinence from sexual relations was part of this process of turning into a monk. For example, Bishop Ulrich of Augsburg, late in his life (and after being severely censured for delegating an illegal amount of authority to a nephew), vowed that he would withdraw to Benedictine observance for the rest of his life. Since he already fasted, rarely ate meat, prayed, neglected his office for pious practices, participated in the daily offices, and celebrated several masses a day, there was little left to distinguish him from a monk of his time, except perhaps physical renunciation.

Certainly some members of the higher clergy emulated the religious practices of monks, although this view must be modified in light of Stephen Jaeger's work emphasizing the class of saints' lives that praised bishops for their public and administrative functions.[23] Nevertheless, it appears that hagiographers emphasized a particular set of virtues in bishops: either administrative care for the people of God (such as in Ruotger's *vita* of Archbishop Bruno of Cologne[24]) or their piety, expressed in extremely monastic ways. These sources do not speak specifically of our issues of fornication, avoidance of women, and so on, but they present a general picture of holiness that is firmly based on that present in monasticism of the time. I believe that it is fair to assume that among other virtues, the subjects of these hagiographical accounts would have adopted the current monastic position on celibacy. What is more, they would have done so for monastic reasons of withdrawal from the world for the sake of nearness to God. Thus Bishop Ulrich of Augsburg (d. 973) showed his special devotion to God with a rigorous round of daily prayers. Not only did he take part in the regular offices of the cathedral clergy; he also recited the daily psalter, a profoundly monastic mode of prayer.[25] He also celebrated the Eucharist—one to three times a day if he was not too busy, but the hagiographer does not mention any special preparation for or grace that Ulrich gained by celebrating these masses.[26] The ninth-century missionary archbishop Ansgar (d. 865), himself a monk by profession, also focused his spirituality on monastic forms. According to his hagiographer, Ansgar developed a special, personalized order of psalms for use during the day—appropriate psalms for walking, dressing, putting shoes on, combing his hair, etc. While Rimbert, the author of the account, includes the fact that Ansgar would celebrate three or four masses a day, his emphasis is on monastic psalmody, clearly the best evidence that Ansgar was a godly man.[27] After all, monastic piety could do anything. There is even a Cluniac story of a monk named Odo (probably not our Abbot Odo) who, while praying before the cross one day, was so caught up in his devotions that he floated in the air for an hour until someone noticed and broke his concentration.[28]

Still, Odo's main interest is in the celibacy of the secular clergy, not of the monks. But he does not simply expect all priests to adopt monastic rules and live up to monastic standards. Instead he proposes a different set of reasons to encourage the secular clergy to celibacy, along with a simpler method of persuasion. It is actions, not thoughts, that play the dominant role in Odo's assessment of the effects of lust, and his concern is not the spiritual rewards of celibacy but with the punishment that awaits those who actively offend God by their sexual proclivities. Odo's position, however, was much more complicated than that monks (or others) should avoid sexual lures as they would serpents. Although his hagiographer is careful to depict the abbot with eyes humbly bent toward earth, following the precepts of the Benedictine Rule, he also has no objection to the youthful Odo consorting with women, without even a companion to act as chaperon. Thus John of Salerno tells how, when Odo was still a simple monk at Baume, a noble woman asked him to save her from her marriage. We know nothing about the husband in the case, but the fact that Odo acquiesced to the woman's wishes suggests that he held matrimonial law and custom in lower esteem than he did the ideals of celibacy. Odo took the woman to an oratory near his monastery. Since Odo had been responsible for "withdrawing her from the world," Abbot Berno ordered him not just to carry food to her regularly but to give her religious instruction, "lest at any time she should repent and at the suggestion of the devil return to the world." Odo did so and a few days later took her to a convent.[29]

It appears that normal relations with a husband could be counted as a lure of the devil. The story also suggests that Odo himself was not particularly afraid of sexual temptation. He

certainly appears more confident than John Cassian, that great
model of monastic life, who told monks above all things to flee from
women and bishops (women because of sexual temptation, bishops
because they were likely to force the monks to become priests and
take them away from their spiritual solitude).[30] For the later Cluniac
monks, such as Abbot Maiolus (d. 994), chastity was a central and
clearly noted part of their spiritual life. For example, Maiolus'
hagiographer Nalgodus stresses that his hero not only vowed
perpetual chastity while he was a boy but kept the vow until the day
he died.[31] But there was a change in attitudes toward human
sexuality in the time between Odo and Maiolus. Chastity had
moved from an assumed part of piety to a major battlefield in the
war for spiritual perfection, not just for monks but for every
Christian with ambitions of spiritual perfection.

It is very interesting that, despite the much-touted emphasis in
the central Middle Ages on sinful deeds rather than intentionality,
these monastic texts with their emphasis on mental purity were
popular reading. Here we can only speculate on how these two
approaches toward sin could function in the same society. It seems
likely that at least reforming monks thought they had attained
sufficient spiritual heights to move beyond the physical to the
spiritual. Those who were not as spiritually advanced, the main run
of the secular clergy and almost all the laity, may well have received
a simpler teaching about sin based on deeds rather than intentions.
They would have been instructed firmly on their overt behavior and
kept in line by the threat of eternal chastisement for lapses. This
attitude marks Odo's works. While the *Collationes* cover a wide
range of topics, the issue of sexual offense or weakness, whether
called fornication, lust, libido, or concupiscence, appears frequently.
In keeping with the spiritual goals of the tenth century, Odo is
concerned with deeds, not thoughts, unlike the more interesting
early monastic authors. Thus his term *luxuria*, usually a catch-all
term for sexual offenses, refers, usually quite explicitly, to
intercourse rather than lustful thoughts.

Odo was not content to make his *Collationes* into a *florilegium*
of monastic views on celibacy, probably because he was not
primarily concerned with educating monks in his treatise. Odo's
discussion of the need for chastity by good Christians owes very
little to the standard works for monks that were available to him.

Unlike such authors as John Cassian, Alcuin, Paulinus of Aquileia, or Smaragdus of St. Mihiel, Odo has little to say about the need to live in celibacy, free from wordly distractions in order to reach closer to God. He does allow that "the elect," those members of the City of God still living out their lives on earth, should conduct themselves in a way that focuses on their attention on eternal glory rather than earthly pleasure. Thus, they should not be duplicitous, avaricious, ostentatious about worldly honors, or glorying in outward things. They should also suffer willingly for the sake of justice while avoiding injury to others. Mixed in with the rest of the list is the admonition that "they ought to keep the body continent."[32] In other words, the point is there, but it is only one of many. A failure of chastity is bad but so is getting too much enjoyment out a newly embroidered chasuble.

What then did Odo teach? Medieval thoroughness very often led authors back to first causes, in this case all the way to the Garden of Eden. Since Augustine, the standard view was that the first humans' sin in the Garden was the starting place for the history of human sexuality.[33] By this interpretation of the early chapters of Genesis, sex got off to a very bad start: it was the punishment for sin. Odo draws heavily on the theological views of Augustine and Gregory the Great, presenting a sophisticated picture of the primal fall and its effects. For Odo as well as for his sources, paradise was a place of beauty, from which erring humanity was driven to a transitory life of exile and prison. Following Augustine, Odo makes it clear that the great punishment for and sign of Adam and Eve's sin against God is the uncontrollable sexual urge.[34] In the *Collationes*, Odo elaborates Augustine's position, explaining that because of the original sin at the dawn of time, vain loves multiplied—including vanity, *luxuria*, and innumerable other vices.[35] In short, Original Sin has tainted all humanity, and man's fallen nature has lowered him to the ranks of the beasts.[36]

There are two interesting differences in Odo's presentation of the primal fall compared with Augustine's which help to explain the distinctiveness of tenth-century thought. Together they suggest an ambivalence in interpretation that, as we shall see, marked much of the reformer's views of celibacy. To begin, Augustine is careful to discuss the transmission of Original Sin from one generation to another through the instrumentality of sexual intercourse. For Odo, however, the sexual act itself is a sin. There are no mitigating circumstances, such as marriage. A child is tainted because of the sexual act that leads to conception. Therefore, Odo is careful to explain that it is just for God to condemn a newborn child who has never had a chance to commit a sin. The reason is not that such children carry the taint of sin within them but that there was sin in the hour of their conception. This passage gives an important view of Odo's almost dualistic view of sexuality as a primary instrument of the devil to control the corrupt human body. As Odo says, "If, therefore, the fault is so great in married concupiscence that infants ought to be punished for that fault alone, how much greater then is the pollution that is perpetrated only because of lust?" In other words, *all* intercourse is sinful. God can damn a legitimate child for the pleasures of its parents; illicit sex is even worse. The abbot cites Paul's authority that God himself will judge fornicators and adulterers. He takes this as evidence that these two sins of intercourse are particularly evil in God's eyes. After all, more important sins have more important judges, and what judge could be more important than God himself?[37] Sexual arousal is itself a punishment for sin and is, therefore, itself sinful, "polluting" a body that God originally created for his own service. In this way, Odo has simplified and starkened monastic teaching about fornication as a chain to worldly things. His attitude has become horrified disgust at the pollution of giving in to flesh, manifestly against God's will.

At the same time, though, the Original Sin in the Garden of Eden was not primarily of a sexual nature. True, the first man and woman suddenly gained sexual awareness when they ate the apple; but, at heart, the sin was one of pride as Odo points out several times in his works. When God confronted Adam for eating the forbidden fruit, he could have atoned for his sin, Odo implies, by making a free confession of this error. Instead Adam dissimulated. He even tried to excuse his behavior by pinning the blame on Eve because she gave him the fruit in the first place, implying that since God created Eve, the blame ultimately rested with God himself, not with poor, gullible Adam.[38] This is the first time that Odo clearly lays out his belief that there are worse sins than lapses from chastity.

This is where Odo's ambivalence, or perhaps reliance on a variety of not fully integrated sources, becomes plain. At times the truly grievous sins a human can commit are those of the mind, such as pride. In other sections, though, the symptomatic vices—lust, gluttony, drunkenness—that reflect a disordered will appear to take on a life of their own, drawing the transgressors to ever greater sins. When he spells out the role of sin in the *Collationes*, at first the situation appears perfectly straightforward. All sin comes down to three vices: pride, *luxuria* (almost always to be equated with sexual lapses), and malice.[39] Nevertheless, Odo goes on immediately to make plain that pride is, in fact, the root of all other sins. He points out specifically that humans would not have a problem with concupiscence if Adam (and one assumes Eve, although Odo does not mention her) had not committed the grievous fault of pride against God. If it had not been for pride, the human genitalia would never have taken on a mind of their own, elevating the power of the body above that of the spirit (again following Augustine).[40] Thus, while pride is a sin of the human spirit, vices such as gluttony and lust are merely sins of the flesh, of weakness rather than evil will.[41] I believe that this is the voice of monastic tradition speaking, emphasized by a tendency to view religious matters in very black-and-white terms.

Soon, though, Odo turns to a different level of discourse on celibacy. When he does so, he appears to contradict his own distinction between sins of body and mind. He states that fornication is graver than other sins. In the resulting discussion, he points out that other sins take place outside the perpetrator's body, while fornication is within the very body of the sinner.[42] The abbot has clearly changed the terms of the discussion here. I believe that, following the long discussion of the issue in Book I, Odo still intends the reader to understand pride as the root of unchastity. He then has moved on to a discussion of the "second string" of sins that would never have appeared to plague the world if it had not been for primal pride and all its later manifestations. Since he is not writing for monks, the religious elite, he emphasizes action rather than intention, as we would expect. Thus, of the sins of deed, rather than thought, giving in to sexual temptation takes first place. *Nothing* debilitates the flesh like *luxuria*.[43] Indeed, the third of Odo's three deadly sins, malice, is almost completely lost. His interest is to weave a tapestry of pride and fornication that forms the backdrop to life in a world where the forces of good and evil are engaged in constant warfare.

It is hardly surprising that Augustin Fliche should have considered the theme of the *Collationes* to be the evil of the world's greatest vices: pride and luxury, leaving malice out of the equation completely.[44] I do not believe, however, that Fliche's assessment that Odo offers no practical advice for correcting the ills of his age is fair to the purposes of the reformer. It is true that Odo sees little to be done with the sin of pride, except for very general statements to beware of it. Still, much of the *Collationes*, as well as Odo's other works, is taken up with admonition, warning and frightening stories all designed to curb the reader's libidinous thoughts. What adds interest to the subject is that Odo's words are not for the most part directed toward a monastic audience. Indeed, his most telling arguments in favor of celibacy are directed toward clergy whether regular or secular, although all sectors of the population are in reach of his pen. Unlike many monastic authors writing for a secular patron, (the *Collationes* is addressed to a bishop, who, as far as we know, was not a monk), Odo molded his text to the interests of the secular clerics.[45]

The main danger of *luxuria* was not that it distracted the mind from God but that it actively offended the deity. A constant reminder of humanity's fall from grace, fornication could be considered the ultimate expression of fallen, carnal nature. On a practical level, Odo appears to consider sexual offenses a greater temptation than other sins. Truly, one gets the sense that it would be a quite measly specimen who would never have occasion to commit a sexual offense. It is also plain that people in many circles did not particularly frown upon sexual vice. Odo takes some pains to demonstrate to the reader that libido can bring about the fall of even the greatest men. For example, Delilah trapped Samson through his sexual weakness.[46] He also expresses frustration that there is so much lust in the world, when it is not even a "natural" sin. As Odo points out, some sins are the result of inevitable necessity, such as theft when one is starving. There is, however, no inevitable necessity that forces a person to lust.[47]

Lust *should* be avoidable by a good person. Still, every human, thanks to Original Sin, has a decided weakness when it comes to sexual offenses. Such a combination makes the world a very uncomfortable place. Odo's own hagiographer points out that his hero earned the nickname "the Digger" because he always kept his head covered and his eyes firmly on the ground.[48] Obviously it was very easy for the allurements of the passing world, including of course sexual temptation, to entrap even a wary person. Where Odo stands out is in his insistence that celibacy was a goal that all ranks in society should strive for, whether monk, cleric, or laymen.

A cleric or layman might indeed be chaste because of special dedication to God in the monastic sense of giving up control even of his own body to God, but Odo does not treat this as a likely occurrence. In the *Collationes* (not in the extremely peculiar *vita* of Gerald of Aurillac[49]), Odo does not expect other orders to act as imitation monks. What sets Odo of Cluny aside is that he enunciated a full doctrine of chastity that not only spread its web beyond monks but was founded upon different premises than traditional monastic spirituality. Probably Odo's horror of "sexual pollution" has its roots in an author such as John Cassian. Still, most of the time abstinence plays a different role in Odo's works than it does in monastic spirituality. Tenth-century authors were not particularly concerned with the role of the individual communing with God and gave very little place to spiritual preparation to commune with the deity. What did interest them, even more than their ninth-century forebears, was state of ritual cleanliness.[50] Following precepts from the Hebrew scriptures, monastic authors such as Odo knew beyond doubt that God wreaks terrible vengeance on those who slight holy things. Any educated churchman could have supplied examples of divine wrath for those who showed disrespect. They knew that it was proper to take off one's shoes before a burning bush (Exod. 3:5), not to touch the ark of the covenant (I Chron. 13:9-10), to avoid Mount Sinai when God was visiting it (Exod. 19:11-25), and had a long list of prescriptions and proscriptions for the Levitical priesthood in attendance on their God, including an entire chapter on their proper consecration (Exod. 28) Overall, there are hundreds of such rules, mostly in the Old Testament, and reformers frequently quoted and adapted them in their efforts to propitiate God. Already the monastic reform movement of the early ninth century had emphasized the need to respect holy places. For example, regulations include strictures against monks spitting in church, "for we are in the sight of God and his angels."[51]

Odo carries ritual respect for holy things several steps further than his ninth-century forebears had. He especially uses every argument he can to emphasize the sanctity of the altar. While people should treat all holy ground with reverence, this is especially true of the altar itself. It is useful to examine the full range of his arguments, even though only some of them are directly connected with our issue of celibacy. Without understanding Odo's eucharistic views, it is not possible to comprehend the force of his teaching on why sexuality and religion should have nothing to do with them. The most important point Odo makes is that a consecrated altar is the most holy thing in the world. Going beyond his Old Testament teachers, he argues that Christian altar is holier than the burning bush of Exodus 3:5. After all, as Odo says, the fire of the bush was a created thing, but upon the altar "is the true body of Christ, in which dwells all plenitude of divinity."[52] The altar, because of the consecration of the Eucharist, is far holier than any other religious symbol of his age. He points this out by trying to convince readers of a point that was by no means generally accepted. Thus he tells a story about a nearby church dedicated to St. Walpurgis. Not surprisingly with the presence of relics belonging to a powerful saint, many miracles were worked at the church. But then some misguided followers of Walpurgis placed her relics on the altar of the church, where they remained for several days. To everyone's consternation, the miracles worked by the relics suddenly ceased. The people soon had an explanation, though. The virgin saint appeared in a vision to one of her disappointed devotees who had failed to obtain a cure. It was not her fault, Walpurgis explained. Relics simply could not work miracles when on an altar—only the divine mystery of the Eucharist could be celebrated there, a superior miracle to all others. Sure enough, when the relics were removed from the altar, they were again able to work miraculous cures. Odo explains that he has included his story to encourage reverence for the Eucharist. If even saints hold the sacrament in such esteem, ordinary Christians should venerate it even more so.[53] This reverence includes purity from sin. As we will see, a particularly important element of this is sexual purity.

Participation in the Eucharist, either as celebrant or recipient, thus called not so much for a special state of mind but for a special cleanliness of body. In his pleas and threats for respect toward the

Eucharist, the abbot of Cluny drew on a firm belief in an angry God who would punish any slights by his people. His direct models were the prescriptions of the Old Testament, but he went far beyond them. For, of course, what the writers of the Old Testament advocated was not a permanent state of celibacy but on the contrary a period of ritual withdrawal from sexual relations while they accomplished a particular religious task. The union of sacerdotal and monastic notions of purity helped to inculcate an official policy of horror in regard to sexual intercourse that was set up as a model about which the vast majority of society could feel guilty even if they did not emulate it.

A very telling anecdote appears in Odo of Cluny's most popular literary work, a hagiographical depiction of Count Gerald of Aurillac, who died in 909. In this *vita*, Gerald is a layman, if an unwilling one; in fact, he was convinced not to enter a monastery only because he could do more good in the world in a position of secular responsibility. Some of Gerald's secret monastic acts, such as cutting part of his hair and beard in imitation of a tonsure or forcing his men to fight with the flats of their swords and butts of their spears, seem rather risible to the modern eye. An interesting note is struck, though, when Odo approaches the issue of sexuality. Odo begins quite simply with a passing statement that Gerald was chaste.[54] Duke William of Aquitaine offered his own sister to Gerald in marriage—a very advantageous alliance and one that, if offspring resulted, would have brought much stability to the region. Gerald refused the alliance. While he may have done so for many reasons, as Odo describes the situation Gerald's motivation was a horror at the thought of defiling himself with sexual relations. As Odo reports, "The horror he [Gerald] felt for carnal obscenity may be judged from the fact that he never incurred a nocturnal illusion without grief." "As St. Martin asserts," concludes Odo, "nothing is to be compared with virginity."[55] What is more, God obviously agrees, since after almost succumbing to the temptation once, Gerald went blind for almost a year.[56]

As with most hagiographical accounts, we cannot know the thoughts or often even the historical actions of the subject, but this tale is very revealing of the state of mind enjoyed by its author. Most important is the simple fact that for the author sex is bad. Other authors were more generous in condoning sexual relations between married couples; Odo simply gives a bare-bones statement that it is not acceptable to someone who wants to lead a life of superior piety. Virginity is simply better. The loss of bodily control evinced by nocturnal emissions is a regrettable reminder of Original Sin. And the emphasis is all on sexual relations, even sexual thoughts, as a form of pollution. But Odo does not show much interest in the traditional view that abstinence clears the mind for other, more important, religious tasks. Instead, celibacy is necessary because God hates fornicators. This is not a temporary withdrawal from intercourse as part of a rite of passage nor even a preparation for a religious task. After all, monasticism, the model into which Odo is working to fit Count Gerald, is a rite of passage with no end in this world.

It has been argued that at least from the mid-tenth century Cluniacs developed a eucharistic spirituality that gave a central place to the presence of Christ in the sacrament, and it was because of this growing emphasis on the doctrine of the Real Presence that they pushed their program of purity among those who approached and especially consecrated the eucharistic Host.[57] This statement is almost certainly true, as far as it goes, but the question of "why celibacy?" remains unanswered. What and when constituted purity? A closer look at Odo's view of the Eucharist may help to reach a solution. There is clear evidence that Odo himself, and perhaps other reform-oriented monks of his time, held the Eucharist in high regard as a cornerstone of spirituality for monks and, indeed, for any Christian. It is interesting, for example, that John of Salerno, Odo's hagiographer, has Odo make a considerable fuss about becoming a priest. By Odo's time, ordination was a normal part of the course of honors for a young choir monk. Usually the rising churchman saved such protests of unworthiness for elevation to the abbacy or to a bishopric. Yet John reports that Abbot Berno ordered Odo to submit for ordination and that the hero of the story was unwilling and submitted only from obedience.[58] This is an interesting hint that our future author held priestly duties in particular esteem. Certainly it was no longer the case, as in the time of John Cassian or Gregory the Great, that ordination to a position in the secular clergy would entail abandoning the monastic life, so Odo's life would have changed little when he became a priest. Unlike the reformers of the next century, there was no sense of worry about possible ordination by a simonist. It seems most likely that ordination was something special and particularly holy, either to John of Salerno or to Odo. Judging from Odo's writings on the subject, I think that the story reflects the abbot's own views.

Other individuals in Odo's time who were connected with monastic reform were also putting greater emphasis on the sacrosanct nature of the Eucharist and the need for an especially holy lifestyle to celebrate it properly. Thus in the *vita* of John of Gorze, which tells of the founding of that great Lotharingian reform center in 933, one of the original circle of founders combined extreme asceticism with eucharistic piety. This man, the archdeacon of Toul, had become a recluse, living in a cemetary near his church (one wonders how he carried out the other duties of an archdeacon). He only emerged from his solitude to celebrate the Eucharist.[59]

A person cannot participate in holy things when he himself is unclean. The consequences are not a loss of special grace but the chance of a very angry encounter with God or one of his saints. This emphasis on the need for ritual purity for everyone, whether monk or lay, appears often in tenth-century literature. For the laity, the role of ritual is plain, and the penalties Odo describes would make almost anyone nervous. One very important lesson he teaches is respect for holy places. Few historians would regard the late ninth and early tenth centuries as particularly peaceful times in Western European history. Still, tenth-century authors do not appear very concerned with murders in cathedrals, many foreign invasions, or even much theft (although Odo tells of one case of larceny). Instead, the moral lesson of choice is the due punishment for sexual promiscuity. Certainly this at least in part reflects a particular abhorrence of fornication as a particular sin against God. Perhaps also authors particularly enjoyed such tales because they gave witness that God would uncover even the most secret sin in time.

Certainly there is no shortage of heavenly wrath for those who ignore God in favor of sins of the flesh. Divine vengeance falls upon those who have sex at the wrong times or in the wrong places or who have made vows of celibacy that they have conveniently forgotten. An interesting example is an early eleventh-century account by Thietmar of Merseburg that purports to tell of events from the reign of King Henry I of Germany (918-36). Henry himself (at the devil's instigation, says Thietmar) had sexual relations with his wife on no less holy a day than Good Friday. They conceived a son, whom the devil claimed in due course. Fortunately, the king was too smart for the devil and had the bishops and priests waiting for the child's birth. They baptized the infant right away, so the demon was frustrated. Even then, though, Henry paid a penalty for his sexual license, since the thwarted demon sent down discord upon Germany.[60] In a similar story, Thietmar tells of a man who conceived a child on Holy Innocents' Day. The child was born with twisted toes—a clear sign of God's anger.[61] Both children's parents had intruded upon holy times with their carnal desires. This is clearly not a case of chastity as a path to greater virtue but of a need for ritual purity on occasions that are especially dedicated to God. In both cases, the author portrays God as taking personal affront because sinners have committed a slight against his divine dignity.

The libidinous layman (I have found no cases of clergy in such a situation) also had to beware of sexual intercourse in the wrong place. Odo tells of a recent occurrence in a nearby monastery. A man of the military class had fled to the monastery for refuge from his enemies, accompanied by his wife. While staying in the abbey guesthouse, they engaged in sexual intercourse. Greatly to their embarrassment, they found that they had become stuck together. The man yelled for help, and, of course, all the monks gathered to enjoy the object lesson of respect for holy places. The couple was only able to uncouple after they had vowed a substantial offering to the patron saint of the place and all the monks had prayed for them. As it was, they were lucky. Odo points out that their punishment for defiling the holy place was only temporary embarrassment since, after all, they were lawfully married. He concludes the story by pointing out that a crime such as incest in a holy place would lead to eternal judgment.[62] The sin committed was one of inappropriate circumstances, rather than a sin (such as murder) that is wrong no matter what the circumstances. Odo appears to be attempting with such a story to warn his readers or hearers that certain places and times are strictly off limits for sexual license. The church is a place that belongs peculiarly to God; his protection extends over the rest of the monastic buildings. Humans should protect these restrictions, especially since, if human means fail, God knows how to take care of his own territory and to do so in a terrible way. It is noteworthy that Odo himself does not appear to have been particularly embarrassed by this tale. He relates it in such a matter-of-fact tone that it sounds as though the sin, if not the miracle, may have been a regular occurrence.

Many sins can make a man or woman unacceptable in a holy place or can insult a holy occasion. These other offenses receive some mention, such as Odo's story from the *History of the Lombards* of an Arian who requested to be buried in a church, only to have his corpse thrown out bodily by the irate saint.[63] There were not any Arians in tenth-century Burgundy. There were, however, many men who were not monks and do not appear to have seen anything particularly repellent about engaging in normal sexual activities. The most obvious, perhaps the most ubiquitous offense in the catalogue of vice is fornication, perhaps in an effort to make people recognize it as a sin. Perhaps because he was a canon of St. Martin of Tours before taking monastic vows, Odo appears more aware of the apparently frequent sexual encounters of the secular clergy, at least those of the upper classes who might have become familiar with his moral admonitions. It must have been clear that monks and secular clerics were perceived as members of two separate worlds. Chastity was a preoccupation of monks, and secular clergy, most of whom were not particularly interested in ritual communion with God, would need a good reason to give up such a pleasant and apparently minor vice.

The best speaking point was ritual purity, especially as applied to the consecrated priesthood. This was of course an issue for which monastic and sacerdotal positions were overlapping ever more. In the tenth century the number of ordained monks was rising steadily, until by the year 1000 it appears to have been the norm for a monk to become a priest at the canonical age.[64] The celebration of the Eucharist was the ultimate ritual—Europe was rapidly moving to the view that Christ's body and blood became physically present during the words of consecration. Therefore it is not surprising that Old Testament laws for ritual cleanliness should be applied to practicing priests.

This was of course nothing new in the tenth century. The principle that one should be pure in either celebrating or partaking of the Eucharist goes back to the apostle Paul. There is a clear statement in I Cor. 11:24-29 that to take communion when unworthy is to eat and drink judgment rather than salvation.

Hrabanus includes a reference to this passage without elaboration in his *De clericorum institutione*.[65] Jonas of Orléans develops this idea in his *De institutione laicali*. As he says, "The most holy body and blood of our lord Jesus Christ, whence comes the redemption and salvation of all, and consists of the mystery of our faith," is used reverently by some but unworthily by others. Regular communion is necessary for salvation, but one must live worthily to receive it. Especially everyone should know the danger that "if one does not eat and drink, he has no life in him; but if he eats and drinks unworthily, he eats and drinks judgment unto himself.[66] Rather of Verona repeats the theme in the second half of the tenth century.[67] It is interesting to note that such accounts do not specify in what way a Christian should be pure to avoid the terrible risk of being damned for engaging in the Eucharist under false pretenses. Paul makes it plain that fornication is one of the forbidden acts; later accounts are not so clear in their condemnations.

The situation was becoming both simpler and more troublesome for Christian priests. Rather than making vague injunctions to purity, authors like Odo were beginning to provide the clergy with clear guidelines. Many of the new rules were based on the Old Testament, but at the same time theologians made it plain that Christian priests played a quite different role. Thus, a Hebrew priest did not engage in sexual relations for a specific period before attending upon the high altar. This was the model for the priests of the Christian era. At the most simple level, that was the answer to the question of whether the clergy should be celibate. As Smaragdus of St. Mihiel points out, Hebrew priests did not engage in their duties every day. Christian priests, however, are expected to celebrate the Eucharist daily. Therefore the only way they can possibly maintain the state of ritual purity necessary for approaching holy things is to abstain from intercourse all the time.[68] He was an early adovcate of sexual abstinence as the key to ritual purity.

Odo of Cluny developed this theme in several ways, which I believe accounts for the power of his statements. First, he strengthened the notions of ritual purity, specifically linking his views on the particular evil of sexual vice to his understanding of the Eucharist. And, perhaps most important, he gave the Old Testament notions of ritual purity a particularly Christocentric slant that certainly pointed the way toward a new mingling of Old and New Testament theology for the next several centuries.

The Eucharist is a sacrifice to God; therefore everything written about the Old Testament priesthood applies to the Mass. This does not, however, lead Odo to the belief that less-frequent celebration of the Eucharist should have called for less frequent practice of celibacy. He is firmly convinced that the early church celebrated the Eucharist less frequently than in his own time. Since it was rarer, though, the office was celebrated more religiously than in the tenth century.[69] Odo never hints that a priest who celebrated Mass perhaps once a month could take an occasional vacation from celibacy. This seems to rest on his belief that the Eucharist is fundamentally of greater holiness than any Old Testament sacrifice. As he states dogmatically: "Those who wish to sacrifice to God at the altar should first make a sacrifice of their vices to God through mortification [of their senses]. . . ."[70]

Not only should priests maintain ritual purity when making their offering, the prophets promised drastic punishments to those who failed in this duty. Odo is particularly scathing when he speaks of negligence in celebrating the Eucharist. His own language is worthy of a particularly disgruntled prophet as he relates God's words through the prophet Malachi and comments on their implication: "Oh priests, that despise my name. . . .You offer polluted bread upon my altar. . . .In that you say, The table of the Lord is contemptible." (Mal. 1:6-7). For Odo, the bread upon the alter is, of course, the consecrated body of Christ. One pollutes it by approaching the altar unworthily. In an overarching denunciation of the state of religion, Odo states that this is the reason many people in his time hold both holy places and the ministers of the church in contempt.[71]

Vice committed by a priest who celebrates the Eucharist is an act of apostasy against God. While one should mourn all apostasy, the offense is particularly grievous when the sinner is a priest. The abbot of Cluny gives two reasons for his view. First, unworthy celebration of the Eucharist is an insult to God—it "daily injures the divine majesty."[72] This is basically the same belief as that expressed by the prophet Malachi. There has been a violation of the laws laid down by God himself for his proper worship. Even if such lapses escape ecclesiastical authority, God will know that the priest has sinned.

The second reason depends very specifically on the nature of the Eucharist itself. The issue here is "the most sacred mystery of the Lord's body." That Christ instituted the Eucharist in the first place, Odo affirms, is a benefice to humanity greater than all the other goods that God ever gave to the human race.[73] Christ is really present in the consecrated elements of the Eucharist. This belief adds an urgency to Odo's pleas for veneration of the Eucharist. The abbot was one of the earliest theologians to incorporate the eucharistic doctrines of the ninth-century Paschasius Radbertus into his own work and it is likely that his sponsorship did much to popularize these views. According to Radbertus' teaching, the elements of the bread and wine in the Eucharist mystically change with the words of consecration to the actual, historical body and blood of Christ.[74] Thus to treat the Eucharist with disrespect is more than dangerous— it is an act similar to Judas' betrayal of Christ himself, and the perpetrator will be damned along with the archtraitor.[75]

Still, one should note that Odo is a careful enough Augustinian to make a clear distinction between the performer of the office and the actual Eucharist or any other sacrament. In several places, Odo is very careful to remind the reader that a sacrament is a sacrament, whoever's hands actually carry it out. Thus a baptism is no better from a holy person than from a sinner, since no matter who performs the act it is Jesus who actually does the baptizing. Similarly with the sacrament of the altar, it is not the just or unjust hands of the priest that consecrate the body and blood of Christ. Christ performs the consecration himself.[76] Although the Eucharist has become more important at Odo's hands, he appears to have recognized the extreme danger of anyone's passing judgment on a priest besides God or his own conscience. Thus he says in praise of Gerald of Aurillac that "if he heard a priest was of evil repute, he did not disdain the Mass, because he knew that the sacred mystery cannot be invalidated by a man who is a sinner."[77]

However, Odo left an ambiguous doorway open to the future. The tenor of his *Collationes* strongly suggests that Odo felt that matters of sin by those in authority, most notably priests, should be handled by God, not by earthly judgment. His tone is one of exhortation for personal improvement, not of public punishment by bishops or any other authority. But at the same time he appears to have acknowledged that eucharisitic laxity was like playing with lightning from heaven. He points out that the apostle Paul would not allow a fornicator to participate in the prayers of the faithful, "lest his impure voice should sully the pure voices of the others in the ears of God."[78] Again, the abbot strikes a note of warning with another reference to Malachi, reminding the reader that God curses the blessings of bad priests (Mal. 2:2, 12).[79] This suggests the opposite of Odo's earlier stand, implying that a person acting in good faith can be damned for the faults of his or her priest. Odo's extreme emphasis on the purity of priests helped point the way to the conflicts of the eleventh century over the effect of a priest's personal morals had on the sacraments he celebrated. Rather of Verona argued, basing his views on Leviticus, that a person in a state of sin cannot act as a priest. (Lev. 21:17-18). He even had the authority of an early ecclesiastical council, that of Neocaesaria, that a person in holy orders who has committed a crime should not exercise his office.[80] It is very likely that rulings such as that of the Synod of Coblenz (1012) that linked the proper celebration of the Eucharist with the personal integrity of the celebrant could have emerged in a society that had not been indoctrinated with the notion of the real presence of Christ in the Eucharist.[81] Certainly there was a tendency to make the efficacy of a sacrament dependent on the purity of the priest celebrating. Arnold Angenendt has argued that this led to a desire to see all priests as ascetics.[82] Still, to judge from Odo's work, the desire for asceticism came first, and the issue of sacramental validity only arose later. Before priests could be condemned as unfit to render true sacraments, there had to be a clear notion of what offenses put a cleric beyond the sacerdotal pale. We can see in Odo's work that the whole nature of what constituted grave sin in a priest had shifted, making the division between good and bad clergy much harder to define. If a priest's sin is not of a public nature but a private act such as a tumble in the hay with a servant girl, an immense door opens for gossip and innuendo.

Why did an author like Odo elevate sexual sin to the pinnacle of vice? There are so many worse things that a priest could do that sexual license appears somewhat trivial to modern eyes. But although other sins received occasional mention, fornication was among the worst to Odo and his successors. As Odo himself said, discord and *luxuria* are the two worst sins for a man presuming to approach the altar. Discord was quickly explained; Odo needed only to cite the gospel text of how a person with hatred in his heart should leave his offering, go make his peace with his enemy, and only then make his sacrifice (Matt. 5:23-24). Instead he focuses his attention on sexual misconduct. But Odo does not explain his reason for elevating *luxuria* to such a high position among the vices. Instead he launches into a general diatribe against the practice, stating plainly that contact with the altar when guilty or either of these sins is worse than approaching the ark of the covenant unworthily.[83]

Why? I think the answer is partly a practical one. Sexual sin is easily hidden. With proper precautions, a congregation need never find out that their priest has lapsed. Thus, it is a sin that almost seems to encourage abuse—what people don't know won't hurt them. Thus, a person truly concerned with proper celebration of holy offices would have to emphasize the pernicious nature of secret sins.

A second reason is the position of sexual indulgence in a society fascinated with the notion of ritual purity. The sacrificial animal must be clean and unblemished; similarly the person making the sacrifice must be free of taint. Looking again to Old Testament models, any tenth-century author would have seen how the Hebrew priesthood went through elaborate ceremonies of ritual purification. Especially emphasized was that their bodies had to be seemly, even to the underwear that was prescribed so the sight of their nakedness would not offend God. Fornication, as already discussed, is a sin that engages the body itself, not just the mind. There was little interest in what the priest was thinking. His body, though, could not be "defiled" by either voluntary or involuntary acts. Since this was a matter over which a priest has control, it would be a much graver sin than sacrificing an unclean animal.

Yet a third reason is that, although Odo was extremely awake to the problems and weaknesses of the secular clergy, he was at heart a monk. Monastic views on abstinence, repeated so often, would have affected not only Odo himself but all who believed that monasticism was the most holy way of life. An important element of monastic spirituality was that anything that gives pleasure must be a trick to lure the soul from God. Under such circumstances, an active sexual life *must* be sinful. The more powerful the attraction, the greater the truly monastic horror of human sexuality. In general, medieval monks had a very healthy respect for the power of human sexuality, assuming that anything so powerful must surely be a lure by the devil. Naturally, sexuality became a focus for those seeking ritual purity, and the two together became an extremely potent combination.

Last, Odo enunciated a view of the nature of Christ himself that emphasized the evil of sexual sin. As he explains, before the incarnation of Christ there was more sexual license in the world, although Odo is careful to point out that good people were always wary of it. But Christ was himself chaste, and set a permanent model for his followers. Christ was born of a virgin. He was the bridegroom of the church, and a bridegroom without spot or stain, virgin and chaste.[84] For Odo, Christ is the "son of the virgin" and, of course, virginal himself. Because of Jesus' model, he admonishes his readers, they too ought to be chaste: "because the commander, the Son of the Virgin, first initiated this with his army. . . ."[85] Humans are called upon to take up the cross with Christ. However, in one of the most telling passages of the *Collationes*, Odo proclaims that a person truly takes up the cross who is chaste, both in heart and in flesh. "For how can anyone take up the cross who does not crucify his own flesh from consupiscence?" The only way to please God is with sacrifice. Abraham offered his son Isaac; Hannah dedicated her son Samuel to the temple. The least a modern Christian can do is to give up the transitory pleasures of the libido.[86]

Thus there was something in Odo's doctrine of human sexuality to cause uneasiness and misgivings in almost anyone who read or heard it. Most people appear to have had at least a sneaking suspicion that monks were better people than they were and certainly that monks knew how to stay on God's good side. This belief is evident from the many donations to monasteries, child oblations, deathbed conversions, and adoptions of at least a partially monastic lifestyle that were so prominent in the Benedictine centuries.[87] Therefore monastic celibacy could be valued, no matter how many or few practiced it. So much for this oldest strand of the church's stand on celibacy. Added to that, the ninth- and tenth-centuries' view on ritual purity made an extremely powerful statement when connected to the Eucharist. And the most novel part of Odo's argument, that the Christian people should look toward a more active imitation of Christ, would appear to have struck a responsive chord. Christ is a more powerful model than even the greatest saint. The belief that Christ was not only the son of the Virgin Mary but was a virgin himself was a powerful argument for abstinence. Odo did not even bother to mention the chastity of lesser characters such as the apostle Paul. Instead he suggests that emulation of Christ is a goal that can truly be attained rather than relying on the mediation of a saint. Thus chastity became an early model of how the pious Christian could imitate Christ. And how better than by imitation could one hope to win the good opinion of the one who would judge your soul in the final days?

NOTES

1. See the introductory epistle to the *Collationes*. Odo abbas Cluniacensis, *Collationes*, *PL* 133 (intro.): 571-18. Odo's *Occupatio* is more monastic in orientation, focusing on the ideal of the contemplative life. I believe that Leclerq was fair in his assessment that the main purpose of the poem was to show how monasticism could give a model of faith and Christian morality rather than combat the ills of the world. As you will see, though, I cannot credit that Odo did not have a more active task in mind when writing the *Collationes*. See Jean Leclerqu, "L'idéal monastique de saint Odon, d'après ses oeuvres," in *A Cluny*, Congrès scientifique (Dijon, 1950), especially 230.

2. Heinz Löwe, "Dialogus de statu sanctae ecclesia. Das Werk eines Iren im Laon des 10. Jahrhunderts," *Deutsches Archiv* 17 (1961): see especially 26-30.

3. Hartmut Hoffmann, "Von Cluny zum Investiturstreit," *Archiv für Kirchengeschichte* 45 (1963): 173. For other assessments of the role played by Odo in reviving the religious consciousness of Europe, see, for example, Raffaello Morghen, "Monastic Reform and Cluniac Spirituality," in Noreen Hunt, ed., *Cluniac Monasticism in the Central Middle Ages* (London, 1971), 13; Noreen Hunt, *Cluny under Saint Hugh, 1049-1109* (London, 1967), 23.

4. John of Salerno, *The Life of St. Odo of Cluny*, in *St. Odo of Cluny*, ed. Gerard Sitwell (London, 1958), (II, 23):66; (III, 10):82.

5. *Pace* Joachim Wollasch, who agrees with Hoffmann, arguing perhaps on the basis of too little evidence that Cluny was bound from its origin not only to monastic reform but to the renewal of all Christianity. But it is Wollasch's contention that Odo's goal was to renew Christianity in a distinctly monkish way. Joachim Wollasch, *Mönchtum des Mittelalters zwischen Kirche und Welt* (Munich, 1973), 147-48.

6. *RB* 58.17. I use Timothy Fry's translation of the difficult second vow of "conversatio morum." *The Rule of St. Benedict*, Latin and English, ed. Timothy Fry (Collegeville, MN, 1981).

7. John Cassian, *Conferences*, especially book 12, *Sources chrétiennes*, vol. 54, 120-46. Edgar Gibson, the translator of Cassian's works for the *Select Library of Nicene and Post-Nicene Fathers of the Christian Church* (Grand Rapids (reprint ed. 1978) declined to translate this section on the grounds that it was unedifying. Of course, all of the issues involving celibacy, except the issue of celebrating the Eucharist, were as applicable to women as they were to men. I follow my sources in using the masculine pronoun except in the rare case when they speak specifically of a woman. I also believe that the sacramental issue is closely enough linked to that of celibacy that a careful adherence to modern non-gendered language would not only be anachronistic but misleading.

8. For one of many examples, see Pierre J. Payer, *Sex and the Penitentials* (Toronto, 1984), 60.

9. Smaragdus abbas s. Michaelis, *Diadema monachorum, PL* 102, 31:626.

10. Alcuin, *De virtutibus et vitiis liber, PL* 101, 18:626.

11. Alcuin, *De virtutibus et vitiis liber, PL* 101, 18:627.

12. Alcuin, *De virtutibus et vitiis liber, PL* 101, 18:627, for example.

13. Smaragdus, *Diadema monachorum*, 18:627.

14. Candidus, *Vita Eigilis abbatis Fuldensis, MGH SS* 15.1, 10:228.

15. Hrabanus Maurus, *Liber de oblatione puerorum, PL* 107, 440.

16. Odo abbas Cluniacensis, *Occupatio*, ed. Antonius Swodoba (Leipzig, 1900), VII, l. 360, p. 159.

17. Odo, *Collationes*, II, 32:577.

18. Odo, *Collationes*, III, 21:605.

19. Ratherius Veronensis, *Praeloquiorum libri VI*, ed. Peter Reid, Corpus Christianorum Continuatio Mediaevalis 46A (1984), II.14:59.

20. Cassian, *Conferences*, 11, 14:118-19.

21. Cassian, *Conferences*, 4, 7-12:172-76.

22. See especially Peter Brown's extensive study *The Body and Society: Men, Women, and Sexual Renunciation in Early Christianity* (New York, 1988) for the development of a distinctively Christian sexual code, which was adopted by early medieval monks.

23. C. Stephen Jaeger, "The Courtier Bishop in *Vitae* from the Tenth to the Twelfth Century," *Speculum* 58 (1983): 291-325.

24. Ruotger, *Vita Brunonis archiepiscopi Colonensis, MGH SS*, new series 10. See also Friedrich Lotter, "Das Bild Brunos I. von Köln in der Vita des Ruotger," *Jahrbuch des kölnischen Geschichtsvereins* 40 (1966): 19-40.

25. Gerhardus, *Vita sancti Oudalrici episcopi, MGH SS*, 4, 3:389.

26. Gerhardus, *Vita sancti Oudalrici episcopi*, 3:389, 9:396.

27. Rimbertus, *Vita Anskarii, MGH SS* 35:68.

28. *Vita s. Hugonis monachi Aeduensi et priore Enziacensi, AASS* Apr. II (II.11): 764.

29. John of Salerno, *Life of St. Odo*, I, 36:38.

30. Cited in Owen Chadwick, *John Cassian: A Study in Primitive Monasticism* (Cambridge, 1950), 64.

31. Nalgodus, *Vita sancti Majoli abbatis Cluniacensis*, AASS Mai II, 3:657.

32. Odo, *Collationes*, I, 31:540.

33. For background, see Elaine Pagels, *Adam, Eve, and the Serpent* (New York, 1988).

34. Odo, *Occupatio*, III, lines 193-221: 36-36; lines 605ff: 48-50.

35. Odo, *Collationes*, I, 6:524.

36. See the discussion of this point in Barbara H. Rosenwein, "Rules and the 'Rule' at Tenth-Century Cluny," *Studia Monastica* 19 (1977): especially 317.

37. Odo, *Collationes*, II, 24: 568-69.

38. Odo, *Occupatio*, II, lines 458ff: 38; Odo, *Collationes*, I, 29:539.

39. Odo, *Collationes*, I, 11:528. In several places, such as *Collationes*, II, 2:567, luxuria plainly includes gluttony and drunkenness besides sexual intercourse.

40. Odo, *Collationes*, I, 12:528.

41. See Odo, *Collationes*, II, 7:554.

42. Odo, *Collationes*, II, 24:569; drawing on I Cor. 6:18.

43. Odo, *Collationes*, II, 15:562.

44. Augustin Fliche, *Le réform grégorienne* (Louvain/Paris, 1924/1926), vol. 1, 46.

45. See Hoffmann, "Von Cluny zum Investiturstreit," 173.

46. Odo, *Collationes*, II, 25:569.

47. Odo, *Collationes*, II, 25:570.

48. John of Salerno, *Life of St. Odo*, II, 9:52.

49. This is not the place to discuss the *Vita Geraldii*. For a thoughtful recent study, see Friedrich Lotter, "Das Ideals Bild adliger Laienfrömmigkeit in den Anfängen Clunys: Odos Vita des Grafen Gerald von Aurillac," in *Benedictine Culture*, 750-1050, eds. W. Lourdaux and D. Verhelst (Leuven, 1983), 76-95.

50. Barbara H. Rosenwein, *Rhinoceros Bound: Cluny in the Tenth Century* (Philadelphia, 1982) discusses Cluny's rise to popularity as a reaction to anomie, giving a stable basis of practice and belief to a region in a state of social flux. Most historians agree that tenth-century writers felt much more fear than love of God, frequently worrying that Christians will anger God through mistaken practice. For a good discussion of this issue, see Hans Martin Klinkenberg, "Versuche und Untersuchungen zur Autobiographie bei Rather von Verona," *Archiv für Kirchengeschichte* 38 (1956): 265-314. See especially p. 305, where he discusses the role of monasticism in a world filled with fear of God. In general, though, little work has been done on this interesting aspect of tenth-century spirituality. For the importance of ritual observance in the ninth century, see especially Adolf Waas, "Karls des Großen Frömmigkeit," *Historische Zeitschrift* 203 (1966): 265-79; Michael McCormick, "The Liturgy of War in the Early Middle Ages: Crisis, Litanies, and the Carolingian Monarchy," *Viator* 15 (1984): 1-23.

51. *Memoriale qualiter*, ed. D. C. Morgand, Corpus Consuetudinem Monasticarum, 1, 1:231-32.

52. Odo, *Collationes*, II, 11:558.

53. Odo, *Collationes*, II, 28:573.

54. Odo, *Vita Geraldii*, 1, 9:102.

55. Odo, *Vita Geraldii*, 1, 34:123-24.

56. Odo, *Vita Geraldii*, 1, 100:104.

57. André Vauchez, *La spiritualité du moyen âge occidental, VIIIe-XIIe siècles* (Paris, 1975), 52. Hunt, *Cluny under Saint Hugh*, 139, suggests that the manner in which Cluny emphasized the Eucharist perhaps made the sacrament more intelligible to the laity.

58. John of Salerno, *Life of St. Odo*, I, 37:39.

59. Iohannes s. Arnulfi, *Vita Iohannis abbatis Gorziensis, MGH, SS* 2, 29:345.

60. Thietmar Merseburgensis episcopus, *Chronicon, MGH, SS* 9, I, 24:32.

61. Thietmar, *Chronicon*, I, 25:32.

62. Odo, *Collationes*, II, 11:558.

63. Odo, *Collationes*, II, 11:559.

64. Cuthbert Butler, *Benedictine Monachism* (London, 1919), 293-94.

65. Hrabanus Maurus, *De clericorum institutione, PL* 107, 31:317-21.

66. Jonas Aurelianensis episcopus, *De institutione laicali, PL* 106, 18:201-4.

67. Ratherius Veronensis, *Excerptum ex dialogo conffesionali cujusdam sceleratissimi, mirum dictu, PL* 136, 13-14:402.

68. Smaragdus, *Diadema monachorum*, 49:647.

69. Odo, *Collationes*, II, 28:572.

70. Odo, *Collationes*, II, 28:573.

71. Odo, *Collationes*, II, 28:572.

72. Odo, *Collationes*, II, 28:572. See also III, 10:598.

73. Odo, *Collationes*, II, 28:572.

74. Odo cites passages from Radbertus' *De corpore et sanguine Domini* throughout the second book of the *Collationes*. See for example II, 30:275-76. See also Ovidio Capitani's article, "Motivi di spiritualità cluniacense e realismo eucharistico in Odone di Cluny," in *Spiritualità cluniacense, Convegni del centro di studi sulla spiritualità medievale* 2 (Todi, 1960), 250-57.

75. Odo, *Collationes*, II, 30:575.

76. Odo, *Collationes*, II, 21:533.

77. Odo, *Vita Geraldi*, II, 14:144. The same view can be found in Jonas of Orléans, *De institutione laicali*, 21:211.

78. Odo, *Collationes*, II, 16:563.

79. Odo, *Collationes*, II, 36:583.

80. Ratherius, *Dialogus confessionali*, 19:407.

81. For Coblenz, see Johannes Laudage, *Priesterbild und Reformspapsttum im 11. Jahrhundert* (Cologne, 1984), 52.

82. Arnold Angenendt, "Religiosität und Theologie. Ein spannungsreiches Verhältnis im Mittelalter," *Archiv für Liturgiewissenschaft* 20/21 (1978/1979): 40-41.

83. Odo, *Collationes*, II, 33:578.

84. Odo, *Collationes*, II, 11:557-58.

85. Odo, *Collationes*, II, 11:559.

86. Odo, *Collationes*, II, 11:558.

87. Gerd Tellenbach, in *Church, State and Christian Society at the Time of the Investiture Contest* (Oxford, 1940), 79 suggests that, moving into the eleventh century, admiration of monks affected people's actions more and more in comparison to their purses, and ever more members of society tried to copy a monastic outlook on life.

Tertius est optimus: Marriage, Continence, and Virginity in the Politics of Late Tenth- and Early Eleventh-Century Francia

Elizabeth Dachowski

Although the development of the doctrine of clerical celibacy is most closely associated with the church reforms of the late eleventh and early twelfth centuries, its roots can be traced back much farther. The very earliest writings of the Christian church exhibited a deep ambivalence towards marriage as may be seen in the epistle of Paul in which he advised that "For the unmarried and the widows I say that it is well for them to remain single as I do. But if they cannot exercise self-control, they should marry. For it is better to marry than to be aflame with passion" (1 Corinthians 8-9). By the fourth century, the church had begun to discourage clerical marriage, and in 419 the Council of Carthage had enjoined continence on "those who touched the mysteries."[1] Although clerical celibacy had long been a theme in theological writing, this theory does not appear to have significantly affected actual clerical practice, especially for the lower levels of the secular clergy, such as priests and deacons.[2] In the tenth century, James Brundage singled out Regino of Prüm, writing in 906, as virtually the only tenth-century canonist to treat questions of sex at any length, though he acknowledged that Abbo of Fleury's collection of canons provided a "cursory treatment of these topics."[3] The official policy of forbidding, rather than merely discouraging, marriage among the clergy evolved slowly from these roots and came to fruition as papal policy in the period of the Gregorian reforms of the late eleventh century.

Among the precursors of the Gregorian ban on clerical marriage are the writings of abbot Abbo of Fleury (d. 1004) in the late tenth century. Abbo's interest in clerical celibacy lay in a very different political context from that of Pope Gregory VII. In Abbo's day, the church's struggle for independence from secular powers lay not with the papacy, which

remained weak despite occasional attempts of popes to assert themselves
but with the monastic reform movement, which sought to free itself
from the rule of local bishops and the interference of their secular
overlords. Abbo's arguments were very much a part of this period of
monastic reform, when Cluny, Fleury, and other monasteries had begun
to claim privileged status within the Christian community by positing
the moral superiority of virgins to the married and even to the non-
virgin continent.[4] In this context, clerical celibacy was less a program of
the papacy or a device for strengthening episcopal authority than an
important component of the power-base of the monastic party in France,
which was, not coincidentally, both the papacy's main supporter in early
Capetian France and engaged in a heated struggle with the French
episcopacy for monastic independence. Just as celibacy later became a
symbol of the purified Christianity which the reformed papacy offered,
in the late tenth century it was a potent argument for the moral
superiority of those monks who sought their independence from an
overly worldly secular clergy.

The career and writings of Abbo, abbot of Fleury (d. 1004), indicate
the central position which clerical and lay marriage held in monastic
politics and spirituality more than half a century before the beginning of
the Gregorian reform movement. For Abbo and his contemporaries,
celibacy was an integral part of the argument for clerical authority. In
particular, monks used their state of virginity as a rationale for their
independence from and spiritual superiority to other clergy as well as the
laity. A careful examination of Abbo's writings on clerical celibacy in
their political context makes clear that Abbo's theory of sexual hierarchy
bolstered his claims for monastic privileges.

Abbo's clearest statement of the moral superiority of virginal monks
is in his *Liber Apologeticus*, written for Kings Hugh Capet and Robert the
Pious, shortly after the council of Saint-Denis in 993.[5] Abbo's ultimate
purpose in composing this work was to defend himself from very
specific charges against him arising from a riot which had broken out at
the council, as becomes clear in the final sections of the work.

The first section of the *Apologeticus*, however, after a brief lament on
the (unspecified) injustices which Abbo had endured, contains a detailed
description of the functional and moral divisions of Christian society.
Abbo began by dividing Christians into three major groups, the virgins,
the continent, and the married. He intended this division to be
understood in terms of a moral hierarchy, with monks, by virtue of their

virginity and withdrawal from the world, occupying the highest position:

> we know that there are from either sex, three orders of the faithful, and if three orders, three grades in the holy and universal church; although none of them is without sin, nevertheless, the first is good, the second better, the third best. And, indeed, the first [order] in either sex is of the married, the second of the continent or widowed, the third of virgins or nuns.[6]

In addition, he made a functional as well as moral distinction between the orders of men, namely the laity, the clergy–which he defined as bishops, priests, and deacons–and the monks. He very briefly treated the further division of the laity into farmers (*agricolae*) and fighters (*agonistae*), who had the duty, respectively, of nourishing and defending the Church. His primary concern, however, was clearly with the function of monks and clergy. He likened the secular clergy to Martha, who did necessary work but was preoccupied with the concerns of the world, and likened monks to Mary, whose removal from the cares of this world brought her close to the contemplative life practiced by monks. He explicitly placed the secular clergy between the monks and the laity, as inferior to the former and superior to the latter.[7] In Abbo's ideal Christian society, each rank played a crucial role without infringing upon the prerogatives of the others: the laity produced food and provided protection, the secular clergy administered the goods of the church without thought of personal gain, and the monks, because of the activities of the first two, led the contemplative life which was so pleasing to God.

Although Abbo's tripartite division did not require secular clergy to be virgins, he clearly believed that the state of virginity was optimal for them, and certainly that they should be continent after assuming ecclesiastical office as deacons, priests, or bishops: "It happens that it was prohibited by the apostles and their successors that clerics (that is, deacons, priests, and bishops) have wives."[8] He did not consider the lower ranks truly clergy, precisely because they could marry, though he admitted that they were frequently included among the clergy by mistake. At least part of his concern is with the possibility that the secular clergy "not beget sons carnally but spiritually."[9] Abbo's attack on clerical marriage went farther than earlier injunctions such as that of the Council of Constantinople in 680 which condemned marriage after ordination, but allowed those married before ordination to keep their wives and required abstinence only from bishops.[10] He did not specifically invoke the fear that clergy might bequeath church offices or property to their sons, although modern scholars have frequently suggested that this fear was a major factor in the increasing attacks on clerical marriage beginning in the tenth century.[11] Nevertheless, the other concerns expressed in Abbo's *Apologeticus* and elsewhere suggest that restricting lay control of ecclesiastical property was of paramount importance to him and may well have lain behind his condemnation of clerical marriage and reproduction.

Recent scholarship has been nearly unanimous in recognizing that Abbo's theoretical formulations regarding the division of Christian society hid more concrete concerns. Jean Batany, for example, has placed Abbo's tripartite division of society in the context of heresies which became troublesome in Orléans in 1022 and in Arras in 1025, a generation after Abbo wrote his *Apologeticus*. Batany believed that there may already have existed in Abbo's day intimations of the complete denial of social and functional divisions within Christendom which eventually characterized the heresy of Orléans and Arras.[12] Georges Duby and Jacques LeGoff looked to the more immediate political situation for an explanation of Abbo's concern with social divisions. They both found clear connections between Abbo's theoretical ordering of Christian society and his claims for increased monastic power in early Capetian France.[13] Marco Mostert, in his much more detailed consideration of Abbo's political thought, went further and characterized Abbo's body of work as a response to "specific situations, which required specific answers, appropriate to the circumstances."[14]

The historical context of this document suggests that Abbo's motivation for writing it lay in the political situation with which he and his monastery were confronted in the early 990s. The final sections of the *Apologeticus* clearly indicate that his primary motive in writing was to defend himself from charges stemming from a riot at the council of Saint-Denis, in which supporters of monastic and lay collection of tithes attacked the assembled bishops, who, it was rumored, intended to do away with this practice.[15] Abbo's position at the council had been in favor of retaining tithes in the hands of the monks (he made no mention of those tithes which had fallen into lay hands) rather than, as the bishops proposed, returning them to episcopal control. Because of Abbo's strong stand against abolishing monastic tithes, Archbishop Gerbert of Reims and Bishop Arnulf of Orléans, both close advisors to the kings and long-standing political adversaries of Abbo and the monks of Fleury, initially suggested that Abbo himself was an instigator of the riots.[16] In light of the serious nature of the charges leveled against him and the accompanying threat of excommunication, Abbo wrote his *Apologeticus* primarily with an eye to clearing himself from these charges.

Ultimately, Abbo's aim in writing the *Apologeticus* was to build a bridge between himself and his political rivals. He never attacked Arnulf of Orléans by name but instead framed his attack in general, theoretical terms. Ultimately, by putting forth his tripartite view of society, he was submitting a pattern for future co-operation between bishops and monks, provided that bishops recognized their role as Martha who merely supported the contemplative Mary.

Abbo's *Apologeticus*, along with Aimoin's comments on this work in his *Vita s. Abbonis* (c. 8), indicate that rather than wishing to encourage those of the laity who had been collecting tithes, as the charges against him implied, the question of lay control of ecclesiastical revenues was at the heart of his complaints to the kings. Indeed, one of Abbo's few allies among the bishops, Archbishop Seguin of Sens, was one of the most seriously injured in the uprising.[17] After specifically denying charges that he was a heretic and professing his faith in the teachings of the apostles, Abbo then went on to point out that even Peter could not claim personal possession of the goods of the church:

> Thence, it was said to Peter the Prince of the apostles "You are Peter and on this rock I will build my church." "My" he said, not "your," and Christ elsewhere [said] "My house is called a house of prayer." The Psalmist also [said]: "Holiness befits your house, Lord." Therefore, if the church is not Peter's, whose would it be? Or will the successors of Peter dare to lay claim to power for themselves which Peter the Prince of the Church did not have?[18]

Abbo had thus shifted the debate from the question of monastic tithes to the much more serious question of how the laity could control the goods of the church.

Events in the months preceding the council of Saint-Denis reinforce the impression that Abbo's concerns lay in protecting monastic property from lay control. Shortly before the siege of Melun in 991, the nephew of Bishop Arnulf of Orléans, Arnulf of Yèvre, had claimed the right to exact payments and carry away goods from Fleury's holdings at Yèvre. The monks of Fleury had initially prevailed upon the kings to force the younger Arnulf to give up his claims. By 991, however, the siege of Melun, arising from a dispute between the Capetians and the comital house of Blois, had altered the political situation in the region. King Hugh Capet now needed dependable supporters in the region. The younger Arnulf took advantage of his strengthened position and had his uncle intervene with the king to reinstate his rights over the monastic lands. Although the monks were able to limit their liability to a relatively modest payment during Bishop Arnulf's lifetime only, Hugh had given the Arnulfs a symbolic victory in their claims against the goods of the monastery.[19] After seeing the damage to monastic property from the elder Arnulf's avuncular advocacy, it is hardly surprising that Abbo would be concerned with limiting the right of clergy to produce legitimate sons, for whom, one would expect, a bishop might exert himself even more strongly.

Abbo likewise, in his *Collectio Canonum*, written shortly after his *Apologeticus*, was primarily concerned with protection of monastic property, which he clearly linked with the issue of clerical celibacy.[20] The *Collectio* consisted of a series of canonical extracts, each introduced with a sentence or two of explanation. Abbo began with extracts which stressed the independence of the church from lay interference and inviolability of church possessions before going on to discuss judicial procedures for elevating and demoting various members of the secular and regular clergy. Within the context of division of church revenues and appointment to ecclesiastical office, Abbo then included several chapters on clerical celibacy and the children of clergy.[21] Chapter 39, entitled "On the Holiness of the Life of Clerics," in fact, included only a decree of Pope Siricius (384-399) making clear that clerical office is not hereditary and that bishops, priests, and deacons should remain continent. Clearly, in Abbo's eyes, "holiness of life" for a cleric could not include passing on one's wealth to children and probably not begetting them in the first place. The following chapter (c. 40) discusses the treatment of the offspring of the clergy: those born before ordination should behave in an exemplary manner to avoid embarrassing the clerical office, while those born after ordination were not only barred from inheritance but were to serve perpetually in the church into which they were born. Abbo re-enforced the point with his next entry (c. 41) which forbade bishops from naming their own successors (a practice which could potentially benefit nephews as well as direct descendants). In his *Collectio Canonum*, Abbo put less emphasis on the moral hierarchy which supported monastic claims for autonomy and more on the practical problems which arose from the entanglement of the secular clergy, particularly the episcopate, in familial obligations.

Abbo more directly addressed the question of clerical marriage in his "Letter to G." in which he gave comfort to an unidentified cleric, "G." and explained G.'s problems in terms of the corruption of his age.[22] The opening paragraphs of this letter once again put his arguments in terms of lay appropriation of ecclesiastical property, which ought to be used to support the "poor of Christ," i.e., the monks. Abbo further emphasized the importance of monastic independence by a series of quotations from the letters of Pope Gregory I the Great, in which the Pope defended monasteries from interference in their affairs by the local episcopate and asserted the inviolability of papal decrees.[23] Abbo finished his letter with a lengthy treatise on the proper behavior of the clergy, with particular emphasis given to clerical celibacy. Mostert has characterized the last section of this lengthy epistle as "a virtual 'rule' for the secular clergy, especially for bishops."[24]

Once again, Abbo's work becomes more clear when viewed in historical context. Although the recipient and date of the letter are unknown,[25] details of Abbo's own political activities suggest a context for understanding his work. Abbo had earlier put the writings of Gregory the Great to use in forging a charter granting wide-ranging privileges to Fleury, including, in addition to the usual recognition of monastic holdings, the status of the abbot of Fleury as the foremost among the abbots of Gaul, right to free election of the abbot, freedom from clerical interference, and the right to receive monks fleeing from other monasteries. He had used this forged charter as a tool to obtain a genuine charter, with similar provisions, from Pope Gregory V (996-999), the young, idealistic successor to the cynical John XV (985-996).[26] Abbo's appeal to the papacy was part of a larger policy of putting ecclesiastical affairs under the Pope's central authority. He had already demonstrated his desire to see serious ecclesiastical issues brought before the Pope and a general council of the church in his efforts to prevent the deposition of Archbishop Arnulf of Reims at the council of Saint-Basle in 991.[27] Arnulf was hardly a model churchman, even by less exacting standards than Abbo's: despite serious concerns about age, education, and character, Hugh Capet had elevated him to the archiepiscopal see for purely political reasons, and Arnulf had almost immediately betrayed the city of Reims to Hugh's rival, Charles of Lorraine. Nevertheless, Abbo argued that a relatively small, regional council, such as that at Saint-Basle, did not have the authority to depose a bishop. That power rested with a council of the entire church and with the pope. In this political context, his quotation of Gregory the Great on the power of the apostolic see and his insistence on clerical celibacy were essential elements in his construction of an ecclesiastical hierarchy in which papacy stood above the rest of the church and the monastic community, with its long practice of celibacy, was located near the top of the pyramid.

The concerns of the papacy and the monasteries were also united in the related question of regulation of lay marriages, though in the face of a relatively weak papacy the main force for the argument came from the monasteries. In the case of King Robert the Pious, for example, the young king's marriage to his cousin, Bertha of Blois, had been condemned by Pope Gregory V. Robert's marriage to Bertha was illicit not only because of her blood ties to him but also because he had stood as godfather to her son by her first husband, thus uniting them in spiritual as well as temporal kinship. Abbo's role in this affair is open to dispute, but it is certain that he had the unenviable job of informing Robert that his petition to the Pope to have his marriage recognized had failed.[28] Abbo's actual role in this was probably much greater than his letter suggests, since the young pope clearly had great deference for Abbo, a long-time champion of the papacy in the Capetian realm and the pope's chosen representative in the restoration of Arnulf of Reims as well as in relaying papal opinion to petitioners in several minor matters.[29] The enforcement of marital righteousness on the secular ruler of France was yet another manifestation of the moral hierarchy which Abbo had established for the promotion of reformed monasticism and pious kingship over pressures from a worldly episcopate and an avaricious laity.

In each of these cases, Abbo's arguments for clerical celibacy and ecclesiastical oversight of marriage also served to reinforce his vision of Christian society, in which the monasteries and the papacy occupied the highest positions of moral authority and worked in cooperation with episcopal and monarchical power. His tripartite divisions of society, produced in the monastic environment of the tenth century, stressed the moral superiority of virgins and the continent, especially monks, to their worldly counterparts. Within this framework, Abbo envisioned all three orders working together for the good of Christian society. Abbo was particularly concerned with differentiating the clergy from the laity, because he saw a tendency in his own day for the laity to become like the clergy, in possessing church property, and the clergy to become like the laity, in being married. That the reforming papacy of Gregory VII took up the cause of clerical celibacy from the monasteries less than a century later should come as no surprise, since many of the most important figures in the reform movement had their roots in the cloister.

NOTES

1. Michael Sheehan, "Sexuality, Marriage, Celibacy, and the Family in Central and Northern Italy: Christian Legal and Moral Guides in the Early Middle Ages," in *The Family in Italy: From Antiquity to the Present*, ed. Richard P. Saller (New Haven, CT, and London: Yale University Press, 1991), 173. See also Jack Goody, *The Development of the Family and Marriage in Europe* (Cambridge and London: Cambridge University Press, 1983), 77-78, and JoAnn McNamara, "Chaste Marriage and Clerical Celibacy," chapter 3 of *Sexual Practices and the Medieval Church* (Buffalo, NY: Prometheus Books, 1982), 22.

2. James Brundage, *Law, Sex, and Christian Society in Medieval Europe* (Chicago: University of Chicago Press, 1987), 150. For a contrary view, see Roman M. T. Cholij, "Married Clergy and Ecclesiastical Continence in Light of the Council in Trullo (691)," *Annuarium Historiae Conciliorum* 19.1 (1987) 71-230 and 19.2 (1987) 241-99.

3. Brundage, *Law*, p. 172. For marriage in general, see David Herlihy, "The Family and Religious Ideologies in Medieval Europe," *Journal of Family History* 12.1-3 (1987), who noted that before the twelfth century, "The Church limited its interventions in marital matters to questions of sin and penitence" (p. 4).

4. This moral preference for virginity can be clearly seen in early medieval hagiography; see Marc Glasser, "Marriage in Medieval Hagiography," *Studies in Medieval and Renaissance History* n.s. 4 (1981), 15-19; and Clarissa W. Atkinson, "'Precious Balsam in a Fragile Glass': The Ideology of Virginity in the Late Middle Ages," *Journal of Family History* 8.2 (Summer 1983), 134-36.

5. London, BL 10972, ff. 15v-22v, published in *PL* 139:473-508.

6. Abbo, *Liber Apologeticus* (*PL* 139:463; BL Add ms 10972, f. 17r): "ex utroque sexu fidelium tres ordines ac si tres gradus in sancta et universali ecclesia esse novimus quorum licet nullus sine peccato sit tamen primus est bonus secundus melior tertius est optimus. et primus quidem ordo est in utroque sexu conjugatorum secundus continentium vel viduarum tertius virginum vel sanctimonialium." All translations of the work of Abbo are my own unless otherwise indicated.

Marco Mostert, *The Political Theology of Abbo of Fleury* (Hilversum, Netherlands: Verloren Publishers, 1987), 89, has pointed out the moral dimension to Abbo's formulation. This distinction is hardly original with Abbo; for his forerunners, see Georges Duby, *The Three Orders: Feudal Society Imagined*, trans. Alfred Goldhammer with a foreword by Thomas N. Bisson (Chicago: University of Chicago Press, 1980).

7. Abbo, *Liber Apologeticus* (*PL* 139:463-5; BL Add ms 10972, ff. 17r-18r).

8. Abbo, *Liber Apologeticus* (*PL* 139:464; BL Add ms 10972 f. 17v): "Constat sane ab apostolis et eorum successoribus esse prohibitum clericos id est diaconos presbiteros et episcopos esse uxorios."

9. Abbo, *Liber Apologeticus* (*PL* 139:464; BL Add ms 10972 f. 18r): "non carnaliter sed spiritaliter filios gignere."

10. Goody, *Family and Marriage*, 79.

11. Goody, *Family and Marriage*, 118; McNamara, "Chaste Marriage," 25-26.

12. Jean Batany, "Abbon de Fleury et les théories des structures sociales vers l'an mille," *Etudes ligériennes d'histoire de d'archéologie médiévales*, Mémoires et exposés présentés à la Semaine d'études médiévales de Saint-Benoît-sur-Loire, du 3 au 10 juillet 1969, et publiés sous la direction de René Louis, Publication de la Société de fouilles archéologiques et des monuments historiques de l'Yonne (Paris: Librairie Clavreuil, 1975), 11.

13. Duby, *Three Orders*, 89; Jacques LeGoff, "A Note on Tripartite Society, Monarchical Ideology, and Economic Renewal in Ninth- to Twelfth-Century Christendom," in *Time, Work, and Culture in the Middle Ages*, trans. Arthur Goldhammer (Chicago: University of Chicago Press, 1980), 54.

14. Marco Mostert, *The Political Theology of Abbo of Fleury* (Hilversum, Neth.: Verloren Publishers, 1987), 127.

15. For a history of the diversion of tithes to monasteries, see Giles Constable, *Monastic Tithes: From Their Origins to the Twelfth Century* (Cambridge, Eng.: Cambridge University Press, 1964).

16. A full account of the riot at Saint-Denis is contained in Aimoin, *Vita s. Abbonis*, c. 9 (*PL* 139:387-414 [c. 9 = 395-7]; Dijon, BM 1118; Monpellier, Faculté de Médecine 68; Paris, BN lat 12606), hereafter, *VsA* (text cited follows that of *PL* with corrections based on manuscripts). Evidence for Gerbert's and Arnulf's involvement may be derived from oblique references to Arnulf in the *Apologeticus* itself, the *VsA*, c. 8, as well as Arnulf's reply to Abbo, in *De Cartilagine*, in P. Lauer, "Le manuscrit des *Annales de Flodoard*, Reg. Lat. 633 du Vatican," *Mélanges, d'archéologie et d'histoire de L'Ecole Française de Rome* 18 (1898), 492-95, and a letter of Gerbert to Arnulf (Fritz Weigle, *Die Briefsammlung Gerberts von Reims*, 2 [*MGH: Die Briefe der Deutschen Kaiserzeit* Berlin: Weidmannsche Verlags, 1966], letter 190; *The Letters of Gerbert with His Papal Privileges as Sylvester II*, English translation in Harriet Lattin [New York: Columbia University Press, 1961], letter 194).

17. Elizabeth Dachowski, "The Serpent and the Dove: The Career of Abbo of Fleury," dissertation, University of Minnesota, 1995, 135-36.

18. Abbo, *Liber Apologeticus* (*PL* 139:465; BL Add ms 10972, f. 18v): "unde Petro apostolorum principi dicitur. tu es Petrus et super hanc petram edificabo ecclesiam meam. meam inquit non tuam et Christus alibi. domus mea domus orationis vocabitur. psalmista quoque. domum tuam domine decet sanctitudo si ergo ecclesia non est Petri cuius erit. aut successores Petri audebunt potestatem sibi vindicare quam non habuit Petrus princeps ecclesiae?"

19. Maurice Prou and Alexandre Vidier, eds., *Recueil des chartes de l'abbaye de Saint-Benoît-sur-Loire*, Documents, Société Historique et Archéologique du Gâtinais 5 and 6 (Paris: A. Picard et fils, 1900-1907), no. 70. See also, Dachowski, "Serpent," pp. 127-31, and Barbara Rosenwein, Thomas Head, and Sharon Farmer, "Monks and Their Enemies: A Comparative Approach," *Speculum* 66 (1991), 781.

20. Abbo, *Collectio Canonum*, "Prefatio" (published in *PL* 139:473-508; Paris, BN lat. 2400, ff. 154r-163r, 172v-173r, 183r), contains a reference to the *Apologeticus*.

21. Abbo, *Collectio Canonum*, cc. 39-42 (published in *PL* 139:473-508; Paris, BN lat. 2400, ff. 154r-163r, 172v-173r, 183r); chapter numbers are from the published edition, as the numeration of the manuscript, especially in the later chapters, contains inconsistencies which the published edition attempts to correct.

22. Abbo, Letter 14 (published in *PL* 139:440-60; London, BL 10972, ff. 23v-38v).

23. Augustin Fliche, *La réforme grégorienne et la reconquête chrétien (1057-1123)*, Histoire de l'Eglise depuis les origine jusqu'à nos jours 8, Augustin Fliche and Victor Martin, general eds. (n.p.: Bloud and Gay, 1950), 62, noted that Pope Gregory I the Great was almost the only Church Father cited by Pope Gregory VII in his writings. The centrality of Gregory I is the focus of Jean-François Lemarignier, "L'exemption monastique," 288-334.

24. Mostert, *Political Theology*, 63.

25. A likely recipient is Gauzbert of Saint-Julien of Tours, a known correspondent of Abbo, though Gauzlin, later abbot of Fleury himself, has also been offered as a possibility. See Patrice Cousin, *Abbon de Fleury-sur-Loire: Un savant, un pasteur, un martyr à la fin du Xe siècle* (Paris: P. Letielleux, 1954), 156 n. 87; Jean-François Lemarigner, "L'exemption monastique," 309-10; and Mostert, *Political Theology*, 63.

26. Marco Mostert, "Die Urkundenfälschungen Abbos von Fleury," in *Fälschungen im Mittelalter: Internationaler Kongress der Monumenta Germaniae Historica*, Munich, 16-19 September 1986, vol 4 (Hanover: Hahnsche Buchhandlung, 1988), 287-318. Mostert elsewhere has suggested that Abbo's interest in securing respect for papal prerogatives arose not only from his desire to secure a charter from Pope Gregory V but also from the need to have a papal charter of this sort accepted by the leaders of the secular and ecclesiastical community of the Loire valley. See Marco Mostert, "L'abbé, l'évêque et le pape: L'image de l'évêque idéal dans les oeuvres d'Abbon de Fleury," *Réligion et culture autour de l'an mil: Royaume capétien et Lotharingie*, ed. Dominique Iogna-Prat and Jean-Charles Picard (Paris: Picard, 1990), 42.

27. For a summary of the proceedings of this council, see Dachowski, "Serpent," 104-25; for its conclusion, see Geoffrey Koziol, *Begging Pardon and Favor: Ritual and Political Order in Early Medieval France* (Ithaca, NY: Cornell University Press,1992), 1-4.

28. Abbo, Letter 1 (*PL* 139:419-21; BL Add ms 10972, ff 1r-1v).

29. Aimoin, *VsA*, c. 12; Abbo, Letters 1 and 3 (*PL* 139:419-422; BL Add ms 10972 ff. 1r-2v).

Heresy, Celibacy, and Reform in the Sermons of Ademar of Chabannes

Michael Frassetto

> And shortly after Manichaeans arose throughout
> Aquitaine seducing the people. . . . Abstaining from
> food, they appeared to be just as monks and faked
> chastity but among themselves practiced every
> depravity.[1]

Recording these words in the late 1020s, Ademar of Chabannes(989-
1034) signaled the emergence not only of some of the first popular
heretics Western Christendom had known in centuries but also a
new religious attitude that laid the foundation for the great reform
efforts to come. The heretics of Aquitaine sought to reform
Christian society or at least the lives of individual Christians. They
hoped to purify society and create a community of the chaste
Christian faithful. But for Ademar and other orthodox ecclesiastics,
this offered a fundamental challenge to the authority and integrity of
the church. Moreover, it challenged the very reforms that church
leaders themselves had attempted to institute at their ecclesiastical
councils. At these councils orthodox leaders attempted to distinguish
between the lay and sacerdotal orders by creating a celibate clergy.
Ademar's work of history and, more importantly, his sermons
provide keen insights into these two phenomena and reveal the
growing interest in purity and clerical celibacy that marked the
eleventh century revolution.[2]

　　Ademar's literary corpus demonstrates that secular and
ecclesiastical authorities throughout Western Europe were not
unaware of the sudden emergence of popular religious dissent after

centuries of dormancy. In fact his account of the appearance of heretics in Aquitaine in 1018 and 1028 is but one of several accounts describing the outbreaks of heresy.[3] As early as 970 heresy emerged in Italy, and other episodes were recorded at Vertus in c. 1000, Orleans in 1022, Arras in 1025, and Monteforte in 1028. Although the origins of heresy at this time remain disputed--and it is a likely combination of internal and external stimuli--the sectaries shared a number of teachings that questioned the authority of the established church.[4] The heretics of the early eleventh century, especially those of the 1020s, posed a clear doctrinal challenge to the established hierarchy.[5] Moreover, they adopted a rigid ascetic code that went far beyond that practiced by many of the secular clergy and, as Ademar notes, was very close to the life of the regular clergy. Indeed, it was this ascetic lifestyle that was most apparent to contemporaries and one that was the greatest affront to the religious hierarchy because it threatened to undermine the distinction between the lay and clerical orders.[6]

It was this rigid ascetic code of the so-called Manichaeans of Aquitaine that attracted the attention of Ademar. As he notes in his history, the heretics of Aquitaine rejected marriage and lived chastely just like monks. In a separate section of the history, he notes that the heretics of Orleans "seemed to be more religious than all the others."[7] But, of course, he suggests that for both groups this lifestyle was intended merely to fool simple Christians into thinking they were pious individuals, accusations he repeats in his sermons.[8] In one sermon he charges that heretics secretly indulge in all forms or bodily pleasure(*cunctas voluptates corporis*) and that they deny that marriage has any worth.[9] For Ademar, these heretics were not true Christians but pseudo-apostles and antichrists whose piety was false and whose intentions were subversive.[10]

Although he accuses the "Manichaeans" in his history and sermons of indulging in all manner of sexual excess, it is likely that he was indulging in a polemic as old as the Christian faith itself. Like other contemporary commentators, including Paul of St. Père de Chartres and Guibert of Nogent, Ademar used this rhetorical device to demonstrate the immorality and inhumanity of heretics who, he felt, stood outside the social order and were intent upon undermining it.[11] The heretics were no libertines but rather adherents of an apostolic lifestyle concerned with matters of spiritual and physical purity.[12] Inspired, in part, by a closer reading of scripture, the heretics sought to live a truly religious life in imitation of Jesus and the first Christians. This evangelical lifestyle included dietary restrictions and sexual abstinence. They rejected earthly pleasures in order to make themselves worthy of heavenly reward and in so doing they rejected marriage, carnal relations and the obligation to produce children. This refusal to participate in the functions of the lay order put them in competition with the clergy. These lay Christians usurped the prerogative of the clerical order by adopting a celibate lifestyle which had been reserved for the secular and regular clergy. In fact, as Ademar notes, the sexual mores of these Manichaeans were more appropriate to monks than to lay Christians. Moreover, by adopting a life of continence, the heretics of Aquitaine undermined the system of social classification many ecclesiastical writers, in various forms, had employed since Carolingian times.[13] Rather than a society based upon separate and distinct social orders, the sectaries of Aquitaine offered a more egalitarian vision of a society rooted in the rejection of the ecclesiastical hierarchy and the shared flight from the material world.[14] The heretics' rejection of marriage, thus, was part of a program that sought to create a more holy society that openly dismissed both the authority of the church and the vision of society being created by ecclesiastical writers.[15]

The rejection of marriage by the heretics of Aquitaine was part of a larger agenda that repudiated the sacramental authority of the clergy and the materialism of the church's teachings concerning the sacraments.[16] In both his history and his sermons, Ademar acknowledges that the heretics rejected baptism, the mass, the Eucharist and all sane doctrine.[17] It is likely that this rejection of baptism and the Eucharist involved more than evangelical protest against the growing authority of the church. There are clear indications that the denial of the sacraments involved questions of the purity of the clergy administering the sacraments and the material of the sacraments themselves. Ademar himself, in his defense of the sacerdotal order, recognized the sexual improprieties of his ecclesiastical brethren and throughout his sermons encouraged them repeatedly to live chastely.[18] In lengthy discussions of baptism and the Eucharist in his sermons, Ademar concentrates on the material components of these sacraments. In the sermon *De Chrismate Sacro*, he describes the necessity of mixing and applying the chrism properly and denounces the errors of heretics concerning this preparation.[19] In that sermon and others, he emphasizes the necessity of using water and chrism at baptism.[20] In a sermon on the workings of the Holy Spirit, Ademar explains that the invisible operation of the Holy Spirit proceeds through the visible material substances to convey the seven graces.[21] And in a long sermon on the Catholic faith in which he denounces the errors of heretics, Saracens and Jews, he cites the Gospel of John to defend the use of water at baptism.[22] He employs similar arguments against the heretics in discussions regarding the Eucharist.[23] Ademar's concerns with defending the material components of the sacraments suggest that the heretics themselves had, at least in part, repudiated them because of a fundamental rejection of worldly, thus impure, substances.

The heretics' rejection of marriage and the sacraments and embrace of an ascetic and celibate lifestyle presented both a doctrinal and ethical challenge to the church and its definition of the social order. It is important to understand the attitudes of the heretics or at least Ademar's perception of those beliefs, because it is in this context that we can understand better the response of the church itself.[24] Indeed, the appearance of religious dissidents who had usurped the privilege of chastity from the clergy forced ecclesiastics, like Ademar, to address the issue of celibacy with renewed zeal.

Reform efforts, of course, antedate the reappearance of religious dissent, but there was an increasing concern within the church that emerged concurrently with the revival of dissent and was manifest in the reform-minded Peace of God movement.[25] Although first emerging as result of the social dislocation of the late tenth century, the Peace movement underwent a rebirth at the same time that the spread of heresy became most virulent, and it is possible that the two movements shared a common source.[26] It is clear from the accounts of several gatherings of the Peace movement that the concerns expressed at these assemblies were similar to those expressed by the heretics. The councils sought not only to curtail violence against the poor and the church but also to reform clerical morality and social organization.[27] The Peace councils, whether directly inspired by the heretics or not, rejected the spiritual egalitarianism of the heretics in favor of a society which recognized the religious authority and uniqueness of the clergy.

The record of the councils of Bourges and Limoges of 1031, perhaps the most famous accounts of Peace assemblies, offer the most valuable account of the revived Peace and the clearest example of the reformist intent of the movement and the growing desire to establish a chaste clergy.[28] The fathers of these councils sought to establish the clergy as a distinct order by removing it from worldly corruption. To that end, they introduced legislation against Nicolaitism and simony, reforms that would become the centerpieces of the program of the next generation and were intended to guarantee the purity of the clergy.[29] These canons also were intended to distinguish the clergy from the other orders in society and, perhaps, were a response to the challenge of the heretics.

The canons of the council of Bourges demonstrate the growing desire within the ecclesiastical elite to define the clergy as a distinct order and to reform the discipline and morality of that order.[30] The most important decisions toward those ends were those that addressed the place of marriage in society. In an attempt to clearly establish boundaries between the lay and clerical orders, several canons were enacted which focused on the general question of the place of marriage in society. These canons prohibit clerical incontinence and clerical marriage and establish specific guidelines concerning marriage among the laity.[31] Legislation regarding lay marriage practices was included alongside prohibitions of clerical marriage to further emphasize the clear separation of the secular and sacerdotal orders and to establish that marriage was an institution reserved specifically for the lay order.

In many ways the real concern was not regulation of marriage among the laity but the restriction of marriage and the establishment of chastity among the clergy. Consequently, the conferees passed some of the most stringent canons concerning clerical marriage. In one canon, the assembled bishops at Bourges declared that "priests, deacons and subdeacons, as canon law rules, may have neither wives nor concubines."[32] They decreed further that if any cleric is currently married or in other way not celibate and does not give up his wife or concubine then he may never ascend to higher orders but must remain among the lectors and cantors.[33] Bishops were ordered not to ordain any subdeacon unless he first promised that he did not have a wife or concubine or agreed to renounce his wife or concubine.[34] Moreover, to guarantee the celibate status of the clergy, it was established that no one may give their daughter in marriage to any priest, deacon, or subdeacon.[35]

The canons of the council of Bourges go beyond legislation against the marriage of priests to include legislation against the children of incontinent or married clergy. These canons were designed to provide further impediments to clerical incontinence. To limit clerical marriage restrictions were placed on the children of priests and deacons. In the same canon that forbade anyone to give their daughters in marriage to members of the sacerdotal order, the assembled bishops also forbade marriage to the sons of members of the clergy of the rank of subdeacon or above. It was also forbidden for anyone to marry the daughter of any priest, deacon, subdeacon, or the daughter of the wife of anyone in higher orders.[36] The council further decreed that the institution of clerical marriage itself was illegitimate, and therefore, as in secular law, no children of such unions could inherit.[37] And not only were the children of clerical unions disinherited and declared illegitimate, but they were assimilated with slaves and could not be ordained to the priesthood.[38] These decrees are surely among the most severe legislation against clerical marriage and the children of clergy and demonstrate the seriousness with which the matter was now being considered.[39]

The growing concern with clerical marriage is further demonstrated in Ademar's *proces-verbal* of the council of Limoges, putatively held the month after the council of Bourges. Indeed, so important was the issue of clerical celibacy to Ademar, and most likely to the church leaders of Aquitaine, that he felt it necessary to have two councils confirm the prohibition. Therefore, according to Ademar, the decrees of the council of Bourges were approved by the bishops at Limoges and incorporated into their decisions.[40] Furthermore, Ademar depicts the members of the council of Limoges returning to the issue after they had already approved the decisions of Bourges. Once again opposition to clerical marriage was expressed by the religious authorities of Aquitaine. Responding to a question concerning judgment of a married cleric, the presiding bishop declared that the canons should be the judge and cited the prohibition of marriage found in the canons of the councils of Toledo and Bourges. Discussion of clerical morality continued, and once again canons were cited which rejected clerical marital unions. These canons confirm the decisions of both Bourges and Limoges: no one who has known his wife or taken a concubine may ascend to the rank of subdeacon or above. These canons make clear too that no bishop may have a wife or concubine and, indeed, that no one who serves at the altar may take a wife or concubine.[41]

Ademar's account of the canons of the councils of Bourges and Limoges of 1031 demonstrates the intention of the ecclesiastics of Aquitaine to distinguish the lay from the clerical order. Indeed, the belief expressed by Ademar that the sacerdotal order was superior to the laity and similar to the order of the heavenly thrones necessitated legislation separating lay and ecclesiastical orders.[42] To accomplish this they sought to create a celibate clergy. But, as Ademar's sermons show, the reasons for creating a celibate clergy went beyond the desire to differentiate the social orders to include moral obligations and scriptural commandments. In one sermon drawn from the Pseudo-Isidorean decretals, Ademar describes the relationship of a bishop and his church. He explains that the relationship is like that of a husband and wife, and just as a husband must not neglect his wife, a bishop must not neglect his church. Indeed, the bishop marries the church, and, like a husband, must love his spouse and keep her chaste.[43] Ademar stresses the responsibility of the bishop to his true spouse and, thus, distinguishes the marriage of a bishop from that of a lay person. To remain faithful to his church the bishop, therefore, could not have an earthly spouse. Indeed, the discussion in this piece reinforces an argument from one of Ademar's earlier sermons. In a sermon celebrating the feast of the Limousin saint Austriclinian, he notes that there are those who say that one should not think ill of bishops and priests and other clergy who marry because, as Paul says, "propter fornicationes autem unusquisque suam uxorem habeat." [44] He explains that marriage is approved for this reason but also that this concession applies only to the laity. The clergy, he argues, should follow the more sublime personal example of Paul and take no wife.[45] And in discussion of scripture in yet another sermon, Ademar explains that God did allow priests to marry under the old law but that under the new covenant brought by Christ priests must not have wives. Clergy must remain chaste to provide the proper moral example to the laity, and it is this example that will encourage others to enter clerical orders.[46]

In several of his sermons, therefore, Ademar found practical, moral, and scriptural support for a celibate clergy. But it is in the *Sermo in sinodo de vita clericorum ex dictis Hieronimi* that Ademar provides some of his clearest arguments for the establishment of a chaste priesthood.[47] In this sermon, he cites scripture and the practices of the church in the apostolic era as precedents for the separation of the clergy from women. He notes that Mary, the mother of Jesus, remained apart from the Apostles and also that Thecla was not permitted to go forward from Antioch with Paul.[48] The precedent of the Apostles is of great importance to Ademar for the priests and bishops are the vicars of the Apostles and, therefore, stands in contrast to the example of those pseudo-apostles in Aquitaine and elsewhere in the West who claim to be true apostles but preach heresy and fake chastity. Furthermore, the responsibility of the Apostles, as it was for the ecclesiastics of Ademar's time, was to defend the orthodox faith and teach the true message of the Gospel. In order not to be distracted from this obligation, the priest must not have a wife. Or as Ademar explains, just as no soldier takes his wife to war, no priest should live with any women in a castle of God.[49] Therefore, Ademar rejected clerical marriage because it would keep the clergy from their fundamental obligation to teach.

In the sermon based on the work of Jerome, Ademar explains further that priests must teach by word and example, and if their example is one of corruption, then they will be scorned by the laity. Clerical incontinence is the root of corruption and the cause of the laity's rejection of the clergy.[50] The source of clerical incontinence and impurity is too close contact with women. Indeed, so threatening to the moral well-being of the clergy are women that Ademar reminds priests that they should not go alone to visit them and bless them.[51] For those in the clerical order, women are "the door of the devil, the way of iniquity, the sting of a scorpion."[52] Women are the source of sin and desire. From the beginning, it was a woman who caused sin to enter the world, and it is women who continue to be the cause of the sin of desire.[53] It is impossible, Ademar says, for anyone to walk across burning coals without burning their feet, and it is equally impossible for anyone to live with a woman without being drawn into the sin of sexual desire.[54] Clerical marriage and access to women, for Ademar, is thus the source of sin and the road to corruption and sexual impurity.

As the sermon on the life of the clergy suggests, members of the sacerdotal order must remain chaste because access to women will distract them from their responsibility to teach and will lead them toward iniquity and impurity. It is this concern with ritual purity that was perhaps the greatest reason that Ademar and his contemporaries were so concerned with the issue of celibacy. It was a matter raised by the heretics who, with their chaste lifestyles, criticized the lives of the clergy and offered a higher moral standard. This concern with purity and the attack on clerical marriage and incontinence was also inspired by the growing interest of Ademar and his contemporaries with the sacrament of the Eucharist.[55] Indeed, it is over the matter of the Eucharist that questions of heresy, ecclesiastical reform, and clerical marriage merge in the writings of Ademar and his contemporaries.

It must be noted that Ademar devotes much attention in his sermons to the issue of the Eucharist. For him acceptance of the truth of the mystery of this sacrament is a matter that divides true Christians from heretics. As we have seen, the heretics of Aquitaine rejected the clergy and the Eucharist because of the impurity of both. Ademar's sermons are his great defense of orthodoxy and as part of that orthodoxy he defends a eucharistic teaching which emphasizes the importance of the material substance of the bread and the wine. He cites biblical history demonstrating the symbolism of the bread and wine.[56] He cites the Gospels as well in which the communion ritual was first performed and in which Jesus informs his disciples to repeat the ritual of the bread and wine in his memory.[57] All of these examples remind us of the centrality of the eucharistic rite in the teaching of the church.

The importance of the sacrament of the Eucharist for Ademar goes beyond its symbolic meaning and visible substance. For Ademar, and his Catholic Christian contemporaries, the sacrament of communion bound the community of the faithful together. In fact, for Ademar, acceptance of the Eucharist is one of the clearest differences between true Christians and heretics, those he calls Manichaeans or messengers of Antichrist. In several sermons Ademar repeats his warning concerning heretics who reject the Eucharist. In the sermon *De Eucharistia*, he cautions his putative audience of those heretics who say that nothing comes from communion at the altar.[58] He also compares the heretics of his day who refused the Eucharist with the Jews of the apostolic period. Citing the Gospel of John, Ademar says that the heretics of his day are just like the Jews who denied that Jesus was the bread descended from heaven.[59]

Ademar's understanding of the importance of the Eucharist comes from his, and his contemporaries', notion of the reality of the physical presence of the body and blood of Christ in the bread and the wine of the sacrament. For Ademar, the sacrament is literally the body and blood transformed by action of the Holy Spirit from the bread and the wine. Throughout the sermons he explains that the bread and wine are the true body and blood of the Lord.[60] As further proof of the real presence in the sacrament, he describes the numerous miracles and visions associated with the performance of the Eucharist. He describes visions of a bleeding infant or lamb above the altar, angels circling the altar, or a boy seated on the altar cloth.[61] Moreover, it is the priest officiating at the mass who is the vehicle for the performance of this miracle. The priest makes a sacrifice of bread and wine just as Abraham and Melchisedech, who prefigured Christ, had.[62] Just as Jesus transformed the bread and wine at the Last Supper, so too do priests when they perform the sacrament of the Eucharist. For Ademar, the priest recreates the incarnation and passion of Christ in the very substance of his body and blood when he blesses and breaks the bread of communion.[63]

Ademar's focus on the Eucharist is thus central to his concerns about the revival of heresy and the integrity of the clergy. This awareness of the physical presence in the Eucharist explains his hostility toward both the heretics of Aquitaine and married clergy. The consecrated host is the pure and holy substance of the body of Christ which cleanses the world of sin.[64] Consequently, all things that come into contact with it must be pure and uncorrupted. Ademar's attention to matters of purity extend to the chalice and paten and even the linen altar cloth which must be clean and consecrated by the bishop to be worthy to hold the host.[65] More important than these items, of course, is the purity of the priest. In a long passage from his *In sermo sinodo*, Ademar explains that ministers at the altar must be ritually and morally pure because they must handle the body and blood of Christ.[66] Priests must be pure of heart and without sin because they handle the body of Christ. It is through them that God sanctifies the bread and wine and thus priests must be pure so that they may worthily perform the eucharistic rite. And, as noted elsewhere in the sermons, the greatest threat to the purity of the clergy is too close contact with women through marriage or concubinage.

Ademar's sermons demonstrate why orthodox clergy were increasingly concerned with abolishing clerical marriage and with reforming the sacerdotal order. The sudden revival of religious dissent forced ecclesiastics like Ademar to examine the doctrinal ethical questions raised by the heretics. The challenge to the sacerdotal authority of the church and its sacramental teachings was a matter of great importance to the orthodox that forced their own examinations of ecclesiastical purity and social organization. The reform stimulated, in part, by the return of heresy, however, also had an orthodox component in the Peace of God movement. The goals of this movement were in some ways similar to those of the heretics but within the well-established societal framework created by ecclesiastical writers. As Ademar's sermons make clear, leaders of the Peace movement sought to reinforce the authority and unique status of the clergy. Opposition to clerical marriage was rooted in this desire to enhance the reputation and status of the clergy. The rejection of what would come to be called Nicolaitism also was based on the pastoral and sacramental responsibilities imposed on the clergy. Their obligation to administer the Eucharist, which as Ademar demonstrated was understood as the physical body and blood of Christ, required greater moral integrity of the sacerdotal order. It was this increasing concern with the purity of the priest officiating at the mass that helped stimulate the desire for fundamental reform. Indeed, as Ademar's writings demonstrate, the great questions regarding purity and orthodoxy and the sacraments and the clergy that would so dominate the discourse of the reformers of the next generation had already begun to form in the early decades of the eleventh century.

NOTES

1. Ademar of Chabannes, *Chronique d'Adémar de Chabannes*, ed. Jules Chavanon, Collection des textes pour servir a l'étude et a l'enseignement de l'histoire, 20 (Paris, 1897), 3:49, p. 173. "Paulo post exorti sunt per Aquitaniam Manichei, seducentes plebem. . . . Abstinentes a cibis, quasi monachi apparebant et castitatem simulabant, sed inter se ipsos omnem luxuriam exercebant."

2. The sermons remain unedited and are now bound in Paris B.N. MS. Lat. 2469, fols. 1r-112v and Berlin D.S. MS. Lat. Phillips 1664, fols. 58r-170r. I am assisting Daniel Callahan in the preparation of an edition of the sermons in two volumes for the series Corpus Christianorum.

3. Useful surveys of this can be found in Macolm Lambert, *Medieval Heresy: Popular Movements from the Gregorian Reform to the Reformation*, 2nd. ed. (Oxford, 1992), 3-32 and R. I. Moore, *The Origins of European Dissent*, rev. ed. (Oxford, 1985), 1-45.

4. For the origins of heresy see Daniel Callahan, "The Manichaeans and the Antichrist in the Writings of Ademar of Chabannes: 'The Terrors of the Year 1000' and the Origins of Popular Medieval Heresy in the Medieval West," *Studies in Medieval and Renaissance History* 15 (1995): 163-223, and Antoine Dondaine, "L'origine de l'hérésie médiévale," *Rivista di storia dell chiesa in Italia* 5 (1951): 47-78 who suggest Bogomil influences and R. I. Moore, *Origins of European Dissent*, 1-45, and Raffaello Morghen, "Problèmes sur l'origine de l'hérésie au moyen âge," *Revue Historique* 236 (1966): 1-26 who reject foreign influences.

5. On the doctrinal characteristics of the heretics see Dondaine, "L'origine de l'hérésie," 47-78, and Heinrich Fichtenau, "Zur Erforschung der Häresien des 11. und 12. Jahrhunderts," *Römische Historische Mitteilungen* 31 (1989): 75-91.

6. Georges Duby, "Marriage in Early Medieval Society," in *Love and Marriage in the Middle Ages*, trans. Jane Dunnett (Chicago, 1994), 15-6; Richard Landes, "Between Aristocracy and Heresy: Popular Participation in the Limousin Peace of God, 994-1033," in *The Peace of God: Social Violence and Religious Response in France around the Year 1000*, ed. Thomas Head and Richard Landes (Ithaca, NY, 1992), 209-10, and Huguette Taviani, "Le mariage dans l'hérésie de l'an mil," *Annales ESC* 29 (1974):1080-2.

7. Ademar, *Chronique*, 3:59, pp. 184-5.

8. It should be noted that issues of heresy and orthodoxy are of central importance in the sermons of Ademar. He wrote the sermons in the late 1020s and early 1030s prior to his departure on pilgrimage to Jerusalem in

1032 from which he did not return. At that time his interest in matters of heresy came from questions about his own orthodoxy and the existence of religious dissidents around him. Consequently, his sensitivity to such matters was particularly heightened, making his sermons an especially valuable source for our understanding of heresy after the turn of the millennium. For further discussion see my "The Sermons of Ademar of Chabannes and the Origins of Medieval Heresy" (Ph.D. diss., University of Delaware, 1993). On the importance of Jerusalem, see Adriaan H. Bredero, "Jersualem in the West," in *Christendom and Christianity in the Middle Ages*, trans. Reinder Bruinsma (Grand Rapids, MI, 1994), 79-104.

9. D.S. MS. Lat. Phillips 1664, fol. 75r.

10. Ademar, Chronique, 3.49, p. 173. ". . .et nuncii Antichristi erant. . . ." He repeats the accusation that the heretics were messengers of Antichrist throughout the sermons. For further discussion and references see Callahan, "The Manichaeans and the Antichrist," 163-223.

11. R. I. Moore, *The Formation of a Persecuting Society* (Oxford, 1987), 6-99.

12. Lambert, *Medieval Heresy*, 28-32, and Richard Landes, "La via apostolique en Aquitqaine au tournant du millennium: Paix de Dieu, culte de reliques et communautés 'hérétiques,'" *Annales ESC* 46 (1991): 573-93.

13. Taviani, "L'hérésie dans l'an mil," 1080-82.

14. Georges Duby, *The Three Orders: Feudal Society Imagined*, trans. Arthur Goldhammer (Chicago, 1980), 130-4.

15. Duby, The Three Orders, 129-66. See also Giles Constable, *Three Studies in Medieval Religious and Social Thought* (Cambridge, 1995), 249-360, esp. 289-323.

16. Georges Duby, *The Knight, the Lady and the Priest: The Making of Modern Marriage in Medieval France*, trans. Barbara Bray (Chicago, 1983), 107-20; Dyan Elliot, *Spiritual Marriage: Sexual Abstinence in Medieval*

Wedlock (Princeton, 1993), 95-8, and Taviani, "Le mariage dans l'hérésie," 1074-89.

17. Ademar, Chronique, 3.49, p. 173. "Negabant baptismum et crucem et quidquid sanae doctrinae est." D.S. MS. Lat. Phillips 1664, fol. 74v. "Ideo cavete ab haereticis qui dicunt nihil prodesse communionem sancti altaris. Et sicut haec sancta abnegant ita baptismi et crucem et ecclesiam abnegant. . . ." For further references see my "The Sermons of Ademar," 230-317.

18. D.S. MS. Lat. Phillips 1664, fols. 115r-116v. It should be noted that Ademar is not alone in responding to heresy by calling on the clergy to live more chastely but is joined by Gerard of Arras-Cambrai. On Gerard, see Moore, *Origns of Dissent*, 9-21; Brian Stock, *The Implications of Literacy: Written Language and Models of Interpretation in the Eleventh and Twelfth Centuries* (Princeton, 1983), 120-39. and Taviani, "L'hérésie dans l'an mil," 1078-82. For a comparison of Ademar and Gerard's reaction to heresy, see my forthcoming article "Reaction and Reform: Reception of Heresy in Arras and Aquitaine in the Early Eleventh Century," *Catholic Historical Review* 83 (1997): 385-400.

19. D.S. MS. Lat. Phillips 1664, fol. 69r.

20. D.S. MS. 1664, fols. 67v, 68v, 79v, 84v, 125r.

21. D.S. MS. 1664, fols. 78v-79r.

22. D.S. MS. 1664, fol. 91v citing John 3:5, "Nemo potest intrare in regnum Dei nisi renatus fuerit ex aqua et Spiritu Sancto."

23. See below, pp. 139-40, for further discussion of the Eucharist.

24. Herbert Grundmann, *Religious Movements in the Middle Ages*, trans. Steven Rowan (Notre Dame, IN, 1995), 7-67.

25. On the Peace movement, see Adriaan H. Bredero, "The Bishop's Peace of God: A Turning Point in Medieval Society?" in *Christendom and Christianity in the Middle Ages*, trans. Reinder Bruinsma (Grand Rapids, MI, 1994), 105-29; Danial Callahan, "Adémar de Chabannes et la Paix de Dieu," *Annales du Midi* 89 (1977): 21-43; H. E. J. Cowdrey, "The Peace and Truce

of God in the Eleventh Century," *Past and Present* 46 (1970): 42-67; the articles in Head and Landes, *The Peace of God*, and my "Violence, Knightly Piety and the Peace of God in Aquitaine," in *The Final Argument: The Imprint of Violence on Society in Medieval and Early Modern Society*, ed. Donald J. Kagay and Andrew Villalon (forthcoming).

26. Landes, "Between Aristocracy and Heresy," 184-218, especially 207-13.

27. Georges Duby, "Laity and the Peace of God," in *The Chivalrous Society*, trans. Cynthia Postan (Los Angeles, 1977), 123-33. For an alternate view of the Peace's reformist intent, see Gerd Tellenbach, *The Church in Western Europe from the Tenth to the Early Twelfth Century*, trans. Timothy Reuter (Cambridge, 1993), 136-8.

28. It should be noted that the canons of these two councils also offer a unique problem. The canons were recorded by Ademar and exist only in B.N. MS. Lat. 2469, who wrote them while in disgrace after his failed effort to declare St. Martial of Limoges an apostle. Much of the record of the councils is clearly a forgery intended to demonstrate the truth of Martial's apostolic status. The reliability of this document and even the existence of these councils, thus, remains open to question. It is, however, likely that Ademar would have intended to give his arguments in favor of Martial's apostolic status the greatest support by surrounding them with the most authentic record of a Peace council as he could and therefore much of the remainder of the accounts is trustworthy. Even if the councils themselves did not occur, the accounts reveal many of the concerns that contemporary ecclesiastics, especially leaders of the Peace movement, shared.

For further discussion of Ademar's activities as a forger, see Michael Frassetto, "The Art of Forgery: The Sermons of Ademar of Chabannes and the Cult of St. Martial of Limoges," *Comitatus* 26 (1995): 11-26; Richard Landes, *Relics, Apocalypse, and the Deceits of History: Ademar of Chabannes, 989-1034* (Cambridge, Mass., 1995), 251-84 and 328-34; Louis Saltet, "Les faux d'Adémar de Chabannes: Prétendues discussions sur Saint Martial au concile de Bourges de 1er novembre 1031," *Bulletin de la littérature ecclésiastique* 27 (1926): 145-60; idem, "Un cas de mythomane bien documenté: Adémar de Chabannes (988-1034)," *Bulletin de la littérature ecclésiastique* 32 (1931): 149-65, and Herbert Schneider, "Ademar von

Chabannes und Pseudoisidor-der 'Mythomane' und der Erzfälscher," in
Gefälschte Rechtstekte der bestrafte Fälscher, vol. 2 of *Fälschungen im
Mittelalter,* 129-50.

29. Amy Remensnyder, "Pollution, Purity, and Peace: An Aspect of
Social Reform between the Late Tenth Century and 1076," in *The Peace of
God,* 280-307. See also Anne Llewellyn Barstow, *Married Priests and the
Reforming Papacy: The Eleventh Century Debates* (New York, 1982), 47-49.

30. B.N. MS. Lat. 2469, fols. 107v-108r contain the canons of the
council of Bourges which are embedded within the *proces-verbal* of the
council of Limoges, fols. 97r-112v. The canons have been edited in Mansi,
vol. 19, cols. 501-506 and will be included in the forthcoming edition I am
preparing with Daniel Callahan.

31. Canons 16-19, Mansi, col. 505, are specifically concerned with
regulation of marriage among the laity.

32. Mansi, col. 503. "Ut presbyteri, et diacones, et subdiacones, sicut
lex canonum praecipit, neque uxores neque concubinas habeant."

33. Mansi, col. 503.

34. Mansi, col. 503.

35. Mansi, col. 505.

36. Mansi, col. 503.

37. Mansi, col. 504. See Heinrich Fichtenau, *Living in the Tenth
Century: Mentalities and Social Orders,* trans. Patrick J. Geary (Chicago,
1991), 115-19, especially 117, who notes that the real reason behind the call
for clerical celibacy was economic.

38. Mansi, 19, col. 504. Remensnyder, "Pollution, Purity and Peace,"
288.

39. Remensnyder, "Pollution, Purity and Peace," p. 288, and Barstow,
Married Priests, 47-48.

40. Mansi, 19, col. 536.

41. Mansi., col. 544-5.

42. D.S. MS. Lat. Phillips 1664, fols. 88v, 97v, 101r and 108v.

43. D.S. MS. 1664, fols. 134r-134v.

44. B.N. MS. Lat. 2469, fol. 8r.

45. B.N. MS. 2469. fol. 8r.

46. D.S. MS. Lat. Phillips 1664, fol. 63r.

47. D.S. MS. 1664, fols. 115r-116r.

48. D.S. MS. 1664, fols. 115r-115v. "Mater Domini de choro apostolorum . . . remota stetit . . . . Tecla post temptationem passionis Antiochiae prohibita est a Paulo pariter pergere."

49. D.S. MS. 1664, fol. 115v. "Sicut nemo miles cum uxore procedit ad bellum ita nemo clericus habitans cum feminis potest vere in clericatu hoc est in castris Dei idoneus permanere."

50. D.S. MS. 1664, fol. 115r. It is possible, of course, that Ademar was thinking of the critique of the clergy made by the example of the heretics of Aquitaine. At several points in the sermons, which focus on questions of heterodoxy and orthodoxy, he makes explicit mention of his concern with heresy, and this passage may be an implicit reference to the challenge of the heretics.

51. D.S. MS. 1664, fol. 115r.

52. D.S. MS. 1664, fol. 115r. ". . . tamquam ianuam diaboli, tamquam viam iniquitatis, tamquam scorpionis percussum."

53. D.S. MS. 1664, fol. 115r.

54. D.S. MS. 1664, fol. 115r. "Si quis ambulaverit super carbones vivos impossibile est ut pedes suos non comburat. Ita qui cum femina habitat impossibile est ut non trahatur ad concupiscentiam mortis hoc est libidinis."

55. Christopher Brooke, "Gregorian Reform in Action: Clerical Marriage in England, 1050-1200," in *Medieval Church and Society: Collected Essays* (New York, 1972), 73.

56. D.S. MS. Lat. Phillips 1664, fols. 110r-110v.

57. D.S. MS. 1664, fol. 106v.

58. D.S. MS. 1664, fol. 75r. "Ideo cavete ab haereticis qui dicunt nihil prodesse communionem sancti altaris." See also fols. 74v, 107v and 114v. For the rejection of the Eucharist by heretics in Aquitaine, see also the recently-discovered, eleventh-century copy of the letter of Heribert edited by Guy Lobrichon in "The Chiaroscuro of Heresy: Early Eleventh-Century Aquitaine as Seen from Auxerre," in *The Peace of God*, 347-8.

59. D.S. MS. Lat. Phillips 1664, fols. 107v-108r.

60. D.S. MS. 1664, fols. 70v, 90r, 103v, 104v and 106v and B.N. MS. Lat. 2469, fol. 90r.

61. D.S. MS. Lat. Phillips 1664, fols. 103r-103v.

62. D.S. MS. 1664, fol. 110r.

63. D.S. MS. 1664, fols. 103v and 108v.

64. D.S. MS. 1664, fols. 90v, 103v and 104v.

65. D.S. MS. 1664, fols. 103r and 123v.

66. D.S. MS. 1664, fol. 109r.

Eschatological Order and the Moral Arguments for Clerical Celibacy in Francia Around the Year 1000

David C. Van Meter

At the turn of the first millennium, the rhetoric of social and ecclesiastical reform was occasionally couched in terms and concepts drawn from the body of eschatological knowledge. Chief among the rhetors who harnessed the emotive and imaginative power associated with the end of this present world were the monks of the reformed monasteries of Francia. Indeed, it was primarily through the ability of these monks to "put the world into words" that the exegetical possibilities of the millennium combined with a series of perceived--and sometimes real--prodigies so as to produce a sense that the world stood on the verge of a profound renovation.[1] Under their influence, a number of the spiritual and ascetic ideals associated with the monastic reform movement spilled out among the laity and the secular clergy. For our present purpose, of course, it will suffice to consider the degree to which the monastic ideal of celibacy figured in the eschatological rhetoric of the monks and thence the manner in which this rhetoric articulated with the movement toward sexual purity that arose in the eleventh century among certain sectors of the laity and especially among the clergy.[2] In particular, eschatology and celibacy converged most visibly in the discourse on the ternary structure of Christendom that occurred around the year 1000. This rhetoric of the monks, when coupled with the currents of apocalyptic expectation that percolated through Francia and Lotharingia around the turn of the millennium[3], inspired nothing less than the beginning of a fundamental reordering of the manner in which contemporaries conceived of the structure of society and lent new force to an argument that celibacy served as a major element of cultic power and sacerdotal identity within the *corpus Christianorum*.

The Moral Three Orders: The Eschatological Dimension of Sexual
Purity

The very ancient idea that a ternary structure governs the social
order exerted a powerful influence on the medieval imagination.
Beginning around the twelfth century, the trifunctional model of
society, according to which there are distinct orders of fighters,
prayers and workers, gained such an intellectual preeminence that it
ultimately shaped the ideological underpinnings of the *ancien régime*
that emerged in early modern France.[4] However, through the
eleventh century the predominant Christian vision of a ternary
society was based not on a functional paradigm but rather on moral
distinctions. In this, it drew its force largely from the theology of St.
Augustine.[5] Proffering the prophecy of Ezechiel 14:13-23 as his
prooftext, Augustine articulated a particularly memorable and
distinctively ecclesiological allegory for Christian society, whereby
the three categories (*genera*) of the faithful who shall endure God's
judgments--executed by sword, famine, plague--may be compared to
Noah, Daniel and Job.[6] That is, Noah stood for the pastors and
rulers of the church, Daniel for the celibate and the virgins who lead
the contemplative life, and Job for the preponderance of the laity
who marry and labor. Augustine also drew yet another, closely
related, allegory for the ternary structure of the church from
amongst the apocalyptic prophecies of Jesus at Luke 17:34-35 and
Matthew 24:40-41: the two men working in the field compare to the
pastors of the church; the two women at the mill, to the laity; and
the two in bed to those who have left the world for the
contemplative life.[7]

Augustine articulated this ternary model, at no less than eight
points in his writings, within the context of his career-long quest to
subsume eschatology into the service of ecclesiology, and
particularly his concept of the church as a *corpus permixtum*.[8] The
great bishop of Hippo seems to have first discovered the utility of
the three moral orders in his quest to justify the Final Judgment in
the face of the texts. A ternary categorization of Christian--priests,
monks and laity--allowed him to represent the hierarchical structure
of the church in his own day in such a manner as to harmonize with
Jesus' apocalyptic allusions, especially at Luke 17:34-35, to the social

contours of peasant society in first-century Palestine. Eventually, however, he came to appreciate this same model as a subtle device for outlining an argument--at once moral and anagogical--that this very structure of the church represented the partial realization of the eschatological hope; within this prophetically-inspired ecclesial environment, the just might both endure periodic judgments of God on human history and await the Final Judgment.

St. Gregory the Great adapted Augustine's ternary model of Christendom, as expressed using the allusion to Ezechiel 14:14, to the religious and societal structures of his own time. To begin, he rejected Augustine's use of the term "categories of the faithful" (*genera fidelium*), and adopted instead a term, "orders of the faithful" (*ordines fidelium*), that suggested that the ternary division of Christians necessarily reflected the existence not only of an ecclesiastical hierarchy but also of relatively fixed religious orders within the church. He also, we should note, largely divested this model of the eschatological connotations that it had either implicitly or explicitly manifested in Augustine's writings, owing to its frequent application as a gloss on Jesus' prophecies on the end. In the *Moralia in Job*, Gregory simply uses this model as a gloss on the allegorical sense of Job's three daughters (Job 1:2).[9] Again, in his homily on the temple prophecies in Ezechiel 40:9-12, he adduces the three moral orders as a gloss on the three chambers (*thalami*) on the eastern gate of the temple (v. 10), explaining that this is an extensive allegory for the infrastructure both of sacred history and the church, before and after the Incarnation. He then goes on to articulate a hierarchy of relative merit and worthiness within this moral schema of three orders. Here he uses as a prooftext the prophecy (Ez. 40:10) that the measure of the three *thalami*--which Gregory has taken to refer, in part, to the three moral orders--shall be one:

> Although the excellence of the preachers is far removed from that of the continent and silent, and although the eminence of the continent stands distinctly apart from the married,...the measure of the three is one, for if there is great diversity in their merits, there is nonetheless no difference in the faith in which they are held.[10]

This to say, that although Gregory admits that all Christians are as one in the faith within the church, he nonetheless unapologetically claims a certain moral supremacy for the priesthood and subsequently places the monks over the laity.

During the Carolingian period, this ternary model of Christian society enjoyed some vogue among the monastic exegetes of Francia and particularly among those of the school of Auxerre. Needless to say, while they adapted Gregory's language regarding the three orders (*ordines*) in preference to Augustine's categories (*genera*), the monks tended to ignore his claims regarding the primacy of the priestly order. They also further expanded the scope of exegetical contexts to which this model might apply; Haimo, for example, adduced Gregory's description of the three moral orders to his own commentary on Isaiah.[11] Haimo's successors, however, tended to employ this ternary scheme in explicitly eschatological contexts. Heric of Auxerre, in discussing the three moral orders in his *Liber glossarum*, placed his exegetical emphasis not on the perdurable structures of salvation history but rather on the expectation of the Day of Judgment.[12] More striking still is the exegetical homily on Matthew 24:27-41 attributed to Remi of Auxerre.[13] Here the discussion of the three moral orders appears in the context of an exegesis of the various apocalyptic signs and events that Jesus prophesied. Interestingly, although this text continues to draw much of its language from Gregory's description of the three moral orders, the eschatological context of the gloss and the prooftexts--that is, Luke 17:34-35 and Ezechiel 14:14--are distinctly Augustinian. While this homily in no way advances any explicit claim for the primacy of one order or the other, it nonetheless elaborates somewhat on the beneficent moral qualities of monasticism. It also, we should note, comes quite close to representing monasticism using the images of a realized eschatology; Daniel represents the order of monks because both spurn earthly marriage and remain continent while serving in the hall of the king.[14]

Toward the year 1000, the Augustinian-Gregorian vision of the three moral orders came to exert an especially strong influence within the monastic milieu and particularly among those monasteries that were caught up in disputes over the issue of exemption. But now the monks applied this model outside of the realm of exegesis, and in so doing, they subjected it to a series of important intellectual mutations. Most significantly, they reconstrued the hierarchical nuances of the three moral orders so as to stress the sense of progression from the earthly to the perfected, thereby producing a vision of the church in which the order of virgin monks stood forth as a realization of the eschatological hope. Thusly construed, the ternary model constituted a remarkably powerful rhetorical tool, in that it might now conflate this imagery of a realized eschatology with both an appreciation of Christian *praxis* and a novel argument for monastic reform.[15] The need for such a rhetorical tool was, indeed, great at that time; as Fulbert of Chartres pointed out towards 1008, it would take "a new rhetor who did not descend but rather fell from heaven" to convince the episcopacy of Gaul to accept the principle that the pope might rightly grant exemption from episcopal oversight and control to the various abbeys.[16]

Among the most important of the ecclesiastical disputes to roil the Frankish church during the eleventh century, one may justly count the question of exemption.[17] The import of this issue extended far beyond the control of monastic properties and abbatial elections; the matter of exemption served as one of the playing fields upon which the advocates of papal primacy and those of episcopal sovereignty arrayed their various arguments. However, while the monastic reform movements of the late tenth and early eleventh century gave new impetus to the efforts of monasteries to assure their exemption by means of papal fiat;[18] this was in reality a much older tactic. By way of example, during the civil wars of the mid-ninth century, the monks of Corbie in Picardy had begun to diligently assemble a portfolio of increasingly powerful papal privileges of exemption.[19] So, too, had the abbey of Fleury in Orléans begun to collect papal privileges in the late ninth and early tenth century, although without gaining, to that point, express independence from the local bishop; it was only in 996/7 that Abbo of Fleury, after much effort, succeeded in winning a papal privilege of exemption from Gregory V.[20] Nonetheless, the Capetian accession, and the ensuing weakening of royal power, only exacerbated the growing inclination of abbots to seek a resolution to the problem of unwanted episcopal oversight at the Holy See in Rome.

Tensions between reform-minded abbots--or, alternately, one might style them as "exemptionist" abbots--and the conservative episcopacy exploded into the open in 991, at the trial of Archbishop Arnulf of Reims at the council of Saint Basle in Verzy. At that council, Abbo, the abbot of Fleury in Orléans, as well as John the *scholasticus* of Auxerre and Abbot Romulfus of Sens, attempted to champion Arnulf's contention that only the pope had the authority to depose an archbishop; for Abbo, at the least, the issue struck close to home, since the rights of his own monastery increasingly depended on the idea of papal primacy.[21] Then, in early 994 this same quarrel between monks and bishops escalated dramatically when an ill-conceived council at Saint-Denis devolved into a riot during which Archbishop Seguinus of Sens suffered injury. In their wrath, the episcopacy identified Abbo as one of the instigators of the riot and excommunicated him. Abbo responded, in part, by writing his well-known *Liber apologeticus*, which he addressed to Kings Hugh and Robert.

In striving, in the *Liber apologeticus*, to gain the moral high ground in his dispute with the episcopacy, Abbo adapted the idea of the three moral orders so as to fabricate an argument by which to claim for the monastic order a spiritual primacy within Christendom. He founded this argument upon a facile syllogism, asserting first the eminence of the virtue of sexual purity, and, secondly, the virginity of the monks:

> We know that in the Holy and universal Church
> there are three orders of the faithful of either sex, as
> if three degrees; although none of these is without
> sin, nonetheless the first is good, the second is
> better and the third is the best. Indeed, the first
> order is that of the married of either sex; the
> second is that of the continent or the widowed; and
> the third is that of the virgins or the pure. Quite
> similar are the three degrees or orders of men, the
> first of which is that of the laity, the second that of
> the clerics, and the third that of the monks.[22]

This passage is very well known, and has been ably treated by such prominent scholars as Georges Duby, Marco Mostert and

Dominique Iogna-Prat.[23] Here let us simply underscore two points that pertain to the present discussion. First, Abbo has imprinted the Augustinian idea of three moral orders with a Hieronimian appreciation of the virtues of chastity. Accordingly, there are three degrees of sexual purity: virginity, continence, and marriage.[24] While in the passage cited above Abbo does not explicitly conflate the moral hierarchy with the ecclesial one, shortly thereafter in the *Liber apologeticus* he plainly draws out the logical conclusion from his premises: "indeed, the order of clerics is in the middle between the laity and the monks; as much as it is higher that the lower, it is that much lower than the higher."[25] Whereas in Gregory's formulation of the three moral orders the priesthood had been first and the monks second, in Abbo's scheme the monks now assumed moral superiority within Christendom, although from the third place-- which is to say the most advanced status, in a neo-Platonic sense of progression toward perfection.

Our second point is to remark on the basis by which Abbo converts a fairly innocuous, moral argument for the relative advantages of virginity and the contemplative life into this sweeping revision of the Gregorian hierarchy of the moral orders of Christianity. In part, he rests his argument on the authority of the Fathers as well as on such conventional scriptural prooftexts as the story of Martha and Mary (Luke 10:38-42).[26] That is to say, the monks have chosen the "better part." Far more striking and resonant with the sorts of apocalyptic anxieties that Abbo claims in this same work have recently troubled Francia and Lotharingia[27] is the manner in which he depicts the monastic profession as a sign of a realized eschatology. In particular, he assimilates the monastic order, by virtue of its institutionalized virginity, with the "college" of the 144,000 of Apocalypse 14:4 who follow the Lamb wherever he goes.[28] Thus, the monks represent the point at which the terrestrial church comes into the closest spiritual contact with the Kingdom of God; while the clergy is laboring in the world and bearing the daily anxieties of all the churches, the monks have abandoned the world to serve in the heavenly court. Although this is certainly not an argument for the religio-political primacy of the monastic order over the clergy, it represents nonetheless an imaginative case for exempting the monasteries from the discipline of the episcopacy, which is comprised of clerics who are *ipso facto* the moral inferiors of monks.

Abbot Odilo of Cluny played a leading role in the monastic reform movement around the year 1000 and, in the process of winning papal exemption for the entire Cluniac order, contributed mightily to the papacy's case for primacy within the Church. Interestingly, the three moral orders were apparently not in vogue at Cluny during this period, although an important liturgical text, the *Sermo de beato Maiolo* adduces the three functional orders as a justification for the social role of the monks.[29] Nonetheless, an eschatologically informed appreciation of their virginity served the monks of Cluny as a central fabric of their self-image. Indeed, even more so than had Abbo of Fleury, the Cluniacs sought in their liturgy and hagiography to conflate the monastic profession with the images of the Apocalypse. In addition to assimilating themselves with the 144,000 who follow the Lamb in the heavenly court, the Cluniacs also depicted their virginity as a sacrificial offering to God which rendered them nothing less than *agni immaculati.* by thus construing the monastic profession as a form of self-sacrifice, the Cluniacs claimed for themselves the voice of those under the altar who, in apocalypse 6:9-11, cry out to the Lamb for justice. That is to say, the monks, having died to the world through a symbolic gesture of martyrdom, perceived themselves as uniquely qualified to serve as the voice of God's judgment that is reserved for the world.[30]

If the monks of Fleury and Cluny found themselves in the position of having to concoct rhetorical arguments to incite a revolutionary fight for liberty, the monks of Corbie enjoyed a much more enviable position. By the year 1000, Corbie already possessed no less than three papal privileges of exemption, which merely confirmed and strengthened a long succession of episcopal, royal, and imperial privileges. The first of these papal privileges, which dates to 855 and was granted by Pope Benedict III, confirms the following for Corbie: the free possession of its goods; the right of the abbot to deny the bishop of Amiens or his ministers access to the monastery and its possessions; the freedom of the monks from episcopal power; the right of the monks to choose the priests who shall bless the altars and consecrate candidates in ecclesiastical offices; and the right to freely elect one of their own monks as abbot.[31] This bull is in fact a remarkable document in that it strikingly foreshadows some of the rhetorical topoi that were to be raised in the struggles for exemption around the year 1000. In particular, it uses strong apocalyptic language to condemn those who would controvert its purposes, comparing them here to the abomination of desolation and calling them the vicars of the antichrist. Throughout the text, the implicit premise that the monks occupy privileged place in the moral hierarchy of the three ecclesiastical orders informs the rhetoric; for example, it is contrary to ecclesiastical order that a layman or a canon be elected as abbot over monks. So too, the monastic life preserves one in a state particularly close to God, and hence monastic affairs must be isolated from external pressures and religio-political considerations; the college of monks is the "sheepfold of Christ," and the only door by which a legitimate pastor may enter is that of regularly constituted elections.[32] In 863, Pope Nicholas I confirmed this privilege, and strengthened it somewhat by explicitly granting the monks the right to appeal their cases to Rome if they did not obtain satisfaction from the bishop of Amiens or the archbishop of Rheims.[33] Finally, in 903 Christopher extended this privilege to encompass the castle and the fortifications built by Abbot Franco in the face of the Norman invasions.[34]

Several times in the early eleventh century, the exemption and immunity of Corbie came under attack. Most seriously, perhaps, towards 1049, Bishop Fulk II of Amiens assaulted one or another of the abbey's privileges, probably by interfering in the right of the monks to have ordinations and consecrations performed by the priest of their choice.[35] Abbot Fulk of Corbie, who attended the dedication of St. Remi in 1049, took full advantage of his timely proximity to Leo IX on that occasion by submitting to the pope the portfolio of Corbie's privileges. On the spot Leo verbally confirmed these privileges and commanded that all of the assembled prelates should also respect them on the pain of anathema.[36] Moreover, Leo commanded both Abbot Fulk and several of his lieutenants to appear in Rome the following year, so as to receive a written bull reconfirming and yet again strengthening Corbie's exemption, and to be ordained as priests.[37] This was a great victory for the monks of Corbie, who long remembered pope Leo IX as a special patron both in life and death.[38]

Within several years of winning the bull of exemption from Pope Leo, a monk of Corbie prepared a recension of Paschasius Radbertus' ninth-century *vita* of St. Adelard and redacted a book of the miracles attributed to this saint. As a whole, these two texts strive to represent the history of Corbie within the greater context of the sanctified process of reconstructing a sense of romanity in Northern Francia.[39] Significantly, this process entailed arguing for the appropriateness of monastic exemption. As had Abbo, the author of the eleventh-century *Vita s. Adelardi* proposes a ternary asceticism and hence proximity to the saints. His source for this line of logic was no doubt St. Gregory the Great's explication of Ezechiel 14, probably as it was mediated by the text of Heric of Auxerre's *Liber glossarum* that was copied immediately after Paschasius Radbertus' *Vita Adelardi* in a late ninth-century manuscript at Corbie.[40] The author of the eleventh-century *Vita Adelardi* optimistically proclaims a vision of Christendom increasing under the reign of the saints:

> [The] Church, adorned numerously with the bud of marriage and thus abounding with a diverse order of sons, furnishes Jerusalem with elect citizens. Jerusalem, is of course the city of heaven, in whose image the terrestrial church is prefigured. Here one has the hope of that city, there the thing desired is held; here the saints are formed, there the elect are reinvigorated. Nor is the Church devoid of those citizens, for God is recognized in their lords, naturally, when emperors bow down before the tombs of fishermen, and when fishermen are honored in the succession of bishops, and bishops in the religion of abbots. Thus, let it delight us to succumb to the highest good; let it be a pleasure to submit to such a great Lord. He is not only a promoter of the growth of those advancing, but also remedially provides for the misfortunes of those falling to ruin when he furnishes us with ceaseless angelic intercessory prayers, and confers the advocacy of the saints. We should not doubt

> that these intercessors--the saints--plead urgently on
> behalf of those who stand accused.[41]

Here a sense of divine progression intrudes itself into the imperfect realm of the terrestrial church through the existence of an ascending hierarchy of three orders--laity, clerics, and monks--which are here represented by their lords. In essence, this hierarchy forms an ongoing, institutional linkage between the heavenly Jerusalem and the terrestrial church.[42] More significantly, this prologue forcefully argues that peace and salvation are to be found in submission to this divinely ordained hierarchy, which itself is a partial manifestation of the eschatological promise of the New Jerusalem (Apoc. 21:2). According to this idealized vision, lay rulers should submit themselves to the apostolic authority of the pontificate, and bishops ought to accept the spiritual preeminence of the very abbots whose holiness and access to the saints are a source of honor and benefit to all of the orders of the terrestrial church. Key to the holiness of the abbots within the hierarchy of the three moral orders, of course, is their sexual purity.

An eschatological construction of celibacy thus played an important part in the monastic reform movement. Certain exemptionist abbots and their apologists used the three moral orders as an ideological device by which to pretend that the monks had by self-sacrifice transcended the corruption of the world and thus might validly challenge the claim of the episcopacy to spiritual preeminence within Christendom. At issue, for the most part, was the degree to which the moral authority inherent in celibacy translated into a conceptual basis of actual ecclesiastical authority and cultic purity. That is to say, the reforming monks of the late tenth and early eleventh century argued that their superior moral status within Christendom necessitated their exemption from episcopal oversight.

Gerard of Cambrai: Eschatological Order and Clerical Celibacy

In some quarters, the episcopacy responded to this campaign for the moral high ground within the ecclesiastical hierarchy with scorn and vicious slanders. Adalbero of Laon's famous satiric poem is a fine example of just such a reflexive response, in that he mocks both the lay nobility for thinking too highly of the virtues of sexual purity, and the monks for pretending to occupy a quasi-eschatological state of virginal unity with the New Jerusalem.[43] But simultaneously there arose among the episcopacy certain voices calling for the reform of the clergy, which was to include eliminating clerical marriage and enforcing celibacy among the priesthood. These voices, of course, eventually prevailed. By the latter half of the eleventh century, the reforming episcopacy and the papacy routinely advanced the argument that the spiritual authority of the priesthood depended, to a certain degree, upon its purification, and that peace and justice could never prevail on earth until a triad of clerical abuses—simony, nicolaitism, and bloodshed—had been eliminated.[44] To the extent that the late eleventh-century reformers radically reconstrued the framework of ecclesiology in their quest for *justitia* and "right order in the world," their program of purification represented a sharp break with the traditions rooted in the Carolingian church.[45]

The episcopal reformers of the early eleventh century, however, called for clerical celibacy not in the hope of subverting the traditional socio-religious order but rather of preserving it against the assaults of those who would seek to erode the authority of the priesthood. In such a task, it appeared necessary, no doubt, to fight fire with fire. Thus, if the exemptionist monks had adduced the powerful imagery of a realized eschatology to their rhetoric, the reforming bishops stood able to counter this with the application of their own eschatological vision of right order. Perhaps the most well-known and effective among these rhetors to interject the prospect of a looming apocalypse into the discussion of celibacy, both lay and clerical, was Gerard I, bishop of Arras-Cambrai (1012-1051).[46]

Gerard, we should note, was no stranger to the problems posed to the episcopacy by the movement for monastic exemption, since he (and even more so his immediate predecessors in the see of Arras-Cambrai) had been caught up in a bitter and highly politicized struggle over the exemption of the rich abbey of St. Vaast in Arras.[47] It should hardly surprise us by now that the topic of sexual purity played a role in this dispute, although in this instance the surviving texts give voice to the episcopal propaganda dismissing the claim of the monastic order to merit exemption on the basis of an elevated moral status. The apologist for the bishops of Arras-Cambrai, writing ca. 1024-1025, claimed that the exemptionist abbot of St. Vaast was scarcely a paragon of sexual purity but rather had squandered the revenues of his abbey in the local whorehouses.[48] The appointment of Richard of St. Vanne to the abbacy of St. Vaast in 1008–an act of *force majeure* on the part of the bishop–temporarily solved the problem, since Richard's style of reform stressed the obligation of monks to submit to episcopal authority. However, Richard's successor, Leduin, once again maneuvered to assert his monastery's immunity and exemption during the episcopacy of Gerard. The tact and skill of both Leduin and Gerard, as well as their mutual respect and even friendship, prevented this renewed impulse for exemption from breaking out into the sort of heated exchanges that had marred abbatial-episcopal relations at Fleury and Corbie and earlier at St. Vaast. Nonetheless, Leduin's gains were real: he parlayed the Peace of God movement into a mechanism for consolidating abbatial holdings abroad;[49] he strengthened the abbey's control over its dependents, as well as its immunity with legislation on the *placitum*;[50] and he successfully forged–or, rather, revised and updated an earlier forgery of–a charter of exemption purportedly granted by bishop Vindician in 680, which Gerard confirmed under some duress in 1031.[51] By the second half of the eleventh century, the disaffected clerics of Cambrai unwittingly testified to the successes enjoyed by Leduin and his successors when they muttered that Vindician had dilapidated their church through his generosity in regards to St. Vaast.[52]

Gerard, in fact, had far greater concerns in Arras than Leduin's relatively amicable efforts to buttress the immunity and exemption of St. Vaast. Throughout the 1020s alarmed churchmen began to notice and take action against pockets of heterodox belief in France and Italy; in their concern, not a few supposed that these outbreaks of heresy were linked to a revival and spread of Manichaeism.[53] Indeed, in 1025, just three years after the notorious trial of the "Manichees" at Orleans, Gerard discovered a pocket of heresy within his own diocese, at Arras. He immediately arrested a group of these heretics and then tried them several days later. The results of this trial are recorded, with much after-the-fact rhetorical elaboration, in the *Acta synodi Atrebatensis in Manichaeos*: after a thorough refutation of their doctrines by Gerard, the confounded heretics renounced their odious doctrines and returned humbly to the mother church.[54] Notwithstanding this optimistic account, this was not the end of the story, for around 1031 we once again find Gerard complaining bitterly, now to Abbot Leduin, of the vitriolic slanders that the heretics in Arras had recently flung against the priesthood.[55]

The origin of the heresy at Arras remains something of a mystery. The *Acta* claim that the heretics were inspired and formed in their doctrines by one or more Italians who had recently arrived in Arras. This is entirely plausible, given the existence of trade contacts between Arras and Italy.[56] But those heretics who were questioned by Gerard claimed simply to follow the evangelical mandates and the precepts of the apostolic life as these had been interpreted for them by these mysterious men of Italy and their leader, Gundolfo. Nonetheless, several of their chief doctrinal points as depicted in the *Acta* can be reduced to a radical piety that was informed by a determined anticlericalism, leading to a denial of clerical authority and moreover sacramental efficacy in matters of salvation. In particular, the heretics claimed that baptisms might be rendered ineffective by the impurities and reprobate lives of the priests.[57] Such anticlerical attitudes were scarcely new to Arras in 1025 and may well have been formed during the bitter conflicts between the exemptionist monks of St. Vaast and the bishops of Arras-Cambrai in the years prior to 1008. Indeed, as early as 1012, Richard of St. Vanne complained bitterly that many among the laity of Arras stubbornly rejected the sacrament of confession, claiming that it is as good to confess to God as it is to confess to men. Since he also aimed exactly this complaint against those monks of St. Vaast who resisted his efforts at reform, we may surmise that this anticlericalism constituted a tactic of resistance on the part of those who continued to seek to limit the power of the see of Cambrai in Arras.[58] Perhaps the laity of Arras--many if not most of whom were dependents of St. Vaast--had been stirred up against the clergy by the former exemptionist abbot, Fuldrad, and his loyalists, who may have attempted to undermine clerical authority by arguing that the priests were impure and hence unworthy repositories for the confessions of the faithful? At any rate, we can be certain that the Italian missionaries whom Gerard railed against found a fertile soil of anti-clericalism in Arras in which to sow the seeds of error.

Among the doctrines of the heretics at Arras, we should note their emphasis on "leaving the world and restraining the flesh from sexual desires."[59] Indeed, as with the exemptionist monks, the heretics of the year 1000 tended to value the state of virginity, even to the point of viewing it in the light of eschatological knowledge.[60] But even so, their pursuit of a quasi-monastic ideal of sexual purity resonated with broader developments in lay piety in the early eleventh century. This ethic of celibacy even left its mark upon the highest circles of lay society. In particular, the early eleventh century witnessed the brief flowering of an odd--and fundamentally unaristocratic--ideal of the virginal ruler. To a certain degree, of course, the development of cults surrounding these rulers was itself a phenomenon of the twelfth century, as the reformed papacy sought to assert the centrality of sexual purity within all modes of holiness, lay and religious alike.[61] But several genuine, eleventh-century voices also seem to have expressed anxiety over whether celibacy was a desirable state among the laity. Most notably, Dudo of St. Quentin recalls that Duke William of Normandy contemplated the three moral orders and consequently wondered how those among the lowest order could possibly enjoy the same reward--salvation--as those in the purest order.[62]

Apparently this same sort of doubt as Duke William expressed underlay the belief of the heretics at Arras that lay celibacy was a virtue to be aggressively pursued, as the author of the *Acta* went out of his way to assert that chaste marriage was a desirable and beneficent state among the laity. Indeed, Gerard is said to have assured the heretics that "whoever uses marriage such that, in fear of God, he directs his efforts toward the love of children rather than fulfilling the appetite of the impudent flesh, shall not be deprived of the lot of the faithful for the fault of marriage."[63] That is to say, while Gerard acknowledges the desirability and hence moral superiority of celibacy and the inherently flawed state of marriage, he excuses this state in the laity when it is coupled with reverence and chastity. To buttress his assertion, he turns to an analysis of the economy of salvation that is founded upon a realized eschatology.

Gerard's argument is manifold and subtle, aimed as much at reassuring the laity and confounding the heretics, as it was at underscoring the eschatological and moral basis of ecclesiastical authority. To begin, Gerard asserts, as a given, that society is to be construed in the terms of a traditional and eminently Carolingian dualism. The *corpus Christianorum* consists of two distinct orders: lay-persons and ecclesiastics.[64] But if this conceptualization of the social order was traditional, Gerard overlaid upon it a radical image of the moral structure of the church. His model did not evoke the ternarity of moral orders that had proved so dear to the monks but rather depended upon a binary paradigm that was far better suited to the religio-political considerations of the episcopacy. While chaste marriage is permitted for the laity, celibacy is the necessary state of ecclesiastics, to include of course the priesthood. Such a moral distinction between socio-religious orders is essential, as Gerard admits, in order to demarcate between those who rule and those who are ruled. But more importantly, this distinction between orders is a reflection of the eschatological nature of the church, which is the realization and prelibation within time of the Kingdom of Heaven.[65] To prove his case, Gerard cites both pseudo-Dionysius's *De caelesti ierarchia* and Gregory the Great's *Regula pastoralis*; just as in heaven there are distinct orders of angels who have varying degrees of authority, so too, within the church the orders of the faithful are inherently unequal. Nonetheless, each of the descending orders of the angels serves in the heavenly court, and each one of the faithful who endures in his or her allotted order persists in the Kingdom, now in the church and eventually in the New Jerusalem.

As we have seen, it is quite likely that Gerard's problem with anticlericalism and even heresy at Arras was related, more or less directly, to the activities and rhetoric of exemptionist monks at St. Vaast. We should therefore note that Gerard, throughout his career, described society in terms that subsumed the order of the monks within the larger ecclesiastical order. In opposing the Peace of God in the 1020s, which was championed by Leduin of St. Vaast among others, he offered up the same dualistic representation of society that he presented to the heretics of Arras; and even when he uttered his famous speech on the three *functional* orders in 1034, he persisted in drawing the fundamental distinction between the laity, comprised of workers and warriors, and those in the church who pray.[66] The recompense for conflating the sexual morality of the priesthood with that of the monks was, however, considerable: such a stance blunted the assault on the moral authority of the clergy by the exemptionist monks and heretics alike. Gerard, in insisting on a celibate clergy in the face of such disturbances in the order of Christendom as heresy and strained diocesan relations, was likely following the lead of Pope Benedict VIII, who in the council at Pavia in 1022 had declared that the incontinence of the priesthood was a chief source of the evils that battered Christendom.[67]

But sophisticated eschatological arguments alone were unlikely to suffice in solving Gerard's problems in Arras. Far more useful, given the tenor of the times, was a fiery apocalyptic rhetoric. Already, Richard of St. Vanne had been forced to adopt a strident rhetoric that conjured up the fire and brimstone that were to befall those who resisted his reforms at St. Vaast.[68] So too Gerard adapted an apocalyptic rhetoric to his purposes. Citing 1 Timothy 4:1-4, he sternly warned the heretics of Arras that to embrace heterodox teachings was to run the risk of damnation as one of heretics of the last days. More striking still is his letter of ca. 1031 to Abbot Leduin, in which he pleads for monastic support of clerical reform in Arras.[69] A fire, caused by lightning, had recently destroyed the church of St. Mary's at Arras, much to the delight of certain "heretics" who held this to be God's just judgment on an unworthy priesthood.[70] In his letter to Leduin, Gerard acknowledges the sad moral and ethical state of the clergy at Arras, but he counters by marshaling an array of apocalyptic texts that insinuate that in the Day of Wrath the judgment will fall first on the priesthood but next and even more ferociously upon the laity. Indeed, Gerard admits to his own fear that the burning of the church is but a sign of far worse things to come, of an impending judgment by sulfurous fire upon all the sons of men. The rhetorical strategy that he laid out before Leduin in this letter is thus to urge ecclesiastical reform in the face of the imminent Apocalypse, so that the laity might hastily return to the embrace of the Mother Church, and the clergy convert and provide worthy moral leadership in a time of great trials.

Gerard's dilemma at Arras--where episcopal authority faced challenges by exemptionist monks, anticlerical lay-persons, and even heretics--provides us with a particularly valuable insight into the manner in which the early eleventh-century movement for a celibate priesthood was energized by ecclesial politics and couched in eschatological rhetoric. The episcopacy did not define the moral issues, in this case, over which the struggle for reform was to be waged. Nonetheless, Gerard was quick to grasp that once the reforming episcopacy adopted the cause of clerical purity as its own, the ability to draw such moral distinctions between laity and cleric might readily be translated into a compelling argument for sacerdotal authority. Just as the reforming monks had first realized, the idea of the moral orders lent itself well to representing the ecclesiastical hierarchy as a partial realization of eschatological prophecies. In the hands of the reforming episcopacy, however, such an eschatological representation of the church served to more fully sanctify the traditional distribution of ecclesiastical power. The full potential of the eschatological rhetoric of sexual purity was realized only in the second half of the eleventh century and the first half of the twelfth and culminated with the decision of Lateran II (1139) that holy orders are universally an impediment to marriage.

NOTES

1. Dominique Iogna-Prat, "Entre anges et hommes: les moines 'doctrinaire' de l'an Mil," in *La France de l'an Mil*, ed. R. Delort (Paris, 1990), 249, 258. See also Roger Bonnaud-Delamare, "Les fondament des institutions de paix au XIe siècle," in *Mélanges d'histoire du moyen âge dédiés a Louis Halphen* (Paris, 1951), 19-26.

2. See Anne Llewellyn Barstow, *Married Priests and the Reforming Papacy: The Eleventh Century Debates*, Texts and Studies in Religion, vol. 12 (Toronto, 1982); Dyan Elliot, "Eleventh-Century Boundaries: The Spirit of Reform and the Cult of the Virgin King," chap. 3 in *Spiritual Marriage: Sexual Abstinence in Medieval Wedlock* (Princeton, 1993).

3. On apocalyptic expectations around the year 1000, see Daniel Callahan, "Ademar of Chabannes, Millennial Fears and the Development of Western Anti-Judaism," *Journal of Ecclesiastical History* 46 (1995): 19-35; Henri Focillon, *L'an Mil* (Paris, 1952, 1984), 45-79; Johannes Fried, "Endzeiterwartung um die Jahrtausendwende," *Deutsches Archiv* 45(1989): 381-473; F. W. N. Hugenholtz, "Les terreurs de l'an mil; Enkele hypothesen," in *Varia Historica aangeboden ann Professor Doctor A. W. Byvanck* (Assen, 1954), 110-23; Richard Landes, *Relics, Apocalypse, and the Deceits of History: Ademar of Chabannes, 989-1034* (Cambridge, MA, 1995).

On some of the literary and exegetical expressions of apocalyptic anxieties, see Daniel Callahan, "Adémar of Chabannes, Apocalypticism and the Peace Council of 1031," *Revue bénédictine* 101 (1991): 32-49; R. B. C. Huygens, "Un témoin de la crainte de l'an 1000: La lettre sur les Hongrois," *Latomus* 15 (1957): 225-39; Richard Landes, "Rodulfus Glaber and the Dawn of the New Millennium: Eschatology, Historiography, and the Year 1000," *Revue Mabillon*, n.s., 7 (1996): 1-21; Daniel Verhelst, "Adso van Montier-en-Der en de angst voor het jaar Duizend," *Tijdschrift voor Geschiedenis* 90 (1977): 1-10; David Van Meter, "Christian of Stavelot on Matthew 24:42, and the Tradition That the World Will End on a March 25th," *Recherches de Théologie ancienne et médiévale* 63 (1996): 58-82.

4. For various approaches to social ternarity, see: Joseph A. Dane, "The Three Estates and Other Medieval Trinities," *Florilegium* 3 (1981): 283-309; Georges Duby, *The Three Orders: Feudal Society Imagined*, trans. Arthur Goldhammer (Chicago, 1980); Georges Dumézil, *Appolon sonore et autres essais* (Paris, 1982); idem, *La courtisane et les seigneurs colorés* (Paris, 1983); Paul Edward Dutton, "*Illustre ciuitatis et populi exemplum*: Plato's Timaeus and the Transmission from Calcidus to the End of the Twelfth Century of a Tripartite Schema of Society," *Medieval Studies* 45 (1983): 79-119; Thomas D. Hill, "*Rigsthula*: Some Medieval Christian Analogues," *Speculum* 61 (1986): 79-89; Dominique Iogna-Prat, "La 'baptême' du schéma des trois ordres fonctionnels: L'Apport de l'école d'Auxerre dans la seconde moitié du Ixe siècle," *Annales ESC* 41 (1986): pp. 101-26; Jacques Le Goff, "Les trois fonctions indo-europeennes, l'historien et l'Europe feodale," *Annales ESC* 34 (1979): 1187-1215; Otto Gerhard Oexle, "*Tria genera hominum*. Zur Geschichte eines Deutungsschemas der sozialen Wirklichkeit in Antike und Mittelalter," in *Institutionen, Kultur und Gesellschaft in Mittelalter. Festschrift für Josef Fleckenstein zum 65. Geburtstag*, ed. L. Fenske, W. Rösener and T. Zotz (Sigmaringen, 1984): 483-500; Edmond Ortigues, "Haymon d'Auxerre, théoricien des trois ordres," in *L'École carolingienne d'Auxerre de Murethach à Remi, 830-908*, ed. Dominique Iogna-Prat, Colette Jeudy, Guy Lobrichon (Paris, 1991), 181-227.

5. Georges Folliet, "Les trois categories des chrétiens, à partir de Luc (17, 34-36), Matthieu (24, 40-41) et Ézéchiel (14,14)," in *Augustinus Magister*, vol. 2 (Paris, 1955), 631-44.

6. *De urbis excidio*, 1.1 (*PL* 40:717); *De peccatorum meritis et remissione*, 11.10.12 (*CSEL* 60:83); *Quaestiones Evangeliorum*, 1.12 (*PL* 35:1326); *Epist*. 111.4 (*CSEL* 34.2:647); *Enarratio in ps.*, 132.4-5 (*PL* 37:1731-32); *Quaestiones Evangeliorum*, 11.44 (*PL* 35 :1357-58).

7. *Enarratio in ps. 36*, sermo 1.2 (*PL* 36:356); *Enarratio in ps. 99*, 13 (*PL*-37:1279-80); *Enarratio in ps. 132*, 4-5 (*PL* 37:1731-32); *Quaestiones Evangeliorum*, 11.44 (*PL* 35:1357-58).

8. Folliet, "Les trois catégories de chrétiens," 638-40; Paula Fredriksen, "Tyconius and Augustine on the Apocalypse," in *The Apocalypse in the Middle Ages*, ed. Richard Emmerson and Bernard McGinn (Ithaca, 1992), 20-37; R. A. Markus, *Saeculum: History and Society in the Theology of St. Augustine* (Cambridge, 1970), 111-26, 154-86.

9. *Moralia in Job*, 1.14 (*PL* 75:535-36).

10. *Homilarum in Ezechielem propheta libri duo*, 2, homily 4.6 (*PL* 76:976-77); cf. Duby, *The Three Orders*, 82.

11. *PL* 111:998; see Ortigues, "Haymon d'Auxerre, théoricien des trois ordres," 202-3.

12. See e.g., the reconstructed Corbie copy of the *Liber glossarum*, ed. Phillipe Delhaye, "Le curieux florilège de Heiric d'Auxerre d'après un manuscrit de Corbie," in *Corbie: Abbaye Royale. Volume de XIIIe centenaire* (Lille, 1963): "Cur Noe, Danihel et Job soli dicuntur in die judicii liberaturi animas suas? Hoc dicto, non tres homines sed tres electorum ordines figuruntur: Noe siquidem qui arcam in diluvio rexit, doctores et prelatos ecclesie; Danihel continentissimus, virgines; Job, qui uxor habuisse legitur, conjugatos." See also David Ganz, "Heiric d'Auxerre, glossateur du *Liber glossarum*," in *L'École Carolingienne d'Auxerre*, ed. Iogna-Prat, et al., 297-309.

13. *PL* 131:871-72. On the matter of authorship, see Colette Jeudy, "L'oeuvre de Remi d'Auxerre: État de la question," in *L'École carolingienne d'Auxerre*, ed. Iogna-Prat et al., 377-78.

14. *Homilia* I (*PL* 131:872).

15. See Iogna-Prat, "Entre anges et hommes," 245-63.

16. *Epistola* 16 (*PL* 141:208).

17. On the political dimensions of the monastic struggle for exemption and immunity in the tenth and eleventh century, see Jean-François Lemarignier, "L'exemption monastique et les origines de la réforme grégorienne," in *Congres scientifique de Cluny* (Mâcon, 1950), 288-334; idem, "La monachisme et l'encadrement religieux des campagnes du royaume de France situées au nord de la Loire, de la fin du Xe à la fin du XIe siècle," in *Le istituzioni ecclesiastiche della "Societas Christiana" del secoli XI-XII. Diocesi, pievi e parrocchie*, Miscellanea del Centro di Studi medievali 8 (Milan, 1977), 363-77; idem, "Structures monastiques et structures politiques dans la France de la fin du Xe et des débuts du XIe siècle," in *Il monachesimo nell'alto Medioevo*, Settimane di studio del Centro italiano di studi sull'alto Medioevo, 4 (Spoleto, 1957), 357-400; Jean-Pierre Poly and Eric Bournazel, *The Feudal Transformation, 900-1200*, trans. Caroline Higgitt (New York, 1991), 163-70; C. Violante, "La réforme ecclésiastique du XIe siècle: une synthèse progressive d'idées et de structures opposées," *Le Moyen Age* 97 (1991): pp. 355-65.

18. Gaston Letonnelier, *L'Abbaye exempte de Cluny et le Saint-Siège: Étude sur le déveloment de l'exemption clunisienne des origines jusqu'à la fin du XIIIe siècle*, Archives de la France monastique, vol. 22 (Paris, 1923).

19. See, e.g., the act of the Eighth Council of Paris and the bulls of Popes Benedict III and Nicholas I, edited by L. Levillain, *Examen critique des chartes mérovingiennes et carolingiennes de l'abbaye de Corbie*, Mémoires et documents publiés par la Société de l'École des Chartes, vol. 5 (Paris, 1902), nos. 28, 29 and 32, pp. 257-65, 266-77, 282-88.

20. Marco Mostert, *The Political Theology of Abbo of Fleury: A Study of the Ideas about Society and Law of the Tenth Century Monastic Reform Movement*, Middeleeuwse Studies en Bronnen, vol. 2 (Hilversum, 1987), 38.

21. Mostert, *The Political Theology of Abbo*, 46-7.

22. Abbo of Fleury, *Liber apologeticus* (*PL* 139:463).

23. Duby, *The Three Orders*, 87-92; Marco Mostert, "The Political Ideas of Abbo of Fleury: Theory and Practice at the End of the Tenth Century," *Francia* 16 (1989): 85-100; idem, *The Political Theology of Abbo*. 88-93; Iogna-Prat, "Entre anges et hommes," 256-59.

24. Jerome, *Adversus Jovinianum* (*PL* 23:225); Duby, *The Three Orders*, 81-2.

25. Abbo of Fleury, *Liber apologeticus* (*PL* 139:464).

26. It is worth noting that Abbo further conflates the anointing of Jesus by Mary the sister of Martha (John 12:2-3) with that by the sinner who was most often assumed to be Mary Magdalene (Luke 7:38). On the cult of Mary Magdalene, see Victor Saxer, *Le culte de Marie-Madeleine en occident des origines à la fin du moyen-âge* (Paris, 1959). It is further interesting that Abbo, in comparing the monks to this hybrid figure of Mary Madgalene explicitly postures the monastic life as the paradigm of penance.

27. Abbo of Fleury, *Liber apologeticus* (*PL* 139:471-72).

28. Abbo of Fleury, *Liber apologeticus* (*PL* 139:464).

29. Dominique Iogna-Prat, "Continence et virginité dans la conception clunisienne de l'ordre du monde autour de l'an Mil," *Académie des Inscriptions & Belles-Lettres*, Comptes rendus des séances de l'année 1985, Janvier-Mars (Paris, 1985), 136-37; idem, "Entre anges et hommes," 256-59.

30. Iogna-Prat, "Continence et virginité," 132-37.

31. Levillain, *Examen critique des chartes ... de Corbie*, no. 29, pp. 266-77. See Ludwig Falkenstein, "Alexander III. und die Abtei Corbie. Ein Beitrag zum Gewohnhietsrecht exemter Kirchen im 12. Jahrhundert," *Archivum historiae pontificae* 27 (1989): 85-195; Laurent Morelle, "Formation et dévelopment d'une juridiction ecclésiastique d'abbaye: les paroisses

exemptes de Saint-Pierre de Corbie (XIe-XIIe siècles), in *L'encadrement religieux des fidèles au Moyen-Age et jusqu'au Concile de Trente,* Actes du 109e Congrès national des sociétés savantes, Dijon, 1984 (Paris, 1985), 597-620.

32. Levillain, *Examen critique des chartes ... de Corbie,* no. 29, pp. 273-74: "Ovile autem Xpsti fore collegium sanctum monachorum, nullus prudentium dubitat. In hoc ovile per hostium ingreditur, quando per electionis ordinem secundum regularem constitutionem aliquis pastorale minsterium soritur."

33. Levillain, *Examen critique des chartes ... de Corbie,* no. 32, 282-88.

34. Levillain, *Examen critique des chartes ... de Corbie,* no. 38, 299-301.

35. See the letter from Fulk to Alexander of ca. 1061 (*Gallia Christiana,* vol. 10, *Instrumenta,* col. 286-87); and the text entitled "Fulco abbas et Ingelrannus de Bova de compositione habita" in the cartulary "Mercator" of Corbie (Paris, B.N. Lat. 17764, fol. 25v).

36. Bishop Fulk was absent and was thus among those bishops upon whom Leo's sentence of excommunication fell. See Anselme de Saint-Remy, *Histoire de la dedicace de St.-Remy,* ed. in *La Champagne bénédictine. Contribution à l'année Saint-Benoit (480-1980),* Travaux de l'academie de Reims, vol. 160 (Reims, 1981), 237, 251.

37. The charter (*PL* 143:641-42) was granted in 1050. On the journey to Rome, see the *Vita s. Geraldi abbatis Silvae-Majoris,* 7-12 (*PL* 147-1028-31). See also Guy Oury, "Gérard de Corbie avant son arrivée à la Sauve-Majeure," *Revue bénédictine* 90 (1980): 306-14.

38. Indeed, an eleventh-century manuscript of Corbie containing the *Miracula beati Leonis noni papae* is our only textual witness to a particularly interesting miracle atibuted to St. Leo and apparently witnessed by some two hundred French and Lotharingian clerics who were in Rome for Palm Sunday (Paris, B.N. Lat. 12257, fol. 123v); cf. the text edited, with several minor omissions, by the Bollandists in the *Catalogus codicum hagiographicorum latinorum antiquiorum saeculo XVI qui asservantur in Bibliotheca Nationali Parisiensi,* vol. 3 (Bruxelles, 1893), 118-19.

39. David C. Van Meter, "St. Adelard and the Return of the *Saturnia Regna*: A Note on the Transformation of a Hagiographical Tradition," *Analect Bollandiana* 113 (1995): 297-316.

40. Delhaye, "Le curieux florilège de Heiric d'Auxerre," 191-210.

41. *Vita s. Adelardi*, Prologus, 1 (*AASS*, Jan. I, p. 111).

42. On the imagery of monastic eschatology, see Adriaan Bredero, "Jérusalem dans l'Occident médéval," in *Mélanges offerts à René Crozet*, ed. P. Gallais and Y.-J. Riou (Poitiers, 1966), 259-71; Jean Leclercq, *The Love of Learning and the Desire for God: A Study in Monastic Culture*, trans. Catharine Misrahi (New York, 1961), 53-68.

43. I.e., Adalbero satirically inverts the moral order by depicting the aristocracy close to the king as having taken up the cowl and embraced chastity and sobriety, while the monks consort with wives and ride off to war; *Poème au Roi Robert*, ed. Claude Carozzi (Paris, 1979), ll. 39-40, 68-79, p. 4, 6.

44. Amy G. Remensnyder, "Pollution, Purity and Peace: An Aspect of Social Reform between the Late Tenth Century and 1076," in *The Peace of God: Social Violence and Religious Response around the Year 1000*, ed. Thomas Head and Richard Landes (Ithaca, 1992), 280-307.

45. See Karl F. Morrison, *Tradition and Authority in the Western Church, 300-1140* (Princeton, 1969), 265-67.

46. Pierre Pierrard, et al., *Les Diocèses de Cambrai et de Lille*, Histoire des diocèses de France, vol. 8 (Pari, 1978), 32-35; Theodor Schieffer, "Ein deutscher Bischof des 11. Jahrhunderts: Gerard I. von Cambrai (1012-1051)," *Deutsches Archiv* 1 (1937): 323-60.

47. See David C. Van Meter, "Count Baldwin IV, Richard of Saint-Vanne, and the Inception of Monastic Reform in Eleventh-Century Flanders," *Revue bénédictine* 107 (1997), forthcoming.

48. *Gesta episcoporum Cameracensium*, 1.107 (*MGH SS* 7:446).

49. Jean-François Lemarignier, "Paix et réforme monastique en Flandre et en Normandie autour de l'année 1030," in *Droit privé et institutions régionales: Études historiques offerts à Jean Yver* (Paris, 1976), 443-68.

50. F.-L. Ganshof, "Les *homines de generali placito* de l'abbaye de Saint-Vaast d'Arras," in *Étude sur les ministeriales en Flandre et en Lotharingie* (Brussels, 1926), 397-414.

51. For the text of Vindician's charter, which is a forgery that seems to have been substantially modified during the abbacy of Leduin, see L. De Bréquigny, F. La Porte du Theil, and J. Pardessus, *Diplomata, Chartae, Epistolae, Leges, aliaque Instrumenta Res Gallo-Francias Spectantia*, vol. 2 (Paris, 1849), 180-82. For Gerard's charter of 1031, see Guimann, *Cartulaire de l'abbaye de Saint-Vaast d'Arras*, ed. E. Van Drival (Arras, 1875), 61-63. However, Van Drival's edition leaves much to be desired; see Henri Stein, *Bibliographie générale des Cartulaires français ou relatif à l'histoire de la France* (Paris, 1907), 30. In 1031, Gerard required the aid of Leduin in waging a rhetorical battle against the "heretical" and anti-heretical sentiments which prevailed among certain lay circles in Arras; see below.

52. Walter of St. Sépulchre, *Vita s. Vindiciani*, 21.1, ed. Joseph van der Straeten, *Les Manuscrits hagiographiques d'Arras et de Boulougne-sur-Mer avec quleques textes inédits* (Brussels, 1971), 113.

53. For a recent review of the problem and the pertinent literature, see Malcolm Lambert, *Medieval Heresy: Popular Movements from the Gregorian Reform to the Reformation*, 2nd ed. (Oxford, 1991), 9-32.

54. *Acta synodi Atrebatensis in Manichaeos* (*PL* 142:1269-1312). On the heretics of Arras, see most recently Michael Frassetto, "Reaction and Reform: Reception of Heresy in Arras and Aquitaine in the Early Eleventh Century," *Catholic Historical Review* 83 (1997): 385-400; see also Erik van Mingroot, "*Acta synodi Atrebatensis* (1025): Problèmes de critique de provenance," *Studia gratiana* 20 (1976): 201-29; Jeffrey Burton Russell, "À propos du synode d'Arras en 1025," *Revue d'histoire ecclésiastique* 57 (1962): 66-87; Brian Stock, *The Implications of Literacy: Written Language and Models*

of Interpretation in the Eleventh and Twelfth Centuries (Princeton, 1983), 120-39.

55. *Gesta episcoporum Cameracensium*, 3.32 (*MHG Scriptores*, 7:478-79).

56. See J. Lestocquoy, *Aux Origines de la bourgeoisie: Les villes de Flandre et d'Italie sous le gouvernement des patriciens (XIe-XVe siècles)*, (Paris, 1952).

57. *Acta*, 1 (*PL* 142:1272).

58. Hugh of Flavigny, *Chronicon*, 2.11 (*MGH SS*, 8:385-86).

59. *Acta*, 1 (*PL* 142:1272): "mundum relinquere, carnem a concupiacentiis frenare."

60. Huguette Taviani, "Le marriage dans le hérésie de l'an Mil," *Annales ESC* 32 (1977): 1074-89; cf. Elliot, *Spiritual Marriage*, 25.

61. Elliot, *Spiritual Marriage*, 113-31.

62. Duby, *The Three Orders*, 85.

63. *Acta*, 10 (*PL* 142:1300).

64. *Acta*, 10 (*PL* 142:1299). On the traditional concepts of dualism, see Karl Morrison, *The Two Kingdoms: Ecclesiology in Carolingian Political Thought* (Princeton, 1964), 36-67; Yves Congar, *L'Ecclesiology du haut Moyen-Age: De Saint Grégoire à la désunion entre Byzance et Rome* (Paris, 1968), 249-323; cf. Duby, *The Three Orders*, 76-80. A most valuable study of the sources of Gerard of Cambrai's pastoral innovations is Bruno Judic, "La diffusion de la Regula Pastoralis de Grégoire le Grand dans l'Église de Cambrai, une première enquête," *Revue du Nord* 76 (1994): 207-30.

65. *Acta*, 15 (*PL* 142:1308).

66. *Gesta episcoporum Cameracensium*, 3.27 (*MGH SS*, 7:474); see Roger Bonnaud-Delamare, "Les institutions de paix dans la province ecclésiastique

de Reims au XIe siècle," *Bulletin philologique et historique du Comité des travaux histoiques et scientifiques. 1955-56* (Paris, 1957), 178-88. On the date and context of Gerard's speech on the three orders, see David C. Van Meter, "The Peace of Amiens-Corbie and Gerard of Cambrai's Oration on the Three Functional Orders: the Date, the Context, the Rhetoric," *Revue belge Philologie et d'Histoire* 75 (1997), forthcoming.

67. Lemarignier, "Paix et réforme," 452-54.

68. Hugh of Flavigny, *Chronicon*, 2.11 (*MGH SS*, 8:379-80).

69. *Gesta episcoporum Cameracensium*, 3,32 (*MGH SS*, 7:478-79).

70. Actually, the manner in which Gerard describes their sentiments here suggests simply a vehement anticlericalism rather than persistence in specific heterodox doctrines.

Gregory VII, Celibacy, and the Eleventh-Century Revolution

Property, Marriage, and the Eleventh-Century Revolution: A Context for Early Medieval Communism

R. I. Moore

For the *literati* of the European Middle Ages, heresy epitomized all that opposed the world and the culture which they had constructed and constituted alike the rallying point of their real enemies and the repository of their imaginary fears. Among those fears, disregard for the integrity of the property and of marriage, the key institutions of Catholic society, figured prominently. It was taken for granted that heretics--if not all heretics, certainly the most dangerous and depraved--shared their women without regard for order or decency. In other words, they were suspected of communism, the principled repudiation of private property and/or exclusive pair-bonding between men and women which has so often been a prominent element of radical social and enthusiastic movements not only in the west but (apparently) in advanced traditional societies embracing all world religions. No apology is necessary, therefore, for beginning the quest for medieval communism among the earliest heretical movements and the literature associated with them.[1]

To do so, however, is at once to evoke one of the most durable and most recalcitrant controversies about the origins of popular heresy in the Latin west--and not, it must be said, hitherto one of the most fruitful. That is the question whether the first popular challenges to the teachings and authority of the Roman church, in the early eleventh century, are to be interpreted as manifestations of class conflict, a direct response to the establishment of the feudal system, or in spiritual terms as a reassertion of the values and aspirations associated with a literal acceptance of the moral and ethical precepts of the New Testament as they were understood and expounded in the lives and traditions of the earliest Christian

ascetics, in particular, the desert fathers.[2] Clearly, it is crucial to that
argument whether the resistance to certain contemporary
developments in the management of property, labor, and marriage
which is occasionally articulated by, or alleged of, the earliest
heretics is to be read as implying opposition to private property and
pair-bonding as such or merely as the advocacy of spiritual elevation
by means of "apostolic poverty" and personal chastity.

However, this venerable debate takes for granted a rather sterile
antithesis between material and spiritual aspirations in the dynamics
of dissent which has tended to dominate interpretation of these early
heresies. This paper will argue, to the contrary, that far from being
directed to the abolition of property, the real significance of the
interpretation of apostolic poverty which prevailed in the eleventh
and early twelfth centuries was that the conditions which it
established for the enjoyment of collective ownership, in turn, made
possible a social regime based on private property. The distinction
between prohibiting personal property as such and forbidding it to
particular sectors of society is not a particularly subtle one. In
general the debate between the Marxist ideal and its critics has been
couched (for excellent reasons) in absolutist terms, as a clear choice
between one principle and the other. But the remarkable and
portentous thing about the social order which emerged in early
medieval Europe was precisely that it presumed and indeed
depended on the legitimacy and utility of two apparently opposite
systems and principles of ownership. It has been agreed on all sides
that the conceptions of private property and public responsibility
which lie at the center of its legal and philosophical systems are
fundamental to the differences between western and other societies
as they developed in modern times.[3] Without becoming ensnarled in
the simplistic and doubtless orientalist commonplaces that early
Islamic law did not conceive of corporate property or Chinese,
individual possession, it may be observed that some of the most
fundamental of the peculiar institutions of *ancien régime* Europe
derived from the clarity with which this distinction between
abstention from private wealth as a private ideal and prohibition of
it as a public requirement was made and the force with which it was
realized in the eleventh and early twelfth centuries.

Although they can be, and commonly have been, considerably
magnified and generalized by adding inferences from the use of

polemical labels such as "manichaean," specific accusations of holding, or wishing to hold, property and women in common are surprisingly few in the period under review--so few, indeed, that they can easily be cited here as a basis for discussion. In listing them I include statements attributed directly to those said to hold such beliefs and allegations reported about them as well as direct references to common holding of property or women in the context of heresy accusations.

> 1. At a synod held at Arras just after Christmas 1024/5 Bishop Gerard of Cambrai examined some people who were reported, among other heresies, to maintain that married people could not be saved. Under examination they "condemned legitimate matrimony" and added that the essential thrust of their teaching was "to abandon the world, to restrain the appetites of the flesh, to prepare our food by the labor of our own hands, to do no injury to anyone. . . ."[4]

> 2. In a letter purporting to have been written by a monk named Heribert, long dated to the middle twelfth century or later but now discovered in an early eleventh-century manuscript from Auxerre, a sect which has appeared in the region of Périgueux is said to include "nobles who have relinquished their property, as well as clerks, priests, monks and nuns."[5]

> 3. c. 1028 Archbishop Aribert of Milan discovered at Monforte d'Asti a community of men and women whose spokesman told him that "we hold all our possessions in common with all men."[6]

> 4. Guibert of Nogent asserts of the heresy of which he believed he had uncovered a cell at Soissons in 1114 that "wherever they are scattered over the Latin world you may see men living with women without the name of husband and wife in such

fashion that one man does not stay with one
woman, each to each, but men are known to lie
with men and women with women, for with them
it is impious for men to go to women."[7]

5. At about the same time in Flanders Manasses, a
follower of Tanchelm, "founded a sort of fraternity
commonly called a guild. It was composed of
twelve men repesenting the twelve apostles and a
woman as the blessed Mary. They say that she used
to be led round the twelve men one by one and
joined with them in foul sin as a sort of
confirmation of their fraternity."[8]

6. A group of heretics discovered at Liege in 1135
"denied legitimate matrimony and held women
ought to be shared in common."[9]

7. The spokesmen of the group discovered at
Cologne in 1142 remarked of Catholics that "Those
who are thought most perfect among you, monks
and canons regular, possess things not individually
but in common; nevertheless, they do possess all of
these things."[10]

On the face of it this list(from which one or two references in minor
accounts of the same episodes may be missing but not more) is
astonishingly short. Where the texts are so few and so fragmentary
speculation has reigned uncontrolled; it has long been customary on
both sides of the argument greatly to increase the apparent weight of
the evidence in two ways. By assuming that the ideas with which we
are concerned (along with heresies such as the denial of marriage as a
sacrament, of infant baptism and the mass, the authority of priests,
the legitimacy of tithes and so forth) go together, a record of one of
them can be taken to imply the rest. Enlarging the field to include
the Cathar and Waldensian communities which appeared in the late
twelfth century and spread rapidly in the early thirteenth brings into
play a period when the sources are much more numerous and
voluminous and when the accusations made against heretics and the

confessions extracted from them are much more comprehensive. It may seem perverse (or simply lazy) to restrict discussion so narrowly when richer resources are readily available. The defense is simple enough. First, from the later part of the twelfth century onwards, the usual issues connected with the nature and reliability of the sources come increasingly to be complicated by questions about the purposes and preconceptions of those who conducted the examinations and constructed the texts and the stereotypes which are fundamental to the history of heresy and to that of persecution generally in our period.[11] Second, there would be an unacceptable circularity in the process of enlarging the implications of a particular text by assuming that it carries with it what is only made explicit in others and then assessing the currency or importance of the ideas in question on the basis of the number and variety of texts in which they appear. I prefer to try, indirect though the means of doing so must necessarily be, to establish the significance of what is said explicitly, however rarely, in its particular contexts before proceeding to consider how widely that significance may be implied elsewhere.

Not only are these accusations few in number and ambiguous in expression, but almost all of them are easily interpreted in terms of conventional piety or of misunderstood or misrepresented versions of it. One of the first things that every undergraduate learns about the Middle Ages is that communal possession of property was not an outlandish or fringe idea. In the eleventh century when (according to the title of what will very likely be the first book she reads on the period[12]) the Middle Ages were being made, it was a principle of the utmost respectability, central to the programs of the most highly regarded and influential religious leaders, and enforced with widespread and vigorous grass-roots support. For this there was good reason. The prime cause of the decay into which religious life was perceived to have fallen in the early tenth century in Burgundy, Flanders, the Rhineland, and Wessex was not, as the myth long had it, the Viking invasions, but the subdivision of the land of churches and monasteries between their clergy and religious. A hundred years or so later, when the Cluniac and many of the other monasteries which flourished in consequence of that reform began to be seen in their turn as having become excessively complacent in their pursuit of spiritual fulfillment, the prime responsibility was placed on the property which they had accumulated, and zealotry in the evasion of its defilements became the hallmark of the new spiritual heroes of the age. The central strategy in the long struggle for ecclesiastical reform, which over the next three or four generations shook every court in Europe, was to wrest every property and source of income upon which the church had a claim out of private hands and place it firmly, and irrevocably, in the proprietorship and direction of religious and ecclesiastical communities. Similarly, and even more notoriously, the avoidance of sexual companionship was seen, with passionate fervor in the eleventh century, both as the surest mark of personal worth and as a primary goal in the general reform of the church and its ministers. Part of the inspiration and nearly all of the rhetoric of this movement was drawn, notoriously, from the history and writings of the early church, which (it is hardly necessary to mention) had embedded in Christian tradition a vigorous strain of communistic sentiment that remained available to any subsequent tendency wishing to make use of it. It is with the tendency and the use in the eleventh and twelfth centuries, not the formation or elaboration of the tradition itself, that this paper is concerned.

There is ample evidence that enthusiasm for the apostolic ideals which animated all this was widely diffused among lay people in many parts of western Europe around the end of the eleventh century and by no means confined to those who were suspected or accused of heresy. A clear statement of their nature and impact is given by Bernold of Constance, writing of the year 1093:

> The common life flourished in many parts of Germany, not only among monks and clerks living together under religious vows but even among lay people who devoutly gave up themselves and their goods to the common life, so that if they have not the monastic or clerical habit they are not inferior to them in merit. As servants (of monks or clerks) they imitate him who came not to be served but to serve, and who taught his followers to attain their salvation through service. Renouncing the world . . . they set themselves to live the common life after the manner of the primitive church. Innumerable men and women have devoted themselves to this

way of life in these times, living in common under
obedience to clerks and monks, and giving
themselves wholly like serving maids to the
performance of their daily duties. In these villages
the daughters of humble people give up marriage
and the world and apply themselves to live under
the direction of a priest. Even the married set
themselves to live religiously, and to obey with as
much devotion as the religious. This way of life
prospers to a tremendous extent in Germany,
where sometimes whole villages hand themselves
over as communities to religion, so that they may
compete ceaselessly to attain holiness in their
lives.[13]

In this light it may appear that a case for reading our tiny handful of
texts as evidence of anything which could properly be called
communism vanishes at once. In the strict sense, the idea that
ecclesiastical property should be held in common was not
communist at all. It prohibited specific categories of individuals
from personal possessions, but it did not advocate or pursue the
abolition of private property as such. Only the last-mentioned of
those listed above, at Cologne in 1142, implicitly did so, while the
reports from the Perigord and Monforte look much more like
conventional avowals of the spiritual notion of apostolic poverty.
Moreover, the Cologne heretics are also the only ones on my list
whose inspiration had clearly come directly and recently from
outside Latin Europe, probably from Constantinople. Similarly,
though general accusations of libertinism against heretics and
deviants of every kind are common enough, charges of the denial of
matrimony are generally to be taken as directed against its
sacramentalism (which is often specifically mentioned) and growing
ecclesiastical control over it rather than against pair-bonding as such.
In the passage cited in the list Guibert's concern was to convict
subjects of homosexuality, not of holding women in common.
Tanchelm, whose associates Manasses and "Mary" were the subjects
of our fifth reference, was apparently prepared to go to considerable
lengths to caricature practices of which he disapproved and showed
impressive imagination and histrionic flair in doing so,[14] but only the

heretics discovered at Liege are accused of associating with their "denial of legitimate matrimony" the proposition that women should be held in common. Whether that is implied by the same accusation against the heretics of Arras in 1024/5 must be conjectural, but it is neither stated nor, so far as I can see, implied in the apparently frank statement of their beliefs which the text presents, most unusually for the period, in what at least purports to be their own words. It is difficult to imagine what reason the bishop could have had for suppressing such a sensational avowal if one had been offered.[15]

The first signs of major conflict over the nature and meaning of landed property in the context of the movement of the Peace of God, which appeared in southwestern France in the closing years of the tenth century. At Le Puy in the Auvergne, at Charroux and Poitiers in Aquitaine, at Anse in Burgundy, popular assemblies were convened by bishops and abbots, at which those who flocked to them swore on the relics brought out from the monasteries for the occasion to protect each other and the church against the *milites* who usurped land, built illicit castles, kidnapped farmers and their families for ransom, stole their flocks, and commandeered their labor. This movement has traditionally been seen as representing an alliance of the church with the poor against a new aristocracy, which was taking advantage of the collapse of public order in the aftermath of the invasions and the decay of Carolingian authority to install itself upon the commanding heights of a new feudal society and economy.[16] Up to a point tradition is correct, but over the years, the picture has become rather more complicated. In the first place, the aristocracy was not new. When the dust began to clear in the twelfth century it became apparent that the castellans and their followers of the eleventh had been, with surprisingly few visible exceptions, the descendants of the counts and vicomtes of the Carolingian age. They were more numerous, because they had divided their lands by partible inheritance to multiply in each generation the households which they formed: thus, in the region of the Maconnais, six ninth-century comital families had engendered twenty-eight or more knightly families of the twelfth century.[17] But, in a startling development whose repercussions one way and another shaped the agenda of the next century or more, in many of the regions this process of division had been halted in the first quarter or so of the eleventh century to be superseded by the practice of primogeniture in the male line which became, increasingly though never universally, the organizing principle of the transmission of landed property among the aristocracy of western Europe.[18] At the same time enormous wealth had been transferred to the church, in the forms of vast tracts of territory, much of it new land to be opened up by clearance but much of it also old and well cultivated and of immense sources of revenue, among which the profits of justice over many men and the collection of tithes from all of them were the most lucrative. The emergence of *de facto* primogeniture and the concession of (in very round and rough terms) something between twenty and thirty percent of landed wealth to the church were not independent of each other. On the contrary, each was conditional upon the other. The terms upon which accommodation between them was secured settled the disposition not only of property-holding but of marriage, at least in northwestern Europe, for the remainder of the *ancien régime*.

It has been apparent for some time that one of the major precipitants of the crisis was the tension arising from a rapidly rising transfer of land to the monasteries as the millennium approached. Barbara Rosenwein's brilliant study of donations to Cluny, in Burgundy, the greatest monastic foundation of them all, has shown how the tension was intensified by a change in the way in which the recipients began to regard the transfers.[19] Up to this time the same tract of land could often be found being given to the monastery over and over again by different members of a family and in different generations. In other words, the donation did not end the family's interest in the land, which had the character, in effect, of being part of a gift exchange circuit, whose purpose was not primarily economic but social, to weave between the great families of the neighborhood a network of association and obligation with the monastery at its center. Now it seems that the monks began to insist that transfers had involved permanent alienation, treating the land increasingly as immovable property with fixed boundaries. Hence the charges and countercharges of usurpation and alienation which monks and laymen hurled at each other with such vehemence at this time arose at least in part from a diverging understanding of the nature and meaning of landed property. It seems reasonable in turn to connect this new attitude with changing use, a stronger identification of the possession of land with the possibility of cultivation. Among the laity, too, it may be that a growing interest in the exploitation of land, beyond mere proprietorship, contributed to a tendency for responsibility for its management to devolve into the hands of a single member of a family and hence to the even more momentous development, which becomes increasingly visible from the third decade or so of the eleventh century, of succession by primogeniture in the male line.

The establishment of a conception of land as comprising defined, fixed, and immovable parcels and of inheritance by a single designated heir contributed essentially to the establishment of the idea of individual ownership. It has long been disputed whether or not the apparent claims of large groups of relatives to sanction the donation of land in this period imply that ownership was vested in the family rather than the individual who normally appears as donor. Stephen D. White has now shown, consistently with the attitudes we have just discussed, that the antithesis is founded on an anachronistically precise conception of ownership and that recognition of the prudence or propriety of associating with the transfer of land anyone who might be thought to have some kind of claim on it was not seen to be inconsistent with the right, or even obligation of the donor to make his gift.[20] Nevertheless, the gradual disappearance of the custom of recording the assent of members of a broad family group to donations, which had fallen out of use in northwestern Europe by the middle of the twelfth century, clearly registers an important stage in the recognition of land as a commodity, open like any other to the uses of the market, and conversely to that of the individual as an independent, legally autonomous agent. This is not to say that such ideas were entirely new or to deny the obvious and indispensable contributions to their establishment of other forces, notably the revival and diffusion of Roman law. But it does suggest that these developments were directly and inextricably the products of the social revolution of the eleventh century. Like all revolutions this one had its victims, and how they were compelled or persuaded to accept their fate remains one of the most obscure questions connected with it. There was, after all, no authority which was recognized as being entitled to pronounce that the claims of younger sons and of daughters on their patrimony were thenceforth abrogated or severely curtailed, let alone with the power to enforce it. On the contrary, we must expect that in a profoundly conservative society every prejudice of tradition and propriety would have reinforced the natural resistance of those whose most fundamental interest was threatened by overturning the customs which governed inheritance.[21] The establishment of the new regime--which did not, of course, happen overnight--required a reconstruction of the norms and values of social life, a propagation and internalization of new ideals and aspirations of awesome power and transcendental scope. The essential elements of the new cosmology thus called forth were the elevation of chastity, the horror of incest, and the creation of a sharp and clear distinction between the clerical and lay domains, as the basis for two distinct and differently organized property-owning elites.

As we have already seen, the great monastery of Cluny was at the eye of the storm. It was Cluny, more than any other house or order, which had caught the imagination of the tenth-century nobility and attracted a tremendous flow of donations to itself and its associates, especially in Burgundy, the Auvergne and Aquitaine.[22] Such flows had happened before and been followed by anti-monastic reactions in which the descendants of the imprudently generous donors endeavored to recover their position. This time, however, it was Cluny's insistence on turning the reciprocal flow of gift and counter-gift into a one-way stream precipitated and sharpened the reaction, and Cluny orchestrated a response that broke away from the previous pattern. In the seventh century or the ninth, the aristocratic reaction had coincided with weakness of the monarchy, under whose protection monastic wealth had burgeoned. At the end of the tenth century the monarchy of France was somewhere near an all-time low. The long erosion of Carolingian power had at last given way, in 987, to the scarcely better-equipped Capetian house, dependent on the support of the northern French bishops who were none too friendly to Cluniac monasticism and, in any case, barely recognized anywhere south of the Loire. By traditional standards the prospects of defending the gains of the last generation were not bright.

The situation was saved for the monasteries by the proclamation of the Peace of God, but the traditional understanding of that movement as an alliance of the oppressed, church and poor, against the nobility, which, aided by the usurpation of royal powers of

taxation and justice, was robbing the monasteries of their lands and
the poor of their freedom is now subject to thorough-going revision.
Royal power was being usurped to create the *seignurie*, certainly, but
Cluny was in the van of the usurpers, as Adalbero of Laon for one
had angrily pointed out.[23] The *pauperes* whose fields were being
protected were most often the monks themselves. And far from
condemning the building of castles, the privatization of taxes and
public services, and the other processes by which the peasantry was
reduced to servitude, the Peace Councils gave them their blessing,
subject to the relatively modest (though certainly not unimportant)
condition that they were carried out by lords on their own land.[24] In
short, the Peace movement represents not a confrontation between
the monks and the new order, but a sanctification of it. Since this
was not the impression which the sources (products of monastic
scriptoria) wished to convey, the terms of the accommodation are
nowhere explained. It is not, however, very difficult to guess what
they were, for by the 1030s the seignurie was in place, the new
family structure was being rapidly established, and the monks once
more enjoyed tranquil possession (relatively speaking) of their
rapidly increasing estates.

      In drawing a new line between the sacred and the profane
celibacy became the primary and indispensable criterion. The
general importance of the idea of chastity (in particular, male
chastity) in the religious movements of the eleventh century has
always been recognized. Dominic Iogna-Prat has directed attention
to a crucial step in its development in the years around the
millennium.[25] Between 999 and 1010 the scriptorium of Cluny and
that of its dependent house of St Germanus of Auxerre produced the
core documents of one of the largest and most widely circulated
hagiographical dossiers of the eleventh century, a life of Majolus,
abbot of Cluny from 954 until 998, a sermon which he had preached,
and a poem describing the election of his successor, Odilo, under
whom Cluny reached its peak of wealth, power, and political
prestige. In Majolus' life, virginity is not only strongly emphasized
but presented as a sacrifice comparable with that of martyrdom. For
the individual monk his sacrifice provided an alternative route to
salvation. For the monastic community as a whole, celibacy defined
its status in the three-fold ordering of society which was now
beginning to be worked out and distinguished it sharply from that of

the warriors (*bellatores*). Hence, among other things it rendered the monks and their possessions untouchable by profane hands.

We have already seen that Cluny under Odilo was at the center of an evolution of the land itself as fixed and immovable property, and Cluny's land, consequently, was now seen as being permanently and absolutely separate from the land of its neighbors. The new elaboration of the idea of celibacy as defining, and so delineating, the monastic community itself and thus underpinning its claim upon society provided a directly equivalent definition and sharpening of cosmological boundaries. It emphasized and entrenched the separation of the monastic community from its lay neighborhood just as the definition of physical boundaries emphasized and entrenched the separation between their lands. It also provided an articulate basis for the provisions of the Peace Councils, which consistently equated the poor, the unarmed, and the celibate as those who fell under their protection. Conversely, that protection was withdrawn not only from armed warriors but also, with increasing firmness, from corrupt and uncelibate clergy. Thus, the frontier of celibacy was extended during the next half century or so to include not only the monks but all clergy and hence, notoriously, to become one of the central issues of the Gregorian reform. For our present purpose another extension is scarcely less important, for by the end of the century and perhaps sooner, celibacy was also being presented as the condition of the ideal knight, whose long quest was ended when his fortitude and valor won at last the wife and, with her land, the possibility of stability and security which he had not obtained from his family.[26]

Increasing emphasis on chastity, and therefore on monogamy, reinforced by the developing ecclesiastical insistence on regarding marriage as a sacrament of the church, also assisted the establishment of the agnatic lineage by distinguishing more clearly between legitimate and illegitimate offspring. It was even more important to define and regulate what marriages might take place. During this period incest prohibitions were not only reinforced but very dramatically extended. The traditional method of calculating the seven prohibited degrees by the "Roman" computation, which counted the acts of generation separating the putative partners and thus allowed marriage between second cousins at one remove, was replaced in the middle of the eleventh century by the "Germanic" method, which forbade marriage between partners with a common ancestor in seven generations. The purpose of the change, which increased the probability that a given match would be prohibited by a factor of about twenty and caused such difficulties that it was virtually reversed by the Lateran Council of 1215, has been a source of some puzzlement. There is no obvious scriptural or theological reason for it, and it is not elucidated by contemporary texts.[27] Nevertheless, one consequence is rather clear. An important general function of incest prohibitions has been to increase the authority of the older generation over the younger by making marriage more difficult to achieve.[28] In combination with the propagation of the ideal of chivalry, which lengthened the apprenticeship of the knight, it provided an element of discipline over him and kept him out of the breeding cycle for longer. No less importantly, it placed the same obstacle in the way of marriage for daughters, whose portions represented a constant threat to the integrity of the patrimony. It is almost superfluous to add that the drive against incest was announced in the canons of the Peace Councils.

The role of the church in rationalizing the transformation of the code of chivalry, is well known.[29] I am now suggesting that it also played a crucial part in fashioning the tools which allowed that transformation to be carried out. Not all younger sons became knights, however. A great many of them became monks and clerks. Hence, as is obvious but seldom stated, the struggle for the recovery of church property was conducted by men whose interest, but for the movement to primogeniture, would often have lain on the other side of the argument. From the very beginning reformers argued that the root of the church's troubles was the alienation of its property and revenues into lay hands, a process that had become almost universal since the middle of the ninth century. At the council at Le Puy in 975, which foreshadowed those of the Peace movement, the restoration of church property and the establishment of a division of the revenues between bishop and chapter was the immediate objective. But everything has its price, and this was coupled with another reform to which it would remain inextricably linked: the members of the cathedral chapter were required thenceforth to lead the common life--that is, to submit themselves to the regime of individual poverty, chastity, and obedience.[30]

There is another way in which lines which had been comfortably blurred in the old world had to be sharply redrawn in the new. Accustomed as we are to the language and values of the eventually triumphant reform we sometimes forget that the old system had its own rationality and harmony. Thus in 983 the Archbishop of Milan enfeoffed the leading families of his diocese with its lands; the cathedral stalls were reserved to members of the same families, from which the archbishop himself was chosen. Following what they venerated as the custom of their patron, St. Ambrose, the clergy of the diocese were not forbidden to marry.[31] This is only the most famous example of a universal pattern. Although it became a powerful source of scandal to the excluded and to those who embraced the new ideals of reform, the lands and office of church and noble families formed, in effect, a coherently organized, fluid, and flexible corporation, positively lubricated by the blurring of the distinction between the secular and the ecclesiastical, whether of land or people.

Once that distinction was defined sharply for one sphere, it was not only logically but practically necessary to define it for the other. A son who abandoned his claim on the family patrimony *qua son* still had to live and discovered a new basis for demanding his portion in the tonsure which he had been persuaded or compelled to adopt. The logic of reform was elegantly completed by granting it to him on the condition of celibacy--that is, not necessarily on his having no children but certainly on his having no heirs. The elder brother who agreed to restore to the church the property which his father or grandfather was said to have usurped might do so with the knowledge that it would not become the patrimony of a rival dynasty and that the monastic stall or prebendary which it supported would not be claimed by the offspring of its present holder but would regularly be vacated with a reasonable expectation that it would become available to the future siblings of his own successors.

These were some of the consequences of the great movement for the reform of the church in the eleventh century. I hope that I have shown, without making any statement whatsoever about the conscious motivation, calculation, or complicity of those who brought it about by means of long, heroic, weary, and often bitter struggles over several generations, that it was inextricably linked with the restructuring of lay society, and that it was so prolonged and so complicated precisely because its ramifications were universal. One thing led to another until, eventually, everything had been changed, and the logic of the new arrangements was complete. By the end of the twelfth century, the dual structure of proprietorship, each with its appropriate system of recruitment and transmission, was in place through most of western Europe. Conflicts between the proprietors were largely reduced to border skirmishes, always capable of flaring unexpectedly and passionately, always good for a headline, but no longer seriously contesting fundamentals.

The alliance between lay princes, church, and people which was mobilized by the Peace of God in the first, critical, stage of the process was quite deliberately constructed. The great monasteries of these regions had for many years skillfully promoted the veneration of their saints--Ste. Foy at Conques, St. Gerald at Aurillac, St. Martial at Limoges, and many more--as a means of arousing and focusing religious fervor and consolidating their influence. The life of their monks, *vita angelica*, was a rehearsal for the heavenly choir. Their liturgy, the *opus dei*, endlessly rehearsed and magnificently performed, provided visitors to their splendid churches with a foretaste of the sight, the sounds, the very smells of heaven. All this was now brought to the support of the peace movement and even adapted in its service. The trope *dona nobis pacem* was added to the common of the mass at this time, and in some churches the liturgy was altered to include the congregation along with the monks in its performance—"and therefore should all people in concert sing the greatness of his praise, those of all ages and of both sexes, ... saying with the angelic spirits, *Gloria dei in altissimis et in terra sit pax hominibus bonae voluntatis.*"[32]

It is hard to imagine a more striking testimony of unity between church and people. Yet within a few years of the composition of those words, from the same monastery and probably from the same pen, that of the liturgist and historian Ademar of Chabannes, we have the first and one of the bitterest accusations of the appearance of heresy among the people:

> Manichaeans appeared in Aquitaine, leading the
> people astray. They denied baptism, the cross and

all sound doctrine. They did not eat meat, as
though they were monks, and pretended to be
celibate, but among themselves they enjoyed every
indulgence. They were messengers of Antichrist,
and caused many to wander from the faith.

The appearance of these "Manichaeans" led rapidly to confrontation
and apparently to violence, for within a short time

Duke William summoned a council of bishops and
abbots to Charroux, to wipe out the heresies which
the Manichaeans had been spreading among the
people. All the princes of Aquitaine were present,
and he ordered them to keep the peace and respect
the Catholic Church.

This is where the history of popular heresy in Europe begins.[33] The
question which it raises is how it had come about that within a few
short years--twenty or thirty at the most and perhaps much less--the
millennial dawn of unity between the church and people which the
chroniclers of the Peace of God described with such enthusiasm had
given way to increasingly bitter hostility, mutual recrimination and
ever-deepening division.

We can dismiss at once the explanation offered by Ademar of
Chabannes in the passage just quoted of subversion by
"Manichaeans." The missionaries of the Bogomil church in Bulgaria
to whom such words were once thought to refer did not appear in
the west until the middle of the twelfth century. We have already
met their first known converts at Cologne in 1142. They had
nothing to do with anything that happened in southwestern France
in the early eleventh century. Augustine and other Fathers of the
Church taught their successors to look out for certain theological
tendencies as typical of that most dangerously seductive of ancient
heresies, particularly if they gave rise to conspicuous abstention from
the pleasures and sins of the flesh, but that was a legacy to the
language of theological debate, not of historical analysis. What
Ademar's use of it tells us is that when the social order and authority
to which he was committed began to be questioned by those upon
whose acquiescence it depended he was inclined, as those whose

authority is challenged often are, to attribute popular unrest to manipulation by sinister external forces. In his case the temptation to do so must have been greatly intensified by his early commitment to the construction of the alliance between church and people and the suddenness and bitterness with which that broke down, for it seems likely that one of the first manifestations of the breakdown, in 1018, may have been the death of forty or fifty people in some kind of protest or demonstration against the costly building program of his own church of St. Martial at Limoges.[34]

These indications that accusations of heresy among the people of Aquitaine at this time had their counterpart in popular charges of avarice against the church point directly to one of the most constant and prominent threads in the history of popular heresy. They also connect it with one of the two great changes in social relations which together reshaped European society in the eleventh century. A few years earlier and in another part of France, Champagne, to the northeast, a peasant named Leutard of Vertus had a vision which led him to leave his wife, break the holy statues in his parish church, and start preaching against the authority of the Old Testament and the payment of tithes.[35] In 1024-5 at Arras, in the first of the affirmations listed above, a group of peasants (or just possibly weavers) told Bishop Gerard of Cambrai, to whom they had been reported as heretics.

> Nobody who is prepared to examine with care the teaching and rules which we have learned from our master will think that they contravene the precepts either of the Gospels or of the Apostles. This is its tenor: to abandon the world, to restrain the appetites of the flesh, to prepare our food by the labor of our own hands, to do no injury to anyone, to extend charity to everyone of our own faith.

It is easy to dismiss such phrases as commonplaces of anticlericalism, though they have not commonly been expressed with the lapidary simplicity of this remarkable series of equations. The accusation of exploiting the poor remained prominent among criticisms of the church by both heretics and Catholic reformers for the rest of the Middle Ages and beyond--but it was new, or at the very least newly vehement, in the eleventh century. In conjunction with the program of the Peace of God, it tells us a great deal.

As we have seen, the declared object of the Peace of God was mutual defense against knights who were concentrating land and its revenues into their hands far more systematically and ruthlessly than had ever been attempted before, reducing free men to serfdom and creating lordships powerful and wealthy enough to sustain a military aristocracy which was better armed, better equipped, more highly trained, and much more sophisticated than its Carolingian predecessors. That is certainly how the Peace was presented to the people whose support it rallied so dramatically. The long lists of practices which the councils condemned included all those which brought Marc Bloch's "first feudal age" into being--the arbitrary seizure of crops and animals, the exaction of fines, the taking of forced labor, holding people to ransom, and building castles without authorization being among the most commonly specified. No wonder that popular enthusiasm could be mobilized on such a scale. But, as we have already seen, there was a contradiction between the general tenor of such prohibitions and the care with which the councils reserved the customary rights of existing lords--a contradiction which corresponded precisely to that between the interests of the monks, bishops and counts who organized the Peace of God and the peasants and small landholders who provided its dynamic force.

It is not in any way surprising that this should have been the case, for the monasteries were also the leaders in the revolution in land use against whose consequences the Peace movement appeared at first to protest. At this time began the great expansion of cultivation which over the next two centuries cleared the forests and drained the swamps of northern and western Europe to bring them under the plow and the vine and to create the additional wealth that would sustain a steady (and by modern standards not spectacular) growth of population, a much higher degree of specialization of skills, and therefore a vastly more varied and sophisticated society and culture--the Europe, as the old cliché has it, of cathedral and crusade. For the cultivators, however, this did not simply mean more people living and working in the same way as before. A large proportion of the additional wealth arose from the extension of arable land, at the expense not only of the wilderness but of the mixture of horticulture, pastoralism and hunting/gathering which was much more typical of the early medieval world. This enabled each cultivator to survive on a much smaller proportion of his output. But, as Marshall Sahlins once pointed out in a classic essay,[36] the highly organized agriculture which was necessary for cereal growing meant that a largely free or semi-free population had to be much more firmly tied to the land, under much harsher conditions than a more primitive economy required. Such conditions were brutally imposed on the working population of Europe in the late tenth and early eleventh centuries, within a framework of property ownership and land management pioneered by the monks of Cluny, among many others, and given sanction through the agency of the Peace of God.[37]

All this naturally gave rise to widespread and lasting resentment, though since the narrative sources of the eleventh century are almost exclusively monastic in provenance, and what record sources there are for most aspects of activity, including judicial activity, are almost by definition themselves part of the new structures of exploitation, intimations of it are few and uninformative. In the late 990s, as the Peace movement was spreading in Aquitaine, assemblies of Norman peasants sent their representatives to appeal to Count Ralph of Evreux against their exclusion from rights to the use of forests and lakes which they had previously enjoyed. By way of reply, he had their hands and feet cut off and let them find their own way home.[38] The collection of tithes which Leutard of Vertus preached against was one of the first claims made on newly cleared and cultivated land. No contemporary judgment on this period is more famous than that of the biographer of Abbot Odilo of Cluny, whom we have already encountered as the inspirer of the dossier of his predecessor Majolus and president of the Council of Anse, where he established the core of his abbey's immense domain, that he found Cluny of brick and left it of marble. The church building which we have seen so close to the earliest expressions of popular anticlericalism was carried out largely by *corvée* labor. It would not be absurd to suppose that the opportunity of extending such demands was one of the many attractions of the building projects to their proprietors. The accounts which the monasteries collected throughout the eleventh century of the miracles worked by their relics--the relics on which the oaths of mutual protection and support had been sworn in the 990s--are full of the dreadful punishments which the saints inflicted on serfs who tried to run away or to give less rent or labor than the monastery claimed as its due.[39]

While all this may provide a plausible context for hostility to property and marriage as such it does not demonstrate its existence and, if it did, would not establish a proven as distinct from a circumstantial explanation of it. Nevertheless, the permanence and peculiarity of the ideas and institutions whose inauguration we have followed not only supplied the womb in which idealistic communism would be nourished for a long time to come but point to some of the elementary conditions (elementary, I suggest grandiosely, in the sense of Bloch or Durkheim) which may need to be taken into account in differentiating European experience from that of other complex agrarian societies. There are indications that communism in respect of property and (indivisibly from it in any agrarian society) the fruits of labor was not only justly feared but in fact advocated, at least by a few, in the call of the Norman peasants for free access to field, wood and stream, for example, and in the insistence of the men of Arras on preparing their food by the labor of their own hands. The universality, rapidity, and brutality of the process of enserfment justify more than a suspicion that in this respect the manifest imperfections of the sources conceal far more of such sentiments than they have preserved. But the renunciation of property, or the opinion that it ought to be renounced, did not invariably imply hostility to property as such and in the not so very long run, became positively and indispensably supportive of it. Sometimes, as in the cases of the Italian monastic reformers of the early eleventh century or later, the Carthusians and Grandmontines (but probably not even the very early Cistercians, as used to be thought[40]) the renunciation of property at individual or institutional level was carried to very great lengths. Even in these cases, its effect was more likely to reinforce property than to undermine it by assisting to define and sustain the dual system whose genesis I have described and tending to divert popular animus against property, and admiration for those who could despise it, into acceptably unsubversive channels.

The place of marriage--and of monogamy--in constructing and sustaining the dual system of property readily explains the fear of sharing of women which was exhibited in descriptions of heretics and others perceived as deviant or threatening. There is no evidence, however, that anyone actually practiced it, least of all the Cathars, who alone espoused a doctrine which would have made chastity desirable as a universal practice, at least in principle.[41] However, as in the case of property, keeping women in common was advocated, and pair-bonding therefore repudiated by some (though by no means all) of the lithest spiritual athletes of the age, albeit on the condition of chastity. Between the proposals that everybody should have sex and that nobody should have it there is a good deal in common. Both deny not only pair-bonding but privileged access to women, and the display of social power which it implies--all the more real a point since Duby's account of the general presumption of the early Middle Ages that women were there for the taking is entirely convincing.[42] Both withdraw the women directly affected by them from marriage used as an instrument in the disposition and protection of property, though the real result of the one may be to sustain that use as surely as the other subverts it.

It must be remembered that like almost everything that has been written on early medieval marriage, which in recent years is a great deal, what is said here about both marriage and celibacy refers to the privileged. On this subject it is even less acceptable than usual to assume that what goes for one class goes for all. It is, of course, both true and important that the church took and was bound to take precisely that view of its teaching, institutions, and discipline. Certainly from the time of the Fourth Lateran Council (1215)--I would say much sooner--it was at least as determined and able to see its preaching practiced in this area as in any other. Nevertheless, in understanding why its efforts were effective and effectively supported by the holders of secular power, it will probably be appropriate to look at questions related to the disposition and control of labor rather than of property and of social order rather than of dynastic continuity. That would open up an entirely new range of questions, which cannot be approached here. However, it is perhaps worth recording that one picturesque episode from this period which apparently reflects popular resentment of both the social and the ecclesiastical changes overtaking marriage also clearly implies that it was not pair-bonding but the placing of constraints upon it that was resented. In 1116 Henry of Lausanne preached against clerical laxity and corruption to such effect at Le Mans that the people rose against the clergy and briefly took over the city. Henry "summoned a sacrilegious meeting at the church of St. Germain and St. Vincent, where he pronounced a new dogma, that women who had not lived chastely must, naked before everybody, burn their clothes and their hair. No one should accept any gold or silver or goods or wedding presents with his wife, or receive any dowry with her; the naked should marry the naked, the sick should marry the sick and the poor should marry the poor without bothering about whether they marry chastely or incestuously."[43] In pursuit of this ideal he commanded the young men of the city to marry its reformed prostitutes(a practice which Innocent III, though not the Le Mans chronicler, would commend as a meritorious work) and took a collection from the bystanders to replace the clothes which had been burned in the ceremony of repentance.[44] It is a remarkable story, and, as we have it, less than complete or consistent, but obvious reading of it as a protest against the impact of clerical interference and social change on family life in a small community is confirmed by Henry's vigorous and articulate insistence, in public debate some twenty years later, that "the consent of the persons involved alone makes a marriage, without any ceremony, and a marriage thus contracted cannot be dissolved by the Church for any reason except adultery."[45] So far as Henry can be regarded as a spokesman for the little community, therefore--and in my view that is a very long way[46]--we must conclude that its response to the forging of an iron link in this age between private property and marriage was not to deny the desirability or propriety of pair-bonding as such but logical necessity and moral acceptability of linking it to the control and transmission of property.

I began by suggesting that it was been characteristic--whether peculiarly characteristic is not for me to say--of communistic teachings in early medieval Europe that they were fervently admired or savagely suppressed not in themselves but in context. I certainly do not maintain that this ambivalence was wholly new in the eleventh century. But, it was very greatly magnified and intensified by the relationships between private and ecclesiastical property and between marriage and celibacy, which required equally that communal holding of property and the avoidance of pair-bonding should be apparently holy, it was, consequently, a question of the greatest moment whether those who displayed spectacular poverty and austerity were saints indeed and entitled to veneration and influence accordingly, or, in the phrase which appears so regularly in these sources, "Satan disguised as an angel of light." Where people of both sexes were involved a simple and infallible test was readily available. That is why the insinuation that a powerful preacher and radical reformer like Robert of Arbrissel slept with his female followers was so damaging,[47] and indeed why the consequences of such accusations among the earliest Cathars in Italy, in the 1170s, precipitated their division into bitterly warring sects.[48] Conversely, it permitted an undoubted saint of unassailable virginity like Christina of Marykate a sustained and intimate relationship with the lord as powerful as the Abbot of St. Albans and allowed her to enjoy considerable influence over him.[49] It does not seem too fanciful to conclude that the twelfth century endowed communism with an ambivalence which it has possessed in European culture ever since. On the one hand, it was correctly identified as radically opposed to the dominant culture and values, which would be utterly destroyed by the general propagation of community either of property or of women; on the other, those same culture and values could be created and sustained only at the price of confirming the moral authority and prestige of certain communist practices. As ever, the danger of purity lay in the impossibility of dispensing with it.

NOTES

1. This paper was written for and discussed by a seminar on pre-modern communism at Cambridge, April 1992, organized by Patricia Crone and John Hall; some of its principal suggestions had been previously adumbrated at a seminar on European Exceptionalism organized by David S. Landes at Harvard in November, 1989. I am grateful to the organizers and to the participants for providing occasions for the opportunity of considering these issues in what were, for me, extraordinarily stimulating cross-cultural and comparative perspectives and to Michael Frassetto for helping me clarify the argument. None of them, of course, is responsible for the errors or obscurities that remain.

2. See: for orthodox Marxist statements, Ernst Werner, *Pauperes Christi. Studien zu sozial-religiösen Bewegungen im Zeitalter des Reformpapsttums* (Berlin, 1956); Gottfried Koch, *Frauenfrage und Ketzertum im Mittelalter* (Berlin, 1962); for the primacy of the spirit, Herbert Grundmann, *Religiöse bewegungen im mittelalter* (2nd ed. Darmstadt, 1961), translated by Steven Rowan as *Religious Movements in the Middle Ages* (Notre Dame, 1995); Raoul Manselli, *L'eresie del male* (Naples, 1963); Jeffrey Burton Russell, *Dissent and Reform in the Early Middle Ages* (Berkeley, 1965); and for woolly liberalism, R. I. Moore, *The Origins of European Dissent* (London, 1977); for bibliography, H. Grundmann, *Bibliographie zur Ketzergeschichte des Mittelalters 1900-66,* Jeffrey B. Russell and Karl Berkhout, *Medieval Heresy: a Bibliography 1960-79* (Toronto, 1981); for balanced general accounts, Malcolm D. Lambert, *Medieval Heresy: Popular Movements from the Gregorian Reform to the Reformation* (2nd. ed. Oxford, 1992) and Colin Morris, *The Papal Monarchy: The Western Church from 1050-1250* (Oxford, 1989), pp. 316-50. Jeffrey B. Russell, "Some Interpretations of the Origins of Medieval Heresy," *Medieval Studies* 25 (1963): 26-53 remains a valuable survey of the historiography up to that point, and both entertainment and instruction in some of its more sensational reaches are generously provided in *Cahiers de Fanjeaux 14: Historiographie du catharisme* (Toulouse, 1979), notably in the contributions of Ch. O. Carbonell and J.-L. Biget.

3. e.g., for preliminary discussion Anthony Giddings, *Capitalism and Modern Social Theory* (Cambridge, 1971); Perry Anderson, *Lineages of the Absolutist State* (London, 1974); John Hall, *Powers and Liberties* (Oxford, 1985); Patricia M. Crone, *Pre-Industrial Societies* (Oxford, 1989).

4. *Acta synodi Atrebatensis,* Migne, PL 142, col. 1272. Despite the agreement of Walter Wakefield and Austin P. Evans, *Heresies of the High Middle Ages* (New York, 1969), 84. I am not confident of my earlier translation of *parare* in the phrase *de laboribus manuum suarum victum parare* as "earn" (R. I. Moore, *The Birth of Popular Heresy* (London, 1975), 17), but the underlying sentiment is the same in either case.

5. Moore, *Birth of Popular Heresy,* 80. For the eleventh-century manuscript Guy Lobrichon, "Le clair obscur de l'hérésie au début du XIe siècle en Aquitaine: une lettre d'Auxerre," *Historical Reflections/Réflexions*

historiques 14 (1987): 423-44. See also his "The Chiaroscuro of Heresy: Early Eleventh-Century Aquitaine as Seen from Auxerre," in *The Peace of God: Social and Religious Response in France around theYear 1000*, eds. Thomas Head and Richard Landes (Ithaca, NY, 1992), 80-103.

6. Moore, *Birth of Popular Heresy*, 19.

7. Cited in the translation of J. F. Benton, *Self and Society in Medieval France: the Memoirs of Abbot Guibert of Nogent* (New York, 1970), 212, but better E. R. Labande, *Guibert de Nogent: Autobiographie* (Paris, 1981). 430-31.

8.Moore, *Birth of Popular Heresy*, 30.

9. Moore, *Birth of Popular Heresy*, 78.

10. Moore, *Birth of Popular Heresy*, 75.

11. For general consideration of these issues, see Moore, *Origins of European Dissent*, 243-63, and R. I. Moore, "Literacy and the Making of Heresy, c. 1000-c. 1150," in *Heresy and Literacy, 1000-1530*, eds. Peter Biller and Anne Hudson (Cambridge, 1994): 19-37; Brian Stock, *The Implications of Literacy: Written Language and Models of Interpretation in the Eleventh and Twelfth Centuries* (Princeton, 1983), 92-151, and the papers collected in A. Dondaine, *Les hérésies et l'inquisition, XIIe-XIIIe siècles*, ed. Yves Dossat (Aldershot, 1990).

12. R. W. Southern, *The Making of the Middle Ages* (London, 1951), frequently reprinted).

13. *MGH, SS* V, p. 452.

14. Moore, *Origins of European Dissent*, 63-66

15. Moore, *Origins of European Dissent*, 9-18.

16. For a comprehensive review of the literature, Frederick C. Paxton, "History, Historians, and the Peace of God," in *The Peace of God*, 21-40.

17 Georges Duby, *The Chivalrous Society*, trans. Cynthia Postan (London, 1977), 66.

18. This fundamental revision is associated especially with the work of Georges Duby, and with that of Gerd Tellenbach and his associates, of which a selection may be found in Timothey Reuter, ed., *The Medieval Nobility: Studies on the Ruling Classes of France and Germany* (Amsterdam, 1978). For Fuller discussion, R. I. Moore, "Duby's Eleventh Century," *History* 69 (1984): 36-49; Thomas H. Bisson, "Nobility and Family in Medieval France: a Review Essay," *French Historical Studies* 16 (1990): 597-613. Note also the significant modification in Constance B. Bouchard's demonstration that the "new man" could and did find their way into the ranks of the tenth-century nobility by marrying its daughters: "The Origins of the French Nobility: a Reassessment," *American Historical Review* 86 (1981): 501-32. The powerful challenge to the prevailing interpretation led by Dominique Barthélemy, "La mutation féodale, a-t-elle eu lieu: Note critique," *Annales E.S.C.* 47 (1992): 776-77 etc. does not affect the present argument, which relates to the structural imperatives of the new society of the eleventh century rather than the suddenness of otherwise of the processes which brought it into being.

19. Barbara Rosenwein, *To Be the Neighbor of Saint Peter: The Social Meaning of Cluny's Property, 909-1049* (Ithaca, NY, 1989).

20. Stephen D. White, *Custom, Kinship and Gifts to Saints: the Laudatio Parentum in Western France, 1050-1150* (Chapel Hill, 1988), 40-85, with comprehensive references to earlier discussion.

21. For examples, Georges Duby, *The Knight, the Lady and the Priest*, trans. Barbara Bray (London, 1983), 93-95.

22. It is also, however, Cluny which has been the subject of most of the research whose results are drawn on here: the rhetoric of this paragraph is certainly not intended to preclude the possibility, indeed the likelihood, that further investigation will reveal similar developments in other regions and under other auspices.

23. Georges Duby, *The Three Orders: Feudal Society Imagined*, trans. Arthur Goldhammer (Chicago, 1980), 141-44.

24. Councils of St. Paulien, 993 (Statuta per Widonem Aniciensem), Mansi, *Concilium collectio*, 19, col. 271-72; Anse, 994, ibid., col. 99-102.

25. Dominic Iogna-Prat, *Agni immaculati: Recherches sur les sources hagiographiques relatives à Saint Maieul de Cluny (954-994)* (Paris, 1988), 305-57.

26. See especially Duby, "Youth in Aristocratic Society," "The Laity and the Peace of God," "The Origins of Knighthood," in *The Chivalrous Society*, 112-22, 123-33, 158-70; I. R. Robinson, "Gregory VII and the Soldiers of Christ," *History* 58 (1973), 197-92; Maurice Keen, *Chivalry* (New Haven and London, 1984), 44-63.

27. Duby, *The Knight, the Lady and the Priest*, 35-36; Jack Goody, *The Development of the Family and Marriage in Europe* (Cambridge, 1983), with a usefully differentiated discussion of the change, 134-46; David Herlihy, *Medieval Households* (Cambridge, Mass, 1985), 82-88.

28. c.f. Robin Fox, *The Red Lamp of Incest* (London, 1980), e.g. at p. 76--a schematic account of the essential function of systems of kinship and marriage which exactly describes the eleventh-century West--and pp. 144-65. Goody, *Family and Marriage in Europe*, chap. 6 ("Church, land and family in the West") points to the mutual interest of the church and the eldest son in reducing the rights of kin and to the extension of the prohibited decrees as contributing to its achievement.

29. Above, n. 23.

30. Chronicle of St. Pierre du Puy, in C. Devic and J. Vaissette, *Histoire du Languedoc* (Toulouse, 1875) V, col. 15, and for discussion.

31. Concisely described by H. E. J. Cowdrey, "The Papacy, the Patarenes and the Church of Milan," *Transactions of the Royal Historical Society* 5/18 (1968): 26-29.

32. Daniel F. Callahan, "The Peace of God and the Cult of the Saints in Aquitaine in the Tenth and Eleventh Centuries," in *The Peace of God*, 165-83.

33. See R. I. Moore, "Heresy, Repression and Social Change in the Age of Gregorian Reform," in. *Christendom and Its Discontents: Exclusion, Persecution, and Rebellion, 1000-1500*, eds. Scott L. Waugh and Peter Diehl (Cambridge, 1996), 19-46.

34. Richard Landes, "The Dynamics of Heresy and Reform in Limoges: A Study of Popular Participation in the 'Peace of God' (994-1033)," *Historical Reflections/Réflexions historiques* 14 (1987): 467-512.

35. Rodulfus Glaber, *Historiarum Libri Quinque*, II.xi in John France et al. *Rodulfus Glaber Opera* (Oxford, 1989), 88-91.

36. Marshall Sahlins, "The Original Affluent Society," *Stone Age Economics* (New York, 1972): pp. 1-39. I owe to Valerie Ramseyer the realization that Sahlins' insights could be applied to Carolingian Europe (without, of course, suggesting a precise parallel between its social organization and that of the purely hunter-gatherer communities of whom he writes).

37. For a recent and brilliant overview of this fundamental and often debated transformation see Pierre Bonnassie, *From Slavery to Feudalism in South-Western Europe*, trans. Jean Birrell (Cambridge, 1991), 149-313.

38. Rodney Hilton, *Bond Men Made Free* (London, 1973), 70-71.

39. For examples, David Rollason, "The Miracles of St. Benedict: a Window on Early Medieval France," Henry Mayr-Harting and R. I. Moore eds., *Studies in Medieval History Presented to R. H. C. Davis* (London, 1985), 73-91.

40. Isabel Alfonso, "Cistercians and Feudalism," *Past and Present* 133 (1991): 3-30.

41. The Monforte group eschewed coition not because reproduction was undesirable in itself, but because a pure world would achieve it without the disagreeable necessity of coition, as bees supposedly did.

42. Duby, *The Knight, the Lady and the Priest*, passim.

43. Moore, *Birth of Popular Heresy*, p. 36.

44. Moore, *Birth of Popular Heresy*, 33-38, and Moore, *Origins of European Dissent*, 86-90.

45. Moore, *Birth of Popular Heresy*, 53-54.

46. See my "Literacy and Heresy"(above, n. 11), 28ff.

47. A piece of seventeenth-century scandal-mongering enthusiastically revived by Jacques Dalarun, *Robert d'Arbrissel, fondateur de Fontevraud* (Paris, 1986); for the defense undoubtedly sound though less fun), J.-M. Bienvenu, *L'étonnant fondateur de Fontevraud, Robert d'Arbrissel* (Paris, 1981), 69-71, 89-93.

48. Moore, *Origins of European Dissent*, 205-09.

49. C. H. Talbot, *The Life of Christina of Marykate* (Oxford, 1959), 135-75.

The Bishop as Bridegroom: Marital Imagery and Clerical Celibacy in the Eleventh and Early Twelfth Centuries

Megan McLaughlin

In the eleventh and early twelfth centuries, the proponents of ecclesiastical reform had marriage very much on their minds. Not only were they trying to prevent members of the clergy from taking wives, but they were also struggling to impose their vision of Christian marriage on a lay population which often thought of wedlock in very different terms. The polemicists of this period devoted considerable attention to the subject of marriage, discussing its role in the divine plan for humanity, the circumstances under which it might properly be entered into, and the purpose and limits of marital relations.[1] At the same time, they often employed marital imagery to describe other relationships with which they were concerned–including the bond that linked a bishop to his church. In the following pages, I propose to examine the ways in which this image of the bishop as bridegroom was used in the polemical literature of the eleventh and early twelfth centuries, the reasons why it appealed so strongly to the proponents of reform, and, finally, its somewhat problematic role in the campaign for clerical celibacy.

The allegory of the bishop's marriage to his church was not new in the eleventh century.[2] In fact, Christian writers first made explicit use of marital imagery to describe the bishop's relationship with the religious community over which he presided in the fourth century.[3] The complex religious politics of that period had led a number of bishops to transfer from one church to another; their opponents sometimes condemned these moves as illegal, citing biblical texts on the indissolubility of marriage in support of their arguments.[4] When Bishop Eusebius transferred from the see of Beirut to Nicomedia, for example, Athanasius of Alexandria used St. Paul's dictum, "Art thou bound to a wife? seek not to be loosed" (1 Cor. 7, 27), to accuse Eusebius of adultery.[5]

The image of the bishop as the spouse of his church reappeared in the ninth century in a context very similar to the one just described. In the important ninth-century compendium of church law (both authentic and falsified) known as the Pseudo-Isidorian Decretals, the writings of St. Paul and other biblical texts on marriage were again invoked against the translation of bishops from one see to another.[6] They were also used to condemn efforts by the members of a church to replace their lawful bishop with another one. Thus:

> Just as a wife may not leave her husband in order to marry another or to commit adultery as long as he lives, even if he is guilty of fornication, but should--according to the Apostle [1 Cor 7,11]--either be reconciled with her husband or remain unmarried, so a church may not leave her bishop or separate him from her in order to take another [bishop] as long as he lives. . . .[7]

As Jean Gaudemet has pointed out, this use of marital imagery reflects the efforts of ninth-century church leaders to ensure the stability of the episcopal office in the face of royal and sometimes noble pressure to replace one bishop with another.

The bishop's marriage to his church was more than just a metaphor, however. At least by the beginning of the tenth century, and probably before, it had acquired a mystical significance as well, which was derived from the ancient and influential allegory of Christ's marriage to the church.[8] This deeper meaning first found expression within a ritual context, in the symbolism of the ceremony of episcopal consecration. It had long been customary for bishops in France and Spain to wear a ring as part of their official attire. This ring was apparently understood at first as nothing more than a "token of episcopal honor"; it was given (along with the crozier, or pastoral staff) to a new bishop during his consecration and taken away from him if he were deposed.[9] In the ninth century, however, Archbishop Hincmar of Rheims, discussing the ceremony for the consecration of bishops, described the ring as a *signum . . . fidei*, a token of faith. The phrase referred to the bishop's role in explaining religious doctrine and concealing the mysteries of the faith when necessary,[10] but it also echoed language Hincmar had used elsewhere to describe an engagement ring--which he saw as a token of plighted faith between the future bride and groom.[11] Perhaps, then, Hincmar had already begun to identify the bishop's ring as a kind of engagement or wedding ring.

A few decades later, this identification was well established, being invoked in a whole series of *ordines*, or ritual directions, for the consecration of bishops.[12] For example, the consecration *ordo* in the pontifical of Aurillac, which dates from about the year 900, includes the following formula, which was to be pronounced during the consecration ceremony by the person who gave the new bishop his ring:

> With this ring of faith *(sub hoc anulo fidei)* we commend to you the bride of Christ, [this] church, so that you may keep her holy and immaculate.[13]

In another tenth-century pontifical, we find a formula that was eventually adopted by the church of Rome for the consecration of the pope:

> Receive this ring, the sign of faith *(fidei . . . signaculum)*, so that, adorned with pure faith, you may preserve without harm the bride of God, namely the holy Church.[14]

The authors of these and other tenth-century rituals apparently envisioned the ring as a sign of the mystical marriage between Christ and the church.[15] In the liturgical context, then, the bishop appeared as the guardian of Christ's bride rather than as her spouse. Only in the eleventh century did the ring come to be seen as the symbol of the bishop's own relationship with his church.

This new understanding of the ring was part of a general elaboration and extension of the allegory of the bishop's marriage to his church in the polemical literature associated with the movement of ecclesiastical reform.[16] This is not to say that this allegory was accepted by every polemicist who wrote during the eleventh and early twelfth centuries. Conservative writers--those who felt uneasy with the increasingly radical changes being proposed for the church in this period--generally avoided the allegory of the bishop as bridegroom, even though they knew and used many of the precedents upon which it was based. On the other hand, the supporters of reform employed it often in a wide variety of contexts and in sometimes quite startling ways.[17]

Marital imagery and marital legislation often appear, for example, in the reformer's discussions of episcopal elections--especially when those elections were controversial. An easy transfer of spiritual power to a single, widely accepted candidate had always been seen as the desirable scenario in such elections, and this scenario had often been achieved (although sometimes only as the result of careful orchestration) in earlier times. In the eleventh century, however, a growing number of episcopal elections were contested, with disputes over the legitimacy of various candidates sometimes lasting for years.[18] While a variety of political issues shaped these contests, often one candidate was favored by the proponents of ecclesiastical reform and another by their conservative opponents. Sometimes there were more than two candidates, which could lead to complex situations, impossible to resolve to anyone's complete satisfaction.

This was certainly the case in Rome in the years from 1045 to 1047.[19] Pope Benedict IX, a member of the powerful Tusculan clan which had controlled the See of St. Peter for several decades, had been driven from Rome by a rebellion in 1044. Early in 1045, another faction in the city arranged for the election of a new pope, who took the name Silvester III. He in turn was forced from office in March 1045, and Benedict was restored. By May, however, Benedict had resigned, and yet a third pope took office as Gregory VI. None of the three popes of 1045 was above reproach. Benedict IX had almost certainly purchased the papal office back in 1032. He is also reported to have led a rather profligate life, although these reports come from later sources and may not have been current in the 1040s. Silvester III's election was clearly irregular. Gregory VI seems to have been regarded as a reform candidate of sorts. But the unpleasant fact remains that someone--it is not clear who--paid a large sum of money to Benedict IX in the spring of 1045 in order to obtain his resignation in Gregory's favor. As a result, many of the reformers concluded that Gregory's election, too, was invalid.

Silvester III's claims to the papacy seems to have been largely ignored after March 1045, but Benedict's resignation was not accepted everywhere. Thus, when King Henry III of Germany crossed the Alps in September of 1046, hoping to be crowned emperor by the successor of St. Peter, it was by no means clear who that successor might be. Henry, a strong supporter of church reform, seems to have recognized Gregory VI as the most likely candidate, for he is said to have received Gregory "honorably" when they met at Piacenza; no such attentions were paid to Benedict IX. However, at the synod held at Sutri in December 1046, Gregory was declared deposed, and at a further synod held at Rome a few days later, Benedict's resignation was confirmed, clearing the way for the election of a new reform candidate, who took the name Clement II. Nevertheless, Gregory VI continued to be widely recognized as the legitimate bishop of Rome until his death in exile in 1047.

Shortly after Gregory's death, either late in 1047 or early in 1048, an unknown author from northern Europe wrote an account of these events in a treatise now generally known as *On Pontifical Ordination*.[20] This "Auctor Gallicus," a supporter of rigorous reform, presents all of the individuals involved in an extremely harsh light. While he admits that it is unlawful for those of inferior rank (including himself) to judge bishops, he justifies the criticism that will follow in the body of his treatise by arguing that none of the men who claimed the papacy between 1045 and 1047 was a legitimate bishop of Rome anyway: they have already been judged by God and by earlier popes. Benedict IX and Gregory VI are represented as simoniacs, men who have tried to purchase ecclesiastical office. Since their elections were irregular, they have no real claim to the papacy. Even so, if anyone could be considered a "real" pope it would be Benedict IX, and after him Gregory VI, for Silvester III was a usurper, and Clement II and his successor Damasus II (who became pope in 1047) were no better.

The author of *On Pontifical Ordination* developed an extended critique of the ways in which popes were being made and unmade between 1045 and 1047. In the process, he managed to deny the legitimacy of five different popes, although he also designated some of them as preferable to others at various points. He based his arguments in favor of particular popes on canon law, primarily on texts drawn from Pseudo-Isidore. However, the Auctor Gallicus goes well beyond his ninth-century predecessors in his application of the law of marriage and sexuality to the relationship of the bishop-- in this case, the bishop of Rome--to his church.

It was clear to the Auctor that Benedict IX remained the most legitimate pope even after he was driven out of Rome in 1044, for at least he had the support of most of the bishops of the west. Here the image of the bishop as bridegroom first comes into play in *On Pontifical Ordination.*

> If it is permitted to compare human to heavenly things . . . the Church is the bride of Christ and bishops fill Christ's place. Therefore they are not the bridegrooms of the Church but her bridegroom . . . . The number of bishops does not obstruct this [for] their unanimity should make them one. But if they are one, they are the bridegroom. He who falls away from unity is neither the bridegroom nor the bridegroom's friend . . . .[21]

A pope like Silvester III, who did not enjoy the support of his fellow bishops, was, then, no true "bridegroom" of the church.

The pope whom he replaced, Benedict IX, had a better claim. The Auctor points out that Benedict's relationship with his church was not ended by his flight from Rome late in 1044, and so when he returned the next spring he had the right to reclaim his office. This is clear from a letter of Pope Leo I:

> For the venerable Pope Leo, writing to Nicetas, bishop of Aquileia, said "If a wife, when her husband has been captured, marries another, if he returns from captivity, let her be united to her former [husband], and let each man receive what is his. Nor shall he be judged culpable who shared in his marriage in the interim. And if the woman is unwilling to return, she is to be expelled from ecclesiastical communion as impious."[22]

Here the Auctor adduces a papal letter on the indissolubility of marriage to undergird his attack on Silvester III and his tentative support for Benedict IX as the preferable pope in early 1045.

He follows the same procedure in his discussion of the election of Gregory VI later that year. While Gregory is described in a later passage of the work as preferable to Clement II, in this passage he is condemned as less legitimate than Benedict IX. Gregory's assumption of the papal title is characterized in strong terms, first as theft and then as rape:

> Indeed, a lesson may be sought in lesser matters. If someone has a daughter and someone else, coming upon her by surprise carries her off--that is, takes her by force--let the abductor, compelled by the law, hand her over to her father or her closest kin, even if she is not betrothed to another. For this was done without the consent of those who were her advocates and against her will. But the Council of Chalcedon decreed that those who cooperated or consented to this, if they were clerics, should be anathema. And he [the abductor] can never legitimately marry the woman who was raped. But if this happens to the Church, it is much worse because she is of much greater dignity. Who would choose him with whom we are dealing? He was not sought out by the "kin" of the Church, who are the bishops. He was not willingly accepted by the Church. Therefore, he is not legitimate . . . .[23]

In the work of the Auctor Gallicus, then, the canon law of marriage is repeatedly invoked in order to evaluate the legitimacy of the various candidates in a hotly contested episcopal election.

The reformers also deployed the allegory of the bishop's marriage to his church in writings directed against specific abuses. In 1058, for example, Cardinal Humbert of Silva Candida finished the last book of his treatise *Against the Simoniacs*. This vitriolic polemic was directed against bishops and other clerics who paid money for their offices, a practice which the reformers as a group abhorred, and which Humbert equated with virtually every crime imaginable.

Indeed, in one notable--but unfortunately rather obscurely worded--passage, he describes the selling of ecclesiastical offices as the abduction and prostitution of the church.[24]

He points out how serious such a crime would be if it were directed against an ordinary woman:

> . . . If some wicked person should, by giving or promising money to her most iniquitous and avaricious guardian, take possession of another man's bride, along with all her household possessions, would not that money be truly said and justly proven to have attacked and overcome all her goods? The harm done by such presumption would--according to the sacred canons--be punished by lifelong excommunication for the rapist, the guardian, and all their supporters, and--according to secular law--by the death penalty or by perpetual exile.[25]

The implication is that the penalties should be much worse if the crime is directed against the church, the bride of Christ. And yet, Humbert continues, no one seems to care about the situation of a church "bought" by a simoniacal bishop and no penalties are currently applied to simoniacs.

> From this observation it may be understood how abject and ignoble the bride of Christ is held to be. No one can be found to mourn her injuries, no one [can be found] to defend her chastity, [which has been] prostituted, sold, assigned to sacrilegious abductors, no on [can be found] even to take her from them and restore her (although defiled) to her spouse.

The bride laments, "My father sold me, the king bought me--to whom shall I complain, who will give me justice?"[26] Indeed, it did often seem to the reformers that there was no help for the church, for many of the most powerful people in Europe were implicated in the sale of ecclesiastical offices. Humbert calls on these people to

give up their unlawful abuse of power and hints that if they fail to
do so, divine wrath will avenge the church's injured chastity:

> And is Jesus supposed to suffer this forever, whom
> no ecclesiastical or lay person now deigns to hear
> and consider complaining about his abducted bride-
> -something which the vilest of men will not endure
> with equanimity?[27]

Humbert's work is reminiscent of the tenth-century consecration
ordines, in that he represents Christ as the legitimate spouse of the
church (with the good bishops as his "friends"[28]). What is novel in
Against the Simoniacs is Humbert's depiction of the simoniacal
bishop, the person to whom the church is sold, as neither the
bridegroom nor the bridegroom's friend but as what would be
called, in the parlance of modern prostitution, a "John."

Around the middle of the eleventh century, some of the more
radical reformers began suggesting that lay interference in the affairs
of the church lay at the root of the problems they were attempting
to eradicate. By the end of the century, opposition to such
interference had crystallized around the practice of lay investiture.
Investiture--the practice through which rulers publicly exercised
their right to approve candidates for ecclesiastical office--reflected
not only the political importance of bishops and abbots but also the
sacrality of kings. In the early Middle Ages, kings were believed to
be very different from ordinary laymen. Through the ceremony of
anointing they acquired an almost priestly character, which gave
them the right to intervene in the religious as well as the secular
affairs of their kingdoms. As long as the sacredness of kings
remained unquestioned, their investiture of bishops and abbots
seemed justified.

By the ninth century, if not earlier, some kings were investing
newly chosen bishops with their staff of office in a ceremony that
took place before the liturgical ritual of consecration. (During his
consecration, the new bishop again received the staff, along with the
ring, from his fellow bishops.)[29] In the early eleventh century, the
German emperors began investing their bishops with the ring as well
as the staff before the consecration ceremony, and this practice was
soon adopted by the kings of France and England.[30] Investiture with

the ring was thus a novelty in the first half of the eleventh century, a fact of which the reformers were well aware. Presumably the introduction of this kind of investiture drew attention to both the object and its symbolic associations, and this may have contributed to the development of the allegory of the bishop's marriage to the church in this period. Certainly opposition to the practice of investiture--which first became manifest around the middle of the century and which was closely related to reformer's denial of sacral kingship--contributed to that development.

Pope Gregory VII (1073-85) and his successors issued a series of decrees forbidding "laymen" (among whom they now included kings) from investing religious leaders with the symbols of their office.[31] The ensuing struggle between the Gregorians and rulers unwilling to give up their traditional rights over ecclesiastical appointments produced both physical and verbal violence, the latter manifested in the flood of polemical treatises produced in the late eleventh and early twelfth centuries.[32] Included among these was a long poem, *On the Ring and the Staff*, by the reforming bishop Ranger of Lucca, probably composed late in 1110.[33] The poem begins and ends with the same lines: "The ring and the staff are two sacred signs: by no means are they to be accepted from the hand of a layman."[34]

In between, Ranger devotes a great deal of attention to the symbolism of the bishop's ring. Its gem, he suggests, represents the bride, and its gold the bridegroom. Just as the two substances are joined together in the ring, so a man and his wife become one flesh (Matt. 19, 5) in the wedding bed, and so the Word of God (the bridegroom) assumed human flesh (the bride) in the Virgin's womb. The ring given to the bishop at his consecration is thus a sign of Christ's "marriage" with the flesh--the Incarnation. "What is so holy, what is so much an image of the Deity" as this ring?[35] Ranger considers it ridiculous for any earthly ruler to possess or give away such a ring, since he is not joined to the church as her spouse (i.e., does not hold clerical office).[36]

Some conservative writers in this period continued to argue that a king could legitimately invest a new bishop with the staff, since it merely represented the temporalities of the see and not the episcopal office itself. But if a king confers authority on a new bishop with a staff, Ranger asks,

then when he gives [him] the bejewelled gold [i.e.
the ring] appropriate to a bridegroom, what is he
doing but offering to make a marriage for him?
And so [the bishop-elect] boldly takes a wife under
the king, before he experiences the Church, the
spouse of Christ, and so is made a bigamist, when
he should be a man of one wife (Titus 1,6).[37]

If lay investiture with the staff serves any real function, then so
must investiture with the ring. And if this is the case, then the
double investiture of new bishops with the ring makes them
bigamists.

But even investiture with the staff is unacceptable to Ranger. He
points out that staff and ring are interdependent, just as the bishop's
pastoral care for his flock and his marriage to his church are
connected.[38] Both objects are holy:

To a bishop solemnly consecrated and anointed,
ring and staff are given as sacred signs. The ring so
that he may know himself to be a bridegroom and
may love the church joined to him, not for his own
sake, but for Christ's. The staff, so that he may
protect Christ's sheepfold, beware of and frighten
off savage wolves. . . .[39]

Thus, Ranger concludes, it is wrong for a secular ruler to invest
new bishops with either the ring or the staff.

In a very striking development, a number of reform-minded
writers in the eleventh and early twelfth centuries argued that
priests, as well as bishops, are married to their churches. For
example, Gerhoh of Reichersberg, in his work *On God's Edifice*
(composed around 1126),condemns simony in the nomination of
priests as well as in the election of bishops. He describes how a new
priest should be chosen for a "widowed" church (*aecclesia viduata*)--
one whose former incumbent has died. In the constitution of a
priest, as in that of a bishop, Gerhoh asserts, no gift should be
involved: "for the church is not to be given like a slave-girl, but
properly married, as is a bride to her legitimate spouse."[40] Thus the

reformers not only used the allegory of the bishop as bridegroom in a wide variety of contexts, they also extended it at times to encompass all members of the sacerdotal order.

The allegory's prominence in reform polemic during the eleventh and early twelfth centuries may be explained in part by the circumstances in which the reformers found themselves. They were reacting to the same kind of complex and confusing power struggles that had led their predecessors to develop the image of the bishop as bridegroom in the first place, so it is hardly surprising that they, too, found it useful.[41] However, other factors probably contributed to the elaboration and extension of the allegory in this period. Growing familiarity with the Pseudo-Isidorian Decretals, which provided clear precedents for the use of marital imagery in discussions of episcopal behavior, may have encouraged the reformers to experiment with such imagery.[42] Their well-documented interest in the Song of Songs, one of the key texts behind the allegory of Christ's marriage to the church, may also have suggested marital (indeed, erotic) interpretations of ecclesiastical relationships.[43] But the reformers were not attracted to marital imagery simply because that imagery was familiar. The allegory of the bishop as bridegroom also offered multiple advantages from the point of view of the reform program. At the same time that it served as a weapon against the evils of invalid elections, simony, and lay investiture, it was also reinforcing the reformers' model of earthly marriage--as properly initiated, consensual, monogamous, loving rather than mercenary, and dissoluble only by death. The extension of the allegory to include priests was clearly intended to encourage the reformation of the lower ranks of the clergy, but it may also have been meant to underline the similarities between priests and their episcopal superiors. For the reformers were eager to show that the sacerdotal order as a whole was different from (and, of course, superior to) the order of the laity.[44] The clergy's intimate relationship with the church was one sign of that superiority.

The conservative writers of the eleventh and early twelfth centuries shared in the same circumstances and were familiar with the same precedents as the reformers. However, they rejected not only the more radical proposals for reform but also many of the assumptions behind those proposals. In particular, most conservative writers were willing to recognize considerable royal authority in ecclesiastical matters.[45] These differences probably explain why most conservative writers avoided the allegory of the bishop or priest as bridegroom, which had already become closely associated with the reform program by the middle of the eleventh century. A few of them do briefly allude to churches as the "brides" or "widows" of clerics.[46] But even in these texts, the identification between clerics and the heavenly bridegroom tends to be more complex than in reform writings. A monk of the pro-imperial monastery of Farfa, for example, writing in 1111, depicted *regnum* and *sacerdotium*, royal power and priestly authority, as the two "arms" with which Christ embraces his bride.[47]

It is, moreover, to the pen of that arch-conservative, the "Norman Anonymous," that we owe the only explicit rejection of the image of clerics as bridegrooms from this period. At a time when theocratic kingship was coming increasingly under attack, the Anonymous defended the sacred character of kings.[48] In his view, the royal anointing ceremony made kings much more than ordinary laymen; they resembled and represented Christ, the Anointed of the Lord. Thus, in the second draft of his treatise *On the Consecration of Pontiffs and Kings*, the Anonymous suggests that Christ married the church not in his capacity as priest but in his role as king:

> Holy Church is the bride of Christ, who is the true king and priest, but she is said to be his bride not in that he is a priest, but in that he is a king. . . That marriage is said to be royal, not sacerdotal, and this bride is called "queen," not "priestess."[49]

The implication is that kings are the proper representatives of Christ in his role as bridegroom:

> And therefore the sacrament of this marriage is more appropriate to the royal than to the sacerdotal office, and therefore kings, who represent the image of Christ the king, are better suited to this marriage, whose sacrament they better represent.[50]

Thus, as part of his defense of royal rights over the church, the Norman Anonymous rejected the identification of priests with the bridegroom.

In general, pro-reform polemicists were much more likely than their conservative opponents to employ the allegory of the clergy's marriage to the church. When we turn to the issue of clerical celibacy, however, the situation becomes more complicated. The celibacy campaign was central to the reform movement, not only as a goal in its own right but also as a way of differentiating the clergy more clearly from the laity. For the reformers the difference between the clergy and laity lay primarily in the clerical office itself and in the rite of ordination, which gave clerics the power to perform the sacraments.[51] But clerical celibacy—which was often contrasted with the expected sexual activity of the laity in reforming treatises—was also a crucial aspect of that difference.[52] Under the circumstances, one might expect the reformers to argue for clerical celibacy by emphasizing the contrast between laymen who married ordinary women and clerics who saved themselves for a heavenly bride.[53] In fact, though, the reformers seem to have been curiously hesitant to interpret the celibate life as another—and higher—form of marriage. While the allegory of the bishop or priest as bridegroom was regularly deployed in their discussion of episcopal elections, simony, and lay investiture, it forms a prominent part of the argument in only one extant work on clerical celibacy.

This was a letter written to Pope Nicholas II in 1059 by Cardinal Peter Damian. Peter urged the pope to take sterner measures against unchaste bishops, those who consorted with women whom Peter calls "whores."[54] It is clear from the other passages in the letter that the bishops in question were simply sleeping with wives taken in what they considered legitimate marriage.[55] However, Peter could not accept the possibility that a bishop could be married to anyone other than his church; for Peter, any ordinary woman with whom a bishop had sexual relations had to be, *ipso facto*, a "whore." Most of the letter is devoted to warning Pope Nicholas that he can expect divine punishment if he fails to do his duty. At one point, however, Peter addresses himself rhetorically to the unchaste bishops themselves. And it is at this point that he invokes the allegory of the bishop's marriage to his church.

The language of this passage plays on a whole series of traditional Christian associations with the word "body." Both the bread consecrated by a bishop or priest during the mass and the church that joins in communion during the mass are identified as the body of Christ, while individual Christians are understood to be members of that body. Also at work in this passage is the assumption that sexual union turns two partners into one flesh. For Peter, working from that assumption, the sexual activities of bishops created an unholy confusion of bodies, which disturbed cosmic boundaries between good and evil, between the divine and the demonic. "By committing fornication," he reminds the bishops,

> you cut yourself off from the members of Christ, and make yourself one with a harlot's body (1 Cor. 6:15). . . . What have you to do with the body of Christ, when by wallowing in the allurements of the flesh you have become a member of Antichrist?[56]

As an extension of this notion of the illicit mingling of bodies, Peter introduces a new accusation into his attack on unchaste bishops. This accusation draws on another traditional image, that of the bishop as a spiritual father, who cares for the individual members of his congregation as his children. That image intersects very neatly with the image of the bishop's marriage to his church, which is the mother of the faithful. As Peter points out to the bishops:

> All the children of the church are undoubtedly your children. . . .Since you are the husband, the spouse of your church, as (at any rate) the ring of your betrothal and the staff of your mandate attest, all who are reborn in her by the sacrament of baptism are likewise related to you as your children.[57]

But if a bishop is the father of the members of his congregation, a bishop who sleeps with one of those members is guilty of incest— indeed, an aggravated form of incest, since the bishop is the spiritual, rather than the physical, father of the woman he sleeps with:

> Clearly, if a father incestuously corrupts his
> daughter, he will be promptly excommunicated,
> deprived of communion, and either cast into prison
> or sent into exile. How much worse, therefore,
> should be your degradation? For you had no fear of
> perishing with your daughter, and not your
> daughter in the flesh—which would be a lesser
> evil—but rather in the spirit. . . .[58]

Peter is horrified by the sacrilege involved in this confusion of
physical and spiritual bodies:

> If you commit incest with your spiritual daughter,
> how in good conscience do you dare perform the
> mystery of the Lord's body [i.e., celebrate mass]?. .
> . At the touch of your hand, the Holy Spirit
> descends—and you use your hand to touch the
> genitals of whores.[59]

Moreover, as Peter points out, the dreadful consequences of the
bishop's sexual activities are not limited to the offender himself.
They extend to his entire church:

> And since you hold all the ecclesiastical orders,
> brought together in one awesome structure, within
> you, you surely defile all of them as you pollute
> yourself by union with a prostitute. And thus you
> contaminate in yourself the doorkeeper, the lector,
> the exorcist, and all the sacred orders [within your
> church] in succession, for all of which you must
> give an account at God's severe judgment.[60]

In Peter Damian's writings, then, the introduction of "incestuous"
sexuality into the bishop's relationship with his church disrupts and
defiles the entire ecclesiastical "family."

    No other reformer in the eleventh or early twelfth century
presents a developed argument against clerical marriage based on the
allegory of the bishop or priest as bridegroom. There are occasional

hints at such arguments in the polemics, but they remain oddly vague and allusive. Some later writers, for example, seem to follow Peter Damian's lead in referring to unchaste bishops and priests as "incestuous." But the term appears in isolation and without elaboration in their works.[61] Similarly, Humbert of Silva Candida uses the term "adultery" to describe the clerical marriages tolerated by the eastern church.[62] Again, though, the term appears in isolation. Neither Humbert nor the reformers who came after him make any effort to explain why clerical marriage might constitute "adultery."

Perhaps, though, such arguments and explanations were developed in works that have not survived or in oral debates that were never written down. Some reformers apparently went beyond Humbert in asserting that priests who married were guilty of "adultery"—or at least that is what we can conclude from the efforts made by conservative authors to refute this suggestion. An unknown writer, active in northern France around 1065, argued that clerical marriages were chaste and sincere, "not, *as the authors of the new dogma claim,* [italics mine] adulterous or even illicit [*fornicaria*]."[63] From this perspective, the reformer's attacks on clerical marriage appeared dangerously novel and disruptive—especially in their call for the laity to boycott the masses by "incontinent priests." He claimed to know of one priest who had been driven from parish to parish by such boycotts. But in taking this action, the reformers had made themselves guilty of the very charge they brought against their priest:

> Just as the Apostle says, "A woman who is with another man while her husband is alive shall be considered an adulteress" (Romans 7:3), so a church which unjustly rejects the priest who is lawfully joined to her is an adulteress, if she is with an alien priest while [her own] is alive. Therefore, [those who call for a boycott of masses performed by married priests] are all adulterers and a worthless band of liars.[64]

While conservative authors generally avoided the image of clerics as bridegrooms, this author gleefully turns accusations of adultery,

which are based on that image, against the very reformers who
proposed them.[65]

Apparently charges of adultery were still being brought against
married clerics some forty years later, for they were again answered,
albeit in a different way, by the Norman Anonymous in his work
On Holy Virginity and the Marriage of Priests:

> For the Apostle also taught that it is proper for a
> bishop to be a man of one wife [1 Timothy 3:21],
> which he would hardly have taught if, *as some
> people assert*, [italics mine] it were adultery for a
> bishop to have both a wife and a church—as it
> were, two wives—at the same time.[66]

The Anonymous exploded the adultery charge by denying—as he did
in his treatise *On the Consecration of Pontiffs and Kings*—that the
bishops ever were married to their churches. "Holy Church is the
wife or bride not of the priest," he asserts, "but of Christ. . . ."

Clearly, then, some reformers were accusing married priests of
infidelity to their heavenly bride during the eleventh and early
twelfth centuries. So why do we find so little trace of this accusation
in the surviving reform treatises? The most plausible explanation is
that the people who brought charges of "adultery" against married
clerics were ardent but relatively unsophisticated supporters of
reform who did not fully realize what those charges implied. Their
views would have been expressed orally and so would not have
survived except in the responses they elicited from conservative
writers like the Norman Anonymous. Most of the attacks on clerical
marriage extant today were composed by better-educated and more
sophisticated men, who would have recognized and avoided the
problems inherent in the "adultery charge."

The celibacy debates of the eleventh and twelfth centuries were
not primarily concerned with whether men had been sexually active
before ordination. Both reformers and conservatives agreed that men
who had been married (only once, of course, and to wives who came
to them as virgins) were entitled to enter the priesthood and even
become bishops. But how could someone whose wife was still
living—even if the couple no longer had sexual relations—"marry"
his church? Reliance on the allegory in this context would surely

have suggested that only virgins and widowers were qualified to become priests and thus would have brought into question the position of many men whom the reformers themselves recognized as legitimate members of the clergy.

If the "adultery charge" excluded too many men from the ranks of the clergy, the "incest charge" brought by Peter Damian excluded too few. For it seemed to leave open the possibility that bishops (and other clerics) could be married, so long as their wives were not their spiritual daughters. Peter actually responds to this problem in the course of his letter on episcopal marriages:

> But perhaps you object that she was born long before you attained the rank of bishop, or that she was baptized in some rural church, and not in your cathedral—as if you were the father only of those to be born in the future, and as if all your diocese were not your church.[67]

But did Peter's response preclude marriage between a bishop and a woman born in another diocese? Or, for that matter, between a priest and a woman born in another parish? It seems likely that later reformers did not actively pursue the argument from "incest" because this argument would not have been effective against many clerical marriages.

The authors of polemics against clerical marriage generally did not base their arguments on the allegory of the bishop or priest as bridegroom—probably because such arguments presented the kind of problems I have just described. Nevertheless, marital imagery continued to play an important role in their work—hovering behind other arguments, appearing and disappearing, shifting in meaning— in ways that suggest both the authors' continued consciousness of the allegory and their reluctance to make explicit use of it in this context. For example, in 1075 Pope Gregory VII wrote to Archbishop Anno of Cologne, urging him to enforce the celibacy of the clergy in his province.[68] His letter includes several references to the allegory of Christ's marriage to the church, but Gregory does not suggest that the clergy represent Christ in this marriage. He identifies them, instead, as members of the heavenly household. Gregory believes that chastity is essential for them, "so that the

service of a pure and unspotted household may be offered to the
bride of Christ who knows neither spot nor wrinkle (Ephesians
5:27)." He suggests that Anno should explain to his clergy ". . . how
great is the virtue of chastity, how necessary it is for every
ecclesiastical position, and how suitable for the chamberlains
[*cubiculariis*] of the virgin bridegroom and the virgin bride." Perhaps
Gregory was not entirely comfortable with the extension of the
allegory to include priests as well as bishops, which was after all still
something of a novelty in his day. Instead he focused on a role that
all members of the sacerdotal order had traditionally shared—that of
God's servants. Nevertheless, Gregory suggests a link between
service and marriage, through his association of the servant's purity
with that of the bride and groom.

     Unlike Gregory, Honorius Augustodunensis actually introduces
the allegory of the priest as bridegroom into one of his works,
although he shies away from it again when he begins to discuss
celibacy.[69] Honorius' *Offendiculum*, which probably dates from the
early twelfth century, begins with a discussion of the marriage of
priests in the Old Testament, based on Leviticus 21:13-14:

> And he shall take a wife in her virginity. A widow,
> or a divorced woman, or profane, or an harlot,
> these shall he not take; but he shall take a virgin of
> his own people to wife.

According to Honorius, this text can be applied literally to the
Christian priesthood, in that men who have married virgins may
become priests, so long as they renounce all carnal relations with
their wives after ordination.[70] But Honorius prefers to understand
the passage "spiritually," in terms of the priest's relationship with his
church. Neither a "harlot" (a church acquired through simony) nor a
"divorcée" (one which has been abandoned by its own priest because
of its heretical views or evil ways), nor a "widow" (a church which
has expelled its own priest *ob religionem*) makes an acceptable "wife"
for a Christian priest. He may properly marry only a "virgin," that
is, a church consecrated by a Catholic bishop and acquired
canonically.[71] Honorius is clearly quite comfortable with the
allegory of the priest's marriage to his church. Yet as soon as he
comes to the issue of clerical continence, the allegory vanishes.

Honorius, like other reformers, bases his argument for clerical celibacy in the *Offendiculum* on Biblical precedents and canon law.[72] He never suggests that a priest's allegorical marriage to his church requires chastity, perhaps because he was conscious of the problems mentioned earlier. Nevertheless, the opening passage of the work clearly places Honorius' discussion of clerical continence within the overall context of the priest's allegorical marriage to his church.

The reformers of the eleventh and early twelfth centuries found in marriage a compelling symbol of the clergy's special relationship with the church and in marital imagery a flexible tool for advancing many aspects of the reform program. They used the old and well-established image of the bishop as bridegroom in new and striking ways, in works on episcopal elections, simony, and lay investiture. At times, they even represented ordinary parish priests as married to their churches. It is true that the reformers rarely based their arguments for clerical celibacy on the allegory of the bishop or priest as bridegroom. Nevertheless, they did represent the church as a bride, draw comparisons between clerical purity and the purity of the bridegroom, and even refer briefly to "incest" and "adultery" when they wrote about this subject. In the end, these glancing allusions may actually be the best indicators of the allegory's profound influence on reforming ideals and reforming rhetoric in the eleventh and early twelfth centuries. For they suggest that the image of the bishop as bridegroom had become so much a part of the reformer's outlook—so much a part of the discourse on reform—that it could not be entirely excluded from the celibacy debate, despite the problems it presented.

NOTES

1. For discussions of marriage in this period, see Georges Duby, *Le Chevalier, la femme et la prêtre* (Paris, 1981), translated by Barbara Bray as *The Knight, the Lady and the Priest: The Making of Modern Marriage in Medieval France* (New York, 1983), 57-185, and James Brundage, *Law, Sex, and Christian Society in Medieval Europe* (Chicago, 1987), 183, 187-202, 207-10.

2. On the early history of this allegory, see Robert L. Benson, *The Bishop-Elect: A Study in Medieval Ecclesiastical Office* (Princeton, 1968), 122-23, and Jean Gaudemet, "Note sur le symbolisme médiéval: le mariage de l'evêque," *L'année canonique* 22 (1978): 71-80; reprinted in his collected essays, *La Société dans l'Occident médiéval* (London, 1980).

3. The third-century writer Cyprian's use of the adjective *adulter* in several letters on ecclesiastical politics may have reflected a similar understanding of the bishop's relationship with his church: see the texts cited by Gaudemet, "Note sur le symbolisme médiéval," 72, n. 4. However, Cyprian makes no explicit reference to the bishop as the spouse of his church.

4. On the controversy within the early church over the translation of bishops, see Kenneth Pennington, *Pope and Bishops: The Papal Monarchy in the Twelfth and Thirteenth Centuries* (Philadelphia, 1984), 75-76.

5. Athanasius, *Apologia contra arianos*, 6 (*PG* 25:260); see also Jerome, *Epistolae*, 69, ed. and trans. (into French) by Jérôme Labourt (Paris, 1953), 197-99.

6. On the Pseudo-Isidorian Decretals, see Horst Fuhrmann, *Einfluß und Verbreitung der pseudo-isidorischen Fälschungen*, 3 vols. (Hanover, 1972-74). On the image of the bishop's marriage to his church in this work, see Gaudemet, "Note sur le symbolisme médiéval," 74-76.

7. Pseudo-Evaristus, *Epsitolae*, 2, in *Decretales Pseudo-Isidorianae et Capitula Angilrammi*, ed. Paul Hinschius, 2 vols. (Leipzig, 1863), 1:90.

8. On the early development of this allegory, see Claude Chavasse, *The Bride of Christ: An Enquiry into the Nuptial Element in Early Christianity* (London, 1939).

9. Odilo Engels, "Der Pontifikatsantritt und seine Zeichen," in *Segni e riti nella chiesa altomedievale occidentale*, Settimane di studio del Centor italiano de studi sull'alto medioevo, 2 vols. (Spoleto, 1987), 2: 754-56; Gaudemet, "Note sur le symbolisme médiéval," 72-73. The phrase *signum*

pontificalis honoris comes from Isidore of Seville, *De eccesiasticis officiis*, 2: 5 (*PL* 83:783).

10. Hincmar, *Epistolae*, 29 (*PL* 126:188): "Signum est enim fidei, ut audientibus se ex divinis mysteriis signet quae et quibus signanda sunt, et aperiat quae et quibus aperienda sunt."

11. The reference is to Hincmar, *Coronatio Judith Caroli filiae* (*PL* 125:811): "Accipe annulum, fidei et dilectionis signum, atque conjugalis conjunctionis vinculum, ut non separet homo quos conjungit Deus." Engels, "Der Pontifikatsantritt, 756, suggests that this change in interpretation may reflect the same tumultuous political situation that encouraged the development of the metaphor of the bishop's marriage to his church in the Pseudo-Isidorian Decretals.

12. Gaudemet, "Note sur le symbolisme médiéval," 73-74.

13. Cited by Gaudemet, "Note sur le symbolisme médiéval," 73.

14. Michel Andrieu, *Les Ordines romain du haut moyen âge*, 5 vols. (Louvain, 1931-61), 4:108. Compare Andrieu, *Les Pontifical romain du haut moyen âge*, 4 vols. (Vatican City, 1938-41), 1:49.

15. Gaudemet, "Note sur le symbolisme médiéval," 74.

16. In addition to the texts discussed below, see those cited by Gerd Tellenbach, *Libertas: Kirche und Weltordnung im Zeitalter des Investiturstreites* (Stuttgart, 1936), trans. R. F. Bennett as *Church, State and Christian Society at the Time of the Investiture Contest* (London, 1959), 129-31.

17. As Gerd Tellenbach has recently pointed out, unreflexive reliance on such conventional terms as "reform movement," "reformers," and "conservatives" may distort our understanding of "the extremely complex reality" of religious change in the eleventh and early twelfth centuries: *The Church in Western Europe from the Tenth to the Early Twelfth Century*, trans. Timothy Reuter (Cambridge, 1993), 157-58. Nevertheless, I have decided to use these terms to classify the writers and texts discussed below, because I

believe that they do serve to identify some fairly consistent affiliations among the intellectuals of the period.

18. This is especially noticeable after the death of Henry III in 1056: Tellenbach, *The Church in Western Europe*, 179ff.

19. For an extended critique of the sources, see Reginald L. Poole, "Benedict IX and Gregory VI," in his *Studies in Chronology and History*, ed. Austin Lane Poole (Oxford, 1934), 185-222. On the events themselves, see Harald Zimmermann, *Papstabsetzungen des Mittelalters* (Graz—Vienna—Cologne, 1968), 119-39; Klaus-Jürgen Herrmann, *Das Tuskulaner Papsttum (1012-1046)*, Päpste und Papsttum, 4 (Stuttgart, 1973), 151-65; F. J. Schmale, "Die 'Absetzung' Gregors VI. in Sutri und die synodale Tradition," *Annuarium historiae conciliorum* 11 (1979): 55-103.

20. Auctor Gallicus, *De ordinando pontifice, MGH, Libelli de lite*, 1:8-14; re-edited by Hans Hubert Anton, *Der Sogenannte Traktat "De ordinando pontifice": Ein Rechtsgutachten in Zusammenhang mit der Synode von Sutri (1046)*, Bonner Historische Forschungen, 48 (Bonn, 1982). The passages discussed below are identical in the Dümmler and Anton texts, so I have cited the Dümmler edition, which is more easily accessible. The exact date of the text is disputed (see Anton, pp. 9-11).

21. Auctor Gallicus, *De ordinando pontifice, MGH, Libelli de lite*, 1:9.

22. Auctor Gallicus, *De ordinando pontifice, MGH, Libelli de lite*, 1:9-10.

23. Auctor Gallicus, *De ordinando pontifice, MGH, Libelli de lite*, 1:11.

24. On the prostitute as a metaphor for the unreformed church, see Jean Leclercq, *Monks and Marriage: A Twelfth-Century View* (New York, 1982), 87-95.

25. Humbert, *Adversus simoniacos*, 3:5, *MGH, Libelli de lite*, 1:203.

26. Humbert, *Adversus simoniacos*, 3:5, *MGH, Libelli de lite*, 1:204.

27. Humbert, *Adversus simoniacos*, 3:5, *MGH, Libelli de lite*, 1:203.

28. Humbert, *Adversus simoniacos*, 3:5, *MGH, Libelli de lite*, 1:205.

29. Engles, "Der Pontifikatsantritt," 758.

30. Uta-Renate Blumenthal claims that Henry III (1039-56) was the first to invest bishops with the ring: *Der Investiturstreit* (Stuttgart, 1982), trans. by the author as *The Investiture Controversy: Church and Monarchy from the Ninth to the Twelfth Century* (Philadelphia, 1988), 35 and 52. Engels, however, attributes this innovation to Henry II (1002-24): "Der Pontifikatsanstritt," 758.

31. Among recent studies of the decrees against lay investiture, see especially Rudolf Schieffer, *Die Entstehung des päpstlichen Investiturverbots für den deutschen König* (Stuttgart, 1981).

32. The pioneering work on this literature by Carl Mirbt, *Die Publizistik im Zeitalter Gregors VII* (Leipzig, 1894) is still useful. Among more recent works, see especially I. S. Robinson, *Authority and Resistance in the Investiture Contest: The Polemical Literature of the Late Eleventh Century* (Manchester, 1978).

33. See also Placidus of Nonantula, *Liber de honore ecclesiae*, 55, *MGH, Libelli de lite*, 2:590; Gerhoh of Reichersberg, *De edificio Dei*, 61 and 133, *MGH, Libelli de lite*, 3:171-182.

34. Ranger of Lucca, *Liber de anulo et baculo, MGH, Libelli de lite*, 2:509 and 533.

35. Ranger of Lucca, *Liber de anulo et baculo, MGH, Libelli de lite*, 2:509-10.

36. Ranger of Lucca, *Liber de anulo et baculo, MGH, Libelli de lite*, 2:511.

37. Ranger of Lucca, *Liber de anulo et baculo, MGH, Libelli de lite*, 2:522-23.

38. "Cum sine coniugio non sit pastoria cura,/ nec pastoris ope coniugium careat": Ranger of Lucca, *Liber de anulo et baculo, MGH, Libelli de lite*, 2:524.

39. Ranger of Lucca, *Liber de anulo et baculo, MGH, Libelli de lite*, 2:527.

40. Gerhoh of Reichersberg, *De edificio Dei*, 61, *MGH, Libelli de lite*, 3:171.

41. As Benson, *The Bishop-Elect*, 203, points out, "At no other time in the Church's history has the episcopal office been the object of such intense scrutiny and deep concern as during the eleventh and twelfth centuries."

42. The influence of the Pseudo-Isidore in the eleventh and twelfth century is discussed in Fuhrmann, *Einfluß und Verbreitung der pseudo-isidorischen Fälschungen*, vol. 2.

43. Friedrich Ohly, *Hohelied-Studien: Grundzüge einer Geschichte der Hoheliedauslegung des Abendlandes bis um 1200* (Wiesbaden, 1958), 94-109; E. Ann Matter, *The Voice of My Beloved: The Song of Songs in Western Medieval Spirituality* (Philadelphia, 1990), 86-122.

44. Johann Laudage, *Priesterbild und Reformpapsttum im 12. Jahrhundert* (Cologne, 1984).

45. For a carefully nuanced discussion of late eleventh-century views on royal authority, see Robinson, *Authority and Resistance*, 60-150.

46. See the anonymous author of the deeds of Bishop Galcher of Cambrai, in *Gesta pontificum cameracensium(Gestes des évêques de Cambrai de 1092-1138)*, ed. C. de Smedt, Publications de la Société de l'histoire de France, 197 (Paris, 1880), 9-10.

47. A Monk of Farfa, *Orthodoxa defensio imperialis*, 3, *MGH, Libelli de lite*, 2:536-37. The editor's attribution of this treatise to Gregory of Catino is no longer accepted: Robinson, *Authority and Resistance*, 142.

48. Ernst Kantorowicz, *The King's Two Bodies: A Study of Mediaeval Political Theology* (Princeton, 1957), 42-61; Karl Pellens, *Das Kirchendenken des Normannischen Anonymus*, Veröffentlichungen des Instituts für europäische Geschichte, Mainz, 69 (Wiesbaden, 1973), 111-19, 225-67.

49. Norman Anonymous, *De consecratione pontificum et regum et de regimine eorum in ecclesia sancta* (J 24), in *Die Texte des Normannischen Anonymus, Die Texte Normannischen Anonymus unter Konsultation der Teilausgaben von H. Böhmer, H. Scherrinsky und G. H. Williams neu aus der Handschrift 415 des Corpus Christi College Cambridge*, Karl Pellens, Veröffentlichungen des Instituts für europäische Geschichte, Mainz, 42 (Weisbaden, 1966), 196-97.

50. Norman Anonymous, *De consecratione pontificum et regum*, in *Die Texte des Normannischen Anonymus*, ed. Pellens, 197.

51. Tellenbach, *Church, State and Christian Society*, 134.

52. This point has been argued most recently by Dyan Elliot, who offers a particularly valuable discussion of what the move towards clerical celibacy meant for women: see her *Spiritual Marriage: Sexual Abstinence in Medieval Wedlock* (Princeton, 1993), 94-131.

53. Indeed, some authors have asserted—without reference to the sources—that this is just what happened: see Henry Charles Lea, *History of Sacerdotal Celibacy in the Christian Church*, 4th rev. ed. (New York, 1966), 162; Tellenbach, *Church, State and Christian Society*, 131.

54. *Die Briefe des Petrus Damiani*, 61, ed. Kurt Reindel, 4 vols. (Munich, 1983-93), 2:206-18.

55. See the references to "fathers-in-law" (*socerorum*) and "mothers-in-law" (*socruum*): *Die Briefe des Petrus Damiani*, 61, ed. Reindel, 2:208.

56. *Die Briefe des Petrus Damiani*, 61, ed. Reindel, 2:214.

57. *Die Briefe des Petrus Damiani*, 61, ed. Reindel, 2:215.

58. *Die Briefe des Petrus Damiani*, 61, ed. Reindel, 2:214-15.

59. *Die Briefe des Petrus Damiani*, 61, ed. Reindel, 2:215-16.

60. *Die Briefe des Petrus Damiani*, 61, ed. Reindel, 2:215.

61. Gerhoh of Reichersberg, *Quod Princeps mundi huius iam iudicatus sit*, MGH, *Libelli de lite*, 3:244-45; idem, *De gloria et honore filii hominis*, ibid., 398; idem, *Commentarius in psalmum X*, idid., 413-15. Sometimes good clerics, characterized as *casti*, are contrasted with the *incestuosi*: see Honorius Augustodunensis, *Offendiculum*, 21 and 33, ibid., 44 and 49. This suggests that the sources may not be Peter Damian, but a letter of Pope Leo IX (*PL* 143:671), which contains very similar language.

62. Humbert, *Adversus Nicetam*, 25 (*PL* 143:996); and see Georg Denzler, *Das Papsttum und der Amtszölibat*, *Päpste und Papsttum*, 5, 2 vols. (Stuttgart, 1973-76), 1:53-54, 160.

63. Anonymous, *Tractatus pro clericorum conubio*, MGH, *Libelli de lite*, 3:588. On this text, see Anne Llewellyn Barstow, *Married Priests and the Reforming Papacy: The Eleventh-Century Debates*, Texts and Studies in Religion, 12 (Lewiston, NY, 1982), 116-19.

64. Anonymous, *Tractatus pro clericorum conubio*, MGH, *Libelli de lite*, 3:594.

65. This argument may reflect the influence of the text from the Pseudo-Isidorian Decretals cited above, n. 6.

66. Norman Anonymous, *De sancta virginitate et de sacerdotum matrimonio* (J 25), in *Die Texte des Normanischen Anonymus*, ed. Pellens, 205.

67. *Die Briefe des Petrus Damiani*, ed. Reindel, 2:215.

68. *Das Register Gregors VII.*, 2:67, ed. Erich Caspar, MGH, *Epistolae selectae*, 2, 2 vols. (Berlin, 1920-23), 223-35.

69. Honorius Augustodunensis, *Offendiculum, MGH, Libelli de lite,* 3:39-57. On the date of this work, see Valerie I. J. Flint, "The Chronology of the Works of Honorius Augustodunensis," *Revue bénédictine* 82 (1972); 219-27, and 241-42; reprinted in her *Ideas in the Medieval West: Texts and Contexts* (London, 1988).

70. Honorius Augustodunensis, *Offendiculum,* 8, *MGH, Libelli de lite,* 3:40-41.

71. Honorius Augustodunensis, *Offendiculum,* 9-12, *MGH, Libelli de lite,* 3:41.

72. On clerical celibacy and canon law in the eleventh century, see Brundage, *Law, Sex, and Christian Society,* 214-23.

Pope Gregory VII and the Prohibition of Nicolaitism

Uta-Renate Blumenthal

The term "reform" to describe the events and ideas of the last half of the eleventh century has lately fallen on hard times.[1] Gerd Tellenbach suggests that we must try "cautiously and patiently to get back the reality itself."[2] This is sound advice, particularly when dealing with Pope Gregory VII (1073-1085) and the enforcement of celibacy among the clergy. It is often claimed that it was due to him, primarily if not exclusively, that the ancient prescription for the celibacy of the clergy became the general standard throughout the western church.

Hildebrand/Gregory VII is seen as the guiding spirit behind papal condemnations of clerical marriage since the 1050s.[3] Such a sweeping statement actually says very little about this pontiff's role in profoundly significant developments. The eleventh and twelfth centuries not only saw the acceptance at least in theory, of celibacy for clergy of all ranks but also the formation of a matrimonial law under ecclesiastical jurisdiction.[4] This essay will be limited in scope. Its focus is an evaluation of the measures of Hildebrand/Gregory VII to enforce celibacy among the clergy in the light of their antecedents. Other important issues in the field of marriage law, consanguineous marriages for instance, will be disregarded here.[5]

One difficulty becomes apparent immediately: the frequent association of simony and nicolaitism.[6] Simony and nicolaitism were the twin issues that dominated efforts to renew the church in the eleventh century, before they were subordinated to the investiture issue after 1075. Sources of the last decades of the eleventh century and thereafter, including the register of Gregory VII, often refer to them in one breath. But simony, a many-headed hydra, could cover a multitude of sins and underwent many transformations,[7] and it is essential for the sake of clarity to distinguish between them to avoid fuzziness and generalities. It should not be overlooked that celibacy for the clergy was an earlier and very different issue, an issue in its own right. Ascetic, monastic, and cultic tendencies inherited from antiquity led to attempts to require clergy to lead celibate lives as early as the fourth century, especially in the West.[8] Indicative of such efforts are the canons of Elvira (306-314) that were taken up in the widely known and influential *Decretum* of Burchard of Worms (1023). Through Burchard's collection they reached Ivo of Chartres, whose *Panormia* (ca. 1093) was the one collection to rival Burchard's influence in the early twelfth century.[9] Burchard's sources, as far as they could be determined, were the *Paenitentiale ad Otgarium* of Hrabannus Maurus and the *Libri duo de synodalis causis* by Regino of Prum, who in his turn was also heavily dependent on the penitentials. The influence of the penitentials on the history of celibacy cannot be overestimated,[10] although efforts at enforcement were sporadic at best and had little success.[11]

Given the influence in particular of Burchard at the time of the Gregorian reform, it is all the more remarkable that such influence appears to be totally lacking in the legislation of the eleventh century here under discussion. Instead, any inquiry into possible antecedents for the decrees of Gregory VII is bound to begin with the synod of Pavia held in 1022 jointly by Pope Benedict VII and Emperor Henry II.[12] Its first two canons go beyond c. 3 of the Ecumenical Council of Nicaea in 325 in their severity, excluding all women from the houses of priests and deposing married clergy including the bishops.[13] Their children and possibly wives, c. 2 of the imperial edict is unclear, are to become serfs of the manor of the cleric concerned.[14] The opening address of the pontiff, presumably composed by Bishop Leo of Vercelli, indeed refers to the "law of Nicaea," but the content of the relevant decree is distorted to bring it into agreement with the new legislation of 1022.[15] In the imperial confirmation unchastity of the clergy is called "the root of all evil" (p. 76, l.39f.), and unfree clerics who father sons with free women are called "the worst enemies of the Church" (p. 71, l.34f.). Up to this point it is readily apparent why some historians are inclined to see the Council of Pavia as an important step towards reform, in line with the legislation of Pope Leo IX (1049-1054), for instance.[16] This view, however, fails to take into account the main thrust of the legislation promulgated in 1022. Despite the rhetoric, significant as a reminder of moral ideals, the issue was not so much the sexual morality of the clergy but rather the great poverty into which the church had fallen despite her generous endowment by emperors and kings (p. 71, l.19-21). The rich estates, patrimonies, and other goods of the church lament the canons of 1022, are acquired by "infamous fathers for infamous sons."[17] Such loss of property was to be prevented at all costs. The bulk of the legislation of 1022, therefore, spells out in detail that sons and daughters of clerics, who were themselves serfs of the church, were to remain forever unfree. They are to belong to the Church as chattel together with all their property.[18]

These concerns, of course, were troubling other regions besides Italy. Given the imperial patronage and the personality of Emperor Henry II (1002-1024), a determined proponent of monastic reform, echoes in the German sees of Hamburg and Goslar are not surprising. Bishop Libentius of Hamburg is warmly praised by the chronicler Adam of Bremen for raising the income of his cathedral through the purchase of estates and the expulsion of the wives of canons from the city. As a result, Adam claimed, it was almost impossible to find a needy person[19]: indicating that once unchaste clergy had ceased to squander ecclesiastical income on their families, there were sufficient funds to assist the poor in the city. To sum up, pressing practical needs, the great poverty of the church, were the dominant theme at Pavia in 1022 and governed the measures of pope and emperor to limit the economic and social dislocations caused by married clergy and their support of their children. Despite the references to a general prohibition of marriage of concubinage for clerics, the theme is not developed in the main body of the decrees in theological terms, nor is there more than an incidental reference to ritual purity.

It is thus hard to find parallels between the canons of 1022 and officially documented papal legislation from the mid-eleventh century. This is true although the economic and social dislocations caused by married clergy had not disappeared by then. A letter of Pope Gregory VII to William the Conqueror is an eloquent witness. In 1076 the pontiff wrote to the king urging him to expel Bishop Juhel from the see of Dol in Brittany.[20] Juhel is said to have acquired the bishopric through simony and, moreover, "was not ashamed to enter openly into marriage" begetting children. Worse was to come:

"he crowned a most frightful crime. . .by adding an abominable sacrilege. For by a monstrous outrage he married off the grown-up daughters of his illicit marriage, bestowing and alienating church lands and revenues by way of their dowries." There is no denying that at least in this particular case the alienation of ecclesiastical property appeared to Gregory VII as the worst offense. The tenor of papal legislation of the mid-eleventh century in general, however, and including that of Gregory VII himself, sets a different emphasis.

A look at the most influential papal-conciliar decree regarding the enforcement of celibacy for the clergy from the period will make this clear. It is preserved verbatim in an encyclical letter sent out by Pope Nicholas II (1059-1061), circulating to a wider audience decrees from the Lateran council of 1059.[21] The relevant c.3 reads as follows:

> Let no one hear the mass of a priest whom he knows with certainty to have a concubine or an unlawful woman. For this reason the holy synod has decreed the following under threat of excommunication, saying: Whoever among priests, deacons, subdeacons publicly married a concubine after the constitution regarding the chastity of the clergy which had been issued by the most holy Pope Leo, our predecessor of blessed memory, or did not dismiss one he had married earlier, shall not sing the mass, nor read the Gospels or the Epistles, as we declare and enjoin on behalf of the omnipotent God and on the authority of the blessed Apostles Peter and Paul; nor shall he remain in the choir room (*presbiterio*) for the divine offices with those who were obedient to the aforementioned constitution; neither shall he obtain a benefice (*partem*) from the church until we have made a judicial decision regarding him, God willing.[22]

The prohibition to unchaste priests and lower clergy to serve at the altar and the then startling innovation of a mass boycott by the populace speak a new language.[23] Such clergy are to be deprived of their benefices and their cases are to be judged by the pope. Gone are all references to unfree clerics and to the exile and/or enslavement of their wives;[24] gone, too, however, is the threat of deposition demanded for unchaste clergy in 1022. The realization that it did not suffice to repeat the simple prescription *feminas non habeatis* as in the Carolingian *Admonitio synodalis* evidently had borne fruit in responsible circles.[25] The assembly of 1059 focused on realistic goals that presumably could be attained by using ecclesiastical discipline. At the same time the measures envisioned avoided major disruptions of the church which had to be anticipated if all unchaste clergy would be deposed on the spot.[26] Historians are usually content to lay the novelties of the 1059 decree, which was included in a re-promulgation of Pope Alexander II (JL 5401),[27] at the feet of the "reform" papacy, and in particular of Pope Gregory VII.

Whether this is correct or not remains to be seen, for the 1059 decree refers clearly to a constitution *de castitate clericorum* of Pope Leo IX (1048-1054). No such text has been preserved, but contemporaries, like the Lateran Council of 1059, were aware of legislation against married clergy at several of Leo's numerous synods.[28] Most explicit is Peter Damian in a letter to Bishop Cunibert of Turin,[29] and his testimony regarding papal legislation against married clergy has always been accepted at face value. The letter is datable to 1064, and three segments in particular are relevant here, one perhaps reflecting the boycott of 1059, another indicating Leo IX (1049-1054) as originator, and a third attributed to Pope Stephen IX (1057-1058).[30] As far as Leo IX is concerned, the fragments reveal first of all that this pontiff prohibited clerical marriage, a decree that was subsequently expanded by Stephen IX.[31] Secondly, we learn that Leo decreed in a full synod that all Roman women who associated with clerics should become serfs of the Lateran.[32] Some historians see here a connection between the Roman council of 1059 and the council of Pavia of 1022, and such a link at least seems plausible.[33] Noteworthy in the present context, however, is the fact that this is precisely the item entirely omitted in c.3 of the 1059 Lateran council. Not so with the third reference in Damian's letter to Cunibert of Turin: the prescription of Pope Stephen IX that unchaste clergy was to be expelled from the community of canons--this would presumably entail a loss of their benefice--and the choir room so that they might desert their women and make amends through penance. Such separation implies the prohibition to celebrate mass or assist at the altar.[34] With slight changes, in particular the reference to papal adjudication, it appears, then, to be a decree of Stephen IX, resuming some legislation of Leo IX, that forms the core for c.3 of 1059.[35] The only source for this decree of Stephen is this passage recorded by Damian.

In his letter to the bishop of Turin in 1064 Damian emphasized that he publicized in all churches the papal decree that "nobody was to hear the mass of a priest, the Gospel from a deacon or, finally the Epsistle from a subdeacon" if these clerics are known to associate with women.[36] Precisely here, however, no derivation is given, other than that it is a papal decree. It seems more likely than not that what Damian had in mind was precisely the introductory proclamation of the decree of 1059 which Damian accepted only after some delay. Both the boycott and the explicit prohibition to say mass, however, are new and radical steps because the first entitled the laity to judge clerical behavior in contradiction to Pseudo-Isidore's clear prohibition and the second deprived clergy of their reason of existence.[37] Pope Leo IX elevated Hildebrand, the later Gregory VII, to the rank of subdeacon, but it must not be forgotten that he was certainly both younger and less influential than other collaborators of the Lotharingian pope.[38] If, therefore, the 1059 legislation is ultimately derived from the pontificate of Leo, Hildebrand would have had little influence. In 1059 the situation changed, however, for Hildebrand had risen to the office of archdeacon of the Roman church, and his influence was marked. Nonetheless, sources for the council of 1059 show us Hildebrand only as delivering an attack on the Aachen rule for canons of 816/817 because it permitted private property.[39] As the historical debate concerning the papal election decree of 1059 has made clear, discussions must have been lively and factionalism was not unheard of. Even the official decrees do not speak in one voice. The threatening posture taken in c.3 is contradicted in clause 10: "ut cuiuslibet ordinis clericos laici non iudicent nec de ecclesiis eiciant." Hildebrand probably was not among the signatories of the election decree.[40] In short, it is impossible to say who among the participants could have been responsible for the important additions made in 1059 to older papal legislation against nicolaitism.

The inspiration for the decree against nicolaitism in 1059 was probably not an earlier papal-conciliar decision but the events in Milan. In 1059 Pope Nicholas II dispatched Peter Damian and Anselm of Lucca (the later Alexander II) as legates to the city to bring about an end to the turmoil there. Our source of information for the legislation is primarily Peter Damian's report to the Archdeacon Hildebrand. He records and requests approval for the measures which he had taken to attain three aims: the subjection of the archbishopric of Milan to the authority of Rome, the elimination of simony, and, finally the elimination of nicolaitism among Milanese clerics.[41] In comparison with the *Liber Gomorrhianus*[42] the very mild condemnation of married clergy at Milan is striking. Even more to the point is the contrasting emphasis in the report itself. To be sure, the heresy of nicolaitism is condemned but almost as an afterthought in the written promise exacted from Archbishop Guido, who has to obligate himself to separate priests, deacons, and subdeacons from their wives or concubines, "in so far as he is able to do so."[43] It should come as no surprise that Damian did not mention at the time the conciliar prohibition to attend masses of married priests: the city of Milan was not unlike a powder keg ready to explode any minute.[44]

The legislation of Peter Damian took place against the backdrop of serious political, social, and religious unrest that convulsed the proud and independent city of Milan.[45] The agitation in Milan was an open secret in Rome. Peter Damian hints as much in his letter to Pope Nicholas II of 1059, encouraging the pope to take steps against nicolaitism, for, he wrote, the *magistri* of the church could not be silent when the common crowd[46] complained loudly and shamelessly about married clergy. He did not see the point of "suppressing in the synod what is publicly proclaimed."[47] The Milanese faction eventually known as the *Pataria* at the head of the agitation had inconspicuous beginnings. Its first leader, the deacon Ariald of Carimate, who began to preach against immorality among the clergy in the countryside around Milan in the early 1050s, was a complete failure at first.[48] In the light of subsequent events it is ironic that it took an invitation from the clergy of Milan in the spring of 1057 for Ariald to find an audience as well as an invaluable ally in Landulf Cotta, a notary of the Ambrosian Church--while the archbishop, Guido, did not take his sermons serious at all.[49] Landulf Cotta, a fiery preacher in his own right, and Ariald concluded a compact under oath that "they would not permit any priests and *levites* (deacons) to have wives from this day on."[50] There is not need here to discuss the well-known history of the *Pataria* once again, but the emphasis on the *luxuria* of the Milanese clergy in the sermons of Ariald and Landulf is often forgotten. *Luxuria* is St. Peter Damian's favorite term to castigate the sinful lives of the clergy. What is condemned root and branch is an entire lifestyle as Ariald makes clear. Ariald's *vita*, composed in 1075 by Andrea of Strumi, faithfully recorded the essential themes of Ariald's first sermons:

> See, Christ says: "Learn from me because I am
> gentle and of humble spirit"; and again he says of
> Himself: "The Son of Man does not have a place to
> lay His head"; and again: "Blessed are the poor in
> spirit, for the kingdom of heaven is theirs." But in
> contrast to this, as you see, your priests consider
> themselves richer because of earthly things, more
> exalted by building towers and houses, prouder
> because of honors, more beautiful because of soft
> and luxurious clothing: they are considered more
> blessed. And they, as you know, marry wives in
> public like laymen, just as accursed laymen follow
> [them in their] debauchery [*stuprum*].[51]

The message of Ariald and Landulf[52] caught on like wildfire. Important in the present context is that it was originally directed exclusively against the wives and concubines of priests and deacons.[53] No one was to attend the masses of married clergy.[54] In vain did the higher clergy try to calm the situation and undermine the authority of Landulf and Ariald. On May 10, 1057, the solemn procession took place in commemoration of the translation of St. Nazaro in the piazza in front of the cathedral. Ariald addressed the crowd of his supporters which followed him into the cathedral to expel unworthy priests who were reciting the office in the choir. On this day a momentous step had been taken: from a boycott to violence against priests and deacons considered unworthy.[55] Ariald then formulated a *phytacium de castitate servanda* that the clergy had to sign under threat of death.[56] As yet, in 1057, simony played no role in the Patarene agitation, it did not become part of it until appeals by both sides forced a reluctant papacy to intervene. Archbishop Guido's synod of Fontaneto near Novara in the fall of 1057 ended with the excommunication of Ariald and Landulf. Ariald subsequently traveled to Rome where he sought and found some limited support, returning to Milan in late 1057, either shortly before or together with two legates: Anselm da Baggio, Bishop of Lucca (1056-1073) and later Pope Alexander II (1061-1073), and Hildebrand. The papal legates were on their way to the imperial court in Germany and stayed only briefly in the city without making any particular impact.[57] It is after his return from Rome that Ariald and Landulf began to preach against simony as well as nicolaitism.[58] It is precisely this program which was reflected in the report of Peter Damian addressed to the Archdeacon Hildebrand in 1059 discussed earlier. In other words, Hildebrand who had visited Milan in 1057 and was familiar with the aims of Ariald, at the vey least supported a papal policy which subordinated the fight against nicolaitism to third place, behind both the assertion of Roman primacy and the battle against simony.[59]

Hildebrand was elected and enthroned by popular acclaim as Pope Gregory VII in the church of S. Pietro in Vincoli during the burial ceremonies for Alexander II in April 1073.[60] His letter to Archibishop Gebhard of Salzburg of November contains the first reference to nicolaitism documented from his pontificate. "There is one issue, however, where we may rightly say your fraternity has been negligent; we have been told that you appear inobedient until now concerning the decrees of the Roman synod which you attended pertaining to the chastity of the clergy." He should use his pastoral powers to enforce these canons among his clergy regardless of consequences (*neque gratiam neque odium alicuius considerans*).[61] The Roman synod to which Gregory referred must have been the council held by Alexander II to repromulgate the decrees of the council of 1059.[62] Gregory VII was referring, therefore, to c.3 of that assembly quoted above. More than a decade had passed, but the decree of 1059 served then and was to serve Gregory throughout his reign as a constant point of reference.[63] Very little is known about the pontiff's first Lenten council in 1074. Two letters of invitation indicate that the state of the church in general constituted the agenda.[64] The chastity of the clergy may well have been discussed, therefore, as the chronicle of Marianus Scottus indicates, but this author unfortunately gives no more than what is essentially a reference to the Ecumenical Council of Nicaea.[65] Details about the work of the legates Gerald of Ostia and Hubert of Palestrina also do not tell us anything specific concerning celibacy of the clergy; they were sent to Germany after the Lenten synod of 1074 to reconcile Henry IV of Germany with the see of Rome and to hold a council reforming the imperial church.[66] We have to wait the Lenten synod

of the following year (February 24-28), when in addition to a brief
formal entry in the official register of Gregory VII, several of his
letters, transmitted within or without the register, preserve the papal
version or summary of part of the legislation issued at that time.[67]
One, or conceivably two, of the letters written in conjunction with
the 1075 council also refer to the Lenten synod of 1074 but only in
terms which equate the legislation against simony and clerical
unchastity of 1074 with that of February 1075.[68] Recent discussion of
the latter council have centered on the question of whether or not
investiture was prohibited as reported by Arnulf of Milan or not.[69]
Such an emphasis, however, is clearly anachronistic. Contemporaries
were practically silent on the question of investiture until after the
second deposition and excommunication of Henry IV in 1080.[70]
They were literally up in arms, however, about the prohibition of
marriage and unchastity among the clergy, in part at least because of
the by-now-familiar linkage with popular boycotts. In a letter sent
immediately after the synod in February 1075 to Archbishop
Siegfried of Mainz the decree reads as follows:

> We, according to the authority of the holy fathers,
> set forth the judgment in our council, that those
> who through simoniacal heresy, that is by the
> intervention of money, are promoted to any rank
> or office of sacred orders should no longer have a
> ministry in the holy church. Those who obtain
> churches by giving money should absolutely
> relinquish them, so that no one henceforth should
> be allowed to buy them. *Those who are guilty of the
> crime of fornication should not celebrate masses or
> serve at the altar in lesser orders. Furthermore, we state
> that if these people ignore our rulings, or rather those of
> the holy fathers, the faithful should in no way receive
> their ministrations, so that whoever is not corrected for
> the love of God and the dignity of office might come to
> his senses by the shame of the world and the reproach of
> the faithful.*(italics mine)[71]

Simony has taken first place in this official summary of the 1075
decrees,[72] and this remains generally true for Gregory's letters
dealing with both simony (here very carefully and conservatively

circumscribed) and nicolaitism. Simonists are to be deposed; unchaste clergy are forbidden to celebrate mass; they have to separate from wives or concubines and do penance before they are allowed to resume their offices in the church; in case of noncompliance the laity is to boycott their services and bring them to their senses. Very few letters deal specifically or exclusively with unchastity.[73] The measures promulgated in February 1075 were sometimes circulated in Germany on the basis of Gregory's letters as part of small propagandist collections[74] as well as in the local councils the pontiff instructed the bishops to hold.[75] A comparison of relevant letters preserved in Gregory's register reveals some variations in emphasis, but even so there are no fundamental differences. Not all issues are mentioned in every letter dispatched after the synod.[76] A letter to Patriarch Sigehard of Aquileia contains the most detailed version of the decree against marriage of clergy, valuable because only here do we find the specific declaration that clergy who disobey the conciliar injunctions are not only excluded from service at the altar but also are not allowed to hold a benefice.[77] The parallel to the 1059 decree, or rather the lost *decretum de castitate* of Leo IX, could not be plainer. Gregory VII insists that he is merely renewing the statutes of the fathers, even though he had the right to create new laws against new ills, and indeed everything indicates that this is indeed what he did.[78] Any hesitation on account of the differences in formulation are removed by the pontiff himself, who points to the legislation of 1059 as the source for the decrees of 1074/75 in a letter written just prior to the Lenten council of dukes Rudolf of Suabia and Bertulf of Carinthia. Since former decrees had fallen into neglect, Gregory wrote, they have to be renewed and their observation has to be stressed, "even by force if necessary."[79]

The same letter reveals that Gregory was fully conscious of the ambiguities of lay intervention. Duke Rudolf and Duke Bertulf are instructed to respond to critics of their use of physical coercion against clergy by a simple reference to "the obedience enjoined upon them" by the pope. Nonetheless, like Nicholas II and the council of 1059 Gregory VII was willing to use the laity in order to enforce papal decrees.[80] The possibility of a papal appeal to the populace enshrined as clause 24 of the *dictatus papae* permitting accusations by "subjects,"[81] was legally significant because it enabled the papacy to intervene unilaterally whenever necessary or desirable.[82] Gregory took the initiative in this manner in the case of Bishop Otto of

Constance.[83] He was one of the recipients of the letters sent out after
the Lenten synod of 1075,[84] and in obedience to the papal request he,
like several of his colleagues, held a local synod to repromulgate the
Roman decrees.[85] But the hostility of the lower clergy to the decree
against nicolaitism was so great that the bishop had to abandon the
promulgation of the relevant segment--interpreted by his critics as an
abandonment of the c. 3 of the council of Nicaea--and indeed go so
far as to allow his clerics to take wives. Gregory's response was
harsh: "O the impudence! O the unparalleled insolence! that a
bishop should despise the decrees of the apostolic see, should set at
naught the precepts of the holy fathers, and in truth should impose
upon his subjects from his lofty place and from his episcopal chair
things contrary to these precepts and opposed to the Christian
faith."[86] Appearances notwithstanding, in the letter Gregory unbent
sufficiently to cite specific authorities in addition to the generic
"precepts of the apostolic see," that is the decrees of the February
synod of 1075. In addition to a reference to St. Paul (1 Cor. 5:11), he
referred to Pope Leo I and to Gregory the Great. Epistle 14 (JK 411),
c. 4: *de subdiaconorum continentia*, of Leo I to Anastasius of
Thessalonica as identified by H. E. J. Cowdrey seems not to have
played a role in the polemics surrounding the issue of nicolaitism--
except among opponents of celibacy, for the same epistle as
transmitted in the Pseudo-Isidorian Decretals demanded that the
bishops could only be married once.[87] Several statements of Gregory
I, however, do, as do several New Testament passages, although
again not this particular passage.[88] The break in the canonistic
tradition as represented by Burchard of Worms and Ivo of Chartres
becomes very clear. Gregory VII appears to have been profoundly
convinced that in the last analysis nothing was needed except a
reference to papal decisions whenever taken. It is pure graciousness
when he condescends to cite anything else as a precedent.[89] In
conclusion he ordered Otto to attend the next Lenten synod
(February 1076). Without waiting the results of this admonition,
which inspired Bernold of Constance's finest writings,[90] Gregory
also wrote to the people of Constance. Moving beyond the
essentially passive boycott of certain masses enjoined by the Lenten
synod of 1075, the pontiff in this letter freed the clergy and laity of
Constance from obedience to the bishop and annulled all oaths of
fealty, "as long as he is a rebel against God and the apostolic see."[91]
The Lenten council of 1076 suspended Otto, and finally in 1080 he

was deposed and excommunicated with other royal supporters.[92] Bishop Altmann of Passau, a firm supporter of Gregory VII, was able to install a papal candidate as bishop of Constance, without, however, putting an end to the struggles over the bishopric which became a center of opposition to the Salian rulers.[93] The degree of influence of Gregory's letter is difficult to gauge almost a millennium later, and it must suffice here to point out Gregory's intentions as expressed in his letter to the clergy and laity of Constance. Remarkable, once again is Gregory's emphasis on obedience and disobedience, respectively, in his letter to the people of Constance:

> Accordingly. . .by apostolic authority we charge all of you, both greater and lesser, who stand by God and St. Peter, that if he is determined to continue in his obduracy you should show him neither respect nor obedience. Nor need you think this a danger to your souls. For if. . .he is determined to resist apostolic precepts, we so absolve you by St. Peter's authority from every yoke of subjection to him that, even if any of you is bound to him by the obligation of an oath, for so long as he is a rebel against God and the apostolic see you are bound to pay him no fealty.[94]

Popular response to the papal decrees like *Statuimus* created strains elsewhere as well, for example in Salzburg, Erfurt, Mainz, Passua, or Thérouanne and Cambrai.[95] Detailed discussions would lead far beyond the present topic, but the situation in Thérouanne and Cambrai deserves some attention, because the events in northern France reflect very much a local and therefore different perspective. At Thérouanne in defense against the popular boycott, Bishop Hubert apparently instructed his cathedral clergy to refuse baptism and burial to opponents of married clergy.[96] Earlier, before Hubert's election to the bishopric in ca. 1079, Gregory had written to Countess Adela of Flanders, asking her to forbid clergy who refused to abandon their wives or concubines to celebrate mass and to expel them from the choir of the cathedral and deprive them from their benefices until they showed the fruit of penitence. She should replace them with chaste priests "from wherever she could find them." In particular she was not to listen to Archdeacon Hubert, the later bishop, who had fallen into heresy due to his incorrect contentions. This letter is dated November 10, 1076 and provides very detailed evidence for the 1075 decree.[97] Conspicuously missing is any reference to the use of coercion or popular threats envisioned by that council. Too much should not be made of this, however, for in a missive sent at the same time to Count Robert, Adela's son, the pope requested that Robert should not obey bishops who themselves did not obey the Apostolic See--very much the same argument as found in the letter to Constance.[98] There is nonetheless a certain shift in emphasis. Instead of calling for the use of force as in the early letter to the German dukes (Reg. 2.45) or addressing the entire population as in the case of Constance, Gregory only demanded a withdrawal of obedience from the ruler in a letter that is pastoral in tone. This trend became stronger in the course of Gregory's pontificate. Perhaps the fierce accusations levied against his reliance upon the laity by the German bishops assembled at Worms had not entirely missed their aim[99] and reconfirmed hesitations that had been present even in 1059.[100] Yet as late as March 1077 Gregory repeated the injunctions proclaimed at the Lenten synod of 1075, including the call of a boycott of the masses of unchaste priests.[101] At the great Roman synod celebrated in November 1078, however, the decree against nicolaitism (c. 12) was exclusively addressed to bishops. Bishops would be suspended if they did not use their disciplinary powers against unchaste priests, deacons, or subdeacons because of bribery.[102] Interestingly it is only in this form that Gregory's measures on behalf of celibacy found an echo in contemporary canonical collections.[103] The pontiff by then indeed had moved away from the reliance on the populace to enforce obedience to papal decrees upon an unwilling clergy. Resistance perhaps was too strong. The case of Ramirdus illustrates the point. The relative early success of the *Pataria* could not necessarily be duplicated elsewhere. Ramirdus was burned alive in Cambrai, simply because "he dared to say that simonists and priests guilty of fornication were not allowed to celebrate mass and that their sacraments are not to be received."[104] In his heart of hearts, however, Gregory continued to favor the laity that took up the case of the papacy and defended papal decrees. In 1081 he wrote to his legates Hugh of Die and Amatus of Oloron, instructing them to allow *milites*, who had supported Hugh's actions against unchaste and simoniac clergy, to retain ecclesiastical tithes and to absolve them from excommunication through a papal dispensation (*discretio*).[105]

The papacy was clearly confronted with an uphill battle in northern France as well as Italy, not to mention Germany.[106] The entrenched custom of clerical marriage, *inveteratum morbum fornicationis clericorum* Gregory called it,[107] was not easily eradicated, especially in the face of a skillful defense, ranging from references to the married clergy of the Old Testament as well as of the eastern church, to the council of Nicaea and its supposed consideration of Paphnutius, to the New Testament itself. Heralds of the papal primacy like Bernold of Constance had an important role to play in face of a determined opposition.[108] To return, finally, to the initial question regarding Gregory VII and his influence on reform and the enforcement of celibacy. If it has been said that Gregory VII was particularly influential, then this is certainly correct in one sense. No pope before him so consistently and systematically sought to enforce obedience to papal decrees. In respect to nicolaitism it must be added, however, that the final legislation promulgated by Pope Innocent II at the Second Lateran Council of 1139, to be taken up in Gratian's *Decretum*, owes nothing original to Pope Gregory VII.[109] The legislation of 1059 served as his guide throughout his pontificate.

NOTES

1. Gerd Tellenbach sarcastically castigated the undifferentiated use of the word "reform," see his *The Church in Western Europe from the Tenth to the Early Twelfth Century*, trans. Timothy Reuter (Cambridge, 1993), 157f. and passim.

2. Tellenbach, *The Church in Western Europe*, 158.

3. Anne Llewellyn Barstow, *Married Priests and the Reforming Papacy: The Eleventh-Century Debates* (New York and Toronto, 1982), 49 and 213 n. 13 with reference to the legislation of 1059 which is described as "Gregorian" on p. 53.

4. Peter Landau, "Ehetrennung als Strafe: Zum Wandel des kanonischen Eherechts im 12. Jahrhundert," *Zeitschrift der Savigny-Stiftung für Rechtsgeschichte, Kan. Abteilung* 81 (1995): 148-88, here esp. 152f. with bibliography.

5. See the examples given by James A. Brundage, *Law, Sex, and Christian Society in Medieval Europe* (Chicago, 1987), 192; Raymond Kottje, "Konkubinat   und   Kommunionwürdigkeit   im   vorgratianischen Kirchenrecht: Zu c.12 der römischen Ostersynode von 1059," *Annuarium Historiae Conciliorum* 7 (1975): 159-65.

6. Simony, briefly defined, is the acquisition of ecclesiastical honors and goods through money; see Hans Meier-Welcker, "Die Simonie im frühen Mittelalter," *Zeitschrift für Kirchengeschichte* 64 (1952-53): 61-93. Nicolaitism took its name from an obscure early Christian sect (see Émile Amann, "Nicolaïtes," in *Dictionnaire de théologie catholique* 11 (1931), col. 499-506.; Johann Michl, "Nikolaiten,: in *Lexikon für Theologie und Kirche* 7 (1962), col. 976) and was popularized and carefully explained by Peter Damian; e.g. letter no. 112 to Archbishop Cunibert of Turin (ed. Kurt Reindel, *Die Briefe des Petrus Damiani, MGH* Die Briefe der deutschen Kaiserzeit IV, parts 1-4 [Munich, 1983-1989], part 3), here p. 286: ". . .Unde et clerici uxorati Nikolaitae vocantur, quoniam a quodam Nikolao, qui hanc dogmatizabat heresim, huiusmodi vocabulum sortiunt." (this edition will be cited Reindel, followed by letter number, below). On nicolaitism see also Brundage, *Law, Sex*, 216 n. 206 with further bibliography.

7. See Meier-Welcker as in n. 6 and cf. Rudolf Schieffer, *"Spirituales Latrones*: Zu den Hintergründen der Simonienprozesse in Deutschland zwischen 1069 und 1075," *Historisches Jahrbuch* 92 (1972): 19-60.

8. For difference with the East see the concise summary by Georg Denzler, *Die Geschichte des Zölibats* (Freiburg, Basel, Wien, 1993), 32f.

9. For Elvira see J. Vives, *Concilios Visigóticos*, pp. 5, 6, 13 and Brundage, *Law, Sex*, p. 69f. (with n. 102 on the disputed date), 75, 110f., 150ff. and 205. For the canonical collections of Burchard and Ivo see Paul Fournier and Gabriel Le Bras, *Histoire des collections canoniques en occident*, 2 vols. (Paris, 1931 and 1932) vol. 1. pp. 364-421 and 2, pp. 55-114, respectively, and for fuller discussion and extensive bibliography Horst

Fuhrmann, *Einfluß und Verbreitung der pseudoisidorischen Fälschungen*, *MGH Schriften* 24, parts 1-3 (Stuttgart, 1972-1974), part 2, pp. 442-85 and pp. 542-62.

10. This is also stressed by Brundage, *Law, Sex*, 152f. and 173-75. Burchard's sources are identified in Hartmutt Hoffmann and Rudolf Pokorny, *Das Dekret des Bischofs Burchard von Worms, MGH* Hilfsmittel 12 (Munich, 1991).

11. Friedrich Kempf, in *The Church in the Age of Feudalism*, eds. F. Kempf, Hans-Georg Beck, Eugen Ewig, and Josef Andreas Jungmann (*Handbook of Church History*, vol. 3), trans. Anselm Biggs (New York, 1969), 341; Carl Mirbt, *Die Publizistik im Zeitalter Gregors VII* (Leipzig, 1894), 239-60; Albert Dresdner, *Kultur- und Sittengeschichte der italienischen Geistlichkeit im 10. und 11. Jahrhundert* (Breslau, 1890), 306-19; Bernhard Schimmelpfennig, "Zölibat und Lage der 'Priestersöhne' vom 11. bis 14. Jahrhundert," *Historische Zeitschrift* 227 (1978): 2-44, here pp. 2-6 with further bibliography; an excellent synthesis is found in Brundage, *Law, Sex*, 150-52.

12. *MGH Const.* 1(*MGH, Legum section IV, Constitutiones et acta publica imperatorum et regum*, vol. 1, ed. Ludwig Weiland, Hanover, 1893 [Cited below, *Const.* 1]), no. 34, pp. 70-78; Schimmelpfennig, "Zölibat," p. 14 for the councils of Bourges (1031)c. 5-6 and Gerona (1068), c. 4, 6-7; Brundage, *Law, Sex*, 218. For a recent evaluation, see Johannes Laudage, *Priesterbild und Reformpapsttum im 11. Jahrhundert* (Beihefte zum Archiv für Kulturgeschichte, vol. 22; Cologne, Vienna, 1984): 84-89 with further literature.

13. *MGH, Const.* 1, p. 75 cc. 1-2 and p. 77 in the imperial version. The reference to the *Codex iuris civilis* is misleading (cf. Novell. 123, c. 14 and Weiland's 73, n. 1) The most likely precedent is c. 10 of the ninth council of Toledo (655), see Schimmelpfennig, "Zölibat," 11f.

14. *Const.* 1, p. 77 c. 2 with note.

15. Nicaea I, c. 3 in *Concilium Oecumenicorum Decreta*, ed. J. Alberigo et al., p. 7; for the general reference to Nicaea see *Const.* 1, no. 34, p. 73, line 15: "lege enim Nicaena quicumque ex clero cum qualibet muliere

habitaverit vel eam turpiter cognoverit vel filium vel filiam genuerit, deponitur." A second reference to Nicaea is found p. 74, line 29.

16. See the references in Laudage, *Priesterbild*, 84, n. 162.

17. *MGH, Const.* 1, p. 71, l. 29ff.: ". . .Ampla itaque praedia, ampla patrimonia et quaecumque bona possunt de bonis ecclesiae. . . infames patres infamibus filiis adquirunt."

18. *MGH, Const.* 1, p. 75f. for the papal version and p. 77f for the imperial confirmation of canons 3-7; Schimmelpfennig, "Zölibat," 12, explains the surprising emphasis on unfree clergy as reflecting the status of priests at rural proprietary churches.

19. Adam of Bremen, *Gesta Hammaburgensis ecclesiae pontificum*, 2nd ed., *MGH, Scriptores rerum germanicarum in usum scholarum* (Hanover, 1876) 2.61, p. 82f. with scholion 43: ". . . vix egens quisquam possit inveniri;" Brundage, *Law, Sex*, 218. For Henry II see vol. 3 of Gebhardt, *Handbuch der deutschen Geschichte*, vol. 3, of Josef Fleckenstein and Marie Luise Bulst (Stuttgart, 1970), 131-36.

20. J. E. H. Cowdrey, ed. and trans., *The Epistolae vagantes of Pope Gregory VII* (Oxford, 1972), no. 16, 44f with translation. Letters edited by Cowdrey will be cited as Cowdrey # below.

21. JL 4405/4406 has been critically edited together with JL 4501 of Pope Alexander II by Rudolf Schieffer, *Die Entstehung des päpstlichen Investiturverbots für den deutschen König (MGH Schriften* 28, Stuttgart, 1981), 208-25; for the council as a whole see Hans-Georg Krause, *Das Papstwahldekret von 1059 und seine Rolle im Investiturstreit* (Studi Gregoriani 7, Rome, 1960) and Laudage, *Priesterbild*, 207-50; see also Detlev Jasper, *Das Papstwahldekret von 1059, Überlieferung und Textgestalt* (Sigmaringen, 1986).

22. Schieffer, *Entstehung*, c.3, pp. 218-22, in 4 recensions with very minor differences. One of the versions is the repromulgation by Pope Alexander II (1063?), JL 4501. The letters of Pope Nicholas II are identified in Jaffe's *Regesta pontificum romanorum* as JL 4405/4406.

23. Schimmelpfennig, "Zölibat," 4 noted that Eustatios of Sebaste (d. 377) had called for a boycott of married clergy; it is most unlikely that the council fathers were aware of the early precedent.

24. This part of the legislation is not picked up until 1089, when Pope Urban II held a council at Melfi and determined in c.12: "Porro eos qui in subdiaconatu uxoribus vacare voluerint, ab omni sacro ordine removemus, offico atque beneficio ecclesiae carere decernimus. Quod si ab episcopo commoniti non se correxerint, principibus licentiam indulgemus, ut eorum feminas mancipent servituri. Si vero episcopi consenserint eorum pravitatibus, ipsi officii interdictione mulctetur." (Mansi, *Amplissima Collectio*, vol. 19, 724). See now Robert Somerville, *Pope Urban II, the Collectio Britannica and the Council of Melfi (1089)*, (Oxford, 1996), 256 for c.12.

25. R. Amiet, "Une 'Admonitio synodalis' de l'époque carolingienne: Étude critique et édition," *Medieval Studies* 26 (1964): 12-82.

26. See Barstow, *Married Priests*, 57ff., 68f.

27. See the edition by R. Schieffer, *Entstehung*, 212ff., col. 4 on each double page and the comments of Laudage, *Priesterbild*, 252f.

28. 11 synods have been documented, see Martin Boye, "Quellen katalog der Synoden Deutschlands und Reichsitaliens von 922-1059," *Neues Archiv* 48 (1930), p. 84ff. For historiographical references, see Reindel, *Briefe* (as in n. 6 above), vol. 2, letter no. 61, p. 207 n.3. Details remain blurred, however, except for letter no. 112 which will be discussed below.

29. Bonizo of Sutri, the second source usually cited for Leo's lost decree *de castitate clericorum*, is much less specific, even though he also reports that masses of married clergy were to be boycotted (*Liber ad amicum*, ed. Ernst Dümmler [*MGH Libelli de lite* 1, 1891, p. 568ff.], p. 589, line 1ff.; cf. also, ibid., p. 588, l.10ff. for the Roman synod of 1049[?]). Bonizo is not only a later writer (ca. 1086) but also often imprecise and tendential; cf. Watler Berschin, *Bonizo von Sutri* (Berlin and New York, 1972), 38ff. A third source is the chronicle of Bernold of Constance (*MGH SS* 5 [1844], 385-467, here 426).

30. Reindel, *Briefe*, letter no. 112, vol. 3, p. 258ff.; see at p. 262., l. 19-p. 263, line 3, recording the mass boycott (=Ryan no. 182): ". . .Nos plane quilibet nimirum apostolicae sedis editui, hoc per omnes publice concionamur aecclesias, ut nemo missas a presbytero, non evangelium a diacono, non denique epistolam a subdiacono prorsus audiat, quos misceri feminis non ignorat. . .;" b) p. 280, l.16-19 (=Ryan no. 197): ". . .In plenaria plane synodo sanctae memoriae Leo papa constituit, ut quaecunque damnabiles feminae intra Romana moenia reperirentur presbyteris prostitutae, ex tunc et deinceps Lateranensi palatio adiudicarentur ancillae. . .;" c) p. 276, l.9-13 (=Ryan no. 196): "Alio quoque tempore, cum papa Stephanus. . .omnes clericos Romae, qui post interdictum papae Leonis incontinentes extiterant, de conventu clericorum et choro aecclesiae praecepisset exire, ut quanquam relictis feminis per paenitentiae se lamenta corrigerent. See J. J. Ryan, *Saint Peter Damiani and His Canonical Sources* (Toronto, 1956), 101f. in particular for segment b; a full bibliography is found in Reindel's edition. In general, see also Barstow, *Married Priests*, 54f.; Laudage, *Priesterbild*, 157f., Schimmelpfennig, "Zölibat," 12f.

31. "Alio quoque tempore. . .omnes clericos Romae, qui post interdictum papae Leonis incontinentes extiterant. . .praecepisset exire." (see the preceding note under c). Bonizo of Sutri recorded for Leo's Roman synod of 1049 a decree "ut sacerdotes et levite et subdiaconi cum uxoribus non coeant" (*Liber ad amicum*, *MGH Libelli de lite* 1, p. 588). The passage and the differing interpretations are discussed by Giuseppe Fornasari, "S. Pier Damiani e lo 'sciopero liturgico,'" *Studi Medievali*, ser. 3, vol. 27 (1976): 815-32, here 818f., n. 10.

32. See n. 30, item b.

33. e.g. Ovidio Capitani, *Immunità vescovili ed ecclesiologia in età "Pregregoriana" e "Gregoriana"* (Spoleto, 1966), 144; the comment in Ryan, *Canonical Sources*, 102, is enlightening and also relevant to the discussion of the legislation of Pavia above. It is not certain at all that this is what contemporaries understood as *constitutum de castitate*. However, some such decree existed, for it was picked up in c.12 of the council of Melfi held by Pope Urban II in 1089: "Porro eos qui in subdiaconatu uxoribus vacare voluerint, ab omni sacro ordine removemus, officio atque beneficio ecclesiae carere decernimus. Quod si ab episcopo commoniti non se correxerint, principibus licentiam indulgemus, ut eorum feminas mancipent

servituri. Si vero episcopi consenserint eorum pravitatibus, ipsi officii interdictione mulctetus." (Mansi, *Amplissima Collectio*, vol. 19, col. 724). See now Robert Somerville, *Pope Urban II*, 256 for c.12.

34. See n. 30, item c.

35. For Stephen IX, see F. Kempf, *The Church in the Age of Feudalism* (as in n.11), 358f.

36. See n.30, item a with Ryan, *Canonical Sources*, no. 182, 94f.

37. Peter Landau, "Die Anklagemöglichkeit Untereordneter vom Dictatus Papae zum Dekret Gratians," in *Ministerium iustitiae: Festschrift für Heribert Heinemann*, ed. A. Gabriels and H. J. F. Reinhardt (Essen, 1985), 373-83; Wilfried Hartmann, "*Discipulus non est super magistrum* (Matth. 10,24)," in *Papsttum, Kirche und Recht im Mittelalter: Festschrift für Horst Fuhrmann*, ed. Hubert Mordek (Tübingen, 1991), 187-200. I do not accept Bonizo's attribution of these segments (*MGH Libelli de lite* 1, p. 589) because of the narrative context. See Ryan, *Canonical Sources*, no. 182, 95 and Fornasari, "Sciopero," 817-19 with detailed bibliography.

38. Contrast Barstow, *Married Priests*, 53 and 213 n.13.

39. Albert Werminghoff, "Die Beschlüsse des Aachener Concils im Jahre 816," IV: "Bruchstück aus den Verhandlungen der Lateransynode im Jahre 1059," *Neues Archiv der Gesellschaft für ältere deutsche Geschichtskunde* 27 (1902), here 669-75. See J. F. A. M. van Waesberghe, *De Akense Regels voor canonici en canonicae uit 816: een antwoord aan Hildebrand-Gregorius VII en zijn geestverwanten* (Assen. 1967).

40. Jasper, *Papstwahldedekret* (as in n. 21), pp. 34-46; see also U.-R. Blumenthal, "History and Tradition in Eleventh-Century Rome," *The Catholic Historical Review* 79 (1993): 185-96.

41. Damian letter no. 65 (ed. Reindel 2, pp. 228-247). The date of the legislation is still debated (Reindel 2, p. 230 and Dressler, *Petrus Damiani*, 130f., n. 221), but Jasper's arguments regarding Hildebrand's elevation to the rank of archdeacon as early as 1058 (*Papstwahldekret*, 39ff.) seem convincing.

42. Reindel, no. 31. See in addition to Reindel's annotation John Boswell, *Christianity, Social Tolerance and Homosexuality: Gay People in Western Europe from the Beginning of the Christian Era to the XIVth Century* (Chicago, 1980), 210-13 and Brundage, *Sex, Law*, 212ff.

43. Letter no. 65, Reindel 2, p. 242, line 2-5.

44. e.g. letter 65, Reindel 2, p. 231 and the following paragraphs. See Cinzio Violante, *La Pataria Milanese e la riforma ecclesiastica, I: Le premesse (1045-1057)*, (Rome, 1955), 190 n.1, for the strict limitations on Milanese attacks on the clergy imposed by Pope Alexander II, who had accompanied Damian on the 1059 legation when he was still bishop of Lucca. The council of 1059, while calling for a boycott (see above at n. 22) emphasized in c.10 that laymen were not allowed to judge clerics ("Ut cuiuslibet ordinis clericos laici non iudicent nec de aecclesiis eiciant;" *Const.* 1, no. 384, p. 548). Peter Damian himself, however, changed his mind and eventually supported a boycott, see letter 112, vol. 3, p. 262 quoted in no.30 as segment a); Barstow, *Married Priests*, 64.

45. H. E. J. Cowdrey, "The Papacy, the Patarenes and the Church of Milan," *Transactions of the Royal Historical Society*, 5th series, 18 (1968): 25-48; repr. In H. E. J. Cowdrey, *Popes, Monks and Crusaders* (London, 1984) as #V, Violante, *Pataria*; Hagen Keller, "Pataria und Stadtverfassung, Stadtgemeinde und Reform: Mailand im 'Investiturstreit,'" in *Investiturstreit und Reichsverfassung*, ed. Josef Fleckenstein (Sigmaringen, 1973), 321-50; Paolo Golinelli, *La Pataria: Lotte religiose e sociali nella Milano dell' XI secolo* (Milan, 1984) is a summary account with translations of the major sources in Italian.

46. *vulgus*: cf. R. I. Moore, "Family, Community and Cult on the Eve of the Gregorian Reform," *Transactions of the Royal Historical Society*, 5th series, 30 (1980): 49-69, esp. 50f. See also Monica Blöcker, "Volkszorn im frühen Mittelalter," *Francia* 13 (1985): 113-49.

47. Letter no. 61, Reindel 2, here p. 208.

48. See Cosimo D. Fonseca, "Arialdo," *Diz. biografico degli Italiani*, 4 (1962), 135-39 for relevant sources and bibliography and n.45 about. Peter

Damian, too, emphasized preaching after his conversion, see Hans Peter Lagua, *Tradition und Leitbilder bei dem Ravennater Reformer Petrus Damiani (1042-1052)* (Munich, 1976), esp. 113ff.

49. Violante, *Pataria*, 181f.

50. Landulfus Senior, *Mediolanensis historiae libri quator*, ed. A. Cutolo Muratori, 4,2 (1942-1950), book 3, c.5, p. 87: "Sub iureiurando constricti mutuo firmaverunt, quatenus sacerdotes omnes et levitas a die illa et deinceps uxorem habere non paterentur. . .;" Violante, *Pataria*, 186.

51. Andrea of Strumi, *Vita sancti Arialdi*, ed. Friedrich Baethgen, *MGH Scriptores*, 30,2 (1926-1934), 1047-1075, here c.19, p. 1063 or c.10, p. 1055; Violante, *Pataria*, 182. See Giovanni Miccoli, "Per la storia della Pataria Milanese," in *Chiesa Gregoriana* (Florence, 1966), 101-60, here 104f. for the characteristics of Andrea's account. For the technical meaning of *stuprum*, see Brundage, *Sex, Law*, 29.

52. Arnulf, *Gesta archiepiscoporum Mediolanensium*, ed. Ludwig C. Bethman and Wilhelm Wattenbach, *MGH Scriptores*, 8 (1848), 1-31, c. 11, p.19, indicates the content of Landulf's sermons.

53. Violante, *Pataria*, 182-86.

54. Violante, *Pataria*, 182-86.

55. Landulf, book 3, c.8, p. 91; Arnulf, book 3, c.12, p. 19; cf. also the late and second-hand account of Bonizo of Sutri, *Liber ad amicum*, ed. Ernst Dümmler, *MGH Libelli de lite* 1 (1891), 568-620, here 591f. Violante, *Pataria*, 188f.

56. See Arnulf, *Gesta*, book 3, c.12, pp. 19f. and the analysis of Violante, *Pataria*, 189-91. Despite the rubric, identical to the lost decree of Leo IX, there is no indication that the two are linked.

57. Violante, *Pataria*, 202,206, 208-12; cf. ibid., p. 210f. for the vague and largely untrustworthy account of Landulf. A "flight" of Archbishop Guido is not supported by independent evidence. For Anselm of Baggio see

Tilmann Schmidt, *Alexander II. (1061-1073) und die römische Reformgruppe seiner Zeit* (Stuttgart, 1977), here 61f.

58. Violante, *Pataria*, 196f.

59. For Alexander II and Milan see now Hartmann, *"Discipulus,"* 195f. with further literature.

60. Reg. 1,1* (=*Das Register Gregors VII.*, ed. Erich Caspar, *MGH Epistolae Selectae* II, 1-2 [Berlin, 1920-1923]); [cited below: Reg. followed by no. and p.].

61. Reg. 1.30; p. 50, lines 20ff.: "Sed est, unde fraternitatem tuam neglegentie merito argui putamus, quod de castitate clericorum, sicut nobis relatum est, preceptis Romane synodi, cui interfuisti, inobediens usque hodie videaris." In all quotes *e-caudata* is transcribed as *e*. Carl Mirbt, *Die Publizistik*, 266, refers to Reg. 1.27 and 1.28 as other examples, but Reg. 1.27 to Bishop Albert of Acqui requests support for Erlembald, the new leader of the Pataria, emphasizes simony. Reg. 1.28 to William of Pavia asks the bishop to fight generally against heresies and to recall his clergy to chastity (p. 45, line 38: ". . .clericos a turpis vite conversatione ad castitatem revocare").

62. Ibid., n.2. For the synods of Alexander II see F. J. Schmale, "Synoden Papst Alexanders II. (1061-1073): Anzahl, Termine, Entscheidungen," *Archivum Historiae Conciliorum* 11 (1979): 307-38.

63. Mirbt, *Die Publizistik*, 269.

64. Reg. 1.42 and 43.

65. Mariani Scotti, *Chronicon*, a. 1074: "papa. . .interdixit presbiteris, diaconus omnibusque clericis, uxores habere et omnino cum feminis habitare, nisi cum eis quas regula vel Nicena synodus concessit." *MGH SS*, 5, 560; Mirbt, *Die Publizistik*. 266 n. 5. The most recent discussion of the 1074 Lenten council is by Robert Somerville, "The councils of Gregory VII," *Studi Gregoriani* 13 (1989): 33-53, here 38f., 41-44; see also Giovanni Borino, "I decreti di Gregorio VII contro i simoniaci e i nicolaiti sono del sinodo quaresimale del 1074," *Studi Gregoriani* 6 (1959-1961): 277-95 and especially

Cowdrey, *Epistolae Vagantes*, 160f., all with further literature. I accept Cowdrey's dating of Gregory's letters to 1075 despite Christian Schneider, *Prophetisches Sacerdotium und heilsgeschichtliches Regnum im Dialog 1073-1077* (Munster, 1972), 79 n. 252 and 118 n. 365; see also I. S. Robinson, "Zur Arbeitsweise Bernolds von Constance und seines Kreises," *Deutsches Archiv* 34 (1978): 51-122, here 71 n. 71 and Rudolf Schieffer, *Die Entstehung des päpstlichen Investiturverbots für den deutschen König* (*MGH Schriften* 28; Stuttgart, 1981), 133 n. 121.

66. Otto Schumann, *Die päpstlichen Legaten in Deutschland zur Zeit Heinrichs IV. und Heinrichs V. (1056-1125)* (1912), 277-95; Schneider, *Sacerdotium* (as in n. 65), 78-85.

67. Reg. 2.52a; Reg. 2.45; Reg. 2.62; Reg. 2.67; Reg. 2.68 and Reg. 3.4. Cowdrey, nos. 6, 7, 8, 9, 10 and 11; see ibid., 160f. for the date of these items.

68. Reg. 2.66 to Bishop Burkhard of Halberstadt, eps. line 19f.: " . . .Sed neque propterea has rursus de eadem re tibi litteras superfluum iudicavimus. . . " Somerville, "Councils," 43 n. 46, assumes that Reg. 2.62 (P. F. Kehr, *Italia Pontificia 7: Venetia et Historia pars 1: Provincia Aquileiensis* (Berlin, 1923), 31, no. 64) also records the decisions of 1074. The letter is dated March 23, 1075. Palm Sunday fell on March 29 and Easter on April 5. Gregory wrote, therefore, during Lent 1075 and the reference to "decreta in peracto concilio preterite quadragesime" could be, but need not be, to Lent 1074: ". . .decrevimus enim, quod, si quis eorum ordinum, qui sacris altaribus administrant, presbyter scilicet diaconus et subdiaconus, uxorem vel concubinam habet, nisi illis omnino dimissis dignam penitentiam agant, sacris altaribus penitus administrare desistant nec aliquo ecclesie beneficio ulterius potiantur sive potitis fruantur. . . ."

69. Schieffer, *Entstehung*, esp. 132-76; cf. Laudage, *Priesterbild*, 260ff. and Uta-Renate Blumenthal, *The Investiture Controversy: Church and Monarchy from the Ninth to the Twelfth Century* (Philadelphia, 1988), 120f. Arnulf, *Gesta*, lib. 4, c. 7, p. 27, lines 18-20; Hans-Eberhard Hilbert, "Zum ersten Investiturverbot nach Arnulf von Mailand," *Deutsches Archiv* 43 (1987): 185ff.

70. Schieffer, *Entstehung*, 179 with literature.

71. Cowdrey no. 6, JL 4931; the translation is that of Somerville, "Councils," 41f. Among the 1075 texts transmitted in the register Reg. 2.66 to Bishop Burkhard of Halberstadt includes the same passage (p. 222, line 20ff.). Cf. n. 68 above.

72. Gregory VII dispatched the letter under seal to back up Siegfried's efforts: ". . .letter. . .bearing our seal, so that by the sanction of its authority you might the more safely and boldly obey our command and drive out from the sanctuary of the Lord the simoniac heresy and the foul defilement of polluting lust" (trans. Cowdrey, 15). Thus it may be considered official and is cited here.

73. e.g., See Cowdrey nos. 11, 16, 32 and 41. Bishop Cunibert of Turin, the recipient of Damian's famous letter 112 (ed. Reindel as in n. 6), was suspended at the council of 1075 (Reg. 2.52a, p. 197, line 1), but the issue was Cunibert's quarrel with the abbey of S. Michele della Chiusa, not nicolaitism.

74. I. S. Robinson, *Authority and Resistance in the Investiture Contest: The Polemical Literature of the Late Eleventh Century* (New York, 1978), 165; Cowdrey, *Epistolae Vagantes*, p. XXV, with ref. to no. 7 (JL 4932) and no. 8 (JL 4933). For an account of the synod, see also Bernold of Constance, *Chronicon* (*MGH SS* 5), 430f.

75. See Cowdrey no. 6 to Siegfried of Mainz, for example (here pp. 14-15). The same instructions were sent to Bishop Werner of Magdeburg (ibid., no. 7), Bishop Burkhard of Halberstadt (Reg. 2.66) and Archbishop Anno of Cologne (Reg. 2.67).

76. See n. 67 above.

77. Reg. 2.62 (p. 217, line 18ff.); "Decrevimus enim, quod si quis eorum ordinum scilicet diaconus et subdiaconus, uxorem vel concubinam habet, nisi illis omnino dimissis dignam penitentiam agant, sacris altaribus penitus administrare desistant nec aliquo ecclesie beneficio ulterius potiantur sive potitis fruantur." The letter omits any reference to the laity. The same omission is found in Reg. 2.67 to Anno of Cologne and Reg. 2.68 to Wezilo

of Magdeburg. Anno and Wezilo are urged to inculcate the chastity of the clergy through preaching.

78. Reg. 2.67, p. 224, line 1ff. Mirbt, *Die Publizistik*, 269.

79. Reg. 2.45, esp. p. 184, line 1ff. and line 25. Caspar points out in the annotation that the content of this clause is equivalent to the passage "Statuimus etiam. . ." translated in the text above.

80. See the preceding note.

81. Reg. 2, 55a, p. 207:"Quod illius precepto et licentia subiectis liceat accusare." Landau, "Anklagemöglichkeit," 374, points out the limitation imposed through the reference to papal permission. This emphasis is further increased in the letters through the papal insistence on obedience.

82. Cf. for Gregory's use of this approach in connection with simony in Germany and northern Italy, Schieffer, "*Spirituales Latrones*," 19-60, here 45f., 51.

83. Josef Fleckenstein, "Heinrich IV und der deutsche Episkopat in den Anfängen des Investiturstreits," in *Adel und Kirche; Festschrift fur Gerd Tellenbach*, ed. J. Fleckenstein and K. Schmid (Freiburg, 1968), 221-36, here 229f.; Helmut Maurer, Die Konstanzer Bürgerschaft im Investiturstreit," in *Investiturstreit und Reichsverfassung* (Konstanzer Arbeitskreis, Vorträge und Forschungen 17; Siegmaringen, 1973), 363-71, here 366.

84. Cowdrey no. 8, pp. 16ff. with the typical *Statuimus* passage, p. 18f. Cf. Reg. 2.60 written in a different context.

85. Robinson, *Authority and Resistance*, 166f.

86. Cowdrey no. 9, here p. 21 in Professor Cowdrey's translation.

87. Paul Hinschius, *Decretales Pseudo-Isidorianae* (Leipzig, 1863; repr. Aelen, 1963), 619 c. 2.

88. We do not know which passages of Gregory I the pope had in mind. Mirbt, *Die Publizistik*, discusses Reg. 1.24 (Feb. 591) and Reg. 1.42

(March 591), pp. 285f. and also p. 296. Cf. the indices found in the three vols. of the *MGH* edition of the *Libelli de lite*.

89. Cf. Horst Furhmann, "Das Reformpapsttum und die Rechtswissenschaft," in *Investitutrstreit und Reichsverfassung*, 175-203.

90. Robinson, *Authority and Resistance*, 165.

91. Cowdrey, no. 10, here p. 25.

92. Reg. 3.10a and 7.14a.

93. Maurer, "Die Konstanzer Bürgerschaft," 366.

94. See also Cowdrey no. 11, p. 26f, to the clergy and laity of Germany, dated 1075. The similarities to the arguments of the encyclical, Cowdrey no. 32, pp. 84ff., dated 1079, are striking. Both items, however, are difficult to date.

95. Mirbt, *Die Publizistik*, 252-55; cf. in general, Barstow, *Married Priests*, 68f. and her chapter 3. For Cambrai, see Gregory VII, Reg. 4.20.

96. Cowdrey no. 41. p. 102f. The letter is dated late 1080, but that date seems uncertain. Reg. 7.16 of March 26, 1080, threatened Hubert with a personal interdict and refused him apostolic greetings. Nothing is known of a reconciliation with Hugh of Die, Gregory's legate in France between March and December 1080.

97. Reg. 4.10. See also n. 66.

98. Reg. 4.11, p. 311, line 5-7.

99. Refutation of obedience, ed. Carl Erdmann, *Die Briefe Heinrichs IV.* (Leipzig, 1937), appendix A, pp. 65-68, here p. 66: ". . .flammamque discordie, quam in Romana ecclesia diris factionibus excitasti, per omnes ecclesias Italie Germanie Gallie et Hispanie furiali dementia sparsisti. Sublata enim, quantum in te fuit, omni potestate ab episcopis. . .omnique rerum ecclesiasticarum administratione plebeio furori per te attributa. . . ."

100. See above at n. 34 and 40.

101. Reg. 4.20 to Bishop Josfred of Paris who is instructed to publicize these decrees throughout France, here p. 328f.

102. Reg. 6.5b, here p. 405f. In an encyclical letter, addressed to the faithful of Italy and Germany, Gregory expelled such clergy from the church until they relented and did penance. Should they persevere in their sin, nobody should dare to attend their offices. The tentative date of 1079 suggested most recently by Cowdrey, *Epistolae vagantes*, no. 32, pp. 84ff., would indicate a return to popular boycott. But the date is uncertain and 1075 would appear more likely.

103. See John Gilchrist, "The Reception of Pope Gregory VII into the Canon Law (1073-1141)," *Zeitschrift der Savigny Stiftung für Rechtsgeschichte*, Kanonistische Abteilung 56 (1973), 35ff., here 71 and table II under 6.5b, cap. 12.

104. Reg. 4.20, p. 328, lines 22ff.: "Item elatum nobis est Cameracenses hominem quendam flammis tradidisse, eo quod symoniacos et presbyteros fornicatores missas non debere celebrare et, quod illorum officium minime suscipiendum foret, dicere ausus fuerit." The letter is dated March 25, 1077. See further R. I. Moore, *The Origins of European Dissent* (London, 1977), 35-41 and 62f.

105. Reg. 9.5, here p. 580, lines 20ff.

106. Mirbt, *Die Publizistik*, 250-59. See now Horst Furhmann, *Überall ist Mittelalter: Von der Geenwart einer vergangenen Zeit* (Munich, 1996), 150-71, esp. 162ff.

107. Reg. 2.30.

108. For Bernold's arguments in defense of the papal prohibition see especially Mirbt, *Die Publizistik*, 284ff. and Robinson, *Authority and Resistance*, 165-69.

109. *Conciliorum Oecumenicorum Decreta*, ed. J. Alberigo et al. (Bologna, 1973), 198, c. 7.

Pope Gregory VII and the Chastity of the Clergy

H. E. J. Cowdrey

Throughout the eleventh century, church reformers from all backgrounds whether laymen, monks, or members of the secular clergy agreed with Pope Gregory VII (1073-1085) in aspiring to extirpate the two "heresies" of simony—the trafficking through money, flattery, or services in ecclesiastical orders and offices, and clerical unchastity—active sexual relationships, whether involving a form of matrimony or not, as engaged in by those in the major orders (including bishops), deacons, or subdeacons.[1] So far as the popes were concerned, measures against them were taken with fresh zeal between the Emperor Henry III's reforming expedition to Rome in 1046 and Archdeacon Hildebrand's succession to the chair of St. Peter as Gregory VII over a quarter of a century later. For example, Pope Leo IX (1049-54) at his Roman synod after Easter 1049 forbade those in major orders to have sexual relations with their wives; a year later, he went so far as to command all clergy and laity to abstain from communion with priests and deacons who were guilty of fornication. At one or other of these synods, he further decreed that priests' harlots within the walls of Rome should be made serfs (*ancillae*) of the Lateran palace. Away from Rome, at his synod of Mainz in October 1049, Leo proscribed "the simoniac heresy and the detestable marriage of priests."[2] Writing in 1051 to the cathedral canons at Lucca, Leo asserted the value of a canonical life with the community of property as a salutary alternative to the moral scandal and material wastefulness of a married clergy.[3] Pope Nicholas II (1059-61) also legislated vigorously at his Roman synod in April 1059. No one might hear the mass of a priest who was known to have a concubine or a woman improperly living with him (*subintroductam mulierem*).⁴ All in major orders who had taken or retained a concubine since Leo IX's ruling were banished from the sanctuary, while to those who duly obeyed Leo's injunction to chastity, Leo commended an apostolic common life both as a daily practice and as a spiritual ideal. Nicholas included his requirements about clerical chastity in an encyclical, *Vigilantia universalis regiminis*, which his successor Alexander II (1061-73) reissued, probably after his own Roman synod in 1063.⁵

Hildebrand witnessed this papal campaign at first hand;⁶ he will also have been familiar with such arguments for clerical chastity as were propagated by two cardinal-bishops: Humbert, formerly a monk of the Lotharingian monastery of Moyenmoutier who from 1050 to 1061 was cardinal-bishop of Silva Candida, and the hermit-monk of Fonteavellana, Peter Damiani, who from 1057 to 1072 was cardinal-bishop of Ostia. Humbert wrote in connection with his legatine journey of 1054 to Constantinople; he replied to a tract by a Studite monk, Nicetas, who attacked the western practice of prohibiting and, if necessary, dissolving the marriages of priests. Humbert's furious onslaught affirmed that, in the Roman church, marriage was permitted to those in minor orders, but those promoted to the subdiaconate or above must thereafter observe perpetual continence. He deprecated the eastern custom of ordaining to the generality of the priesthood only those who were married; it was unseemly that new husbands made weak by recent sexual delight should handle the immaculate body of Christ and that they should quickly return their consecrated hands to caressing the bodies of women. The bull of excommunication that Humbert left on the altar of Sancta Sophia included a reference to the error of the Byzantines in permitting and defending the carnal marriages of those who minister at the holy altar.⁷

In a number of his letters, Peter Damiani concerned himself with the need for absolute continence in all who were in major orders in the west and especially Italy.⁸ He did not spare the bishops from his strictures;⁹ all in authority—popes, bishops, and lay rulers like Countess Adelaide of Turin—were to eradicate fornication. All sexual activity was included in this term; for the women of the clergy could not legally marry and were, therefore, concubines or whores. No one might hear the mass of a priest, the gospel read by a deacon, or the epistle read by a subdeacon whom he knew to consort with women. Peter repeatedly gave reasons of cultic purity for such a prohibition: because Christ's natural body was formed in the temple of a virgin's womb, he looks to his ministers nowadays to be continent and clean in the presence of his sacramental body; with regard to bishops in particular, hands that confer the Holy Spirit should not touch the genitals of harlots. Peter looked for moral, as well as cultic, purity in the clergy but this tended to be the subject of separate letters to those of exemplary life.[10]

If Hildebrand lived in the midst of such zeal for clerical chastity at Rome, he was also acquainted at first hand with the popular movement of the Patarenes which, from the mid-1050s, gathered strength in Lombardy and especially at Milan.[11] At first resisting clerical incontinence and soon also simony, the Patarene leaders proclaimed that only clerks of pure and humble life were true ministers of Christ. The sacraments of the rest were without benefit: one spokesman said that their sacrifices were like dogs' dung while their churches were stables for horses.[12] The Patarenes, therefore, proclaimed a kind of lay strike against offending clergy. The faithful were to boycott their churches; Milanese clerks were forced to sign a bond promising chastity; if they were impenitent, their houses were ransacked; access to the altar was barred; those who tried to approach the altar were dragged away.[13] The Patarene leader Ariald also established a *canonica* or center of common life and worship, where exemplary clergy might minister.[14] Both before and after he became pope, Hildebrand was a strong supporter of the Patarenes and, especially, of the knight Erlembald, their most militant leader.[15]

In view of both of this support for the Patarenes and of the concern at Rome on the part of the popes and others between 1046 and 1073 to commend and to enforce clerical chastity, the distribution by date of reference to it in surviving letters of Gregory VII is surprising. It is as follows:[16]

Year	Reg.	Epp. vag.	Total
1073	1.27, 28, 30	-	3
1074	1.77, 2.10, 11, 25, 29, 30	-	6
1075	2.45, 47, 55, 61, 62, 66, 67, 68, 3.3, 4	6, 7, 8, 9, 10, 11	16

1076	4.10, 11	16	3
1077	4.20	-	1
1078	5.18	-	1
1079	-	32	1
1080	-	41	1
1081	9.5	-	1

No less remarkable is the distribution of regions with which Gregory's letters were concerned:

Region	*Reg.*	*Epp. vag.*	Total
Germany	1.30, 2.10,11, 25, 29, 30, 45, 61, 66, 67, 68, 3.3, 4, 5.18	6, 7, 8, 9, 10, 11, 58	21
Germany and the kingdom of Italy	-	32	1
The kingdom of Italy	1.27, 28, 77, 2.47, 55, 62	-	6
France (excluding Normandy)	4.10, 11, 20, 9.5	41	5
The Anglo-Norman kingdom	-	16	1

Even when allowance is made for possible gaps in the registration or survival of letters, it is apparent that, so far as his own *acta* are concerned, Gregory concentrated heavily on the German and Italian kingdoms of Henry IV. Even so, most of his surviving letters date from the rather less than two years between his Lent synod at Rome in early March 1074 and the worsening of relations between pope and king which led, in February 1076, to Gregory's first sentence of deposition and excommunication. Otherwise put, the promotion of clerical chastity was at the forefront of Gregory's direct personal attention only during the short period that his attention was not diverted by the struggle of pope and king in Germany or by matters related to it. Thus, his campaign against clerical celibacy was slow to start. For almost the first year of his pontificate, he referred to it only in two letters of the same date to Italian bishops, Albert, bishop-elect of Acqui and Bishop William of Pavia, whom he urged to support his own long-standing ally, Erlembald of Milan.[17] Otherwise, his sole reference was in a letter to one of Gebhard's clerks having come to Gregory in Capua.[18] Gregory's letters leave no doubt of his profound and sustained commitment to strive against clerical fornication. But he spent most of the second half of 1073 in South Italy in an endeavor to compose the affairs of the papacy's Norman allies whose loyalty mattered when Henry IV's disposition was uncertain. From 1076, Gregory was usually too much preoccupied by his contest with Henry IV for him to give his mind strenuously to the enforcement of clerical chastity; after his second excommunication and deposition of Henry in 1080, the subject almost completely vanished from his letters.

Gregory passed decrees about clerical chastity at his Lent synods of 1074 and 1075. His campaign in these years was his major endeavor to enforce it. It built up gradually. The sole report of the synod of 1074 is, significantly, from Germany: the Mainz recluse, Marianus Scottus, recorded that Gregory forbade priests, deacons, and all clerks to have wives or at all to live with women, save those "whom the Rule or the Nicene synod allowed."[19] Marianus wrote of no sanctions that Gregory may have imposed. In 1074, Gregory dispatched to Germany as legates the cardinal-bishops Gerald of Ostia and Hubert of Palestrina. After Easter, they released Henry IV from the excommunication that he had incurred by associating with excommunicated counselors. They were also commissioned to teach obedience to the strict rule of clerical chastity.[20] The legates encountered resistance from the German bishops and were unable to hold a synod. But upon returning to Rome, they added their testimony to that of the Empress-mother Agnes that Henry was minded to cooperate in eradicating simony and in remedying "the chronic disease of the fornication of the clergy."[21]

Hitherto in 1074, Gregory's letters to Germany about clerical fornication had been occasional. There were none before October. Then he ordered Archbishop Udo of Trier to investitgate the charges of the cathedral clergy of Toul that their bishop, Pibo, had a record of simony and of living with a woman in fornication. Archbishop Udo and his colleagues found the charges to be groundless, and Udo pleaded with Gregory never again to be given a similar commission.[22] The matter did nothing to commend papal intervention to the German bishops. Also in October, a German count and his wife, almost certainly Count Albert of Calw and his wife Wiltrud, received a letter from Gregory in which he complained of the slackness of the German bishops in enforcing the laws of God; as a consequence, the clergy were guilty of many transgressions, including sexual uncleanness. Gregory exhorted his lay correspondents to stand fast in the truth and constancy of faith; they were to cleave to what the apostolic see had decreed about bishops and priests who were simoniacal or who lay in fornication.[23] Gregory named no sanctions, but, if he was referring to the decree of Leo IX, Nicholas II, and Alexander II, the implication was that godly laity should avoid the ministrations of sinful clergy. In November, Gregory wrote to Archbishop Anno of Cologne about a tithe dispute. He added an exhortation to Anno to proclaim in his own diocese and in those of his suffragans the duty of all priests, deacons, and subdeacons to live chastely.[24] Once again, he added no sanctions against offending clergy, but his sense of the regency of the matter was clear.

During the twelve months or so that followed, three reasons can be suggested to explain why Gregory should have directed a much more sustained campaign in Germany and, to a lesser extent, in the kingdom of Italy,[25] against simony and clerical fornication. First, it should be remembered that Gregory enjoyed the one period of, as he supposed, good relations with Henry IV that occurred during his pontificate. He was increasingly persuaded of Henry's goodwill and cooperation. The exigencies of the Saxon war in Germany compelled Henry to profess docility. Gregory, for his part, hoped soon to welcome Henry to Rome for imperial coronation and to find him willing to deserve coronation by furthering his purposes.[26] Secondly, Gregory could not afford to leave unheeded the failure of his legates of 1074 to make headway with the reform of the besetting evils of the German church.[27] Thirdly, as a consequence, Gregory was determined to call to active obedience the German episcopate which, in the latter months of 1074, was showing resistance to his aspirations and methods for the reform of the church.[28] Except that, in 1075, he sent no more legates, he now sought to use every means at his disposal to strive against simony and clerical fornication.

Even so, the terms of Gregory's decree against clerical unchastity at his Lent synod of 1075 are far from certain. The brief record of the synod in the Register does not give them,[29] and they seem to have been differently formulated for Italian and German destinations. The principal sources are Gregory's letters. Writing on 23 March to the Italian metropolitan Sigehard of Aquileia, Gregory expressed himself relatively mildly. A priest, deacon, or subdeacon who had a wife or concubine (*uxorem vel concubinam*—this is one of only two instances in Gregory's letters of the word *uxor* being unequivocally conceded to a clerk's partner) must altogether put her away and do penance; the refractory must cease from ministering at that altar, and henceforth they might not receive or enjoy the fruits of an ecclesiastical benefice. Such ecclesiastical sanctions as brought to bear by the metropolitan or his suffragans were the only ones invoked. There was no word of coercive action on the part of the laity.[30] But in undated but probably almost contemporary letters to the German archbishops Siegfried of Metz and Werner of Magdeburg, Gregory required, without distinguishing wives from other women, that "all who were guilty of the crime of fornication" must cease from service at the altar. As his prime sanction against those who disobeyed, Gregory prescribed that the people should in no way accept their ministrations, "so that those who are not corrected from the love of God and the honor of their office may be brought to their senses by the shame of the world and the reproof of the people (*verecundia saeculi et obiurgatione populi resipiscant*)." The archbishops were also to exercise their own pastoral zeal.[31] On 29 May, and so six days after his mild letter to the archbishop of Aquileia, Gregory wrote of his measures against offending German clergy in similar terms; if, after episcopal admonitions, they did not repent, the laity should altogether shun their ministrations.[32] To Germany, Gregory wrote as though his synod had, like those of Nicholas II and Alexander II, called for at least a passive boycott by the laity of the ministrations of incontinent clergy.

Following his letter to Anno of Cologne in November 1074,[33] it was principally to German archbishops—Sigehard of Aquileia is the only known exception—that Gregory looked for support, both in their dioceses and in their provinces, against the "heresies" of simony and clerical fornication. First and foremost, he looked to the senior German metropolitan, Archbishop Siegfried of Mainz. At the beginning of December 1074, he summoned him with his suffragans urgently to come to Rome for his next Lent synod. By way of preparation, he was searchingly to investigate how his suffragans had come by their bishoprics and how they had lived since acquiring them (*introitum et conversationem predictorum episcoporum diligentissime inquiras*), and he was to send an advance report to Gregory; for Gregory knew that some of their reputations were not praiseworthy.[34] Siegfried excused his own attendance on grounds of ill-health. He promised obedience to God and to Gregory in the matters of clerical chastity and simony, but he pleaded with Gregory to exercise mildness and discretion.[35] But, after the Lent synod, Gregory wrote to Siegfried that the Roman decree (*hoc decretum*), of which he seems to have circulated a copy, must be zealously taught to the whole clergy and inviolably obeyed by them.[36] Archbishop Werner of Magdeburg, and perhaps other archbishops, received an identical letter.[37] On 29 March, Gregory again wrote to Archbishop Werner, exhorting him to emulate Joshua of old:

> By apostolic authority we enjoin and command
> you that, in order to preach and the more zealously
> inculcate the chastity of the clergy, you strenuously
> and urgently sound upon the priestly trumpet, until
> you shatter and raze the wall of Jericho, that is, the
> works of rebellion and the pollution of filthy lust.[38]

On the same day, he wrote again to Archbishop Anno of Cologne, calling upon him and his suffragans to gird themselves more strongly to secure the chastity of the clergy; Anno should summon a provincial synod at which he should resolutely preach it.[39]

It was not only to the German metropolitans that Gregory in 1075 addressed his letters about clerical unchastity. Again on 29 March, he wrote to Bishop Burchard II of Halberstadt with a view to confirming the bishop's assiduousness in favoring chaste and religious clerks as fellow-workers in his task. As for the lewd and incontinent, they should either be offered fatherly correction or, if they were incorrigible, they should be excluded from the holy altars; unless they duly repented, the laity should in no wise hear their ministrations.[40] If Gregory showed in the case of Burchard how he encouraged a bishop whom he thought to be properly active, his dealings with the diocese of Constance reveal his approach to one whom he deemed recalcitrant. Its bishop, Otto, did not come to the Lent synod of 1075; Gregory was quick to send him individual notice of his measure against simony and clerical fornication, which he was urged to uproot from his diocese. Later in the year, Gregory sent Otto a letter of stern rebuke for not only conniving at the retention by clerks of their women (*mulierculae*) but also for allowing them to begin new relationships. Gregory summoned Otto to account for himself at the Lent synod of 1076. He also wrote to the clergy and laity of his diocese; he explained his own position and instructed them, if the bishop persisted in his obduracy, to show him neither respect nor obedience.[41]

So far as the German laity are concerned, Gregory sought to incite all ranks to resist unchaste clerks by words and by actions. For much of 1075, Gregory was persuaded of King Henry IV's willing cooperation. He rejoiced about it in December 1074;[42] in July 1075, he included amongst Henry's supposed virtues his willing purpose effectively to promote the chastity that became the clergy as servants of God.[43] At the beginning of the year, he had addressed the South German dukes, Rudolf of Swabia, Berthold of Carinthia, and Welf of Bavaria, with a view to stimulating all-out lay action. He castigated the weakness of the German archbishops and bishops in allowing the ministrations of clerks guilty of simony and fornication and in disregarding the sanctions imposed by successive popes since Leo IX. Whatever the bishops might or might not say, Gregory therefore looked to the dukes as to other reliable laity on no account to accept the ministrations of offending clerks. Their resistance was to go further than merely boycotting them. Under the sanction of obedience, they were to strive to publish and to argue for papal measures both in the king's court and in other places and assemblies in the German kingdom. They were to exclude offending clerks from participating in the holy mysteries, "even by force should it prove necessary (*etiam vi si opportuerit*)." This phrase was an incitement to the laity to use such active force as was familiar in Italy but as had not hitherto been called for in Germany. Gregory laid down that, should this new departure meet with the objection that it was not the laity's business to act in such a way, the reply should be that the objectors should not obstruct the dukes' and the people's salvation; let the objectors come and dispute with Gregory at Rome about the obedience that he was imposing upon the laity.[44]

By early in 1075, Gregory was thus seeking to mount a two-pronged attack in Germany upon simony and clerical unchastity—an attack by the archbishops and bishops acting through their synods, and an attack by the laity both great and small acting through the king's court and their own assemblies. At much the same time, Gregory was also seizing his opportunities to enlist Italian laity in the same cause. The laity of the county of Chiusi were to take all necessary steps to expel from the cathedral a provost guilty of perjury and notorious fornication and to do what was necessary to renew the pristine state of their church.[45] The people of Lodi, on the other hand, were to help their exemplary bishop, Opizo, to extirpate simony and clerical fornication from his diocese and to do so with all their strength (*totis viribus*).[46]

By the end of 1075, Gregory was urging the clergy and laity of the kingdom of Germany not to obey bishops who continued to condone or to ignore clerical fornication. The faithful were told neither to obey such bishops or to follow their precepts.[47] In the same year, the Augsburg Annals, a source unfriendly to Gregory, commented on the wandering preachers who were everywhere sowing discord as well as on the preposterous papal decree that clerical continence should be enforced through laymen.[48] A letter such as Gregory's to all clergy and laity reads like his sanction for such a campaign.

The events of the winter of 1075-76, which included the German and Lombard bishops' renunciation of obedience to Gregory followed by Gregory's deposition and excommunication of King Henry IV, brought to an abrupt end Gregory's writing of letters to Germany and Italy about clerical chastity. In letters to these kingdoms, the subject reappears only in a brief letter, probably early in 1079. It is addressed to "all who show due obedience to St. Peter throughout the whole kingdom of Italy and of the Germans"; it forbade all priests, deacons, and subdeacons who were guilty of the crime of fornication entry to the church until they repented and mended their ways, while the laity were not to hear their offices.[49] The letter seems to have been associated with Gregory's endeavor at his Lateran synods of 1078-80 to promote the moral improvement of the Christian life; in November of 1078, a decree required that a bishop who connived at clerical fornication or who failed to punish it should himself be suspended.[50] At this stage, Gregory seems to have demanded of the laity only abstention from the ministration of offending clergy, not the active and forcible resistance which he countenanced in his letter to the South German dukes. His restraint may have been deliberate, for after the election of Rudolf of Swabia in 1077 as anti-king, he was disturbed by the ravages and the perils of civil strife in Germany.[51] He may have recoiled from adding to it by fomenting aggressive action against offending clergy.

Not until November 1076 did Gregory refer in letters relating to France to the subject of clerical fornication; it was brought to his attention by reports of controversy in Flanders about whether or not clerks who persisted in fornication might celebrate mass. Gregory wrote letters on the same day to Countess Adela and to her son Count Robert I le Frison in which he insisted that they might not do so but that they should be expelled from the sanctuary until they had duly repented; where possible, they should be replaced by priests who lived chastely. Gregory called upon the count to be diligent in resisting clerical fornication and simony, but he employed no phrases that implied the use of physical violence.[52] A letter of 1080 to Bishop Hubert of Thérouanne shows Gregory reacting to a report of a Flemish bishop's consenting to clerical fornication.[53]

As concerns France more widely, only once do Gregory's letters record a general initiative against clerical fornication. In March 1077, and so just before the full deployment of the authority of Gregory's papal vicars in France, Bishops Hugh of Die and Amatus of Oloron, Gregory entrusted Bishop Josfred of Paris with a number of commissions on his behalf. At the end of this letter, he urgently called upon Josfred to urge bishops throughout France to act as he had required German bishops to act after his Lent synod of 1075. The bishops were altogether to prohibit from ministering at the altar priests who would not desist from fornication, while Josfred himself was not to desist from publishing this prohibition in every place and assembly. If Josfred found the bishops to be lukewarm or if errant clerks were rebellious, he was to forbid the whole people from receiving their ministrations until they were shamed into amendment of life or compelled to return to a life of chastity (*ad castitatem religiose continentie redire cogantur*).[54] This phrase carries more than a hint that the laity should not only boycott their ministrations but should proceed to physical coercion. It is surprising that, two months later when Gregory sent Bishop Hugh of Die his first major agenda in French affairs, he made no mention of clerical fornication.[55]

In letters involving the Anglo-Norman kingdom, Gregory's references were occasional and in reaction to circumstances. In 1076, Gregory sought the cooperation of King William I to secure the expulsion from the Breton see of Dol of Bishop Juhel, whose offenses included marriage and the alienation of church property in order to provide his daughters with dowries.[56] In 1081, Gregory instructed his legates Hugh of Die and Amatus of Oloron to be restrained in their dealings with the king whom Gregory praised, amongst other things, for compelling priests under oath to separate from their wives (*uxores*); Gregory may have had in mind the canons of the council of Lillebonne (1080) which William had held.[57]

The limits of time and place within which Gregory wrote in his surviving letters about clerical chastity are thus surprisingly narrow. But the concern about it amongst reformers everywhere and Gregory's own zeal to enforce it, not least in his letter of 1077 to Bishop Josfred of Paris, make it more than unlikely that he ceased to work for it. The contest between *sacerdotium* and *regnum* of which his dealings with the German monarchy were an expression brought other business to the forefront of Gregory's own attention. But the legates and papal vicars of whom he made increasing use had a responsibility for ensuring that the momentum of Gregory's drive was maintained. Three examples may be given by way of illustration.

First, between 1077 and 1079, the Roman subdeacon Bernard and Abbot Bernard of Saint-Victor of Marseilles served as Gregory's legates in Germany. Their principal concern was with the high matter of the German kingdom, and Gregory's letters to them said nothing of clerical chastity. Yet they were concerned to promote it. In 1077, they held an assembly at Constance to which Bishop Otto had returned and had exceeded the limited powers that were allowed him. The legates took the opportunity to condemn the simony and the clerical fornication that were rampant in the diocese according to the terms of Gregory's synodal ruling. They insisted that no Christian should receive the ministrations of clerks who had been condemned for incontinence.[58]

Secondly, in France and northern Spain, Bishops Hugh of Die and Amatus of Oloron became widely active as papal vicars from this time and they held a number of legatine councils. The few records of the canons that were enacted make clear their zeal to enforce clerical chastity. At Poitiers in 1078, Hugh decreed that sons of priests and others born in fornication might not be admitted to holy orders or become monks and regular canons. No deacon, priest, or subdeacon was to have a concubine or to have under his roof any woman who might give rise to suspicion of evil; whoever knowingly heard the mass of an offending priest was to be deemed excommunicate.[59] At Gerona in the same year, Amatus ruled that, if any clerk henceforth married or took a concubine, both his orders and his office would be in jeopardy; he must withdraw from the clergy until he had done canonical satisfaction.[60] A letter of 1081 from Gregory to the two legates referred to "many knights" who had won their favor by coercing fornicating and simoniacal clergy.[61] The letter confirms the indication in Gregory's letter to Bishop Josfred of Paris that, whatever restraint he may have adopted in Germany, in France Gregory continued to countenance, if not call for, the bringing to bear of lay violence against offending clergy, and that his papal vicars undertook a militant campaign.

Thirdly, one of Gregory's staunchest supporters in south Germany was Bishop Altmann of Passau (1065-91) who, by 1081, was Gregory's papal vicar in that region. He was greatly concerned to implement Gregory's requirements of the clergy, especially their chastity.[62] He loyally, and in face of bitter opposition, proclaimed in his diocese Gregory's decree of 1075.[63] He wrote to Gregory for advice about the ecclesiastical position of clerks who had offended.[64] But he was remembered as one whose approach was by no means only negative; it was said of him that as in some places he destroyed the service of the devil, so in others he established the service of Christ.[65] Throughout his episcopate, he did so by establishing houses of regular canons which at once set a standard of clerical life for others to follow and provided places of refuge and society for those who came under persecution. During and after Gregory's pontificate, such houses bore continual witness to his demands on the clergy. It was a Bavarian regular canon, Paul of Bernried, who c. 1128 wrote a Life of Gregory which testified to and applauded his measures in Germany against simony and clerical fornication.[66]

These three examples show how, when Gregory himself was diverted by events from interventions to promote the chastity of the clergy, his legates and papal vicars, as well as other agents, maintained the impetus that he began in 1074 and 1075.

A final aspect of Gregory's concern for clerical chastity calls for comment. By contrast with the writings of Cardinal Humbert,[67] Gregory made no reference whatsoever to the custom of marriage amongst the parish clergy of the eastern churches. He did not mention it when writing about points of difference between Latins and Greeks; in view of his tolerance, though not approval, of the Greeks' use of leavened bread in the Eucharist as well as of his genuine desire to promote better relations, it is probably that his silence is a deliberate one.[68] Certainly, in this as in other matters, he was far from being a disciple of Cardinal Humbert.

Such, in summary, was the course of Gregory's actions, on his own part and through papal legates and vicars, to promote the chastity of the clergy. In the light of this evidence, it is possible to investigate Gregory's reasons for so strenuously acting to achieve it.

Undoubtedly, one of his reasons was his conception of the need for cultic purity in those who ministered at the altar. He said as much in 1076 in his letter to Count Robert of Flanders after he received reports of priests in his county who engaged in fornication but nevertheless when singing mass handled the body and blood of Christ. He said that such priests paid no heed to the great insanity and crime of at one and the same time handling the body of a harlot and the body of Christ.[69] Yet, by contrast with the emphasis laid upon this argument by Cardinals Humbert and Peter Damiani, this is the sole occurrence of it in Gregory's letters. Characteristically, he used emotive phrases of a general kind, such as "a base manner of life (*turpis vite conversatio*)," "the pollutions of filthy lust (*sordide libidinis pollutiones*)," or "the foul pollution of lustful contagion (*feda libidinosae contagionis pollutio*)."[70] Gregory also applied such language to simony. It, too, was a "contagion (*contagium*)."[71] He bracketed together "these detestable plagues—the simoniac heresy and the fornication of ministers of the sacred altar."[72] Gregory usually did not dwell upon the cultic inappropriateness of clerks having intercourse with women but sought to set up an overall emotive barrier against both fornication and simony which, by deterring clerks from these "heresies," would free them as an order of the church to cultivate the moral character that befitted their ministrations.

Gregory distanced himself from the polemic of Humbert and Peter Damiani in another respect. They, like some other late eleventh-century and twelfth-century reformers, campaigned against clerical unchastity by branding it as "Nicolaitism." The word was derived from references in the book of Revelation, 2.6, 14-15, to a sect of the Nicolaitans which the Lord, and all right-thinking Christians, abhored; its offences included fornication. From the second century, the name was thought to be derived from that of Nicholas, the last-named of the seven original deacons of the apostolic church (Acts 6.1-6). Despite his blameless character as described in scripture, he acquired the reputation of having been the first fornicator among the clergy. The revival of the term "Nicolaitans" in the eleventh century was owing to Cardinal Humbert in his polemic of 1053 against the Studite monk Nicetas. The learned cardinal consulted the compendium of ancient heresies which was compiled by the fourth-century Greek author Epiphanius of Constantia (Salamis). It enabled him to remind Nicetas of "the accuresed deacon Nicholas, the leader of this heresy [what he called adultery, rather than marriage, of priests] whom we thing came forth from hell"; according to Epiphanius, Humbert pointed out, Nicholas had taught that priests should both have and sexually enjoy wives as laymen did.[73] Peter Damiani eagerly followed Humbert by writing against *Nicolaitae*.[74] In 1059, he saw to it that Archdeacon Hildebrand was familiar with the term; he wrote to him:

> Now, clerks are called Nicolaites when they have intercourse with women against the law of ecclesiastical chastity. Obviously, they become fornicators when they couple together in this foul commerce; they are rightly called Nicolaites when they defend their death-bringing plague as though by authority. For a vice is turned into a heresy when it is confirmed by the defense of misguided teaching.[75]

Despite such instruction, Gregory as pope never used the word "Nicholaite" in letters in his Register, and it occurs only once outside; in 1076, Bishop Juhel of Dol was stigmatized as a simoniac and a Nicolaite (*Nicolaita*) on account of his publicly notorious marriage.[76] Gregory was similarly reticent about the legends of Simon Magus, the father of all simoniacs.[77] It is probable that Gregory deliberately played down such legends and that, despite the prominence of the Nicolaitans in the writings of Humbert and Peter Damiani, he preferred to campaign against clerical unchastity by using other arguments.

Characteristically, the other arguments that Gregory advanced were moral or tended in the direction of seeing chastity as a virtue. While Gregory would certainly not have distinguished so sharply as would the present-day commentator between cultic and moral considerations, he showed a tendency to stress the latter, as being appropriate to the nature of the church in relation to Christ. He did so with regard to the clergy whom he was trying to win for a life of chastity. Especially in his letters to Archbishop Anno of Cologne, he turned from the state of the individual clerk day by day as he ministered at the altar to focus upon the corporate, moral purity which befitted the church as the bride of Christ. St. Paul declared that, as bride, the church should "know no stain or wrinkle (Eph. 5.27)." Its clergy should bring to such a church the gracious service of a spotless and unstained household. Within the ministering household, chastity was, for the clergy, a virtue of the chamberlains of Christ as the virgin husband and of the church as the virgin spouse. Chastity became more than simply the suitability to handle the sacrament; it was conformity to Christ and his bride the church in the completeness of their union. Such conformity presented moral demands of the widest kind; as Gregory commented to Anno, "the other virtues are of no value before God without chastity, neither is chastity of value without the other virtue."[78] Chastity took its place as part of the overall vision for the church that Gregory, in 1084, declared to have always been his concern: "that the holy church, the bride of Christ, our lady and mother, should return to her former glory and stand free, chaste and catholic."[79]

Gregory set clerical chastity in a moral context yet more decisively in the arguments that he directed, not towards offending clerks themselves but to all in authority, clerical and lay, great and small, through whom he wished to discipline them by whatever means. He appealed insistently to their duty of obedience to the directions of the church and especially of the apostolic see. Gregory's conception of obedience was not mainly one of outward conformity to the positive laws of the church but rather an inner commitment to the injunctions of a personal superior as within the monastic context.[80] Thus, he grounded his requirement of obedience in the Bible and in the comment upon it of his predecessor Pope Gregory the Great. In letters about clerical chastity, he five times urged his correspondents to be obedient in promoting it by citing part or the whole of one of his favorite biblical citations. It was from the prophet Samuel's rebuke of the disobedient King Saul when he had wrongly spared the king and the spoil of the Amalekites: "To obey is better than sacrifices and to hearken than to offer the fat of rams. For rebellion is as the sin of witchcraft, and stubbornness is as iniquity and idolatry (1 Sam. 15.22-23)." With this text, Gregory associated the comment of Pope Gregory the Great, that obedience constitutes true sacrifice, and that it carries the reward of faith.[81]

To the South German dukes in 1074, Gregory used Samuel's rebuke of disobedience in order to condemn the German bishops' slackness against sinful clergy, so that sacred ministrations were unworthily performed and the people were led astray. To the clergy and people of Constance in 1075, Gregory cited at length Gregory the Great's homily on obedience. In the same year, he communicated Samuel's rebuke and Gregory I's comment to Bishop Burchard of Halberstadt. In 1076, he used the same combination of text and explanation to comment to Count Robert of Flanders upon the indivisibility of obedience among all Christians: if bishops did not obey the admonitions of the church by enforcing clerical chastity, lay princes were absolved from obedience to their bishops. In his encyclical of 1079 to all the faithful in Italy and Germany, Samuel's words and Gregory I's commentary were again cited, this time to extend the duty of obedience in opposing clerical fornication to all true Christians.[82] By thus setting the campaign against clerical unchastity in a context of obedience to the church and its authorities, Gregory directed it from cultic considerations towards obedience and the gaining of human salvation. "I beseech you," Gregory ended his encyclical of 1079, "obey your apostolic precepts that you may attain to your inheritance in the heavenly kingdom."

Compatibly with these considerations about the chastity of the clergy, Gregory in his letter of 1075 to Bishop Otto of Constance presented it as simply part of the right constitution of things as manifested in the church. He stated as an evident fact that there were three orders in the church, so that men were either virgins, or continent, or married (*aut virgines sunt aut continentes aut coniuges*). Whoever stood outside these three orders was not numbered among the sons of the church or within the boundaries of the Christian religion.[83] Gregory argued from the inherent duties and constraints that arose for each order. He ruled out the possibility of clerical marriage by a characteristic *a fortiori* argument. If the least of laymen were known to keep a mistress, he transgressed the law of his order and was debarred from the sacraments of the altar until he repented as a member severed from the Lord's body. That being so, no one could dispense or minister the holy sacraments when, by having transgressed the bounds of his order, he could not even be a partaker of them. Clerical chastity was part of the necessity of things.

Gregory's argument from the three orders of society makes clear why he normally subsumed all relationships of clerks with women under the term "fornication."[84] Only the laity could be *coniuges* and so enter into marriages. Thus, all clerical relationships with women, including their apparent marriages, were contrary to the right ordering of society and therefore not what they purported to be. The argument from the three orders also makes clear why, unlike Cardinal Humbert, Gregory did not seek warrant in the Bible for his demands upon the clergy, nor was he concerned to establish that clerical continence was the rule from the earliest days of the church.[85] For him, it was enough that it was required by the nature of the orders of men in the church; to warrant it, he appealed to rulings by the greatest rather than by the earliest of the popes of antiquity—Leo the Great (440-61) and Gregory the Great (590-604).[86]

Gregory's reasons for requiring the chastity of the clergy may be summarized as follows. He was at one with his contemporaries in demanding it for the cultic reason that it was not fitting for hands that ministered at the altar also to handle the bodies of women. Yet he was reticent about this reason and almost always expressed the cultic aspect by using emotive language of a general character about the polluting effect of lust upon the clerk's manner of life. He made very little use indeed of language and arguments of a legendary nature which were based on New Testament texts about the Nicolaitans. In this as in other respects, he was not the disciple of

Cardinal Humbert of Cardinal Peter Damiani. Instead, he showed a clear tendency to move from cultic arguments towards moral ones. With an eye to the final perfection of the church, he demanded that the clergy should cultivate chastity as a virtue together with the other virtues that befitted the household servants of Christ and his bride, the church. All those, clerical or lay, great or small, who could in any way enforce it were to do so as an exercise of their own Christian obedience within the church. The pattern to be followed was that of the three orders of the church—the virgins, the continent, and the married, each of which had its separate manner of life; this manner of life must not be infringed or confused with that of the others.

Gregory's energetically promoted campaign to enforce clerical chastity, especially in the years 1074 and 1075, added to the resistance that clerks were already offering to the endeavors of reforming churchmen to make them abandon their wives and companions.[87] Thus, probably at a council of Paris in 1074, Abbot Walter of Saint-Martin of Pontoise resisted the overwhelming majority of those present who declared that Hildebrand's decree about married priests was unsupportable and unreasonable, so that it should not be obeyed. Significantly in view of Gregory's own arguments, Walter urged the duty of obedience to papal authority. The upshot of the debate was that Walter was seized and carried off to the king's palace.[88]

A sharp picture of similar happenings in Germany is presented by the monastic annalist Lampert of Hersfeld. According to him, the whole company of the clergy (*tota factio clericorum*) was incensed by Gregory's demands. For them, he was a man who was palpably heretical and a proclaimer of insensate teaching. By his violent demands, he was trying to make men live after the manner of angels; if he denied them the use of nature to which they were habituated, he would loosen the reins of fornication and all uncleanness. Anyhow, the clergy would rather desert their priesthood than their marriage; it would remain to be seen how Gregory, in whose eyes men were unclean, would summon up enough angels to staff the parishes of the church. Lampert wrote of the dilemma of Archbishop Siegfried of Mains, caught between the mandate of the pope rigorously to enforce a rule of chastity and the fury of a recalcitrant clergy.[89] Probably in October 1074, Siegfried held a synod at Erfurt at which he found no support among the bishops.[90] A year later, he convened another synod at Mainz at which Bishop Henry of Chur produced Gregory's latest stern letter to Siegfried.[91] When Siegfried declared himself minded to implement Gregory's demands, the reaction was so violent that, according to Lampert, he barely escaped with his life.

Lampert's picture is complemented by other evidence. At about the time of the synod of Mainz, Siegfried's suffragan, Bishop Otto of Constance, held a diocesan synod at which the clergy rejected the canon of the council of Nicaea about clerical chastity.[92] Gregory's anger at Otto's acquiescence in his clergy's rejection elicited Gregory's three forceful letters to Constance of late 1075.[93] Bishop Altmann of Passau, on the other hand, behaved as Gregory would have wished. At a synod almost certainly held late in 1075, he resolutely upheld Gregory's position. On St. Stephen's Day (26 December), he reiterated it in a sermon at the cathedral, thereby provoking a tumult from which he, like Siegfried of Mainz, had difficulty in escaping.[94]

Such incidents were of more than local and temporary significance. They served to make Gregory's demands for clerical chastity a subject of widespread debate and therefore notoriety. The debate was conducted through polemical writings which further fueled concern. A full consideration of them would exceed the scope of the present study,[95] but some of the literature both for and against Gregory's demands may be noticed by way of example.

Against Gregory, between 1074 and 1079, there was written in Germany an *Epistola de continentia clericorum* which purported to be addressed by the saintly Bishop Ulrich of Augsburg (923-73) to a Pope Nicholas.[96] In Ulrich's lifetime, there was no pope of this name. The reference was clearly to Pope Nicholas II in view of the measures of 1059-60 concerning clerical continence, with regard to which the pope was said to have dealt "not legitimately but wrongfully, not canonically but injudiciously (*non iuste, sed impie, non canonice, sed indiscrete*)." Pseudo-Ulrich argued that the duty of the pope was to commend but not to command continence. Compulsion was alien to scripture and to the canonical tradition; the author deployed arguments such as Lampert of Hersfeld recorded amongst the clergy that enforced continence was fraught with moral perils for the clergy and raised the danger of scandal in the church at large. A detail of the letter was its reference to the supposed intervention at the council of Nicaea of the martyr-figure and bishop of Upper Thebes, Paphnutius, who persuaded the council to permit married clergy the liberty of abstaining from their wives or not.[97] According to the chronicler Bernold of St. Blasien, at his Lent synod of 1079, Gregory VII condemned the so-called rescript of Ulrich to Pope Nicholas about the marriage of priests and especially the precedent allegedly set by Paphnutius' intervention at Nicaea.[98]

A further illustration of opposition to Gregory's measures is provided by two letters, evidently of 1078, which survive from what seems to have been a widespread riposte in northern France to Bishop Hugh of Die's legatine action against married clergy.[99] The first is addressed by a circle of clergy at Cambrai to the church of the province of Rheims. The senders expressed an intention of defending the public liberty of the clergy. One respect in which they sought to do this was by protecting their liberty to marry. They strongly resisted any attempt to prohibit marriage to all ranks of the clergy in major orders; clerks who had not vowed themselves to continence had the right to be the husband of one wife. Probably under the influence of Pseudo-Ulrich, the letter cited in justification the supposed intervention of Paphnutius at the council of Nicaea. The reply of the clergy of Noyon to those of Cambrai survives. It is couched in cautious terms; while it defended the ordination of the sons of clergy, it did not go so far as to justify clerical marriage as such but pleaded for further consideration. The points that stand out from this exchange of letters are, first, the resistance of the clergy as expressed by the clerks of Cambrai to the rigor of Gregory's demands as transmitted by his legates, second, the rapid dissemination of such a supposed precedent for questioning it as the incident of Paphnutius' swaying the council of Nicaea, but, third, the reluctance of the clergy of Noyon to commit themselves to the resistance canvassed by their brothers at Cambrai. There was genuine debate, and minds were not closed against such reform as Hugh of Die was seeking.

On the side of Gregory VII, particular significance attaches to the writings of Bernold of St. Blasien and his circle.[100] Bernold's career adds to the interest of his writings. He was born c. 1050 the son of a priest; this circumstance made him, like others of his time, sensitive as to the propriety of clerical marriage. By 1075, he was a canon of Constance. The attitudes of the bishop and clergy of the diocese concentrated his mind so that he became a dedicated advocate of a strictly Gregorian persuasion, not least in matters of clerical discipline. In the cathedral school at Constance, he had been well educated in biblical and canonical studies and in the skills of literary presentation, and his education was reinforced by good personal character. In 1084, he was ordained priest by Cardinal Odo of Ostia, and he became the close associate of Bishop Gebhard III of Constance whom Odo also ordained. By the time of Gregory VII's death, he had become a monk of the reformed house of St. Blasien. The polemical tracts that he wrote while at Constance included his *De incontinentia sacerdotum* of 1075-76, which had the form of an exchange of letters with a priest named Alboin.[101] Whereas Bernold defended canon three of the council of Nicaea, Alboin took his stand upon the intervention of Paphnutius. It was, in effect, a scholarly answer to Pseudo-Ulrich. Soon afterwards, Bernold wrote his *Apologeticus;*[102] in it, he defended Gregory's synodal decrees against simoniacs and incontinent ministers at the altar and sought to demonstrate with a wealth of detail and argument their complete compatibility with the sacred canons of holy scripture. Bernold took as his starting point the letter of "our pope" Gregory VII to Bishop Otto of Constance in the spring of 1075.[103] Bernold's apologetic was important not only for its inherent qualities of learning and presentation but through his connections with the networks provided by the cathedral school at Constance and then by south German reformed monasticism. It was enhanced by his visit to Gregory at Rome in 1079 and by his contact in Germany with Cardinal Odo of Ostia, the future Pope Urban II.[104] Bernold illustrates the force and freedom with which Gregory's demand for clerical chastity, along with other demands that he made, could circulate and find commendation in Germany. Further afield, similar channels of long-term communication opened up; for example, the spiritual force of such newer orders as the Carthusians was effective in gradually commending Gregory's objectives, particularly clerical chastity, in France.[105]

Posterity has ascribed to Gregory VII an epoch-making role in demanding and enforcing the chastity of the clergy and in thereby establishing in the Latin church the closest possible association between priesthood and celibacy. There are some grounds for considering such a claim to be excessive. As regards his synodal decrees and the methods by which he sought to procure their enforcement, it is impossible to point to any element that was not present in the work of his papal predecessors from Leo IX to Alexander II or in the activities of groups like the Patarenes which were well established before he became pope. Moreover, after his death, the problem of clerical chastity remained an endemic one. Yet it is probably correct to regard Gregory's pontificate as a turning point. His stringent requirement of chastity was advanced, particularly in 1075, with a force and insistence that were new. Compared with the enthusiastic crudeness of Peter Damiani's advocacy of it and the heavy and legendary vehemence of Humbert's, Gregory's tendency to shift the emphasis from the cultic to the moral in arguing for continence and his close association between the chastity of the individual clerk and the quest for a church which was truly the bride of Christ, without stain or wrinkle, added fresh depth to the concept of chastity as proposed to the clergy. Far more than before 1073, the networks of communication by which papal aims and aspirations were disseminated caused them to strike home with the clergy and laity. The developments of Gregory's pontificate challenged the life-style of every clerk, both in respect of his relationship with women and also in respect of the standards by which his ministry should be governed. No one who reads Gregory's letters can fail to grasp the unprecedented impact that was made by the spiritual and moral demands that they conveyed.

This impact was not lost upon the world of the later reform papacy. When, in 1139, Pope Innocent II sought to consolidate its work in the canons of the Second Lateran Council, the canon on clerical chastity was said to have been drawn up "following in the footsteps or our predecessors Gregory VII, Urban [II], and Paschal [II]," without mention of Gregory's predecessors. It forbade anyone to hear the masses of those whom he knew to have wives or concubines. In order that the law of continence and the cleanness that was pleasing to God might be spread abroad among ecclesiastical persons and holy orders, all clergy and others who had presumed to take wives in transgression of their sacred purpose were to separate from them. Innocent took the step of stating definitively that unions of this kind, which were manifestly contracted against the rule of the church, could not be regarded as marriages at all. Those who rightly separated from their partners must perform due penance for such great sins.[106] If the canon lacked the moral force of Gregory's own pronouncements, it confirmed the actions that he had taken and took them to their conclusion by definitively stating that marriages of clerks were null and void. Celibacy was the rule to which all in major orders were expected to conform in purpose and in actuality.

NOTES

1. For a general survey of the history of clerical celibacy, see Georg Denzler, *Das Papsttum der Amtszölibat*, Päpste und Papsttum 5, 2 vols. (Stuttgart, 1973-76). For Gregory VII and his age, Carl Mirbt, *Die Publizistik im Zeitalter Gregors VII.* (Leipzig, 1894), remains fundamental. For Gregory's letters, the most recent editions are *Das Register Gregors VII.*, ed. Erich Caspar, *MGH Epistolae selectae* 2 (Berlin, 1920-23) [hereafter *REG.*], and *The Epistolae vagantes of Pope Gregory VII*, ed. Herbert Edward John Cowdrey (Oxford, 1972) [hereafter *Epp. Vag.*].

2. Bonizo of Sutri, *Liber ad amicum* 5, ed. Ernest Dümmler, *MGH Libelli de lite imperatorum et pontificum* 1: 588-89, *Die Briefe des Petrus Damiani* no. 112, ed. Kurt Reindel, *MGH* Die Briefe der Deutschen Kaiserzeit 4, 3:280-81, Adam of Bremen, *Gesta Hammaburgensis ecclesiae pontificum* 3.30, ed. Werner Trillmich, in *Quellen des 9. Und 11. Jahrhunderts zur Geschichte der Hamburgischen Kirche und des Reiches*, ed. Werner Trillmich and Rudolf Buchner, Ausgewählte Quellen zur Deutschen Geschichte des Mittelatlers 11 (Darmstadt, 1961), 364.

3. *Ep.* 55, *PL* 143:671-72.

4. In the early church, the term *mulieres subintroductae* had originally been used of women who lived with men in spiritual marriage. In this context, however, the reference was to a canon of the council of Nicaea (325) which forbade clerks to dwell with any *subintroducta mulier*, unless perhaps a mother, sister, or aunt, or other such person as was above suspicion: canon 3, *Conciliorum oecumenicorum decreta*, ed. Guiseppe Alberigo et al. (3rd edn., Bologna, 1973), 7.

5. The best text of the encyclicals is in Rudolf Schieffer, *Die Entstehung des päpstlichen Investiturverbots für den Deutschen König*, Schriften der *MGH* 28 (Stuttgart, 1981), 208-25; see caps 3-4, pp. 218-21.

6. At the synod of 1059, he made an impassioned plea for the adoption at Rome of a strict form of canonical life, although his concern was to exclude private property and he is not recorded as having mentioned the subject of chastity; Albert Werminghoff, "Die Beschlüsse des Aachener Concils im Jahre 816," *Neues Archiv der Gesellschaft für altere Deutsche Geschichtskunde* 27 (1902), 605-75, at 669-71.

7. Nicetas' *Libellus contra Latinos*, caps. 15-16, Humbert's *Responsio sive contradictio adversus Nicetae Pectorati libellum*, caps. 25-34, and the bull of excommunication are edited in Cornelius Will, *Acta et scripta quae de controversiis ecclesiae Graecae et Latinae saeculo undecimo composita extant* (Leipzig and Marburg, 1861), pp. 133-35, 147-50, 153-54. Leo IX drew upon Humbert's reply in a letter of his own to Nicetas, fragments of which survive as his *Ep.* 105 *bis*, *PL* 143:781-82.

8. See esp. *Die Briefe des Petrus Damiani* no. 61, 2:206-18, no. 65, 2:228-47, no. 112, 3:258-88, no. 114, 3:295-306, no. 141, 3:488-502, no. 162, 4:145-62.

9. Thus, in 1059, he told Pope Nicholas II that "Nuper habens cum nonnullis episcopis ex vestrae maiestatis auctoritate colloquium, sanctis eorum femoribus volui seras apponere, temptavi genitalibus sacerdotum, ut ita loquar, continentiae fibulas adhibere": *Ep.* 61, 2:207. Their lack of response led him to write the tract that followed.

10. e.g. *Die Briefe des Petrus Damiani* no. 59, 2:195-202.

11. Of the various sources for the Patarenes, see esp. Arnulf of Milan, *Liber gestorum recentium*, ed. Claudia Zey, *MGH Scriptores rerum Germanicarum in usum scholarum separatim editi* 67 (Hanover, 1994), Andrew of Sturmi, *Vita sancti Arialdi*, ed. Friedrich Baethgen, *MGH SS*, 30/2 (1929), 1049-75, and (for Peter Damiani's report to Hildebrand on his visit in 1059) *Die Briefe des Petrus Damiani* no. 65, 2:228-47. For a brief

account of the Patarenes, see H. E. J. Cowdrey, "The Papacy, the Patarenes and the Church of Milan," *Transactions of the Royal Historical Society*, 5th ser. 18 (1968), 25-48, repr. H. E. J. Cowdrey, *Popes, Monks and Crusaders* (London, 1984), no. V.

12. Arnulf, *Liber gestorum recentium*, 3.9, p. 177.

13. Arnulf, *Liber gestorum recentium*, 3.10, pp. 178-79.

14. Andrew of Sturmi, *Vita sancti Arialdi*, caps. 11-12, pp. 1057-58.

15. Hildebrand's support is disapprovingly traced by Arnulf, *Liber gestorum recentium*.

16. This table is based upon the list in Mirbt, *Die Publizistik*, 268, n. 4. In records of Gregory's Lateran synods, the matter is expressly referred to only in *Reg.* 6.5*b* (Nov. 1078). There are no references to it in letters of or after 1082. *Epp. vag.* no. 58 is omitted from this table because it is a fragment and undatable.

17. *Reg.* 1.27-28, 13 Oct. 1073, pp. 44-45; in each case, Gregory replied to messages that came to him.

18. *Reg.* 1.30, 15 Nov. 1073, pp. 50-51.

19. Marianus Scottus, *Chronicon a.* 1096 (1074), ed. Georg Waitz, *MGH SS* 5 (1844), 560. For the legislation at Nicaea, see above n. 3; it was incorporated by Carolingian reformers into the documents of their day, e. g., *Institutio canonicorum Aquisgranense* (816) cap. 39, *MGH Conc.* 2,1:360.

20. *Reg.* 2.66, p. 221, cf. 2.12, pp. 143-44 for the lack of response to the legates in the German church.

21. *Reg.* 2.30, p. 163.

22. *Reg.* 2.10, pp. 140-42, *Die Hannoversche Briefsammlun (1. Hildesheimer Briefe)* no. 17, *Briefsammlungen der Zeit Heinrichs IV.*, ed. Carl

Erdmann and Norbert Fickermann, *MGH* Die Briefe der Deutschen Kaiserzeit 5 (1950), 38-41.

23. *Reg.* 2.11, pp. 142-43.

24. *Reg.* 2.25, p. 157.

25. In Lombardy, the vicissitudes of the Patarenes should be borne in mind: as n. 11.

26. See esp. 3.7, pp. 256-58.

27. As n. 20.

28. See, e. g., Archbishop Liemar of Bremen's letter to Bishop Hezilo of Hildesheim, with its protest against Gregory, "Periculosus homo vult iubere, que vult, episcopis ut villicis suis": *Die Hanoversche Briefsammlung,* no. 15, pp. 33-35.

29. *Reg.* 2.25*a*, pp. 196-97.

30. *Reg.* 2.62, p. 217. For further comment upon it, see Giusepp Fornasari, "La riforma gregoriana nel 'regnum Italiae'," *Studi Gregoriani* 12 (1989): 314-16. The word *uxor* also occurs in *Reg.* 9.5, p. 580.

31. *Epp. vag.* nos. 6-7, pp. 14-17. The case for dating *Epp. vag.* nos. 6-11, pp. 14-27, to 1075 is presented by Cowdrey, *Epp. vag.* pp. 160-61. For the Lent synod of 1075, see also Berthold, *Annales a.* 1075, ed. Georg. H. Pertz, *MGH SS* 5 (1844), 277-78.

32. *Reg.* 2.66, pp. 221-22.

33. *Reg.* 2.25.

34. *Reg.* 2.29, pp. 161-62.

35. *Codex Udalrici* no. 42 *Monumenta Bambergensia*, Bibliotheca rerum Germanicarum, ed. Philipp Jaffé, 6 vols. (Berlin, 1864-73), 5:88-91. See also

Reg. 3.4. pp. 248-50, for a further summons to Siegfried resolutely to implement papal directives by punishing and eliminating clerical fornication.

36. *Epp. vag.* no. 6.

37. *Epp. vag.* no. 7.

38. *Reg.* 2.68, pp. 225-26.

39. *Reg.* 2.67, pp. 223-24.

40. *Reg.* 2.66, pp. 221-22.

41. *Epp. vag.* nos. 8-10, pp. 16-27.

42. *Reg.* 2.30. p. 163.

43. *Reg.* 3.3, p. 246.

44. *Reg.* 2.45, p. 182-85.

45. *Reg.* 2.47, pp. 186-87.

46. *Reg.* 2.55, pp. 200-1. For evidence that Gregory disapproved of extremer forms of lay coercion of clergy in Italy, see Guy of Ferrara, *De scismate Hildebrandi* 1.10, ed. Roger Wilmans and Ernst Dümmler, *MGH Libelli de lite* 1.543-44.

47. *Epp. vag.* no. 11, pp. 26-27.

48. "Girovagi sub specie religionis discurrentes, maximam ubique seminant discordiam. Papae decretum enorme de continentia clericorum per laicos divulgatur": *Annales Augustani a.* 1075, ed. Georg Pertz, *MGH SS* 3:128.

49. *Epp. vag.* no. 32, pp. 84-87.

50. *Reg*, 6.5*b*, pp. 401, 405-6. For Gregory's synods of 1078 and 1079, see Berthold, *Annales*, pp. 306-9, 313-15, 316-18. For Gregory's concern with moral reform at such synods, see H. E. J. Cowdrey, "The Reform Papacy and the Origin of the Crusades," forthcoming, *Le Concile de Clermont de 1095 et l'appel à la croisade.*

51. e. g. *Reg*. 5.7, p. 356.

52. *Reg*. 4.10-11, pp. 309-11.

53. *Epp. vag.* no. 41, pp. 102-3.

54. *Reg*. 4.20, pp. 328-29.

55. *Reg*. 4.22, pp. 330-34.

56. *Epp. vag.* no. 16, pp. 44-47. This letter does not have the assurance of authenticity which is conferred by inclusion in Gregory's Register; its somewhat unusual vocabulary may give rise to some caution about it.

57. *Reg*. 9.5, pp. 579-80. For the canons of Lillebonne, see *The Ecclesiastical History of Orderic Vitalis* 5.5, ed. Marjorie Chibnall, 6 vols. (Oxford, 1969-80), 3:24-29, where the use of lay accusations and of compurgation with regard to clerks and the collocation of canons about clerical chastity and the lay possession of tithes are significant. In 1080, Gregory and William were in close touch; the king may have sought goodwill by seeing that Gregory knew about the canons of Lillebonne: *Reg*. 7.23, 25-27, pp. 499-502, 505-8, *The Letters of Lanfranc Archbishop of Canterbury*, ed. Helen Clover and Margaret Gibson (Oxford, 1979), nos. 38-39, pp. 128-33.

58. Berthold, *Annales a*. 1077, pp. 293-94.

59. Canons 8-9, Mansi, 20:498-99.

60. Canon 1, Mansi, 20:517.

61. *Reg*. 9.5, p. 580.

62. The principal source for Altmann's work is *Vita Altmanni episcopi Pataviensis*, ed. Wilhlem Wattenbach, *MGH SS* 12 (1856), 226-43.

63. *Vita Altmanni*, caps. 11, 17, pp. 232-33, 234.

64. *Epp, vag.* no. 58, pp. 140-41.

65. *Vita Altmanni*, cap. 8. P. 231.

66. Paul of Bernried, *Vita Gregorii VII*, in Johann M. Watterich, *Pontificum Romanorum . . .vitae* 2 vols. (Leipzig, 1862), 1:476-546. See esp. caps. 26, 36-42, pp. 484, 489-96.

67. See above, p. 270.

68. Gregory's most important letter about the eastern churches is *Reg.* 8.1, pp. 510-14, where Gregory admittedly did not cover all aspects of the *Graecorum temeritas*.

69. *Reg.* 4.11, p. 310.

70. *Reg.* 1.27, 28, 2.68, pp. 45, 226, *Epp. vag.* nos. 6, p. 14, 9, p. 20; in the last letter, Gregory invoked St. Paul's prohibition of even eating with vicious men (1 Cor. 5.11).

71. *Reg.* 3.4, p. 249. Gregory seems to have regarded simony as the graver sin, e.g. the penalty for simony as Gregory prescribed it to Archbishop Sigehard of Aquileia was deposition, while that for disobedient fornicators was suspension from their office: *Reg.* 2.62, p. 217.

72. *Reg.* 2.55, p. 200.

73. *Responsio* caps. 25-26, 34, pp. 147-50. For Epiphanius, see his *Panarion* 25.1.1-6.6, esp. 1,4-5, in *Epiphanius von Constantia, Ancoratus, Panarion, De fide*, ed. Karl Holl, GCS 25, 31, 37, 3 vols. (Leipzig, 1915-33), 1:267-74, esp. 267-68.

74. *Die Briefe des Petrus Damiani* nos. 61, 65, 112, 129, 2: 216-18, 230-31, 235, 242-45, 3:286, 432-33.

75. *Die Briefe des Petrus Damiani* no. 65, pp. 230-31.

76. *Epp. vag.* no. 16, pp. 44-45.

77. See H. E. J. Cowdrey, "Simon Magus in South Italy," *Anglo-Norman Studies* 15 (1992-93): 77-90.

78. *Reg.* 2.25, 67, pp. 157-223-24. For the bridal imagery, see also 2.55, p. 200. In the citation, Gregory was following Pope Gregory the Great, *Moralia in Iob* 21.3, ed. Marc Adriaen, CC 143, 143A, 143B, 3 vols. (Turnhout, 1979-85), 2:1068.

79. *Epp vag.* no. 54, pp. 132-33.

80. For such an interpretation of Gregory's concept of obedience, see Karl J. Benz, "Kirche und Gehorsam bei Papst Gregor VII. Neue Überlegungen zu einem alten Thema," in *Papsttum und Kirchenreform. Historische Beiträge. Festschrift für Georg Schwaiger zum 65. Geburtstag*, ed. Manfred Weitlauff and Karl Hausberger (St. Ottilien, 1990), 97-150.

81. *Moralia in Iob*, 35.14, 3:1792-93.

82. The five letters are *Reg.* 2.45, p. 184, 2.66, p. 222, 4.11, pp. 310-11, *Epp. vag.* nos. 10, pp. 24-25, 32, pp. 86-87.

83. *Epp. vag.* no. 9, pp. 20-21. For the three orders, see Giles Constable, *Three Studies in Medieval Religious and Social Thought* (Cambridge, 1995), 305-13.

84. Gregory used the word *uxor* of clerical partners only twice: *Reg.* 2.62, p. 217, p. 5, p. 580. On the other hand, he used the more unfavorable language only when bishops were involved; Juhel of Dol "nuptiis publice celebraris scortum potius quam sponsam ducere non erubuit, ex qua et filios

procreavit": _Epp. vag._ no. 16, pp. 44-45; cf. his comments on Bishop Pibo of Toul: _Reg._ 2.10, pp. 140-41.

85. See Humbert, _Responsio_ caps. 25-27, pp. 147-48.

86. The principal references to clerical chastity in the writings of these popes are: Leo I, _Epp._ 14.4, 167.3, _PL_ 54:672-73, 1204; _S. Gregorii Magni, Registrum epsitularum_ 1.52, ed. Dag Norberg, CC 140, 140A, 2 vols. (Turnhout, 1982), 1:54-55.

87. e.g. the violence that Archbishop John of Avranches is said to have experienced as a synod at Rouen had as its background earlier Norman synodal legislation against clerical marriage; whatever the date of the synod, which may have been 1072 or 1074, it is unlikely to have been a reaction against Gregory's decrees: Orderic Vitalis, _Ecclesiastical History_ 4, 2:200-1 and n. 5.

88. The source for Walter's intervention is his twelfth-century _Lives_, which present considerable critical difficulties: _Vita Galteri longior_ and the later _Vita Galteri brevior_, in Joseph Depoin, _Cartulaire de l'abbaye de Saint-Martin de Pontoise_ (Pontoise, 1895-1901), 185-201, 174-184, at 193, 179. The evidence of these Lives indicates that the incident should be dated to the council of Paris in 1074 rather than that in 1092: Ienje van 't Spijker, _Als door een speciaal stempel. Traditie en vernieuwing in heiligenlevens uit Noordwest-Frankrijk (1050-1150)_ (Hilversum, 1990), 42-44. (I am grateful to Dr. van 't Spijker for advice and information about Abbot Walter.)

89. _Lamperti monachi Hersfeldensis Annals aa._ 1074-75, ed. Oswald Holder-Egger, revised by Wolfgang D. Fritz, Ausgewählte Quellen zur Deutschen Geschichte des Mittelalters 13 (Berlin, n.d.), pp. 256-61, 302-3. Lampert may have confused events of these two years.

90. Siegfried's problems with his clergy are further illustrated by his letters to Gregory: _Codex Udalrici_ nos. 42, 45, 5:88-91, 97-100, and by his letter to the leading clergy of his province: _Mainzer Urkundenbuch_, 1: _bis 1137_, ed. Manfred Stimming (Darmstadt, 1932), no. 343, p. 239.

91. _Reg._ 3.4, pp. 248-50.

92. *De damnatio scismaticorum* 2.2, ed. Friedrich Thaner, *MGH Libelli de lite* 2:45; for the canon of Nicaea, see above, n. 4.

93. *Epp. vag.* nos. 9-11, pp. 18-27.

94. *Vita Altmanni* caps. 11, 17, 12:232-34.

95. For fuller discussion, see Mirbt, *Die Publizistik*, 12-16, 36-44. 270-342; Ian S. Robinson, *Authority and Resistance in the Investiture Contest: the Polemical Literature of the Late Eleventh Century* (Manchester and New York, 1978), 165-68.

96. *Pseudo-Udalrici Epistola de continentia clericorum*, ed. Lothar von Heinemann, *MGH Libelli de lite* 1: 244-60.

97. Pseudo-Ulrich owed his knowledge of this matter to Cassiodorus, *Historia ecclesiastica tripartita* 2.14, ed. Walther Jacob and Rudolf Hanslik, CSEL 71 (Vienna, 1952), 107-8. The Greek sources that lie behind Cassiodorus are Socrates, *Historia ecclesiastica* 1.11, *PG* 67:101-4, and Sozomen, *Historia ecclesiastica* 1.23.1, ed. Joseph Bidez and Günther C. Hansen, GCS 50 (Berlin, 1960), 44-45.

98. Bernold, *Chronicon a.* 1079, p. 436. Bernold was present at the synod.

99. *Cameracensium et Noviomensium clericorum epistolae*, ed. Heinrich Böhmer, *MGH Libelli de lite* 3:573-78. The diocese of Cambrai at this time was subject ecclesiastically to the metropolitan see of Rheims, but it was divided politically between Germany and France.

100. See esp. *Libelli Bernoldi presbyteri monachi* ed. Frederick Thaner, *MGH Libelli de lite* 2:1-168.

101. *Libelli* 1, pp. 7-26.

102. *Libelli* 3, pp. 59-88.

103. *Epp. vag.* no. 8, pp. 16-19.

104. For a survey of the Gregorian networks and friendships, see I. S. Robinson, "The Friendship Network of Gregory VII," *History* 62 (1978): 1-22, and I. S. Robinson, "The Dissemination of the Letters of Pope Gregory VII During the Investiture Contest," *Journal of Ecclesiastical History* 34 (1983): 175-93.

105. See H. E. J. Cowdrey, "The Carthusians and their Contemporary World: the Evidence of Twelfth-Century Bishops' *Vitae*," in *Die Kartäuser und ihre Welt-Kontakte und gegenseitige Einflüsse*, ed. James Hogg, Analecta Carthusaina 62, 2 vols. (Salzburg, 1993), 1: 26-43.

106. Canon 7, *Conciliorum oecumenicorum decreta*, p. 198.

Medieval and Modern Consequences of
Clerical Celibacy

Clerical Identity and Reform: Notarial Descriptions of the Secular Clergy in the Po Valley, 750-1200*

Maureen C. Miller

Late in April of 882, a priest named Dominic traveled a short distance along the Via Emilia from his village of Modolena into the city of Reggio. Although he may have had other errands in the city, we know certainly that he came to exchange lands with the bishop. In the presence of over a dozen witnesses and with the consent of his father, Dominic gave three pieces of his land to Bishop Aron and received ten *sestaria* of land belonging to the church of San Prospero in Modolena. In the charter recording this transaction, the notary identified Dominic as "priest, son of Atrepertus of Modolena."[1] A little over three centuries later, a priest named Ildeprandus made that same journey into the city of Reggio with a similar purpose. On May 12, 1198 he exchanged one piece of land belonging to the parish (*plebs*) of San Michele of Modolena for all that Peter Astese held in Calcinara. Ildeprandus acted with the consent of his "brothers" (three other priests and two clerics from the parish and a priest from another church). The notary identified him as "Ildeprandus, archpriest of the parish of San Michele ofModolena."[2]

The differences between these two men, Dominic and Ildeprandus, are the subject of this essay. Although they shared the same vocation, the conception of what it meant to exercise that vocation--to be a priest--changed dramatically over the three centuries that elapsed between their visits to Reggio. A notable reform movement had occurred in the eleventh and early twelfth centuries. The changes it sought to effect in the lives of the medieval clergy were numerous, far-reaching, and tremendously significant for the subsequent history of western Christianity.

At root, the reform movement demanded a profound

reorientation of loyalties. Both of the "heresies" it refined and aimed to eradicate were outgrowths of clerical participation in kin and clientage networks. Simony--the buying or selling of ecclesiastical offices or services--was really the application of common early medieval notions of gift exchange to religious contexts. A cleric gave a *donum* upon ordination to a church, and expected gifts at the performance of major rites like baptism or burial. The wider use of coinage in the early eleventh century, in these exchanges and more generally in the increasingly commercialized western European economy, provoked growing opposition to these practices that formed and cemented relationships.[3] Nicolaitism--clerical marriage and concubinage--obviously involved clerics and church property in kin relations and lineage strategies.[4] As many have pointed out, kin groups were under increasing pressure to marshal resources in this period and one important means was the more careful control of marriage. Marital alliances became a tool in the preservation and expansion of lineages, and clerical marriages involved church lands and tithes in familial strategies to provide for progeny.[5]

Certainly then, in the early eleventh century, clerics were deeply enmeshed in the complex social networks of feudal Europe. The reformers' demands for clerical celibacy and the cessation of simony, therefore, had far-reaching economic, social, institutional, and emotional implications. They required clerics to find new means to support themselves; to rearrange their day-to-day domestic lives; to change how, and often where, they lived; to disrupt kinship patterns and alliances; to reorder their relationships with the individuals closest to them and with the communities they served.

Traditionally, historians have seen and described this revolutionary struggle as a dramatic clash of ideas fought out by popes, emperors, bishops, and theologians. Augustin Fliche's classic *La réforme grégorienne* is the most enduring example of this approach.[6] The clearly defined sides--popes vs. emperors, reform vs. corruption-- and triumphalist papal perspective that characterize this narrative have given way in the past two decades to a more complex and pluralistic approach. Giuseppe Fornasari's contribution to the 1985 Salerno conference on the Gregorian Reform and Europe exemplifies this recognition of the uneven fortunes of the movement and the quite varied local experiences and conditions that shaped its results.[7]

Fornasari also stresses popular spirituality in his analysis of the

reform, and this is another salutary trend in more recent work.[8]
Particularly fruitful have been considerations of eleventh-century
spirituality in the context of changing social structures: R. I.
Moore's "Family, Community and Cult on the Eve of the Gregorian Reform,"
for example, insightfully connects changes in settlement and fractured
communities to the new importance of the priesthood and obsessive
concern for cultic purity.[9] Probably most important for our
understanding of the secular clergy in the reform era, however, is
Johannes Laudage's *Priesterbild und Reformpapsttum im 11.
Jahrhundert.*[10] Laudage argues that a new awareness and understanding
of the priestly office had already emerged in the early eleventh century
in Italy and Germany, and that this widely diffused new *Priesterbild*
was an important cause of the reform movement.

One of the strongest aspects of Laudage's work is his use of the
sources central to the traditional school--canon law, theological and
polemical tracts, papal letters--and some of the sources favored by the
new religious history—saints' lives and liturgical texts. What follows is
an attempt to explore and expand upon Laudage's emphasis upon "self-
understanding" (*Selbstverständnis*) and priestly renewal by bringing
more of the sources of social history to bear upon the issue of clerical
reform in the eleventh and twelfth centuries.

The type of source I will rely upon here is the notarial charter.
Social historians have long used charters and their name-ladened
witness lists to reconstruct kinship and clientage ties.[11] How clerics
appear in these documents, and with whom, can tell us about clerical
loyalties and how these changed over the eleventh and twelfth
centuries. The priest Dominic, for example, was described as "filius
Atreperti de Motolena"; he was identified in relation to his blood kin
and to a community where he resided and was known. The archpriest
Ildeprandus, on the other hand, was described as "de plebe Sancti
Micaelis de Mutilena;" he was identified in relation to a specific church
in which he served. This change in how clerics were identified occurs
in charter collections throughout the Po Valley.[12] Let us first consider
the pattern of change and variations in the evidence of different
northern Italian cities. Then we can explore what this change means.

The Earliest Evidence and the Early Medieval Pattern

The earliest extant notarial charters for northern Italy, of course, date from the sixth and seventh centuries, but it is not until the eighth century that their authenticity and frequency allow us to draw any conclusions.[13] This evidence, in fact, suggests that priests were sometimes identified by their churches in late antiquity and the very early Middle Ages. A series of documents selling or donating lands to the church of San Pietro in Varsi near Piacenza and charters concerning several churches in the diocese of Lucca identify priests by reference to their church alone.[14] Contemporaneously, however, clerics were also identified through kinship ties–most commonly by reference to their fathers (such as "Filipert clirico filio q(uon)d(am) F[i]l[imari fabro]) but also by reference to their brothers (as when Anuald donated goods to "Anecardo v(iro) v(enerabili) pr(es)b(itero) germano meo").[15] But no clear and entirely consistent pattern emerges that reveals the circumstances determining whether a cleric was identified by church or by kin. Some priests and deacons were identified by kinship ties, and while some of these may not have overseen a church,[16] some clearly did but were not identified with reference to it.[17] A donation of 763 raises the possibility that the status of the land involved determined the means of identification. In this charter Barruccio and the priest Teuderisci, identified as "germanis filii q(uon)d(am) Donati," donated their house to Rachiprand, priest of the church of Santa Maria di Sesto, acting on behalf of his church.[18] Indeed, most of the priests identified by church were acting on behalf of their institutions (receiving or exchanging lands identified as part of the church's property),[19] but some were disposing of their own personal property.[20]

Perhaps the mixed usage in these eighth-century charters indicates a transition from a late antique or patristic-era custom of identifying clerics by their churches to an early medieval pattern of using kinship ties. This would give some weight to the assertions of later reformers that they were reviving "apostolic traditions." Unfortunately, the sources do not survive that would allow us to establish the conventions used to identify clerics from the fourth to the seventh centuries. Clearly, however, by the early ninth century the practice of identifying clerics by their churches was eclipsed by identification through kin (see Figure 1 and Appendix).

The triumph of this pattern in the early Carolingian era meant that clergy were identified in notarial documents exactly as were lay persons--only the addition of their clerical rank (priest, deacon, etc.) distinguished them. This was true for all levels of the clergy, from simple acolytes to priests. There are even several examples of bishops being identified in relation to their fathers: in a donation of 954, Bishop Odelricus of Bergamo is identified as "son of the well remembered Aroaldus of Belusco."[21]

Not only are clerics identified through kin relations, but they very frequently appear in charters with members of their families. One of the earliest surviving documents from Reggio (dated 6 December 767) reveals a cleric, the subdeacon John, making a donation to the monastery of San Salvatore in Brescia with five of his "cognati."[22] While it is most common for clerics to appear in charters with their brothers, they sometimes appear with their wives and children.[23]

There are two highly significant exceptions to this early medieval pattern of identifying clerics through kin relations. The first is when many clerics appear together in a charter. In August of 913, for example, when Bishop Adalbert of Bergamo exchanged lands with the 27 "custodians and rectors" of the hospital (*xenodochium*) called Casanova, only the first names and ecclesiastical ranks of each of the clerics were given.[24] There are numerous examples of such groups among the "decumani" of the Milanese church (the lower clergy attached to urban churches who exercised care of souls).[25]

The second, at least partial, exception is cathedral canons. Even when appearing alone in charters, canons are often identified solely by reference to their church. This is particularly true of chapter leaders (provosts, archpriests, or archdeacons) acting on behalf of the chapter, but ordinary canons disposing of personal property may also be identified by their church alone.[26] It was not uncommon, however, for cathedral clergy to identify themselves by their church and their kin: in a charter of 1063, "Arardus deacon of the holy Bolognese church" is also "son of the deceased Richizo."[27] Local conventions varied greatly. In the charters of the chapter of Ferrara, canons are never identified with patronymics.[28] In those of the chapter of San Antonino in Piacenza, they are identified with patronymics until the late ninth century, then without them beginning in the 880s.[29] The canons of San Giovanni in Monza are identified without patronymics in the first half of the eleventh century and increasingly with them in the second half.[30] In Bergamo, the provost acting on behalf of the chapter is identified without a patronymic while ordinary members are identified with one.[31]

The Change

With these two exceptions--groups of clerics and cathedral canons--identification of clerics by kin relations was the norm in the early medieval Po Valley. By the mid-twelfth century, however, a different convention had become dominant: when clerics appeared in notarial documents, they were identified only with the name of their church. Several kinds of language are used in doing so. A cleric might simply be "de ecclesie," "de plebe," or "de ordine ecclesie/plebe" (+ title of church). Priests could be identified as "officialis," "ordinatus," "prepositus," "custus," "rector," or "pastor" of a church.

In some cities, (see Figure 1) the emergence of this new formula was quite gradual: in Verona the kin-formula and the church-formula coexisted for centuries, and in Parma for roughly forty years.[32] The changeover was most abrupt in the cities where it occurred latest: in Modena and Bergamo the new pattern appears nearly without precedent in the mid-twelfth century.[33] In Cremona, Piacenza, Reggio, and Bologna both patterns overlap for ten to twenty years. In all the cities of the Val Padana here considered, the custom of identifying clerics by their church supplanted other conventions by the mid-twelfth century.[34]

Some difference between the higher and lower orders of the clergy is also evident in the disappearance of kinship identification in several cities. In Bergamo, for example, the last priest to give his father's name appears in 1078; only simple *clerici* seem to use patronymics after that.[35] Priests also abandoned the use of parental names in Reggio after 1097 and in Padua after 1114.[36] In both these cities, *clerici* continued to identify themselves through kin relations for a period.[37]

In several cities, transitional patterns are evident (see Figure 2). In Piacenza, for example, some clerics in the middle decades of the eleventh century (1015-1076) use a combination of identification by church and kin. In Reggio, Parma, and Padua some clerics lose their patronymics and are identified solely by place ("habitator in," "de loco") from the late tenth to the early twelfth century. Identification by title alone is also used for almost a century in Padua. Verona shows the greatest concurrent variety of identification formulas for the longest period of time. Rather than a clear transition from one pattern to another, Veronese usage suggests the long coexistence of multiple formulas with one (identification by church) emerging as dominant in the second half of the twelfth century. What is important to note, however, is that the eleventh century is the period throughout the Po Valley when the greatest variety of formulas for identifying clerics coexists.

Meaning

This general chronology and the character of the change suggest some link to the "Gregorian" Reform. The reform movement had, indeed, attempted to separate the sacred from the profane, mainly by clarifying the spheres of ecclesiastical and secular authority and by reclaiming ecclesiastical lands and rights from lay persons. This concern to separate the sacred from the profane led to the articulation of a new code of clerical deportment--stressing celibacy and the communal life--and to a reorientation of clerical loyalties from their kin group to the more powerfully centralized institution of the church. In this context, the substitution of references to kin with references to churches when identifying clerics seems yet another attempt to set the clergy apart from the lay world.

Closer scrutiny of the data does support a link between reform and the identification of clerics by churches. The earliest identifications of clerics by their churches are usually associated with institutions cultivating a communal life. The earliest examples at Parma describe clerics at the churches of San Antonino (1057), San Matteo (1067), and Sant'Anastasia (1071).[38] All three were urban churches under the control of the reformed part of the cathedral chapter (a schism in the chapter between those who lived the communal life and those who did not began in 1039 and persisted into the early twelfth century).[39] The charter of 1071 was a donation by "Guido, officiating priest of the church of Sant'Anastasia of the city of Parma" specifically to the communal *mensa* of the reformed canons.[40] Links to reformed institutions may also be found for Cremona. One of the earliest examples for Cremona was a priest of the church and hospital of Sant'Agata, which Pope Gregory VII took under his special protection in 1077.[41]

The new formula also seems to appear early among the *plebes*, the baptismal churches of the countryside, where communities of secular clerics were developing in the eleventh century.[42] Two of the earliest examples from Milan (both dated 1018) describe priests serving rural *plebes*, San Protasio in Seveso and Sant'Alessandro in Brivio.[43] The archpriest Lambert, identified as "of the order and parish (*plebe*) of San Lorenzo of Genivolta," bought part of a castle and manor near Cremona in 1058 and another Cremonese priest drawing up his will in 1059 was identified by his *plebs*.[44] Rural parishes also figure prominently among Veronese examples.[45]

This connection between early examples of the new notarial formula and churches cultivating some sort of communal life accords well with the exceptions to the early medieval pattern of identification by kin. Both these exceptions--groups of clerics and cathedral canons--were clerical communities with at least the possibility of sharing a life in common. It seems then that membership in a community is what may determine identification in notarial documents--one is either a member of a lineage (a family) or member of an ecclesiastical community (which in its nomenclature of relationships, of course, mimics a "family").

The most precocious case of the transition to this new notarial convention, Verona, further elucidates this connection. In Verona, the use and spread of this formula are definitely linked to the formation of clerical communities. The earliest consistent usage of this means of identifying clerics occurs at the church of San Lorenzo in Sezano, which was founded in the early ninth century by Audo, archdeacon and later bishop of Verona. Audo had specifically founded and endowed San Lorenzo to foster the education and formation of secular clerics ("scolam habeat et clericos nutriant" in the language of Audo's charter),[46] and there was a sizeable clerical community there by the second half of the ninth century. From the late ninth century, the clergy of San Lorenzo are identified in charters by their church.[47]

Audo's idea of fostering the development of secular clerics by endowing a *scola* was taken up by the feisty Bishop Ratherius in the tenth century as a means of reforming the clergy. This is why, I believe, Verona develops the widest usage of this notarial formula earliest. Numerous clerical communities formed in the Veronese diocese over the tenth and eleventh centuries, and these *scole* and rural *plebes* were the first to adopt identification by church.[48] Bishop Ratherius's promotion of clerical communities, however, underscores the importance of the economic underpinnings of communal life. One of the reasons Ratherius lost imperial support and, consequently, the diocese of Verona in 968 was that he tried to use lands usually granted as fiefs to imperial retainers to endow a *scola* for the minor clergy.[49] Financial support was key in reforming the clergy; if ecclesiastical institutions were to replace the families of clerics, they had to provide support for the clergy. This is why, of course, the reformers were so interested in property, in the reclamation of tithes and church lands. It is also why, it seems to me, lay people begin to make donations to churches of the secular clergy in the eleventh century.[50]

This change in the way in which clerics are identified in notarial documents suggests two related changes in the secular clergy. First is the triumph of the idea that the clergy should be supported by their churches. This was made possible by the integration of proprietary churches into the diocesan structure, the restoration of tithes to parishes, and greater precision in distinguishing personal from ecclesiastical property. Note that in our original example of the twelfth-century priest Ildeprandus, the lands exchanged clearly belonged to the church of San Michele. The second change, intimately related to the development of adequate means of support for the secular clergy, is the increased tendency for clerics to live together in communities. Ildeprandus acted with the consent of his "brothers," the priests Vivianus, John, and Peter, and the clerics Bernardus and Morengus--all of the parish ofModolena.

By the mid-twelfth century then, the church and its community had, at least to some degree, replaced the families of secular clerics. A priest was supposed to receive his sustenance from his church and his most intimate day-to-day relations were with his spiritual "brothers," the other clerics attached to his church, not his blood brothers. This does not mean that clerics ceased owning personal property and severed all ties with their kin when they entered holy orders. Clerics from noble families, particularly numerous in cathedral chapters, continue to appear in charters administering private property. But similar kinds of documentation for parish priests and clerics attached to urban churches--abundant in the early Middle Ages--decrease in the late twelfth century. The spread of this ideal that the church and its community replaced the cleric's natal family is indicated in the new notarial practice of identifying clergy by their church.

But who made this change? Was it the clergy who, finding their identity and status in their vocation, identified themselves as from a certain church? Or was it the laity, most directly notaries, who insisted that clerics be shorn of their lineage affiliations in public documents? Although the evidence is somewhat mixed, I think the clergy themselves are responsible for the change. It is true that notaries generally determined the form and formula of the documents and solicited the details of the transaction--the names of the parties, the property involved, its location, etc. (often taking this information down in a brief dorsal redaction before writing the full charter on the flesh side of the parchment). I have found several examples of notaries having drawn up a charter for a cleric expecting to identify him by his kin: in a Veronese charter of 1075, the notary Salomon wrote "Martin archpriest of the church of Santo Stefano and son of the deceased," and then left a blank for the name of Martin's father.[51] But this shows that notaries' instincts were conservative: they assumed that clerics would be identified with a patronymic. I have not found a case where the notary identified a cleric by his church and then inserted a patronymic above the line or in the margin.

If we look at individual notaries and how they identified clerics, there is not the kind of uniformity that would suggest an ideological notarial position. The notary John, working in Verona in the early eleventh century identified one priest with a patronymic and placename, another with the name of a church and a patronymic, another with just the name of a church and yet another simply as "Ingelmarius presbiter."[52] A similar variety of formulas marks the charters of the notary Vuido, active in Parma in the mid-eleventh century. In a charter he redacted in 1057, Vuido identified the priest Azo by his church, but in a charter of 1066 he identified another priest with a patronymic (both were disposing of personal property).[53] Such variation suggests that clerics identified themselves, and this interpretation makes more sense given the association of the new formula with reformed institutions.

To conclude, what we have in these mundane bits of formulary seems to be some indication of how secular clerics conceived of themselves and how they represented themselves in public. That this conception changed over time in ways consonant with reform ideals suggests that the impact of the reform movement was deep and widespread. That this change occurred in various cities of the Po Valley regardless of papal or imperial affiliation, suggests that significant changes in the organization and mentality of the secular clergy occurred from the ground up. Note that the change happened earliest in Verona, a city that remained loyal to the emperors to the very end of the investiture conflict. A stronghold of Canossan influence such as Mantua[54] experienced this change later than did Parma, seat of the anti-pope Honorius II. This dissonance between indicators of change on a local level and the politics of the investiture conflict should caution us to look beyond the politics of reform to understand reform.

Appendix

Listed below are the sources used for each of the principal cities in this
study. In defining this group, I chose those towns with early medieval
charters so that changes could be charted before and after the
millennium. Where I have had to be selective in examining archival
sources, I concentrated on *fondi* likely to yield references to secular
clerics (those of cathedral chapters or clerical congregations). I have
also indicated the specific charters that yield the chronological patterns
represented in Figures 1 and 2. Since cathedral canons figured
differently in the documentation, references to them were analyzed
separately and are not included here (nor represented in the figures).

Bergamo
    Sources
1. *Le pergamene degli archivi di Bergamo a. 740-1000.* Edited by
    Mariarosa Cortesi. Bergamo, 1988.
2. *Archivio Vescovile,* Diplomata seu Jura Episcopatus
    Bergomensis, Raccolte 1-2.
3. *Biblioteca Civica "Angelo Mai,"* Pergamene del Comune 354,
    364, 382, 467, 474, 477, 498, 502, 514, 534, 537, 538, 568,
    569, 575, 599, 602, 676, 907, 1205, 1211, 1234, 1252, 1312,
    1891, 1955, 2098.
    Data
    Kin Relations (800-1125): S1 6, 7, 17, 24, 25, 29, 33, 47, 53, 56, 59,
61, 64, 71, 74, 81, 95, 96, 112, 125, 126, 134, 144, 151, 165, 184, 207;
S2 Rac. 1, 23, 24, Rac. 2, 22; S3 602, 676, 534, 599, 477, 514, 502, 474,
5680I.
    Church (977, 985, 1149-): S1 141, 152; S2 Rac. 2, 62, 64; S3 1891,
1252, 2105, 2098, 537, 364, 1312.
    Other: Place: S1 18, 23, 26; S3 467, 538, 575.

Bologna
    Sources
1. Savioli, Lodovico Vittorio. *Annali bolognesi.* 3 volumes in
    6. Bassano, 1784-1795.
2. "Le carte bolognesi del secolo decimo." Edited by Giorgio
    Cencetti. In *Notariato medievale bolognese* 1: 1-132. 2

vols. Rome, 1977.
3. "Le carte del secolo XI dell'Archiviodi S. Giovanni in Monte
   e S. Vittore." Edited byGiorgio Cencetti. In *Notariato
   medievale bolognese* 1: 133-182.
4. *Archivio di Stato*, a. Capitolo di San Pietro b. 1 (1054-1189);
   b. San Stefano b. 2-16 (1069-1196); c. San Giovanni in
   Monte b. 1-8 (363-1178).
   Data
   Kin Relations (986-1143): S2 15; S1 61, 69; S3 9; S4a 10; S4b b. 2:
3, 7; b. 3: 4, 10, 16, 17bis, 24; b. 4: 4, 6, 15, 16; b. 5: 14; b. 8: 9; b. 10:
6; S4c b. 2: 4, 8, 9, 27.
   Church (1065, 1133-): S4a 11; S4c b. 2: 29, 32, 38, 39, 49; b. 3: 40;
b. 6: 2, 26, 44; S4b b. 9: 26; b. 10: 12; b. 12: 21; b. 15: 8, 30; b. 16: 23.

Cremona
Sources
1. *Le carte cremonesi dei secoli VIII-XII*. Edited by Ettore
   Falconi. 4 vols. Ministero per i beni culturali e
   ambientali, Biblioteca statale di Cremona, Fonti e sussidi
I/1-4. Cremona, 1979-88.
   Data
   Kin Relations (941-1078): 53, 71, 116, 117, 119, 122, 132, 141,
151, 153, 157, 160, 165, 184, 219, 223.
   Church (1018, 1019, 1158-): 130, 131, 202, 203, 206, 211, 272,
277, 285, 295, 300, 320, 324, 325, 326, 337, 351, 404, 405, 537, 606,
794.
   Other: Kin Relations + Church: 111, 199, 226; Place: 218.

Modena
Sources
Regesto della chiesa cattedrale di Modena. Edited by Emilio
   Paolo Vicini. 2 vols. Regesta Chartarum Italiae 16 and 21. Rome,
1931-36.
   Data
   Kin Relations (979-1136): 58, 77, 81, 117, 120, 124, 135, 139, 146,
150, 151, 165, 167, 170, 171, 176, 186, 200, 208, 213, 215, 250, 251,
254, 264, 270, 386.
   Church (1145-): 431, 435, 440, 460, 461, 463, 554, 558, 816.
   Other: Place: 63, 158, 286, 323.

Padua
Sources
Codice diplomatico padovano. Edited by Andrea Gloria. 3 volumes.
Venice, 1877-81.
Data
Kin Relations (978-1155): 1: 50, 70, 84, 124, 169, 180, 191, 196,
220, 221, 254, 280, 286, 318, 329; 2: 25, 29, 46, 65, 67, 606, 633, app.
1517.
Church (968, 1008, 1072, 1129, 1153-): 1: 51, 85, 214; 2: 185, 582,
632, 734, 1005, 1004.
Place (1027-1148, 1170): 1: 119, 156, 161, 181, 242, 248, 272, 309;
2: 230, 263, 316, 387, 486, 503, 1006, app. 1496.
Title Alone (1050-1138): 1: 155, 217, 255, 299; 2: 38, 56, 159, 338.

Parma
Sources
1. *Codice diplomatico parmense. Volume primo, secolo VIIII.*
   Edited by Umberto Benassi. Parma, 1910.
2. "Le carte degli Archivi Parmensi dei secoli X-XI." Edited by
   Giovanni Drei. *Archivio storico per le province parmensi* ns
   22bis (1922): 536-559 [901-920]; 23 (1923): 225-353 [921-
   968]; 24 (1924): 221-295 [969-1000].
3. Ibid. 25 (1925): 228-334 [1001-1032]; 26 (1926): 135-239
   [1032-1055]; 28 (1928): 109-273 [1055-1100].
4. *Le carte degli Archivi Parmensi del sec. XII.* Edited by
   Giovanni Drei. Parma, 1950.
Data
Kin Relations (860-1095): S1 10, 11, 15bis; S2 6, 16, 18, 46, 51, 75,
82; S3 14, 15, 21, 36, 44, 46, 54, 75, 80, 103, 109, 112, 114, 143, 145,
146, 150, 159, 161.
Church (991, 1057-): S2 78; S3 101, 115, 125; S4 14, 27, 52, 59, 69,
80, 83, 98, 99, 110, 111, 118, 139, 158, 160, 169, 188, 200, 225, 353,
355, 383, 506, 509, 602, 606, 752, 753, 763, 818, 829, 845, app. 140.
Place (979-1039): S2 69, 72; S3 48, 68.

Piacenza
Sources
1. *Le carte più antiche di S. Antonino di Piacenza (secoli VIII e*

IX). Edited by Ettore Falconi. Parma, 1959.
2. *Le carte private della cattedrale di Piacenza I (784-848)*.
Transcription by Paola Galetti. Parma, 1978.
3. *Archivio della Cattedrale* [microfilm in Archivio di Stato],
cassetoni 5-6, 11-12, 14-16, G.
4. Dal Verme, Giuseppe. *Indice cronologico con breve regesto
delle pergamene dello Archivio Capitolare della Cattedrale
di Piacenza* (1820) [photocopy in Archivio di Stato].
5. *Archivio Capitolare S. Antonino* [microfilm in Archivio di
Stato] Atti Privati nos. 499-588.
6. Cerati, Giulia. *Per un biografia di Aldo Vescovo di Piacenza
1096-1121*, Tesi di Laurea, rel. Piero Zerbi, Università
Cattolica del S. Cuore, Facoltà di Lettere e Filosofia, a.a.
1978-79.
7. Rossi, Simona. *Arduino Vescovo di Piacenza (1121-1147)*. Tesi
di Laurea, rel. Annamaria Ambrosioni, Università Cattolica
del S. Cuore, Facoltà di Lettere e Filosofia, a.a. 1990-91.
Data
Kin Relations (816-1093): S1 3, 7-8, 10, 17, 26-28, 40, 47, 51-52,
74-78, 83; S2 15; S5 509, 512, 527, 551, 556; S6 app. 1.
Church (788-839, 1051, 1083-): S2 2, 7-8, 16, 23, 24, 30; S4 pp.
379, 382; S5 588; S7 app. 4, 21, 37, 77; S3 cass. 16 1143 nov. 24, cass. 6
1194 mar. 13 (orig. 26).
Kin and Church (1015-1076): S4 pp. 375-7; S5 499, 501, 513, 518,
527, 528, 531, 540.
Other: Place: S1 67; S5 588.

Reggio Emilia
Sources
1. *Le carte degli archivi reggiani fino al 100*. Edited by
Pietro Torelli. Reggio-Emilia, 1921.
2. *Le carte degli archivi reggiani (1051-1060)*. Edited by Pietro
Torelli and F. S. Gatta. Reggio-Emilia, 1938.
3. "Le carte degli archivi reggiani (1061-1066)." In *R.
Deputazione di Storia patria per l'Emilia e l Romagna - Sez.
di Modena e Reggio--Studi e documenti* 2 (1938): 46-64, 239-
86; 3 (1939): 51-64, 113-29, 239-50.
4. *Edizione diplomatica delle pergamene degli archivi di Reggio
Emilia dal 1067 al 1075*. Transcribed by Loretta Marmiroli.

Tesi di Laurea, rel. Ettore Falconi, Università degli Studi
di Parma, Facoltà di Magistero, a.a. 1969-1970.

5. *Edizione diplomatica dei documenti degli archivi di Reggio
   Emilia dal 1076 al 1080.* Transcribed by Rossana Patroncini.
   Tesi di Laurea, rel. Ettore Falconi, Università degli Studi
   di Parma, Facoltà di Magistero, a.a. 1969-1970.

6. *Edizione dei documenti degli archivi di Reggio Emilia dal 1081
   al 1090.* Transcribed by Miranda Valli. Tesi di Laurea, rel.
   Ettore Falconi, Università degli Studi di Parma, Facoltà di
   Magistero, a.a. 1973-1974.

7. *Edizione dei documenti diplomatici degli archivi di Reggio
   Emilia dal 1091 al 1099.* Transcribed by Valeria Pastore.
   Tesi di Laurea, rel. Ettore Falconi, Università degli Studi
   di Parma, Facoltà di Magistero, a.a. 1976-77.

8. *Edizione dei documenti degli archivi di Reggio Emilia dal 1100
   al 1106.* Transcribed by Anna Messori. Tesi di Laurea, rel.
   Ettore Falconi, Università degli Studi di Parma, Facoltà di
   Magistero, a.a. 1974-1975.

9. *Edizione dei documenti diplomatici degli archivi di Reggio
   Emilia dal 1107 al 1115.* Transcribed by Erminio Magnani.
   Tesi di Laurea, rel. Ettore Falconi, Università degli Studi
   di Parma, Facoltà di Magistero, a.a. 1976-1977.

10. *Archivio di Stato, Reggio,* a. Benedettine di S. Tommaso,
    b. 1-2; b. Monastero dei SS. Pietro e Prospero, b.
    1121-1150.

11. *Archivio Capitolare del Duomo* passim.
    Data
    Kin Relations (767-1115): S1 2, 19, 48, 90-91, 108, 123, 137, 144,
    148, 151, 168; S2 13, 15, 43; S3 54, 56, 59, 67, 86; S3 7, 18, 27, 42, 46,
    51; S4 19, 37; S5 11, 19, 31, 34; S6 32, 44; S7 41; S8 5, 55.
    Church (1013, 1098-): S1 107; S7 50; S10b 24, 55, 60; S10a 74, 80,
    82, 86I, 87-88, 90-91, 93, 112, 135; 11 1150 sett., 1154 feb. 5.
    Place (993-1105): S1 81, 111, 130, 149, 152, 184; S2 4, 14, 30, 39;
    S5 2; S6 37-39; S7 17, 29; S8 47; S10a 67.

Verona
    Sources
1. *Codice diplomatico veronese.* Edited by Vittorio Fainelli. 2
   volumes. Venice, 1940-63.
2. *Archivio Capitolare* pergamene 962-1200

3. *Archivio di Stato* all fondi 962-1158; examples in a. S.Maria
in Organo, b. Ospedale Civico, c. S. Michele inCampagna, d.
S. Stefano, e. Clero Intrinseco, Ist. Ant. Reg., f. S.
Nazaro e Celso, g. S. Anastasia, h. SS.Apostoli.
4. *Archivio Segreto Vaticano*, Fondo Veneto (San Giorgio in
Braida, San Pietro in Castello, 962-1185).
5. "Documenti per la storia del priorato di S. Colombano in
Bardolino." Edited by Carlo Cipolla. *Atti e memorie della
Accademia di agricoltura, scienze e lettere di Verona* 80
(1903-4): 89-227.
Data
Kin Relations (814-1128): S1 1: 115, 125, 131-34, 172, 184, 229,
231, 282; 2: 12, 59, 111; S4 6756, 6760; S3a 27, 51; S2 I-6-2v (BC 10
m4 n6), III-7-7r (AC 34 m3 n5).
Church (839-): S1 1: 153, 229; 2: 159, 210, 224, 234, 259; S2 III-5-
1v (AC 11 m9 n15), II-4-5r (AC 61 mp n6), II-5-1r (BC 23 m4 n2), II-
5-4 (AC 38 m2 n4), II-5-3v (24 ag. 1066), II-5-7v (AC 72 m3 n8), I-5-5r
(AC 47 m13 n9), II-5-6v (30 jan. 1098), II-6-3r (BC 14 m5 n7), II-6-3r
(BC 24 m3 n7), I-6-3r (AC 52 m2 n14), II-6-4v (BC 12 m3 n3), I-5-6v
(AC 20 m4 n5), III-7-6r (AC 68 m4 n6), I-6-2v (AC 31 m2 n1), III-7-7v
(AC 70 m4 n12); S4 6535, 6765, 6790, 6755; S3a 47app*, 72; S3b 40,
42, 51, 55, 44, 58; S3c 6, 8, 23a, 26, 34; S3d 4, 7, 13, 16, 19, 22, 27-28,
32, 35, 46, 50; S3e I 16-18, 47, 107, 114, II 64, 196, III 42, 70, 100, 101;
S3f 630, 1207, 803, 1213b; S3g 4, 10, 13-14, 16-17; Sh 1, 3, 8, 12,
Famiglia Maggio 3, S. Nicolo 1-2, Scalzi nos. 2-2, S. Pietro in
Monastero 1-2, S. Tommaso 1.
Church and Kin Relations (915-1116): S1 2: 136, 240; S4 6536; S2
Mss. Muselli 3 lugl. 1043, III-6-6r (AC 66 m3 n8), II-5-4v (BC 29 m4
n9), III-6-8 (AC 72 m2 n1), II-6-3r (BC 24 m3 n7), II-6-8r (BC 32 m5
n15), II-5-74 (AC 66 m5 n3), I-6-2r (AC 41 m3 n5), Mss. Muselli 11
gen. 1116; S3a repertorio 1721, 165; S3b 50, 60; S3e I 18 II 66; S3 San
Salvar in Corte Regio 3app*.
Place (907-1135): S1 2: 80; S2 II-6-8r (BC 44 m2 n14); S4 6779,
6762, 6788; S3a 57; S3b 23; S3e II 63 III 100; S5 7.

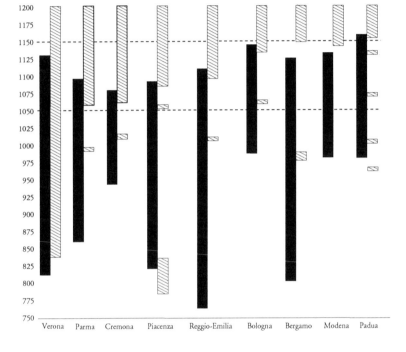

Figure 1: Transition from Identification by Kin to Identification by Church

kin relation, or kin relation and place ("filius quondam ___" or "filius quondam ___de loco ___")

church only ("rector/officialis ecclesie ___")

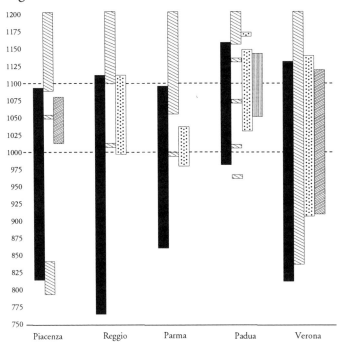

Figure 2: Transitional Patterns of Identification

■ kin relation, or kin relation and place ("filius quondam ___" or "filius quondam ___ de loco ___")

⬚ place only ("de loco ___" or "abitator in ___")

▨ kin relation and church ("filius quondam ___ et rector/officialis ecclesie ___")

▧ church only ("rector/officialis ecclesie ___")

▥ clerical rank only ("presbiter," "diaconus" etc.)

NOTES

˚I would like to thank Bill Bowsky, Duane Osheim, and George Dameron for their comments and suggestions on an early version of this work, and the members of Mark Edwards' History of Christianity Seminar at the Divinity School, Harvard University for feedback on the primordial edition. I am also grateful to Chris Ingersoll of Hamilton College for constructing the figures and to Peter and Nancy Rabinowitz for crucial encouraging interventions in the final revisions.

Charters throughout are cited by document or parchment number; "b." = busta/e.

1. 28 April 882, "Dominicus presbiter filio [sic] Atreperti de Motelena": *Le carte degli archivi reggiani fino al 1050*, ed. Pietro Torelli (Reggio-Emilia, 1921), 19.

2. *Archivio di Stato, Reggio Emilia*, S. Tommaso, b. 2, 93: 12 May 1198, "Ildeprandum archipresbiterum de plebe sancti micaelis / de mutilena."

3. On simony in general, see Jean Leclercq, "Simoniaca Heresis," *Studi Gregoriani* 1 (1947): 522-30; Joseph H. Lynch, *Simoniacal Entry into Religious Life from 1000 to 1260: A Social, Economic, and Legal Study* (Columbus, OH, 1976). On simony and the gift economy see Amy G. Remensnyder, "Pollution, Purity, and Peace: An Aspect of Social Reform between the Late Tenth Century and 1076," in *The Peace of God: Social Violence and Religious Response in France around the Year 1000*, eds. Thomas Head, Richard Landes (Ithaca, NY, 1992), esp. 283-84 and accompanying annotation. On the increased usage of coin and these transactions, see R. I. Moore, "Family, Cult and Community on the Eve of the Gregorian Reform," *Transactions of the Royal Historical Society* ser. 5, 30 (1980): 66.

4. On the development of clerical celibacy and the definition of clerical marriage as "heresy," see Henry C. Lea, *History of Sacerdotal Celibacy in the Christian Church* (Philadelphia, 1867); John E. Lynch, "Marriage and Celibacy of the Clergy--The Discipline of the Western Church: An Historico-

Canonical Synopsis," *The Jurist* 32 (1972): 14-38, 189-212; Gabriella Rossetti, "Il matrimonio del clero nella società altomedievale," in *Il matrimonio nella società altomedievale*, 2 vols. (Spoleto, 1977) 1: 473-576; Giuseppe Fornasari, *Celibato sacerdotale e «autocoscienza» ecclesiale: per la storia della «nicolaitica haeresis» nell'occidente medievale* (Udine, 1981); Jean Gaudemet, "Le célibat ecclésiastique: Le droit et la pratique du XIe au XIIIe s.," *Zeitschrift der Savigny-Stiftung für Rechtsgeschichte, Kanonistische Abteilung* 68 (1982): 1-31.

5. David Herlihy, "The Agrarian Revolution in Southern France and Italy, 801-1150," *Speculum* 33 (1958): 23-37; Georges Duby, *Le Chevalier, la femme et le prêtre* (Paris, 1981) chapters 5-6; David Herlihy, *Medieval Households* (Cambridge, MA, 1985), chapter 4; Moore, "Family, Community and Cult," 61.

6. Augustin Fliche, *La réforme grégorienne*, 3 vols. (Louvain, Paris, 1924-37). Also Gerd Tellenbach, *Libertas: Kirche und Weltordnung in Zeitalter des Investiturstreites* (Leipzig, 1936); Norman F. Cantor, *Church, Kingship, and Lay Investiture in England: 1089-1135* (Princeton, NJ, 1958); Uta-Renate Blumenthal, *Die Investiturstreit* (Stuttgart, 1982).

7. Giuseppe Fornasari, "La riforma gregoriana nel «Regnum Italiae»" *Studi Gregoriani* 13 (1982): 281-320. I place my own work in this vein: Maureen C. Miller, *The Formation of a Medieval Church: Ecclesiastical Change in Verona, 950-1150* (Ithaca, NY, 1993). Much work has also emphasized resistance to "reform" and the negative results of the Gregorian program: Anne Llewellyn Barstow, *Married Priests and the Reforming Papacy: The Eleventh-Century Debates* (New York, 1982); Elisabeth Magnou-Nortier, *La société laïque et l'Église dans la province ecclésiastique de Narbonne (zone cispyrénéene) de la fin du VIIIe à la fin du XIe siècle* (Toulouse, 1974).

8. Giuseppe Fornasari, "Coscienza ecclesiale e storia della spiritualità: Per una redefinizione della riforma di Gregorio VII," *Benedictina* 33 (1986): 25-50; E. Werner, *Pauperes Christi. Studien zur sozialreligiösen Bewegungen im Zeitalter des Reformpapsttums* (Leipzig, 1956); Cinzio Violante, "I laici nel movimento patarino," in *I laici nella «societas christiana» dei secoli XI e XII*, Atti della terza Settimana internazionale di studio, Mendola, 21-27 agosto 1965 (Milan, 1968); Étienne Delaruelle, *La piété populaire au moyen âge* (Turin, 1980), 3-26, 81-124, 161-194; André Vauchez traces the origins of a lay

spirituality to this period: *Les laïcs au moyen âge: Pratiques et expériences religieuses* (Paris, 1987), or in a more condensed form in "Comparsa e affermazione di una religiosità laica," *Storia dell'Italia religiosa, I: L'antichità e il medioevo*, eds. G. de Rosa, T. Gregory, A.Vauchez (Rome, 1993), 397-425.

9. Cited above note 3; other examples include, of course, Cinzio Violante's *La società milanese nell'età precomunale* (Bari, 1953), part II, chapter III.1 and *La pataria milanese e la riforma ecclesiastica, I: Le premesse (1045-1057)* (Rome, 1955); also Remensnyder, "Pollution, Purity, and Peace" (note 3 above); Bruce Lanier Venarde, "La réforme à Apt (Xe-XIIe siècles): Patrimoine, patronage etfamille," *ProvenceHistorique* 152 (1988): 131-47.

10. Johannes Laudage, *Priesterbild und Reformpapsttum im 11. Jahrhundert* (Cologne, 1984). The essays collected in *Le clerc séculier au moyen âge*, XXIIe Congrès de la Société des Historiens Médiévistes de l'Enseignment Supérieur Public (Paris, 1993) make a solid contribution to the disappointingly meagre work done on the secular clergy. On this literature, see Miller, *The Formation of a Medieval Church* 40-41.

11. Obvious good examples being Georges Duby, *La Société aux XIe et XIIe siècles dans la région mâconnaise* (Paris, 1953); Hansmartin Schwarzmaier, *Lucca und das Reich bis zum Ende des 11. Jahrhunderts; Studien zur Sozialstruktur einer Herzogstadt in der Toscana* (Tubingen, 1972); Pierre Toubert, , *Les structures du Latium médiéval. Le Latium méridional et la Sabine du IXe à la fin du XIIe siècle*, 2 vols. (Rome, 1973); *Famille et parenté dans l'occident médiéval*, Actes du colloque de Paris (6-8 Juin 1974) organisé par l'École pratique des hautes études (VIe section) en collaboration avec le Collège de France et l'École française de Rome, Collection de l'École française de Rome 30 (Rome, 1977).

12. The observations made here are based primarily upon the good collections of notarial charters that survive for Bergamo, Bologna, Cremona, Modena, Padua, Parma, Piacenza, Reggio-Emilia, and Verona. See the appendix for a list of the published and archival sources consulted for these cities. I have also drawn upon materials from Brescia, Como, Faenza, Ferrara, Mantua, Rimini, and Treviso, but the number of early charters for these towns is insufficient to establish broad patterns of change. Their evidence is

summarized in note 34. The published eleventh-century charters of Milan have also been consulted.

13. The Ravenna papyri, of course, predate the parchments published in the *Codice diplomatico langobardo*, but they offer only a few references to clerics and these are cathedral canons: Jan-Olof Tjäder, *Die nichtliterarischen lateinischen Papyri Italiens aus der Zeit 445-700* 2 vols. (Lund, 1955-1982) 1: 25, 2: 33, 34. The CDL documents commence in 620, but only 2 of the 11 seventh-century charters are authentic: *Codice diplomatico longobardo* ed. Luigi Schiaparelli, 3 vols., Fonti per la storia d'Italia 62, 63, 64 (Rome, 1929-) 1: 371-72.

14. *CDL* 52, 54, 60, 64, 79, 87, 111, 160, 164, 210, 219, 227, 232, 241, 258, 265, 279, 281.

15. *CDL* 38, 58.

16. In a charter of 763, for example, "Ratpert pr(es)b(iter)o filio q(uon)d(am) Ansfridi" petitioned Bishop Peredeo of Lucca to ordain him rector of the church of San Geneso: *CDL* 173.

17. In 764, for example, the priest Sunipert "filio Ferduli" asked Bishop Peredeo to transfer him from the *plebs* of S. Martino (in Colline) to one of its dependent churches, San Quirico: *CDL* 181. In 769 in Pavia, the deacon Grato "filio b(one) m(emorie) Simplitio" willed his property to the church and xenodochium he founded and oversaw in Monza: *CDL* 231.

18. *CDL* 169.

19. *CDL* 52, 54, 60, 64, 79, 87, 111, 160, 161, 241, 260, 265, 279.

20. *CDL* 219, 227, 232, 258.

21. "Ego in Dei nomine Odelricus sancte Bergomensis ecclesie episcopus et filius bone memorie Aroaldi de Be/lusco," *Le pergamene degli archivi di Bergamo a. 740-1000*, ed. Mariarosa Cortesi (Bergamo, 1988), 95. Other examples: in 1006, Bishop Landulph of Brescia is identified in a lease as "Landulfo Christi misericordia episcopo sanctae Brixiensis ecclesiae, filio

quondam Dagiberti, qui fuit de loco Arciaco"; Archbishop Aribert of Milan is identified in five different documents as "filius bone memorie Gariardi qui fuit de loco Antimiano"; *Gli atti privati milanesi e comaschi del sec. XI*, 4 vols., ed. G. Vittani, C. Manaresi, C. Santoro (Milan, 1933-64), 21, 169, 218, 248, 294, 310.

22. *Le carte degli archivi reggiani fino al 1050*, 2. Another example of a cleric acting with relatives is in *Le carte degli archivi reggiani (1051-1060)*, ed. Pietro Torelli, F. S. Gatta (Reggio-Emilia, 1938), 5, 4 April 1052: the subdeacon Vuibertus and his brothers Vuido and Albertus renounced any claim to property donated to San Prospero. Evidence of clergy deeply imbedded in kin networks is particularly strong in the charters of Modena: *Regesto della chiesa cattedrale di Modena*, 2 vols., ed. Emilio Paolo Vicini, Regesta Chartarum Italiae 16 (Rome, 1931-36) 1: 35, 63, 69, 77, 117, 120, 135, 139, 146, 150, 167, 176, 183, 208, 213, 215, 250, 254, 259, 260, 264, 270, 274.

23. In 907, "Ioannes clericus de Panicale filio quondam Aguste et Elena iugalis seu filiis et nepotibus nostris" leased two vineyards near Bologna: "Le carte degli archivi parmensi dei secoli X-XI," ed. Giovanni Drei, *Archivio storico per le province parmense* [hereafter, *ASPP*] ns 22bis (1922): 6. As late as 1101, a priest in Treviso made a gift to his daughter, acting with the girl's mother: *Archivio Capitolare di Treviso*, 9.

24. "Aribertus archipresbiter et Leo, Petrus, Benedictus, Dagibertus, Lupus, Adelgisus, Garibaldus et item Lupus, Salo, Gisilbertus, Lampertus presbiteris, Anspertus archidiaconus, Teoderulfus, Benedictus, Adelbertus, Leo, Tado, Aldo diaconibus, Adelbertus, Andreas, Anderatus, Amelfredus, Ardemannus, Agimo, Gumpertus subdiaconibus, ordinariis de infra eadem civitate Bergamo, custodes et rectores senodochio sito infra civitate in loco ubi nominatur Arena, quod vocatur Casanova." *Le pergamene degli archivi di Bergamo*, 57.

25. *Gli atti privati milanesi*, 4, 29, 48, 84, 136, 446, 516, 634, 727. These groups are usually comprised entirely of priests who are identified as "de ordine decumanorum sancte Mediolanensis ecclesie." On the "decumani," see *Dizionario della chiesa ambrosiana* (Milan, 1987) sv decumani.

26. From Parma, for example, there are several documents enacted by "Azo diaconus et prepositus canonice Parmense" in the early tenth century ("Le carte...," *ASPP* ns 23 (1923): 23, 24, 41, 45, 46) but also documents by individual canons identified as "de ordine sancte Parmensis ecclesie" purchasing property ("Le carte . . ." *ASPP* ns 25 (1925): 24 and ns 26 (1926): 66).

27. Lodovico Vittorio Savioli, *Annali bolognesi* 3 vols. (Bassano, 1784-1795) 1, part 2, 63: "arardus diaconus sancte bononiensis ecclesie filius quondam richizo."

28. *Le carte ferraresi più importanti anteriori al 1117*, ed. Italo Marzola (Città del Vaticano, 1983), 5 (956), 6 (956), 8 (969), 12 (993), 17 (999), 18 (999), 21 (1014), 26 (1027), 27 (1028), 28 (1028), 30 (1037), 31 (1037), 33 (1041), 34 (1041), 35 (1043), 39 (1048), 41 (1058), 43 (1062), 45 (1046), 46-47 (1066), 49 (1067), 51 (1068), 55 (1071), 56 (1071), 57 (1074), 63 (1084), 66 (1088), 67 (1088), 69 (1091), 71 (1091), 72 (1092, 73 (1092), 74 (1092), 75 (1092), 76 (1093), 77 (1094), 78 (1095), 80 (1097), 81 (1097), 82 (1097), 83 (1100), 88 (1117), 90 (1117).

29. *Le carte più antiche di S. Antonino di Piacenza (secoli VIII e IX)*, ed. Ettore Falconi (Parma, 1959), 8 (825), 30 (872), 32 (873), 33 (873), with patronymics; 56 (886), 66 (892), 84 (899), without.

30. *Gli atti privati milanesi*, 6 (1003), 16 (1005), 30 (1008), 70 (1014), 99 (1019), 430 (1062), 668 (1095), without; 375 (1054), 415-416 (1060), 544 (1074), 640 (1083), with.

31. Provost (without patronymic): *Le pergamene degli archivi di Bergamo*, 40 (905), 44 (908), 58 (915), 59 (917), 62 (918), 64 (920), 96 (955), 99 (957), 113 (962), 125 (971), 135 (975), 144 (979), 145 (979), 154 (986), 173 (996), 177 (997); other canons (with patronymic): Ibid., 91 (952), 99 (957), 116 (966). This seems also to be the pattern at Reggio: *Le carte degli archivi reggiani*, 23, 47, 48, 59, 72, 73, 75, 77, 78, 85 (all provost, without patronymic); but in 58 the provost exchanged lands with a member of the chapter identified with a patronymic.

32. Both patterns, plus a combination of the two, also coexisted in Milan for the entire eleventh century: *Gli atti privati milanesi*, by kin alone, 1007-1098: 24, 54, 78, 121, 130, 173, 205-6, 220, 327, 341, 362, 367, 378, 481, 489, 502, 506, 524, 538, 542, 571, 685, 693, 698, 732-33, 763, 807, 815-6, 821, 823, 829, 839, 844, 851, 855; by both church and kin, 1001-1095: 1, 8, 17, 25, 31, 35, 38, 43, 46, 49, 51, 59, 66, 74, 78, 83, 87, 95, 97, 101, 106, 109-10, 114, 117, 122, 128, 142, 155-7, 163, 165-6, 169, 171-2, 174, 176, 188-9, 194, 197, 199, 207-8, 216, 218, 224, 234, 240, 248-9, 254, 257, 261-2, 270-1, 273, 275, 281-82, 290, 293-94, 302, 304, 308-10, 316-17, 320-21, 326, 333, 339, 340, 345, 350-54, 358, 361, 371, 373, 375, 383, 386, 389, 397-9, 404, 406, 409-10, 415-416, 420, 425, 427, 432-5, 445, 449, 452, 454, 463, 470, 473-4, 485, 496, 500-1, 503, 505, 511, 512, 514, 518, 520, 536, 544, 559, 561, 566, 577, 659, 681, 688, 701, 712-13, 717, 723, 758-60, 802, 810-11, 814, 828; by church alone, 1018-1100: 91, 93, 105, 126, 284, 295, 336, 367, 430, 450, 459, 525-6, 543, 630, 651, 668, 679, 683-4, 756, 768, 793, 829, 862, 886.

33. From 800-1125, the early medieval kin formula reigns in Bergamo. There is one example in 977 of a priest identified only by his church, another in 985 of a priest identified by both church and kin, and then from 1145 on clergy are only identified by church. In Modena, identification by church occurs for the first time in 1145 and then is the norm. See Appendix for specific document citations.

34. In Brescia, the first identification of a cleric by church alone was in 1016, but this usage was not dominant until 1120: Federico Odorici, *Storie bresciane*, 11 vols. (Brescia, 1953-65) 5: 22, 54; 6: 136, 161; *Le pergamene del monastero di S. Giulia di Brescia ora di proprietà Bettoni-Lechi, 1043-1590: Regesti*, ed. Rosa Zilioli Faden, Monumenta Brixiae historica fontes 7 (Brescia, 1984) 9, 14, 18, 20, 22, 23, 27, 30; Giovanni Girolamo Gradenigo, *Brixia Sacra* (Brescia, 1755), 225-6.

The earliest identification of a priest by church alone in Como was in 1079, but not until the third decade of the twelfth century is there evidence of this usage being dominant: *Gli atti privati milanesi*, 590 (1079); *Archivio di Stato di Milano*, Fondo di Religione b. 104 (S. Abbondio di Como), 21 (1136), 36 (1160, 41 (1167); *Carte di S. Fedele in Como*, ed. D. Santo Monti (Como, 1913), 13 (1138), 19 (1147), 20 (2247), 50 (1196).

In Faenza, clerics are identified by church from 1111: *Archivio Storico Comunale di Ravenna*, Biblioteca Classense, 12bis; *Archivio Capitolare di*

Faenza, 1123 gen. 24, 1185 feb. 9, 1185 apr. 20; *Biblioteca Comunale di Faenza*, Schedario Cronologico di Mons. Dott. Giuseppe Rossini, 1159 dic. 8, 1181 feb. 25.

Ferrarese clerics seem to have been identified by church from the very end of the eleventh century: *Le carte ferraresi*, 69 (1091); *Biblioteca Comunale "Ariosto" di Ferrara*, mss. G. A. Scalabrini, cl. I 459, Quat. VI f. 4r (1154), Quat. VIII f. 15 r (1197), and cl. I 445 vol. 2, f. 276 (1143).

In Mantua there is one early identification by church in 1011, and then this usage becomes the norm from 1160 on: *Regesto mantovano*, ed. Pietro Torelli, Regesta Chartarum Italia 12 (Rome, 1914), 47, 317, 354, 390, 394.

Although I've only been able to scratch the surface of the enormously rich archival sources for Ravenna, the published charters and some materials from the *Archivio storico arcivescovile di Ravenna* suggest the transition from identification by kin to identification by church occurred in the early twelfth century: *Regesto di S. Apollinare Nuovo*, ed. Vincenzo Federici, Regesta Chartarum Italiae 3 (Rome, 1907), 40 (1103), 61 (1137), 62 (1138); *Monumenti Ravennati de' secoli di mezzo per la maggior parte inediti*, ed. Marco Fantuzzi, 2 vols. (Venice, 1801-1802) 2: 51 (1109), 1: 128 (1134), 80-81 [p. 396] (1143, 1157), and 144 (1189); *Archivio storico arcivescovile di Ravenna*, 1785 (1122), 1737 (1123), 3689 (1124); *Regesto della chiesa di Ravenna; Le carte dell'Archivio Estense*, eds. V. Federici, G. Buzzi, 2 vols, Regesta Chartarum Italiae 7 and 15 (Rome, 1911-1931), 57 (1174), 59 (1175), 99 (1188).

The documentation for Rimini is not plentiful enough to establish a pattern, but a priest is identified as "ministratori et / dispensatori Sancti Iohannis Baptiste" in a charter of 1142: *Archivio Capitolare di Rimini*, Biblioteca del Seminario Vescovile, 21[A] (transcription by Dottsa. Cecilia Antoni and Dott. Nicola Matteini, whom I thank along with Dott. Giampiero Lascaro for allowing me to consult their computerized edition of these charters).

There are so very few references to priests other than canons in the documentation of the *Archivio Capitolare di Treviso* that no pattern is evident: 2 (1069) does identify a priest by his church, but the clerics in 6, 9, and 11 are either identified only by title or by title and place.

35. Last *presbiter*: *Archivio Vescovile, Bergamo*, Diplomata seu Jura Episcopatus Bergomensis, Raccolta 2: 22; later *clerici*: *Biblioteca Civica "Angelo Mai*,*"* Pergamene del Comune, 534, 599, 477, 514, 502, 474, 568-0I.

36. Valeria Pastore, *Edizione dei documenti diplomatici degli archivi di Reggio Emilia dal 1091 al 1099,* Tesi di Laurea, rel. E. Falconi, Università degli Studi di Parma, Facoltà di Magistero, a.a. 1976-77, 44; *Codice diplomatico padovano,* ed. Andrea Gloria, 3 vols. (Venice, 1877-1881), 67.

37. In Reggio, until 1113: Anna Messori, *Edizione dei documenti degli archivi di Reggio Emilia dal 1100 al 1106,* Tesi di Laurea, rel. E. Falconi, Università degli Studi di Parma, Facoltà di Magistero, a.a. 1974-75, 41; Erminio Magnani, *Edizione dei documenti diplomatici degli archivi di Reggio Emilia dal 1107 al 1115,* Tesi di Laurea, rel. E. Falconi, Università degli Studi di Parma, Facoltà di Magistero, a.a. 1976-77, 5, 55; in Padua, until 1155: *Codice diplomatico padovano,* 606, 633.

38. "Le carte . . ." *ASPP* ns 28 (1928): 101, 115, 125.

39. Beginning in 1039, many donations specify that the properties granted be used for the support of those canons living the communal life. They donate goods "a communi mensa fratrum canonicorum" or "canonici Parmensis ecclesie in ea comuniter viventes." ["Le carte . . ." *ASPP* 26 (1926): 68 (other examples, 74, 79, 91, 114, 124, 140, 144, 173) and *Le carte degli Archivi Parmensi del sec. XII,* ed. Giovanni Drei (Parma, 1950), 31.] As Reinhold Schumann has carefully demonstrated, this schism in the chapter persisted into the early twelfth century. [Reinhold Schumann, *Authority and the Commune, Parma 833-1133 (Impero e comune, Parma 833-1133)* (Parma, 1973), appendix E, "The Common Life in the Chapter of Parma in the Eleventh Century," 297-302.] I differ from Schumann's reading of the evidence only on the matter of the provost Ado the Second. Schumann hypothesizes that this provost united the canons briefly under one head leading the common life. It was, however, this Ado who was redacting documents in a private residence, and for this reason I would place this provost on the unreformed side. None of the donations to the reformed part of the chapter mention this provost. Given its duration, the division was probably healed through attrition rather than moral suasion.

40. "Le carte . . ." *ASPP* ns 26 (1926): 125.

41. *Le carte cremonesi dei secoli VIII-XII,* ed. Ettore Falconi, 4 vols. (Cremona, 1979-88), 272, 221. Matilda of Canossa was also an early patron of

this hospital; by 1090 the "religiosi viri et mulieres" of Gregory's bull had formed a house of canons regular. Lorenzo Manini, *Memorie storiche della città di Cremona* (Cremona, 1819), 106-110.

42. In addition to the examples cited below, *Codice diplomatico padovano*, 214 (1072); "Le carte . . ." *ASPP*, ns 25 (1925): 33 (1025); *Archivio di Stato, Reggio Emilia*, San Tommaso, b. 2, 67, 74, 80, 82, 86, 88, 90, 91, 93; *Biblioteca Civica "Angelo Mai,"* Pergamene del Comune, 1891. On communities of secular clerics at *plebes*, see Miller, *The Formation*, 51-52; exactly the same sort of evidence found in Verona occurs in the examples cited above.

43. *Gli atti privati milanesi,* 91 ("Giselbertus presbiter de ordine et plebis sancti Protasii / sita loco Seuse"), 93 ("Odelricus presbiter de ordine sancte Mediolanensis eclesie et custus eclesie et plebe / sancti Alexandri sita loco Brivio").

44. *Carte cremonesi,* 203 ("Lamberto archipresbitero de ordine et plebe Sancti Laurentii sita loco Iovisalta"), 206 ("Ego in Dei nomine Ingezo presbiter de ordine et plebe Littera Iohanni").

45. *Archivio Capitolare, Verona* III-5-1v (AC 11 m9 m15): "johannes presbiter de plebe sancti firmi habitator in biunda" (972), II-5-3v: "salvester presbiter de plebe sancti petri sita infra castro albuciano, abitator in suprascripto vico" (1066); *Archivio di Stato, Verona*, Famiglia Maggio, 3: "silvester presbiter de plebe sancte marie est sita in castro surgada" (1011); S. Maria in Organo 47app*: "ingelbertus qui ingelbeldo dicitur presbiter de plebe sancti martini et est abitator in vico gerciano ubi dicitur petinisale" (1026); Ospitale Civico, 42: "rodemundo presbiter de ecclesia et plebe sancte marie tulis et est abitator in vico bardolinus" (1056); *Archivio Segreto Vaticano*, Fondo Veneto, 6765: "arozo presbiter de plebe sancti iustini sita colonge" (1028).

46. *Codice diplomatico veronese* 1: 217.

47. *Codice diplomatico veronese* 1: 229 (865); 2: 210 (931), 234 (946); *Archivio di Stato, Verona*, S. Maria in Organo, 34app* (963), 38'app* (978), 47app* (1026), 50app* (1036), 22 (1037).

48. Miller, *The Formation*, 50-51; *Codice diplomatico veronese* 2: 159; *Archivio Capitolare, Verona* III-5-1v (AC 11 m9 m15), II-5-4r (AC 38 m2 n4); *Archivio di Stato, Verona*, S. Anastasia, 4; Famiglia Maggio, 3; S. Maria in Organo, 47app*; Ospitale Civico, 42; S. Stefano, 7, 13; *Archivio Segreto Vaticano*, Fondo Veneto, 6765.

49. Ratherius of Verona, "Urkunden und Akten zur Geschichte Rathers in Verona," ed. Fritz Weigle, *Quellen und Forschungen aus italienischen Archiven und Bibliotheken* 29 (1938-39): 26-27; Fitz Weigle, "Il processo di Raterio di Verona," *Studi storici veronesi* 4 (1953): 39.

50. Miller, *The Formation*, 111-113; examples from other dioceses: Rossana Patroncini, *Edizione diplomatica dei documenti degli archivi di Reggio Emilia dal 1076 al 1080*, rel. E. Falcone, Università degli Studi di Parma, Falcoltà di Magistero, a.a. 1969-70, 24 (1078); Miranda Valli, *Edizione dei documenti degli archivi di Reggio Emilia dal 1081 al 1090*, rel. E. Falcone, Università degli Studi di Parma, Falcoltà di Magistero, a.a. 1973-74, 49 (1089); *Atti privati milanesi*, 31 (1008), 253 (1036), 387 (1056), 393 (1057), 395 (1057), 396 (1057).

51. *Archivio di Stato, Verona*, Clero Intrinseco, II, 192, 2 June 1075: "Martinus archipresbiter de ecclesia sancti stephani et filius condam [blank]"; another example dated 18 April 1101: *Archivio Capitolare, Verona* II-6-3r (BC 33 m5 n1). Other examples: Loretta Marmiroli, *Edizione diplomatica delle pergamene degli archivi di Reggio Emilia dal 1067 al 1075*, Tesi di Laurea, rel. E. Falconi, Università degli Studi di Parma, Facoltà di Magistero, a.a. 1969-70, 51 (1075), "Aginus presbiter filius quondam *** de civitate regii"; *Atti privati milanesi*, 357 (1052), "ego Andreas presbiter de ordine eclesie et plebe sancti stefani, scito in loco Segrate et filius quondam ***"; 816 (1094), "Galtio presbitero et filius quondam *** de locoBaniolo."

52. *Archivio di Stato, Verona*, S. Maria in Organo, 27 ("ego iohannes presbiter qui rufino dicitur filius quondam ursoni de villa que nominatur marleo locum ubi dicitur glare"); Ospitale Civico, 21 ("dominicus diaconus de plebe sancti martini sito in vico pescaria filius quondam pedelberto habitator in suprascripto vico"); *Archivio Capitolare, Verona* II-5-1r (BC 23 m4 n2) ("iohannis presbitero officiale basilica ecclesia sanctorum apostolorum sita foris urbium veronensis"); I-5-6v (AC 71 m4 n4).

53. "Le carte . . ." *ASPP* 28 (1928): 101 ("Azo presbiter, qui est oficiale de ecclesia Sancti Antonini de civitate Parma"), 114 ("Iohannes presbiter filius quondam Petroni de loco Sancto Vitali"). Both were making donations of private property to ecclesiastical institutions.

54. See note 34 above.

Owe armiu phaffheite: Heinrich's von Melk Views on Clerical Life

Francis G. Gentry

Although there is much, besides time, that separates the European eleventh and twelfth centuries from the end of the twentieth century, there are also many issues and theses that span the chronological gulf, demonstrating once again, if demonstration were needed, that there is at least as much that binds disparate generations and even peoples as separates them. One obvious matter of concern in both eras, and one that is pertinent to the matter at hand, is the struggle of the larger part of humanity to deal with the extraordinarily difficult task of living in an age of upheaval. Just as European society did in the eleventh and twelfth centuries, so also now modern society, especially in the west, is making slow progress through a protracted era of social and, at times, emotional transition (*Umbruchszeitalter*). Then as now, a major role in the transition is assumed by the conflict between religious and secular authority for control over the hearts and minds of people. True, the confrontation between papacy and empire in the eleventh and twelfth centuries was of a wholly different nature than the present debate in the west. The former involved no less than the conflict of the fundamental theses as to who is best suited to rule God's people, the pope or the emperor. Thus, it cannot be equated with the modern "church/state" conflict which is defined by the impulses emanating from the Reformation, later filtered through the sieve of the Enlightenment, and tempered by the Industrial Revolution. Nonetheless, certain tangential phenomena are common to both eras. One very important point of correspondence is the issue of the reform of the Roman church. In the twentieth century the question of moral reform, especially in the area of sex, has dominated public

and private Christian agendas and has led to mass "defections" from
mainstream Christian churches, even on the part of respected
theologians. Similar incidents occurred in the eleventh and twelfth
centuries. On the other hand, a major difference between then and
now was that many individuals who repudiated the Roman Church
and banded together into groups not sympathetic to the claims of
dominance of the church (or of the nobility, for that matter) were
most often branded as heretics, excommunicated, persecuted, and
not seldom executed. Reform of the Roman Church in the eleventh
and twelfth centuries, and especially the issue of clerical celibacy,
were primarily matters of concern to theologians writing in Latin,
not to the laity, quite unlike the situation that prevails in the
modern, post-Vatican II age. Yet there were critics in twelfth-
century Germany, lay persons writing in the vernacular, who called
for greater vigilance and participation on the part of the laity. We
will turn our attention to the sharpest of these critics, Heinrich von
Melk, after a brief discussion of salient events in German lands in
the eleventh and twelfth centuries and their reflection in other
German vernacular writings.

Clearly, the eleventh-century events that were to have lasting
influence in German lands were the Investiture Controversy and the
reforms of Gregory VII and his predecessors that acted as its
catalyst.[1] These phenomena were accompanied by other
fundamental social innovations that likewise contributed to make
the eleventh century significant in the history of social development
in the German sphere. Here I am thinking specifically of the rise of
the ministerial class, the opening up of new lands for colonization,
the struggle for reform in monastic orders, and the rise of popular
religious movements dominated by lay persons. A further milestone
in the intellectual history of the German Middle Ages was the
emergence of a vernacular literature after a "silence" lasting more
than a century.[2] An otherwise unidentified cleric named Ezzo
ushered in the new age with the self-assured words:[3]

> Der guote biscoph Guntere vone Babenberch,
> der hiez machen ein vil guot werch:
> er hiez di sine phaphen
> ein guot liet machen.
> eines liedes si begunden,

want si di buoch chunden.
Ezzo begunde scriben,
Wille vant die wise.
duo er die wise duo gewan,
duo ilten si sich aller munechen. (V, 1-10)

(The worthy Bishop of Bamberg, Gunther, directed that a splendid
work be written. He bade his priests to write a lofty hymn. They
began [working on] a hymn because they were well familiar with the
books [i.e., the Bible]. Ezzo began to write, and Wille composed the
music. When he had created the melody, they all rushed to become
monks.]

The *Ezzolied* stands at the beginning of the resurgence of the
vernacular as a vehicle of literary discourse, but it also stands at the
end of a period of relative political stability in the Empire. Unlike
the later eleventh-century *Memento mori* or the twelfth-century
moralists (e.g. Heinrich von Melk) whose focus is strictly on earthly
existence and its potential as an inhibiting factor for the salvation of
the soul, the *Ezzolied* is a "child of its time," a joyous celebration of
the triumph of Christ over death (*von dem tode starp der tot*: "death
died as a result of death," V 347) and Satan, who is portrayed as the
Leviathan snapping at and getting snared on the Cross. Emphasized
is not the suffering Christ of later Gothic centuries with his crucifix
of pain and martyrdom, but rather the majestic Christ the King,
triumphantly wearing a crown on a victorious Romanesque cross.

How different then is the *Memento mori*, a penitential rhymed
sermon (19 strophes, 76 long lines) composed between 1080 and 1090
by a monk named Notker, possibly the later abbot of the reform
monastery of Zwiefalten. Shifting his gaze from heaven to earth,
Notker deals with this life as well as its beauties and attendant
dangers. He leaves no doubt about his intentions right from the
start:[4]

nu denchent, wip unde man, war ir sulint werdan.
(Now reflect, o women and men, upon where you will be
journeying!)

Unlike the *Ezzolied*, there is no ambiguity about the intended
audience of the *Memento mori*. For Notker makes clear that his work

is not meant for monastic listeners. "Wip unde man" is a typical circumlocution for "everyone," but it also implies exactly what it says: "men and women." In addition, many of the themes that Notker takes up in his work are those that would have more application to lay persons, i.e., the correct disposition of wealth so that it does not prevent the salvation of the soul and the responsibility of the powerful to secure and protect the rights of the powerless. Composed of three parts, the *Memento mori* evidences a logical internal cohesion proceeding from the death of the body to the possible death of the soul and ending with the purpose of existence, reunion with God. Nonetheless, the work deals with life and not death. Notker's concern is to impart to his noble listeners the type of behavior that they must evidence in order to attain Paradise, and that form of behavior is, simply, to follow the commandment of God, namely to love one's fellow human beings. The commandment demands active engagement in the affairs of life and active charity on the part of those in power toward those in a less advantaged position in society. The fact that the *Memento mori* was composed during a period of great unrest in the German empire doubtless profoundly influenced its content, for, as noted above, it was a time of chaos.[5] Indeed, the reverberations of the Gregorian reforms and the Investiture Controversy were felt in the most concrete spheres of human activity. For the clash of weapons was involved, and, as would be expected, it was the poor and powerless who suffered greatly and who would continue to suffer for much time to come. It was against this background that Notker wrote the *Memento mori*. And in an era when it appears that the powerful of a land were failing to carry out their duties as Christian princes, it should not come as a surprise that a churchman would concern himself with admonitions to the rich and powerful to return to the proper path. For people's souls and the well-being of the church on earth itself were seen to be gravely threatened.

Of the more than ninety works from the Early Middle High German period (ca. 1060-1170), those that contain a reflection of external events follow the model of the *Memento mori*, namely the events themselves are not depicted or discussed directly but rather the dangers that the effects of these events posed toward the immortal souls of the poets' listeners, who were, for the most part, members of the lay nobility. It is also probable that for some of the works, e.g., the retelling of *Genesis* and *Exodus*, both early twelfth century, a monastic audience was envisaged. Irrespective of the intended audience, however, contemporary historical or social events are not directly portrayed in any of these works, with the exception of the *Annolied* (ca.1080). One scene in particular (strophe 40) is offered here to demonstrate that contemporary events were occasionally directly addressed in vernacular literature, if the general topic of the work was also contemporary, in this case the life of Archbishop Anno of Cologne (d. December 4, 1075). With barely concealed rage, the poet presents his listeners with a raw, powerful description of the desolation and the lamentable state of the German empire in the 1080s:[6]

> Dar nâch vîng sich ane der ubile strît,
> den manig man virlôs den lîph,
> duo demi vierden Heinrîche
> virworrin wart diz rîche.
> mort, roub unti brant
> civûrtin kirichin unti lant
> von Tenemarc unz in Apuliam,
> van Kerlingin unz an Ungerin.
> den nîman nimohte widir stên,
> obi si woltin mit trûwin unsamit gên,
> die stiftin heriverte grôze
> wider nevin unti hûsgenôze.
> diz rîche alliz bikêrte sîn gewêfine
> in sîn eigin inâdere.
> mit siginuftlîcher ceswe
> ubirwant iz sich selbe,
> daz dî gedouftin lîchamin
> umbigravin ciworfin lägin
> ci âse den bellindin,
> den grâwin walthundin. (40, 1-20)

(Then began the evil conflict in which many a man lost his life. At the time of Henry IV the Empire was brought into total disarray. Murder, robbery, and arson devastated churches and lands from Denmark to Apulia, from France to Hungary. No one was able to withstand them, even if they wished to keep faith with each other.

They organized great military campaigns against relatives and countrymen. The whole Empire plunged its weapons into its own innards. With a victorious hand it [sc. the Empire] overcame itself so that the cadavers of the baptized lay scattered and unburied--as carrion for the baying gray wolves.)

The above lines could refer to the disruptions in society brought about by the fierce and savage war against the Saxons, or they might also be a hyperbolic reaction to the beginning trauma of the Investiture Contest. Whatever the catalyst for their composition may have been, it is clear that the poet is incensed and views Henry IV as the wellspring of calamity from which all the turmoil besetting the empire flows, and since the *Annolied* is also a decidedly political work, the poet seized the opportunity to deride a significant opponent of his hero.

The *Annolied* occupies an isolated position within Early Middle High German literature, however, and it will not find a kindred saga until the massive *Kaiserchronik* from the mid-twelfth century. As indicated above, most works from this period have a pastoral purpose and admonish the rich and powerful to be just judges and guarantors of the rights of the less privileged. The great themes of the Gregorian reform, simony and celibacy, are apparently not considered to be subjects appropriate to pastoral admonitions to the laity, and are, thus, scarcely touched upon in the vernacular before Heinrich von Melk, and then only fleetingly.

Heinrich von Melk is, without doubt, the most colorful and gifted of the Early Middle High German authors. Two works are transmitted under his name in the Viennese Codex 2696 from the fourteenth century, *Von des Todes gehugde* (Concerning the Remembrance of Death) and the *Priesterleben* (Life of Priests). Both works are distinguished by a refined verse and rhyme technique (a very high percentage of pure rhymes, a minimum of overlong lines of 12-14 syllables), unrelenting invective against all Estates, but especially secular priests, merciless satire, and an abundance of several core scenes within the narrative that display a remarkable gift for dramatic staging. As far as the identity of the poet is concerned, a few verses from *Von des todes gehugde* seemed to provide the answer:[7]

> dar bringe du, got here,
> durch diner muoter ere

und durch aller diner heiligen reht
Heinrichen, dinen armen chneht;
unt den abt Erchenfride . . . . (1029-1033)

(Lord God, bring to that place [i.e., Paradise] for the glory of your
mother and for the sake of all your saints Heinrich, your humble
servant, and the abbot Erkenfried.)
Clearly, these lines represent a biographical disclosure, and from
them a most ingenious biography was constructed for Heinrich, the
humble servant. Heinrich was "identified" as a *conversus*, a lay
brother associated with a monastery. The monastery in question was
postulated to be the Benedictine monastery of Melk in Austria since
an abbot Erkenfried ruled that monastery 1122-1163. Because of the
sharpness of his attacks and the depth of his acquaintanceship with
courtly life, Heinrich was deemed to be a noble who, becoming
progressively repelled by the world and rejected by ungrateful
children, withdrew as an older man to a monastery, where he
immersed himself in studies and saw it as his duty to admonish all
classes of society regarding their duties as Christians. Unworthy
priests became his particular target. There can be no doubt that this
is an impressive biography. Unfortunately, it is not an accurate one
for a myriad of reasons. Abbot Erkenfried of Melk could scarcely
come into question as Heinrich's patron since the above-mentioned
poetic refinement of the two works reflects a period later than 1163.
In addition, the contents of the poems underscore concerns and
display conventions of a time more accurately located within the last
quarter of the twelfth century (e.g., court customs, secular love
lyrics, validity of sacraments administered by unworthy priests,
etc.). Thus, who the author was, whether his name was Heinrich
von Melk, or whether both works are by the same individual is
unknown. Although the virtual identity of lines 397-402 in *Vom
Priesterleben* with lines 181-186 in *Von des todes gehugde* as well as the
closely-related subject matter suggest that the two poems are
composed by the same individual,[8] the matter of common
authorship of both items continues to be the subject of lively
speculation.[9] For the present discussion, Heinrich von Melk will be
considered as one person and, consequently, as the author of *Vom
Priesterleben*, if for no other reason than stylistic ease.

Although only a fragment (746 lines), *Vom Priesterleben* is
distinguished from all other works of the Early Middle High
German period, with the exception, of course, of *Von des todes
gehugde*, by the sharpness of its tone and the directness of its
invective against unworthy priests.

Borrowing the image of the sentry who is to warn God's people
of impending danger from Ezekiel 33, 1-9, Heinrich begins his work
(the surviving fragment, that is) lamenting the lack of this type of
vigilance on the part of priests toward the perils that beset
Christians:

> Owe, getorst ich des gewehenen,
> daz nu bisiuften und betrehenen
> solden alle die, die christen sint!
> die uns da lerent, die sint blint,
> ir ougen diu sint ane lieht.
> si hant munt unt sprechent nieht.
> wir hoeren dehein horen von in scellen,
> si sin hunde die niht mugen bellen. (9-16)

(Alas, that I feel compelled to say that all those who are Christian
must now lament and weep! Those who instruct us are blind; their
eyes are without sight. They have mouths and [yet] they do not
speak. We do not hear any horn from them resounding; they are
dogs that cannot bark.)

The priests, who should be the sentries, hardly man their
lookout posts, and severely neglect their duty:

> owe, leider wie selten
> die phaffen stent an der warte. (30-31)
> (Alas how rarely the priests stand watch.)

And what keeps them from being watchful? Where are the
guardians?

> [they are in] die mouchelzellen,
> da si sich inne mestent,
> so die liut die vient chestent.
> si ziehent sich uz dem gitraebe.
> der in allez daz gaebe,
> des si in erdenchen mehten,

> so waere der bouch wol ir trehtin. (54-60)

(They are hiding in their dens where they feast while the demons torment the people. They [the priests] withdraw from the fray. If they were able to conceive of the one who would give them all things, the belly would doubtless be their lord.)

These are, of course, sharp words, but do not necessarily refer to the transgressions of simony or unchaste behavior. By the middle of the twelfth century, the drinking of priests and monks, especially, belonged to the long-established lore of European humorous balladry. But Heinrich is leading up to precisely these two sins. Before taking on these theological issues, however, he wants to depict the complete abandonment of pastoral care by priests. He concentrates thus in the first 110 lines on the drinking and feasting of priests in their comfortable lodgings and their aping of noble customs while the laity is left unprotected and unsuccored outside.[10]

The remaining 636 lines of the work are taken up with a relentless, scathing, and bitter attack on unchaste and simoniacal priests. He scornfully rejects the argument of nicolaite priests and their sympathizers that St. Paul's words "it is better to marry than to be tortured" (I Corinthians 7, 9) apply to them and their wives and concubines:

> Paulus sprichet, bezzer si minnen denne brinnen.
> der rede sulen si sich versinnen
> wen er da mit meine.
> er meinte dehein minnen wan die eine,
> den got dar zuo geordnent hat,
> daz er mit elicher hirat
> muge chomen ze siner rehten e. (188-194)

(Paul says that it is better to marry than to burn. They [the priests] should know whom he [Paul] was addressing [with these words]. He meant no marriage except the one that God ordained for him [the layman in the marriage] so that he could achieve his correct station in life through lawful marriage.)

Thus, according to Heinrich, the words of Paul do not provide the authority for priests to marry or have any closer relationship with a woman unless she be a mother or sister (121-122). Indeed, a true priest and servant of God will spend his time in fasting and mortification of the body (219-222; 540-541). After all, the priest is supposed to be the pure light leading his flock. If a priest is carousing with women and setting a bad example, how can he admonish his parishioners to practice the correct form of life?[11] The answer is, of course, he cannot. The wives and concubines of priests also do not escape Heinrich's scathing remarks, and while his criticism of them is severe (718-721), it is not quite as harsh as others, Peter Damian's, for example. Nonetheless, Heinrich is quite clear about what awaits them in the afterlife:

> man biginnet si stetenen
> in fiurine chetene
> nach diesem broedem libe
> die briester mit ir wiben. (726-729)

(After this transitory life the priests and their women will be held in fiery chains.)

Closely connected with this theme, in Heinrich's thought, is the issue of simony. For one of the results of this abuse is that the elaborate dress and hair styles of the priests' women are financed from the alms given to the Church and the payments made by penitents for forgiveness (700-717).

Heinrich also discusses the general issue of simony and its implications quite apart from his diatribe against unchaste priests. Simony is the sin of Judas for it involves nothing less than the selling of Christ Himself. Referring to Christ's words at the Last Supper, "and yet, here with me on the table is the hand of the man who betrays me" (Luke 22, 21), Heinrich writes:

> 'sin hant diu mit mir izzet
> diu ist, diu mich verchouffen wil.'
> diu rede dunchet siu niht ze vil,
> die hiut chouffent and verchoufent
> und durch miete toufent
> unt den scaz nement von der erde,
> daz des toten bivilde werde
> deste vlizchlicher begangen. (356-363)

('The hand that eats with me is the one that intends to sell me.'
These words make little impression upon those today who buy and
sell [church offices, sacraments, etc.] and who perform baptisms
[only] for payment. They also take the treasure from the [heirs][12] so
that the burial of a dead [relative] will be carried out all the quicker.)

Having said that, Heinrich then retreats from the extreme and
heterodox position that the sacraments administered by an
unworthy priest are invalid. This subject was a hotly debated one at
the time of Gregory VII, and was waged on both sides in the twelfth
century by such luminaries as Arnold of Brescia, Hugo of Rouen,
Honorius of Autun, and Gerhoch von Reichersberg, among others.
Heinrich appears to share the basic opinion of the latter three
teachers, namely, that the sacraments administered by an unworthy
cleric were valid as long as the priest's sins were not *widely known*.
Heinrich writes:

> swenne der briester so sere missevert,
> so sprechent si [laypersons], sin misse si unreine.
> daz ist ein groezlichiu meine. . . .
> wir sulen niht vorscen umb sin leben,
> der daz ampt da fur bringet. (370-372; 382-383)

(whenever the priest goes greatly astray, they claim that his Mass is
invalid. That is a gross falsehood. . . . We should not minutely
scrutinize deeply the life of the man who says the Mass.)

Although stingingly critical of unworthy priests in general,
Heinrich stands firmly within accepted orthodox teaching. As long
as the priest was legitimately consecrated, that is, he did not acquire
his office through simoniacal means, he is able to administer valid
sacraments:

> swa daz gotes wort und diu giwihte hant
> wurchent ob dem gotes tisce ensant,
> da wirt gotes lichnamen in der misse
> von einem suntaere sin gewisse
> sam von dem heiligstem man
> der briesters namen ie gewan. (397-402)

(Wherever the word of God and the consecrated hand act together at the altar of God, there will come into being the body of God [i.e., the transubstantiation] in the Mass [said] by a sinner as certainly as [in one said] by the most pious man who ever attained the name of priest.)

Basically identical lines appear in *Von des todes gehugde* (181-186; see Note 9 above), and their appearance in both works bears witness not only to the orthodoxy of the poet but also to the fact that this issue was of paramount interest in the latter half of the twelfth century--and not just among the clergy.

Although religious works continued to be written in German, Heinrich von Melk stands at the end and not at the beginning of a tradition. Nonetheless, Heinrich's passionate engagement in the matters of church and social reform provides eloquent testimony to the maturing of the laity. The issues of celibacy and simony are no longer the concern solely of theologians writing in Latin. Unfortunately, he had no successors, for the literary expectations of the lay audience was changing and the age of the Court and its literature was dawning. However, both Heinrich von Melk and later poets like Walther von der Vogelweide, Hartmann von Aue, and Wolfram von Eschenbach, to name but a few, are connected by the self-assuredness with which they employ the vernacular as a vehicle of literary endeavor.

The Heinrich of *Von des todes gehugde* and *Vom Priesterleben* is a masterful narrator, fully conscious of himself as a writer who is able to put vernacular expression on a stylistic par with Latin. He is a layman who speaks about theological matters on an equal level with members of the clergy. He not only addresses a noble, lay audience in the one work (*Von des todes gehugde*), but he also represents the interests of this group to a clerical audience in the other. His writing is an affirmation of the worth of the lay nobility itself and its view of the vital role that it plays *within* the Christian order of things, a role that it shares with the clergy--and will soon have as a dominant partner. This confidence and positive self-concept will find its quintessential expression, of course, in the secular tales of the Courtly period, where society is improved by the actions of members of the nobility and not by representatives of the institutionalized church. There the path to salvation will not lead solely through the priests but also--and primarily--through the good works of each individual.

Approximately a century after the turmoil of the late eleventh century, relative political stability engendered a new attitude among lay people, a sense of empowerment, to use a modern term. The church and its priesthood are, however, not demonized or treated contemptuously. On the contrary, the church is honored but viewed to be in need of guidance, guidance that can come from lay people following the age-old lessons of Christianity. In this respect, Heinrich stands squarely within the currents of popular piety that were aswirl in his age.

NOTES

1. There is, of course, no necessity for a literary historian to explain the significance of this event to historians. Thus, I offer the comments in this essay in the spirit of Karl Bosl's call for a cooperative effort on the part of historians and literary historians:

> Methodisch gesagt ist also der Literaturhistoriker darauf angewiesen, vom Historiker eine Analyse der jeweiligen Gegenwart mit ihrer Vergangenheit und Zukunft entfaltet zu bekommen, um innere hintergründige Bewegungen und Trends im Literatur--(und auch im Kunst-) Werk bestimmen, deuten zu können. Der Historiker seinerseits aber findet in der Spiegelung und im literarischen Seismographen eine notwendige, aber indirekte Bestätigung oder Korrektur seiner Analyse [. . .].

Karl Bosl, "Arbeit, Armut und Emanzipation: Zu den Hintergründen der geistigen und literarischen Bewegung vom 11. bis zum 13. Jahrhundert," *Beiträge zur Wirtschafts- und Sozialgeschichte des Mittelalters. Festschrift für Herbert Helbig zum 65. Geburtstag*, ed. Knut Scholz (Köln/Wien: Böhlau Verlag, 1976), 129.

2. The *Ezzolied* was truly an unusual event for its time. Not only did Ezzo produce a striking and well-structured hymn, but more importantly the work demonstrates that the vernacular was again deemed a vehicle

worthy of *written* literary religious expression–disregarding for the purposes of this discussion the ingenious *translations* of Notker Labeo from the end of the tenth/beginning of the eleventh century. For the first time since the Old High German *Christus und die Samariterin* (ca. 900), a German work of mature quality quite literally burst upon the scene and forever changed literary convention in Germany.

3. Werner Schröder, ed., *Kleinere deutsche Gedichte des 11. und 12. Jahrhunderts* (Tübingen: Niemeyer, 1972), 10. The lines are from the later Vorau version (V) of the Ezzolied (34 strophes, 420 lines). The earlier, and much shorter Straßburg version (S) (7 strophes, 76 lines) begins with:

> Nu wil ih iu herron
>   heina war reda vor tuon:
>   von dem anegenge,
>   von alem manchunne, . . . (1-4)

(Now I intend to relate to you, my lords, a true tale about Creation and about all mankind. . . .)

A brief note to the above *iu herron*: The term of address, "my lords," would be quite proper for the postulated audience of the original *Ezzolied*, namely members of the higher clergy, of the lay nobility, or of the members of the about-to-be-regularized Bamberg cathedral Chapter (1057-1061).

The lines from the Vorau version are of interest because they bring together the names of the poet and his patron, a supposition that is borne out by the *Vita Altmanni*. The *Vita*, written around 1130 in the monastery of Göttweig at the behest of the abbot Chadalhoh, reports on the life of the Passau Bishop Altmann, who died in 1091. One of the episodes from Altmann's life contains a description of a pilgrimage to the Holy Land, in which he took part, under the direction of Bishop Gunther of Bamberg and Archbishop Siegfried of Mainz in 1064/65. Also participating in this pilgrimage, according to the *Vita*, was a certain cleric named Ezzo who wrote the above-mentioned *cantilena de miraculis Christi*, and, with regard to Ezzo and the hymn, the *Vita* writer adds the statement, *[Ezzo] patria lingua nobiliter composuit* (". . . he composed [the hymn] splendidly in his

mother tongue"). That the "cantilena" in the vernacular by someone named
Ezzo and the *Ezzolied* are one and the same thing is a virtual certainty.

4. Friedrich Maurer, ed., *Die religiösen Dichtungen des 11. und 12.
Jahrhunderts. Nach ihren Formen besprochen und herausgegeben*, Volume I
(Tübingen: Niemeyer, 1964), 249-59. See also: Rudolf Schützeichel, *Das
alemannische Memento Mori: Das Gedicht und der geistig-historische
Hintergrund* (Tübingen: Niemeyer Verlag, 1962); Francis G. Gentry,
"Notker's *Memento mori* and the Desire for Peace," *Amsterdamer Beiträge
zur älteren Germanistik* 16 (1981): 25-62.

5. In the roughly twenty years between the *Ezzolied* and the *Memento
mori*, a young king had been kidnapped (Henry IV at Kaiserswerth in 1062
by Bishop Anno of Cologne), a minority rule in which Empress Agnes,
Henry's mother, ceded enormous portions of Salian lands, and with them
power, to great nobles who would prove to be a threat to the Crown,
savage wars with the Saxons, and perhaps most importantly the struggle
between Henry IV and Pope Gregory VII, the so-called "Investiture
Controversy." Overshadowing all these matters was the on-going effort to
reform the church.

6. Eberhard Nellmann, ed., *Das Annolied. Mittelhochdeutsch und
Neuhochdeutsch* (Stuttgart: Reclam, [1975] 1986): 52-54.

7. All quotations from *Von des todes gehugde* and *Vom Priesterleben*
from: Friedrich Maurer, ed., *Die religiösen Dichtungen des 11. und 12.
Jahrhunderts. Nach ihren Formen besprochen*, Volume III (Tübingen:
Niemeyer, 1970), 258-359.

8. swa daz gotes wort und diu giwihte hant
     wurchent ob dem gotes tisce ensant,
     da wirt gotes lichnamen in der misse
     von einem suntaere sin gewisse
     sam von dem heiligstem man
     der briesters namen ie gewan. (*Priesterleben*, 397-402)

     swa aber daz gotes wort unt diu gewihte hant
ob dem gotes tisce wurchent ensant,

da wirt der gotes lichnamen in der misse
von einem sundaer so gewisse,
so von dem heiligstem man,
der briesterlichen namen ie gewan. (*Von des todes gehugde*, 181-186)

9. See: Peter-Erich *Neuser, Zum sogenannten "Heinrich von Melk":
Überlieferung, Forschungsgeschichte und Verfasserfrage der Dichtungen Vom
Priesterleben und Von des todes gehugde* (Köln/Wien: Böhlau Verlag, 1973);
and Gisela Vollmann-Profe, *Geschichte der deutschen Literatur von den
Anfängen bis zum Beginn der Neuzeit. Band I: Von den Anfängen zum hohen
Mittelalter. Teil 2: Wiederbeginn volkssprachiger Schriftlichkeit im hohen
Mittelalter, 1050/60- 1160/70* (Königstein/Ts.: Athenäum, 1986), 166; repr.
Tübingen: Niemeyer Verlag, 1994, 130; Wiebke Freytag, "Das Priesterleben
des sogenannten Heinrich von Melk: Redeformen, Rezeptionsmodus und
Gattung," Deutsche *Vierteljahresschrift für Literaturwissenschaft und
Geistesgeschichte* 52 (1978): 558-80.

10. For example, a priest will not admit the halt, lame, or blind
knocking at his door because he is in the process of being leeched. Of
course, when the cleric's friends arrive, they are let in immediately. They
recline on luxurious bolsters, overeat, drink mead and wine, and speak of
"minne," courtly love (90-103). The latter is a topic also mentioned with
contempt in *Von des todes gehugde* and provides evidence that the poet(s)
knew courtly customs.

11. Heinrich argues that a lawfully married layman must refrain from
sexual congress five days before receiving communion and for some days
afterwards to boot. (267-271) How could a priest, who sings the Mass every
day, possibly abide by this rule if he has a woman? (273-278).

12. The word in the manuscript "erde" (earth, ground) makes no sense
in the context. I agree with Henschel (*Theologia Viatorum* 4 [1952], 267-273)
that the line is corrupt and use his suggestion "erbe" (heir) in the
translation.

Gender, Celibacy, and Proscriptions of Sacred Space: Symbol and Practice

Jane Tibbetts Schulenburg

Space is neither inert nor neutral, nor is its organization, articulation, or the formulation of its boundaries a natural phenomenon. Rather, spatial constructs are the historical and cultural products of an age. As metaphors and symbolic systems, they embody the basic values and meaning of a culture. Operating as a mechanism for classification, spatial arrangements attempt to demarcate and intensify the hierarchical ordering of society, to define and clarify social roles and relations, and to regulate social behavior. Spatial constructions are therefore fundamental statements of power and authority, and they have been used to serve a wide range of special interests. Moreover, once space has been constituted—bounded and shaped—it, in turn, exerts its own influence on society.

Medieval churchmen had more than a passing interest in the construction of sacred space. On one level, the medieval church as ritual center was much more than a mere building. It was seen as a symbolic code: a "model" of the cosmos and image of the Celestial City, imbued with divine order and harmony as were the heavenly spheres.[1] In their attempts to reflect the symbolic interconnection between the Celestial City and the church as its earthly representation, churchmen throughout the Middle Ages were concerned with the "divine" ordering as well as the necessary protection of sacred space.

Central to many of the church's most holy beliefs and rituals, sacred space was seen as a type of privileged, efficacious space set apart from that which was profane or desacralized.[2] Cathedrals, churches, chapels, and monasteries, along with their precincts and cemeteries, were consecrated in formal religious ceremonies and were perceived as occupying special sacralized space. According to Peter of Celle, Abbot of St. Remi (twelfth century), "the cloister lies on the border of angelic purity and earthly contamination."[3] Thus in order to maintain the sacred quality of this privileged and ordered space, and to avoid desecration or pollution from outside forces, certain symbolic or physical boundaries were established. Moreover, beliefs in explicit dangers or divine punishment were formulated and circulated by churchmen to deter or threaten potential transgressors (especially women) who might plot to defy these policies and cross the forbidden thresholds.[4]

Although deeply affected by spatial policies, women have historically been denied the opportunity to exercise a direct role in determining or controlling religious or sacred space. Furthermore, women have been particularly vulnerable to changes or reforms in the articulation of space. Thus the adoption of gender based spatial proscriptions can be seen as an indirect index of ecclesiastical authority over women: they embody underlying values/attitudes and fears of the church hierarchy towards female sexuality and the perceived disruptive nature and "uncontainability" of women.[5]

During the past several decades scholars in a number of disciplines have explored the various aspects of space, place, and symbolic classification.[6] However, the phenomenon of gender as the determinant in the formulation of proscriptions of sacred space in the medieval world seems to have been taken for granted; and perhaps for that reason, the gender-based ordering of sacred space has not received the kind of attention it deserves. Through a study of several thousand saints' lives, canons of church councils, cartularies, liturgical collections, handbooks of ecclesiastical offices, penitentials, chronicles, correspondence, architectural and archeological data, enough evidence is available to provide a rough index of the various attempts at ordering and negotiating sacred space; and particularly the development of exclusionary policies as practiced by the medieval church. This study will survey one aspect of the sexual division of sacred space: the placement and displacement, and the general exclusion of women from male monastic churches from ca. 500-1200.

The Exclusion of Women from Monastic Churches

In general, parish churches and cathedrals, as public centers of worship and pilgrimage, encouraged the participation of women in various religious activities and rituals. Although within these churches space was heavily inflected by gender: for example, the clergy attempted to strictly segregate the sexes, provide preferential space to the male laity, and severely limit female participation within sacred spaces (i.e., the altar area, etc.), women still assumed essential functions and were valued for their contributions to the faith.[7] However, in contrast to these public centers of worship, many major medieval churches and chapels, even cemeteries and holy wells, were designated as strictly off limits to all members of the female sex. Women were prohibited from entering these sacred spaces and therefore found themselves at a distinct disadvantage in their need to practice their religion, i.e., to hear mass, make confession, or to personally visit the tombs of relatives or saints located in these churches. This gender-based discriminatory policy appears to have been particularly difficult for women during the period from the ninth through the twelfth centuries, an era which witnessed a growing popularity of the cult of relics as well as the proliferation of male monastic foundations which also served as major cult centers.

Influenced by ancient Greek, Jewish, and early Christian practices, the origins of these gender-based exclusionary policies are found in the early eremetic and monastic milieu and pertained particularly to male monastic churches and their precincts. With their emphasis on leading the life of "impatient angels" with strict asceticism and celibacy and their exaggerated fear of female sexuality, one of the major monastic characteristics was the rigorous avoidance of women. Many of these holy men/founders of monastic communities had espoused the eremetic life, fleeing to the "desert," to escape from the distractions of the "fleshy" world—which included the myriad of dangers traditionally associated with women. Therefore the *vitae* of these hermit saints frequently provide us with vivid descriptions of "brash" female intruders who allegedly attempted to seduce these holy men. The negative hagiographic portrayals of extreme female behavior marginalized women as the dangerous "other." The *Lives*, however, recounted in glowing detail the heroics of these spiritual athletes, that is their personal or private struggles with female distractions, temptation, concupiscence, the creative "ruses of Satan," and their ultimate success at "becoming dead to the world."[8] Over time this blatant fear of female sanctity, which often assumed the dimensions of a full-blown misogynism, became spatialized in the institutionalization of strict codes of female avoidance adopted by male monastic communities.

Monastic *regulae* and canons of church councils were especially concerned with the strict prohibition of female entry into monastic cloisters as well as monastic churches. St. Caesarius in his *Regula ad Monachos* notes that women were forbidden to enter the monastery; the *Regula S. Ferreoli* warns that no women, including nuns and young women, were to be allowed within the monastery.[9] The Carolingian reformer, St. Benedict of Aniane, notes that under no circumstances were women to enter the basilica of the monastery of Aniane.[10] The Camaldolese Benedictines not only forbid women entry into their churches but, according to a sermon by St. Romuald (d. 1027) prohibited them (under penalty of excommunication) from setting foot in the forests in which the monks' cells and churches were located.[11] The Cistercians were equally severe in forbidding all women entry into their monasteries.[12] A number of canons, for example, warned that the abbot must not allow any female to come into his monastery, not even to attend a solemn religious service. The severity of this policy is underscored by the fact that if the abbot disobeyed this injunction, he would be excommunicated or sent to another monastery where he would be condemned to bread and water for three months.[13] Many other records, (e.g., cartularies, chronicles, saints' lives, etc.), especially those relating to individual Benedictine houses, underscore the importance of these exclusionary policies for these communities and their reputations.

Sources of the period, however, seem indirectly to reflect the fact that despite their strict policies, churchmen often experienced difficulties putting them into practice; problems resulted in policing their restrictive barriers and keeping women from disturbing their sacred space. They therefore tried to enforce their authority and exclusionary policies by threats of divine wrath or supernatural punishment. Thus the popular saints' lives and chronicles of the period record a series of fascinating yet gruesome cautionary tales intended to serve as strong deterrents to potential female transgressors. They describe, for example, brazen women , who, daring to overstep these forbidden thresholds or boundaries of sacred space, found themselves subject to swift visible punishments by the "wronged" saints. Frequently these retaliatory acts were recorded as posthumous miracles of the saints whose churches/sacred space had been violated by these female intruders. When St. Siviard was abbot of the monastery Anisole (Maine) and wrote the *vita* of its founder, St. Calais (d. 545), a contemporary of the woman named Gunda attempted to enter the monastery and its church which had always been strictly off limits to all women. She was interested in discovering, if, after some one hundred years, St. Calais still enforced this gender-based restriction. According to the saints' *Life*, she therefore cut off her hair and disguised herself as a man in order to enter the cloister without being noticed. She coordinated her entry with that of the monks going to divine office, namely, when the doors of the church were open. Gunda then went into the oratory where their patron St. Calais' body was located. Suddenly, according to the *vita*, she was miraculously struck down by God—she lost her sight and black blood flowed from her breast. She also let out such a horrible scream that she attracted the attention of all of those who were present in the church. When interrogated by the monks, Gunda admitted her crime. The author then notes that this punishment had in fact a salutary effect in that it prevented other women, who might have been tempted, from trying a similar stunt.[14]

According to tradition, the hermit saint Goeznou had such a fear of women that he erected a huge stone as a marker beyond which no female was to tread under penalty of death. (Here the concept of the "threshold" was seen not simply as a metaphor but a point of maximum tension. It was at this spot that special vigilance was demanded against infiltration.) As noted in the saint's *vita*, in order to test this policy, a woman was said to have pushed another past this barrier; whereupon the assailant fell dead, while the woman who had reluctantly transgressed remained unharmed.[15] The tradition associated with the oratory of St. Goulven warned that all female transgressors would be struck blind by the saint. Those female trespassers of St. Fiacre's chapel were said through the posthumous intervention of the angry saint to go mad on the spot.[16] Similarly, we are told that in 1091, Queen-Saint Margaret of

Scotland was prohibited from entering the church of St. Lawrence from which all members of the female sex were rejected. When she attempted to ignore this policy and enter the church with her offerings, she was said to have been suddenly smitten and repelled. Fortunately, she was restored to health by the prayers of the clergy and was then able to present them with her offerings.[17]

Further cautionary examples derive from Symeon of Durham's defense of the exclusionary reform policies adopted at the cathedral of Durham (twelfth century) Briefly, the proscriptive policy at Durham was tied to the post-Conquest reform and the replacement in 1083 of the married clergy/canons by reformed Benedictine monks. It appears that with the reform initiated by William of St. Calais, who had previously been a monk at the monastery of St. Carileph (St. Calais) in Maine, the famous seventh-century patron St. Cuthbert was conveniently provided with a posthumous abhorrence of females (in the tradition of St. Calais.)[18] Thus the reform writings of Symeon of Durham served to reshape the patron saint of Durham according to the blatant prejudices of the period. Although this new reform type clearly conflicted with the historical Cuthbert, who was known to have befriended many women during his lifetime; this "historical inaccuracy" or creative reconstruction was apparently not problematic for the reformers. Symeon contended that Cuthbert had in fact been a blatant misogynist all of his life, and because of his great aversion toward women, it was well known that women were unable to enter any of the churches with the saint had been associated. He also noted that "This custom is so diligently observed, even unto the present day, that it is unlawful for women to set foot even within the cemeteries of those churches in which his body obtained a temporary resting-place, unless, indeed, compelled to do so by the approach of any enemy or the dread of fire."[19] Moreover, with the reformers' emphasis on celibacy and cultic purity, as well as the need to control or contain and segregate women from the monks/male clergy and sacred space, they established in the name of St. Cuthbert's alleged misogynism a line of a local blue frosterly marble in the floor of the second bay of the nave of Durham Cathedral. This line can still be seen today, stretching across the pavement from north to south—approximately one foot wide with a cross at its center. Beyond this "holy barrier," or impenetrable threshold, women were forbidden to pass. And according to the later "Rites of Durham," if by chance any woman crossed it into the body of the church, she would be taken straightaway and punished for some days![20]

Symeon of Durham then provides a lively description of a number of frightening punishments inflicted posthumously by the angry saint (from his feretory) on "shameless" women who dared to test the sacrosanct space of the cathedral, churchyard, or cemetery of Durham. He tells of a certain Sungeova who defied this sacred space by venturing across the churchyard: she immediately lost her senses and died the same evening.[21] Another disrespectful woman who dared to pass through the cemetery of Durham became mad and ended her life by cutting her own throat.[22] Symeon also relates in detail the story of Judith, wife of Earl Tostig:

> An honorable and devout woman (who) exceedingly loved St. Cuthbert, and contributed many ornaments to his church; and promised that she would add yet more together with landed possessions, if permission were granted her to enter within its walls, and to pray at his sepulcher. Not venturing to do such a thing as this in her own person, she had planned to send one of her waiting-maids before her, concluding that if the girl could do this in safety, she herself, the mistress, who was to follow after her, would incur no danger.

However, when the maid secretly attempted to enter the sacred churchyard she was struck by a violent gust of wind and suddenly became ill. She had scarcely returned home when she died. Symeon adds that the countess was terrified by this turn of events and to make amends, she and her husband commissioned a crucifix and images of Mary and St. John the Evangelist, covered in gold and silver, which they presented along with a number of other ornaments for the decoration of the church.[23] Thus after introducing a number of cautionary examples, Symeon notes that "Many other instances might easily be added to these, showing how the audacity of women was punished from heaven; but let these suffice, since we must proceed to other matters."[24]

Reginald, monk of Durham (twelfth century), relates another case in which a woman dared to defy the spatial barriers of Durham. Here Helisend, the chambermaid of the Queen of Scotland, disguised in a black cope and hood, secretly entered the cathedral. However the Sacristan, Bernard, intercepted her with the objurations of the coarsest kind and she was forcibly ejected from the church.[25]

Later sources which describe the building of the Lady Chapel at Durham in the early twelfth century further reinforce these popular antifeminist reform attitudes and the apparent need to rationalize and protect the cathedral's exclusionary policies of sacred space. During the construction of the Lady Chapel, originally located at the far east end of the church behind St. Cuthbert's shrine, the foundations and lower walls began to shrink and crack. This basic structural problem was attributed by churchmen to supernatural causes, namely, Cuthbert's great hatred of women. They believed or contended that the saint was simply objecting in his own subtle way to having a chapel of the Virgin (which would attract hordes of women) built so uncomfortably close to his own tomb. Thus contrary to the traditional spatial arrangement which placed the Lady Chapel at the east end of the church, the Lady Chapel at Durham came to be situated in a unique location; outside the west wall of the cathedral, thus keeping women physically as far as possible from the sacred east end of the church and the feretory or shrine of the holy St. Cuthbert.[26]

Similar cautionary tales can be found in other sources of this period. The contemporary *vita* of St. Bartholomew of Farne (d. 1193) recounts, for example, the story of a Flemish woman who had been a close friend of the saint in his early years. Later, after he had adopted the life of a hermit, she came to visit him on the island of the Inner Farne which had been made famous by St. Cuthbert. When she was forbidden to enter the saintly man's chapel, she became enraged, fiercely complaining that she was treated like a dog. Attempting to defy this sacred boundary or threshold and set foot into the chapel, she was suddenly thrown down on her back "as if by a whirlwind." We are told that it was only through St. Bartholomew's intervention that she recovered.[27]

Perhaps one of the most marvelous examples of these didactic tales can be found in Goscelin of Canterbury's *History of St. Augustine.*[28] In describing Augustine and his companions' trip from Rome to England, he relates their adventures during their overnight stay at Sai on the Loire. Here the missionaries were attacked by the inhabitants; particularly violent were the women who attempted to drive them out of the area. As described by Goscelin,

> But the women gathered together at the same time and rampaged against God's saints not just with irreverence but with so much madness, wailing, contempt, mockery, and derision, that men seemed in some sense harmless in comparison with them. It was not enough to cast them out, but they ran them down, dragged and pushed them along, exhausted them, and drove them out with mocking impudence.

Later the newly converted at Sai, inspired by miracles, established a church on the very site where Augustine had spent the night. In recounting or rationalizing its gender-based exclusionary policy (in contrast to the policy of Canterbury where the saint's tomb was located and women could enter "freely and legitimately"), Goscelin relates that a "perpetual miracle endures whereby no woman is ever able to enter that church or to draw water from the fountain, to the end that the world may know how greatly this gender offended God in the injury shown his servants."[29]

Goscelin then provides in some detail a wonderfully frightening example of a woman who dared to defy this policy established at the church of Sai and her "just" punishment, namely, an exploding womb followed by death! According to Goscelin,

> A prestigious matron attempted to enter here with a large wax candle, as if the saint would be flattered by her power and wealth. To those who stood by and attempted to frighten her off she responded that she had not sinned against the saint but desired to do him honor, and she pressed on in her presumptuous intention. And so she had scarcely

reached the forbidden boundary and sacred threshold when her entrails suddenly burst out; the secret parts of her womb flowed upon the earth, and she fell down miserably and died. The dead woman was dragged outside and taught everyone in horrific fashion what she herself had believed of no one. By such a rebuke all women have been instructed that they should fear touching open doors more than closed ones.[30]

While the expressed purpose of these cautionary tales was to serve as a deterrent to others contemplating similar actions—their repetition might also provide us with an indirect index of oblique strategies actually adopted by women who resented these discriminatory policies and thus attempted to test or challenge the boundaries of ecclesiastical/patriarchal authority. These stories might also have been designed as propaganda or subtle advertisement for these exclusive male monasteries whose famous churches housed the tombs of popular saints and important collections of relics. Thus they were used to underscore the overwhelming attraction or fame of the saint or church and to make the monastery or pilgrimage site all the more valued.

However, in general, these sources taken together underscore the church's enduring concern (sometimes more exaggerated than others) with the "necessary" segregation, containment, and exclusion of women from sacred space. With the emphasis on celibacy, cultic purity, and the underlying fear of female sexuality and threat of moral contagion, the church was highly suspicious of women assuming the privilege of entering monastic churches and their precincts. This was seen as a dangerous precedent; one which could only have a ruinous effect on the moral tenor of the monastery and its life of celibacy—also as a source of rumor and scandal, it would destroy their hard-won reputations. Moreover, on a practical level, some monks clearly did not see any need for women or a female presence (except for that of the Virgin Mary and female saints) in their monasteries. In fact, many felt they were better off without any women within miles of their monasteries as they would only provide a source of distraction and temptation. The churchmen therefore had the luxury to cultivate a totally masculine religious milieu or a "world without women."[31]

Although female monasteries frequently adopted policies of strict active and passive enclosure, they were unable to get along without a male presence, for on the bottom line they required a priest for at least sacramental functions and confession. Therefore their rules stipulate, for example, that with the exception of bishops, provisores, suppliers, priests, deacons, aged lectors, builders, etc., men were forbidden entry into the secret parts of the monastery and in the oratory. [32] In addition it appears that, at least in many of the early female monasteries, there is a basic difference in the ordering of sacred space; for in contrast to the male communities, women's houses made provision for the laity (male and female) to be allowed into their main ecclesia and burial churches. This is the case of La Balme, discussed later in this study, and this arrangement can be further corroborated by a variety of evidence from other female foundations of the period.[33] It also appears that many of the early (Merovingian/ Carolingian) female monasteries had several churches including a separate church for the abbess and nuns (the abbatial church), a funerary church, one for the laity, and another for churchmen; or, if the community had one major church it would frequently be divided so as to have separate space partitioned off for nuns to remove them from the distractions of the outside world; however, it would allow the laity, pilgrims, etc., entrance into the nave and chapels and access to the saints' tombs.[34] It therefore appears that the more inclusive spatial policies of the women's communities in regard to entry into their churches did not have the same effect on men as the male policies of exclusion had on women. I have not found, for example, parallel cases of alleged spiritual deprivations for men or male attempts to break into convents to worship or to venerate relics found in female monastic churches. Rather these exclusionary policies adopted by male communities placed a disproportionate burden or special hardship on women who wished to visit male monastic or pilgrimage churches for prayer and religious services, to visit the tombs of their male relatives, and particularly to receive the special benefits of the holy dead—the saints and their relics.

Policies of Negotiation and Accommodation of Sacred Space

Although we find a proliferation of monastic churches which
were officially designated as strictly off limits to women, there is
also some evidence or perhaps a certain awareness in regard to the
special problems which these policies might create for women as
well as a flexibility on the part of some churchmen to make
provisions for female worshippers who would otherwise find
themselves shut out from the church without opportunities for
worship, communion, or the veneration of saints and relics.

One solution to the problem of the exclusion of women from
sacred space was to provide a separate or alternative sacred space,
namely, a special chapel or small church, built just outside of the
monastery's walls, to accommodate female worshippers. According
to Symeon of Durham, a small church of this type was built by St.
Cuthbert on Lindisfarne Island. Inhabitants called it the "grene
cyrice" because it was situated upon a green plain. Cuthbert directed
"that the women who wished to hear masses and the word of God
should assemble there and that they should never approach the
church frequented by himself and the monks."[35] This chapel was
therefore to serve the religious needs of women; however, it was also
to keep them from attempting to enter the monastery's church. The
Regula of the monastery of Tarnatensis notes that women are
forbidden to enter into the monastery; however, they could go into
the oratory or guest house.[36] Similar arrangements were made in the
tenth century at the great reform center of Cluny. As noted in *The
Life of St. Odo of Cluny*, "Now, not far from it [the monastery of
Cluny] there was an oratory to which women were admitted to
pray. . . ."[37] The Cistercians also made special provisions for female
worshippers. According to their *Consuetudines*, in many of their
abbeys they built near the porterage a chapel for women which
opened to the outside of the monastery's wall. (This location also
allowed the porter to dispense bread and nourishment to women
travelers without allowing them within the monastic precinct.)[38]

Other sources record special concessions made to accommodate
female worshippers. The *vita* of St. Theofroi (d. ca. 728) explains
that although women were not permitted to enter his monastery's
church, the abbot allowed them to come near to the church doors

("haberent sedem circa templi januam"), and there they might receive special instructions on the merits of salvation.[39] Similarly, Goscelin of Canterbury notes in regard to the exclusionary policy of the monastic church of Sai: "But lest women there should seem entirely deprived of the holy father's grace, the inhabitants built a suitable holding-area for them before the doors of the church, (pro foribus ecclesiae receptaculum illis congruum aedificavere) where they would be able to gather, pray, pay their offerings and vows, and approach the holy mysteries."[40]

However, in general these exclusionary policies must have been particularly generous for those women who personally sought cures and miracles from a particular saint whose tomb was located within a male monastery. A moving description of the special hardships which these spatial prohibitions could cause for women can be found in the *vita* of the abbot saint Leutfridus (d. ca. 738). The *Life* notes that Leutfridus' church contained the relics of a number of saints, but its access was strictly forbidden to women. One day a blind woman on pilgrimage approached the monastery searching for a cure. When she learned that no women were admitted into the church and that she would be unable to approach the saint's relics for a cure, she was forced to give a candle in memory of God to a man. He then (serving as the woman's proxy) placed the candle before the tomb of St. Leutfridus. According to Leutfridus' miracles, only in this "indirect" way did the blind woman receive an immediate cure.[41]

Our sources also provide a few exceptional examples of perhaps a certain sympathy and enlightened sensitivity toward women's problems with exclusionary space and their need for equal access to saints and their intercessory powers. One early case can be found in Gregory of Tours' *Life of the Fathers*. In this work he relates a discussion between the aged brother-abbots Lupicinus and Romanus making preparations for their burials. Romanus said to his brother, "'I do not want to have my tomb in a monastery which women are forbidden to enter. As you know, the Lord had given me the grace of bringing cures, although I am unworthy and do not deserve it, and many have been snatched from various illnesses by the imposition of my hands and the power of the Lord's cross. Thus many people will gather at my tomb when I leave the light of this life. That is why I ask to rest far from the monastery.' For that reason, when he died he was buried ten miles from the monastery, on a small hill. At length a great church was built over the tomb, and large crowds came there every day. Many miracles are now accomplished there in the name of God: the blind find light, the deaf their hearing, the paralysed the use of their limbs."[42] Thus according to Gregory of Tours, Romanus chose not to be buried in his own monastery (which would have excluded female pilgrims) but rather at a site located at a safe distance from his monastery. It is interesting to note that the church in which the saint's tomb found its resting place was La Balme, a large convent where Romanus' sister held the office of abbess. Therefore, in contrast to his monastic church, this church was then open to female and male pilgrims.[43]

The case of the monastic church of Elnone is also of interest. According to the *Life of St. Amand* (d. ca. 679), sixteen years after the death of the saint, a new church was built because the old one was too inadequate or small and inaccessible to women.[44]

The formulation of policies of exclusion and an awareness of the difficulties they might cause for women are also recorded in the *vita* of St. Alto, abbot of Altomunster (d. ca. 760). Here Alto is described as strongly objecting to the plans of his superior, the reformer St. Boniface, who insisted that women be forbidden entry into Alto's new church. Boniface finally consented to the Abbot's petition and consecrated this new monastic church; allowing women as well as men to worship there in common. Perhaps reflecting a compromise in their negotiations, the sacred foundation, located next to the church, was consecrated with the proviso that no woman be permitted to approach it or drink from it.[45]

During the translation of the relics of St. Vincent to the monastery of Castres, we learn that the martyr's body was not immediately brought into the monastic church (which was closed to women) but rather placed in the church of the Genitricis Dei where many devoted women flocked to see the relics. Later a new church in the saint's honor was built near to the monastery which was open to both sexes.[46]

A unique and fascinating case of special concessions made in response to women's insistence on access to holy relics is found in the monastery of Fleury/St-Benoît-sur-Loire. According to the *Miracles of St. Benedict*, when the popular relics of Sts. Denis and

Sebastian were brought to the monastery of Fleury (ninth century), a large crowd of men and women followed the saints' relics because of certain miracles which occurred. Ancient authority had forbidden women's admittance within the outer gates of the monastery, thus entreaties were made so that women be permitted to enter the church where the relics were in order to pray and carry out their vows. But since this went against monastic discipline, they were refused. The women persisted in their request and caused an impressive disturbance which could not be ignored. Others joined them and with great difficulty they were able to persuade the abbot to have a tent set up outside the monastery gates on the eastern side where the relics would be displayed for twenty-four hours, beginning at the vigil of Sunday, after which time they were then taken back inside the monastic church. When this arrangement was carried out, crowds of people from near by and distant places flocked to Fleury to secure healing for the soul and body.[47] It then appears from this account that the women did not passively accept the restrictive spatial policies of the monastery rather they staged an angry protest. It was only under that pressure that the abbot and monks of Fleury begrudgingly granted these women this rather limited privilege.[48]

Other sources note special concessions made by churchmen or religious communities to individual noblewomen or abbesses, who under unique circumstances, were allowed entrance into their churches. The *vita* of St. Lioba notes: "Sometimes Lioba came to the monastery of Fulda [St. Boniface's monastery] to say her prayers, a privilege never granted any women either before or since, because from the day that monks began to dwell there, entrance was forbidden to women. Permission was only granted to her for the simple reason that the holy martyr St. Boniface had commended her to the seniors of the monastery and because he had ordered her remains to be buried there."[49]

Similarly we learn that the monastery of St. Bertin made special concessions to allow a noblewoman to enter the monastery's church. Thus in 938, despite the strict prohibitions against female entry, Adela, countess of Flanders was allowed to enter the church. Apparently in a state of extreme illness, the countess had petitioned the monastery to allow her to pray for a cure before the altar of their patron, St. Bertin. Although we are assured that in the entire history of the monastery no woman had ever crossed its threshold, the countess was given special permission to enter the church by the advocatus of the bishop, the treasurer of the monastery (who no doubt exercised an important role in this decision), and the monks. She was brought into the monastery during Easter week by the bishop "not without great trembling." She prostrated herself before the altar of St. Bertin where she prayed and her "body received health." The saint's *Life* adds that after the countess' miraculous cure, she brought them many ornaments and as long as she lived never ceased to make generous donations to the monastery.[50] Thus, at least from an economic standpoint, the granting of this special privilege proved beneficial to the monastery.

The chronicle of Hugh of Flavigny refers to another exceptional case in which a woman was allowed within a male monastery. Apparently, in order to learn more about the reform practices of monasticism, Ava, abbess of St. Maur of Verdun, was permitted to observe monastic life at the great reform center of Cluny. Although St. Odo and the rules of the monastery apparently forbade any woman entrance to the cloister of the great church, out of friendship for Abbot Richard, founder of Ava's community of St. Maur, Abbot Odilo of Cluny, brought Ava not only into the cloister but also into the chapter. In addition, on Sunday she was received in the procession of brothers. The chronicler, Hugh of Flavigny, however, underscores the exceptional character of this event, "for continually up until today" (ca. 1100) he writes, "the memory of this visit still remains at Cluny."[51]

Other sources note special ajustments or a relaxation of these strict policies which excluded women from male monastic space. One concession made at the General Chapter of the Cistercians in 1157, for example, allowed women to visit a new church of the Order during the nine days following its dedication but stressed that this period of time could not under any circumstances be extended and that women guests were not allowed to remain in the church over night.[52] (This limited provision which permitted women to visit newly constructed Cistercian churches appears to have been based on economic expediency with the intent that in the enthusiasm of these "open houses" the female visitors would be moved to make generous contributions to the community.) A number of cases however reveal the punishments imposed upon Cistercian abbots for their "excessive" hospitality to female religious and other women. The abbot of Savigny was severely punished for inviting a group of nuns to sing in his monastery's new choir and eat in their refectory on the day of the dedication of his church.[53]

Similarly, economic motivation appears to have provided the rationale for the manipulation of exclusionary policies of sacred space at the abbey of Ottobeuren. Here the reform abbot "nevertheless. . . admitted noble women to parts of the monastery; and since these were wealthy, they abundantly endowed the monastery."[54]

Perhaps one of the most dramatic public challenges to the gender-based proscriptions of the sacred space is described in the *Miracles of Robert of Arbrissel*. Upon learning that women were prohibited from entering the Abbey Church of Menelay (where he was slated to preach), Robert of Arbrissel publicly defended their policies and brought many women along with him into the church. He thus blatantly provoked those in charge of guarding the church doors (whose job it was to turn women away); they then loudly invoked their patron Saint Menelay to avenge this insult. As described in the *Miracles*, Robert of Arbrissel responded to their threats with a stirring defense of women and their nature, arguing that in fact the saints are not enemies of the Brides of Christ. He then demanded: "who is it who dared to say that there would be any church in which women would not be permitted to enter because of their transgressions and guilt. Which is more important, the material temple of God or the spiritual temple in which God lives? If the woman takes and eats the body and blood of Christ, think what folly it is to believe that she must not enter the church!" And according to Robert of Arbrissel's *Miracles*, "In this manner, after he had publicly demonstrated the truth, this error stopped and became totally extinct."[55]

Thus while many of the institutional sources from this period describe strict policies of women's exclusion from monastic churches and cloisters and their precincts, at the same time, under certain conditions, they also reveal a flexibility on the part of some churchmen—special provisions of alternate space and adjustments in the boundaries of sacred space made for women with religious leanings. In some cases these concessions were forced upon reluctant churchmen by determined women who were intent on having equal opportunities in their access to saints. Not infrequently these manipulations of sacred space appear to have been the result of crass economic considerations; other cases, however, reveal a sensitivity and sympathy toward women, an awareness of the special difficulties brought about by these proscriptive policies.

While there is a continuity of these gender-based exclusionary policies from ca. 500-1200, it appears that they became especially problematic for women from the ninth through the twelfth centuries. For it was during this period that there emerged a growing popularity of the cult of the saints, pilgrimages, along with the establishment of many new or reformed male monasteries which housed famous collections of relics. Women were strongly attracted to the cults of saints; they needed access to the saints' tombs, their special intercessory powers and miraculous cures.[56] At the same time the reform movements of the period, for example, the Carolingian, Cluniac, and Gregorian reforms, placed an increased emphasis on the regularization of monastic life, on celibacy with an exaggerated fear of female sexuality and threat of moral contagion, which resulted in a full-blown misogynism; all of which underscored the need to re-emphasize and attempt to implement severe policies of exclusion from male monasteries. Thus during this period the sources frequently focus on exacting codes which defined/limited sacred space; they concurrently underscore the various threats, challenges, negotiations in regard to women and their limited access to sacred space, especially admission to the tombs of the holy dead.

Despite harsh, uncompromising policies and threats of divine intervention, it appears that during this period, churchmen frequently experienced difficulties in their attempts to enforce their agendas of exclusion. Women did not acquiesce or accept quietly, without protesting, these spatial restrictions. This is underscored by the repetition of canons warning ecclesiastics that they must use their authority to stop women from threatening their special prerogatives or from encroaching on sacred space. In addition, many of the sources, especially male saints' lives, frequently condemn "imprudent," disruptive females who dared to test, challenge, or ignore the "sacred" prohibitions, who refused to be scared off by the "divine deterrents." These defiant women perhaps saw these discriminatory measures exactly as what they were—not divinely inspired, natural or inevitable but rather culturally determined man-made proscriptions of sacred space used to exercise control, regulate social behavior, or accommodate financial gain. In their acts of insubordination, in overstepping the arbitrary thresholds or boundaries and pushing aside the man-made barriers which were designed to cordon off sacred space, these medieval women dared to protest publicly the inequities of these policies for themselves and their sex.

NOTES

1. See especially Otto von Simpson, *The Gothic Cathedral: Origins of Gothic Architecture and the Medieval Concept of Order*, 2nd ed. (New York, 1962), 8, 35-38.

2. Mircea Eliade, *The Sacred and the Profane: The Nature of Religion*, trans. Willard R. Trask (New York, 1959); Mary Douglas, *Purity and Danger: An Analysis of the Concepts of Pollution and Taboo* (Harmondsworth, 1970), esp. 1-22, 121-39.

3. Peter of Celle, "The School and the Cloister," in *Selected Works*, trans. Hugh Feiss, Cistercian Publications (Kalamazoo, 1987), 79.

4. Douglas, *Purity and Danger*, 1-22, 121-39.

5. Carol J. Clover notes the "uncontainability" of the independent woman of early Scandinavia in "The Politics of Scarcity: Notes on the Sex Ratio in Early Scandinavia," in *New Readings on Women in Old English Literature*, eds. Helen Damico and Alexandra Hennessy Olson (Bloomington and Indianapolis, 1990), 128.

6. See for example, Margaret Aston, "Segregation in Church," *Women in the Church: Studies in Church History 27*, eds. W. J. Sheils and Diana Wood (Oxford, 1990), 237-94; Roberta Gilchrist, *Gender and Material Culture: The Archeology of Religious Women* (London and New York, 1994); Sofia Goesch Gajano and Lucetta Scaraffia, *Luoghi sacri e spàzi délla santità* (Turin, 1990). I would like to thank Mary Martin McLaughlin for this

reference. GESTA (The International Center for Medieval Art), XXXI/2, 1992—this issue is devoted to medieval women's religious and sacred space. *Sexuality and Space: Princeton Papers on Architecture*, ed. Beatriz Colomina (New York, 1992); Peter Brown. *The Body and Society: Men, Women, and Sexual Renunciation in Early Christianity* (New York, 1988); R. I. Moore, *The Formation of a Persecuting Society: Power and Deviance in Western Europe, 950-1250* (Oxford and New York, 1987).

7. Jane Tibbetts Schulenburg, "Medieval Women and Sacred Space: Symbol and Practice," paper delivered at the Seventh Berkshire Conference on the History of Women," Wellesley College, June 21, 1987. See Margaret Aston, "Segregation in Church," pp. 237-94. I am presently working on a book on medieval women and sacred space, ca. 500-1200. It will also include an examination of the spatial arrangements of double monasteries and affiliated houses, anchorholds, etc.

8. See my forthcoming book, *"Forgetful of Their Sex": Female Sanctity and Society, ca. 500-1100* (Chicago, 1995), ch. VIII. See also Jane Tibbetts Schulenburg, "Saints and Sex, ca. 500-1100: Striding down the Nettled Path of Life," in *Sex in the Middle Ages: A Book of Essays*, ed. Joyce E. Salisbury (New York, 1991), 203-31.

9. *PL*, 66, ch. 154, col. 337.

10. *PL*, 66, ch. 159, col. 341.

11. *PL*, 66, ch. 164, col. 345.

12. *PL*, 66, ch. 155, cols. 338-39.

13. Hefele Leclerq, *Histoire des Conciles*, 3, 1, Council of Auxerre (587), p. 220.

14. *Acta Sanctorum*, hereafter cited as *AASS*, Julii I (July 1), p. 87.

15. *AASS*, Oct. XI (Oct. 25), p. 691.

16. *AASS*, Aug. VI (Aug. 30), pp. 598-620.

17. Johanne Mabillon, *Acta Ordinis S. Benedicti* (Luca, 1740), V, p. 269.

18. See Schulenburg, *"Forgetful of Their Sex"*, ch. 8; Joan Nicholson, *"Feminae Gloriosae*: Women in the Age of Bede," in *Medieval Women*, ed. Derek Baker, esp. p. 28 where she notes this posthumous antifeminism; Victoria Tudor, "The Misogyny of Saint Cuthbert," *Archaelogia Aeliana*, 5th series, 12 (1984), 157-67; Victoria Tudor, "The Cult of St. Cuthbert in the Twelfth Century: The Evidence of Reginald of Durham," in *Saint Cuthbert. His Cult and His Community to AD 1200*, eds. Gerald Bonner, David Rollason, and Clare Stancliffe (Woodbridge, Suffolk, and Wolfboro, New Hampshire, 1989), 447-67.

19. *The Historical Works of Simeon of Durham: The Church Historians of England*, trans. Joseph Stevenson (London, 1855), 3, pt. 2, ch. 22, pp. 657-58.

20. *Rites of Durham* (1593): Surtees Society: CVII (Durham and Edinburgh, 1902), ch. 17, p. 35.

21. *The Historical Works of Simeon of Durham*, ch. 23, p. 658.

22. *The Historical Works of Simeon of Durham*, ch. 24, pp. 658-59.

23. *The Historical Works of Simeon of Durham*, ch. 46, pp. 682-83.

24. *The Historical Works of Simeon of Durham*, ch. 24, p. 659.

25. Reginald of Durham, *Libellus de Admirandis Beati Cuthberti Virtutibus* (London, 1835), ch. 74, pp. 151-54.

26. *Rites of Durham*, ch. 22, p. 43.

27. David Hugh Farmer, *The Oxford Dictionary of Saints* (Oxford, 1978/82), 30; *AASS*, Iun. V, pp. 714-21.

28. I would like to express my extreme gratitude to David Townsend for sharing this wonderful example with me. This is also David Townsend's

translation of Goscelin's *Life of St. Augustine Bishop of Canterbury, AASS,* Maii, VI (May, 26), p. 377.

29. *AASS*, Maii, VI (May 26), p. 377.

30. *AASS*, Maii, VI (May 26), p. 377.

31. See David F. Noble, *A World Without Women: The Christian Clerical Culture of Western Science* (New York, 1992).

32. For a survey of various policies of active and passive enclosure, see Jane Tibbetts Schulenburg, "Strict Active Enclosure and Its Effects on the Female Monastic Experience (ca. 500-1100) in *Distant Echoes: Medieval Religious Women*, I, ed. John A. Nichols and Lillian Thomas Shank (Kalamazoo, 1984), 51-86. See also Cesaire d'Arles, *Oeuvres Monastiques: Oeuvres pour les Moniales*, I, Sources Chrétiennes, no. 345, ed./trans. Adalbert de Vogue and Joel Correau (Paris, 1988), especially pp. 35-273; Sr. Maria Caritas McCarthy, *The Rule for Nuns of St. Caesarius of Arles: A Translation with a Critical Introduction* (Washington D.C., 1960); R. Naz, "Cesaire d'Arles (règles de saint)" in *Dictionnaire de droit canonique* 3 (Paris, 1938), 260-78; *The Ordeal of Community: Rule of Donatus of Besançon*, Peregrina Translation Series, no. 5, 2nd ed., trans. Jo Ann McNamara and John Halborg (Toronto, 1993), ch. 55, p. 62.

33. See Cesaire d'Arles, *Oeuvres Monastiques: Oeuvres pour les moniales*, 98-113; Marquise de Maille, "Les monasteres colombaniens des femmes," in *Les Cryptes des Jouarre* (Paris, 1977), 26ff; Yvonne Labande-Mailfert, "Les débuts de Sainte-Croix," in *Histoire de l'Abbaye Sainte-Croix de Poitiers: Quatorze siècles de vie monastique*, in *Mémoires de la Société des Antiquaires de l'Ouest*, 4 serie, 19 (1986-1987), 25-116.

34. Laband-Maillfert, "Les débuts de Sainte-Croix," 25-116; for the later period see also *GESTA*, 31/2, 1992.

35. *Historical Works of Simeon of Durham*, ch. 22, pp. 657-58.

36. *PL*, 66, ch. 154, col. 337.

37. John of Salerno, *The Life of St. Odo of Cluny* in *St. Odo of Cluny: The Makers of Christendom*, ed. Dom Gerard Sitwell (London and New York, 1958), ch. 36, p. 37.

38. Marcel Aubert, *L'Architecture Cistercienne en France* (Paris, 1947), I, p. 47.

39. *Acta Sanctorum Ordinis S. Benedicti*, 3, p. 481.

40. *AASS*, Maii, VI (May 26), p. 377.

41. *Acta Sanctorum Ordinis S. Benedicti*, 3, p. 593.

42. Gregory of Tours, *Life of the Fathers*, trans. Edward James, bk. I, ch. 6, p. 34.

43. Gregory of Tours, *Life of the Fathers*, bk. I, ch. 6, pp. 34, 137, no. 11.

44. *PL*, 66, ch. 161, col. 343; see also Maille, *Les Cryptes de Jouarre*, 27.

45. *PL*, 66, ch. 163, cols. 344-45.

46. *PL*, ch. 159, col. 341.

47. *Les miracles de Saint Benoît*, ed. E. De Certain (Paris, 1888), I, pp. 64-65.

48. This case is also noted by Janet L. Nelson in her interesting study, "Women and the Word in the Earlier Middle Ages," in *Women in the Church: Studies in Church History*, 27 (1990), 68.

49. Rudolf, *The Life of St. Leoba* in *The Anglo-Saxon Missionaries in Germany*, trans. and ed. C. H. Talbot (New York, 1954), 233.

50. *Acta Sanctorum ordinis S. Benedicti*, 3, p. 139.

51. *Chronicon Hugonis, PL*, 154, col. 239.

52. Aubert, *L'Architecture Cistercienne en France*, 47.

53. Aubert, *L'Architecture Cistercienne en France*, 47.

54. G. G. Coulton, *Five Centuries of Religion: The Friars and the Dead Weight of Tradition, 1200-1400 A.D.* (Cambridge, 1927), 649.

55. J. Dalarun, "Robert d'Arbrissel et les femmes," *Annales ESC* 39 (1984): esp. 152-53. I would like to thank André Vauchez for bringing this study to my attention.

56. See Jane Tibbetts Schulenburg, "Saints, Gender and the Production of Miracles in Medieval Europe," paper presented at the Ninth Berkshire Conference on the History of Women, June 1992, Vassar College; Tudor, "The Cult of St. Cuthbert in the Twelfth Century," 447-67; Pierre-André Sigal, *L'Homme et les miracles dan la France médiévale (XI-XII siècle)* (Paris, 1985), especially 259-61; Ronald C. Finucane, *Miracles and Pilgrims: Popular Beliefs in Medieval England* (London, 1977), 118, 104-106, 152-51, 166-67, 183-86: Caroline Walker Bynum, *Fragmentation and Redemption* (New York, 1991), 188-89.

Ecclesia Semper Reformanda: Clerical Celibacy and Reform in the Church

Daniel F. Callahan

In his final work, translated into English as *Fifty Years of Catholic Theology: Conversations with Yves Congar*, the late Dominican theologian, one of the most influential Catholic thinkers of the twentieth century and a central figure behind the scenes at the Second Vatican Council, makes the extraordinary statement that ". . . by the end of the century there will be no more priests in the whole of France than there are taxi drivers in Paris–14,000," a truly disturbing figure for the country known as the eldest daughter of the church.[1] Yet a similar situation is found in many countries throughout the developed world.[2] Recent figures on the Catholic Church in the United States indicate a probable decline of forty per cent in the number of diocesan priests over a forty-year period, from 35,000 active diocesan priests in 1966 to c. 21,000 by 2005.[3] Just as troubling is the problem of an aging clergy, with almost half fifty-five or older and only an eighth thirty-four or younger by 2005.[4] At the same time the number of Catholic laity in the United States continues to grow. There will be c. 2,200 parishioners for each priest in 2005 as compared to 1,100 per priest in 1966.[5] Moreover, it has been noted that Roman Catholicism worldwide seems to be the only major religion having serious difficulty filling the ranks of its ministers.[6]

The reasons for the precipitous fall in numbers of priests are many. The extraordinary changes resulting from Vatican II undoubtedly have played a role in destabilizing many clergy unwilling or unable to deal with the new order. The growing involvement of the laity at all levels in the Catholic Church also has diminished the role of the priest, especially in parish life. The inability of a number of priests to deal with the increasing centralization in the church and the rigid conservatism of Rome, especially in sexual matters, surely plays a significant role in the

departure of many clergy from the priesthood.[7] The growing push of
women for more responsibilities and authority has also caused a
reexamination of the nature of Holy Orders. Studies indicating that one
third of all priests are homosexual, with an even higher percentage in the
seminaries, have also raised questions about who is attracted to the
priesthood.[8] Most disturbing of all have been accusations of pedophilia
against a number of clergymen in the past decade, especially in the
United States, not even sparing the hierarchy, charges that have greatly
stained the image of the priest.[9] All these factors have altered the
sacerdotal persona and made it less attractive for many. The requirement
of celibacy also plays an important role in the large number of
individuals leaving the priesthood and for those unwilling to consider
the priesthood as a calling. A recent study has indicated that if celibacy
were made optional there would be at least a fourfold increase in the
number of young Catholic men who would be seriously interested in
becoming priests.[10] The obligation of celibacy is quite simply the major
obstacle in their pursuing this path.

Any significant reform of the Roman Catholic Church requires that
the issue of celibacy be squarely addressed. Yet to have done so in the
post-Tridentine Catholic Church prior to Pope John XXIII's
summoning of the Second Vatican Council in 1959 would have been
virtually unthinkable. It was his call for *aggiornamento*, the bringing up-
to-date of the Catholic Church, that focused attention on the idea of
ecclesia semper reformanda, an idea so dear to John Calvin and the
Protestant reformers in the sixteenth century.[11]

The eminent theologian Hans Küng in his seminal work *The
Council, Reform and Reunion* indicated the importance of Pope John
XXIII's idea of *aggiornamento* and the central position of the theme of
the ever reforming church.[12] *Aggiornamento* did not end with the
completion of Vatican II but is on-going, comparable to the Protestant
reformers' idea of *Ecclesia semper reformanda*. *Aggiornamento* is not a
crude relativism but an attempt to renew the church in the light of
modern needs, yet remaining true to Sacred Scripture and the traditions
of the church through the guidance of the Holy Spirit. Küng sought to
show the scriptural roots for this idea of reform and to indicate that it
was not totally alien to the theology of the church from the thirteenth
century onwards. The theme of reform often appeared in the writings of
the patristic church and in the early Middle Ages, as Gerhard Ladner
demonstrated in a number of his writings, especially in *The Idea of*

Reform: Its Impact on Christian Thought and Action in the Age of the Fathers.[13] The early medieval ideas of reform were espoused by Pope Leo IX and his circle toward the middle of the eleventh century when they sought to end simony and nicolaitism within the western church.[14] Yet as several essays in this volume have indicated, ecclesiastical reform and efforts to impose clerical celibacy were conjoined in the minds of a number of churchmen in the three centuries before Leo IX and Gregory VII.[15] And it is clear in most of the essays in this book that the attempts, even before the First and Second Lateran Councils, to require celibacy for the clergy in the church in the west became central to the development of further efforts for reform, even if that reform was not yet regarded as an ever present necessity for the church in the world.

I wish to take this opportunity to express my gratitude to Michael Frassetto for asking me to read the essays in this volume and comment on their contributions. When one recalls that the pieces were not commissioned, that they were submitted by their authors without having received any guidelines about content and that the contributors did not know who else was submitting a piece, the finished product is a remarkable mosaic forming a coherent picture. What is clearly seen is the status of the obligation of celibacy in the early Middle Ages and the growing awareness of many churchmen in the tenth and eleventh centuries of the importance of its central position in the life of the western church and the need to enforce it if the church was to be reformed and restored to its original purity. Although there is, not surprisingly, a certain amount of overlapping material, each essay stands on its own as a valid and important contribution to the formation of the full image.

The essays by Edward Peters and Paul Beaudette offer valuable overviews of the issue of celibacy in the history of the western church–the former for what it says about the evolution of the historiography on the issue after the Middle Ages, the latter for its focus on the central position of celibacy to many throughout the Middle Ages. Edward Peters' rich essay, incorporating much recent scholarship, owes much to his studies of the career of Henry Charles Lea, whose own writings on celibacy played so important a role in the study of the issue in the late nineteenth and early twentieth century. One of the great strengths of Peters' essay is its success in considering the scholarship in the light of the period in which it was produced. It is helpful to be reminded about the difficulty of scholarly detachment on so controversial an issue. To this reader the greatest strength of Paul Beaudette's essay is the material on the centrality of the third and fourth century for the history of celibacy in the western church. In seeking to understand what the canons of Elvira reflect, he examines the roles of asceticism, sacralization and the negative attitudes toward sexuality, but sees as the principal factor the role of ritual or cultic purity. The last point is one which a number of the authors in the collection rightly point to as central in explaining the continuing importance of the celibate life for the sacred ministers. Their debt to the writings of Mary Douglas and Peter Brown is constantly acknowledged.

The second section, "Episcopal and Monastic Attitudes toward Celibacy in the Early Middle Ages," might just as easily be viewed as the early medieval roots of the eleventh-century papal reform stand on celibacy. These essays are by a group of young scholars, the work of most not yet well known. Some of the most important and fascinating findings in the entire volume are presented in this part of the book. Picking up on several themes from Beaudette's essay, Mayke de Jong in her essay on the Carolingians and celibacy has much on the continuing importance of the emphasis on ritual purity, especially in the monasteries as centers for such an interest. The importance of the Old Testament in the period receives quite properly much attention. Valuable also is her consideration of the debt of the Carolingians to the earlier reform efforts of such figures as Gregory of Tours, Caesarius of Arles, and Boniface.

As in the preceding essay, the study of the spirituality of Odo and Cluny by Phyllis Jestice emphasizes the essential importance of ritual purity. She presents the reformed monks of the tenth century as ". . . the first firmly self-motivated reforming group in the medieval church."[16] Not only the ritual purity in Cluny's spirituality, with its emphasis on the Eucharist, was important for the Cluniac reform, but so also was a Christian perspective, evident in the writings of Odo and Odilo, in which there is attention to the emulation of Christ. She additionally indicates Odo's roots in the secular clergy and his continuing interest in reforming their sexual mores.

Elizabeth Dachowski continues the study of the central importance of the monastic reform movement of the tenth and early eleventh century in her piece on Abbo of Fleury and celibacy. Using his tripartite division of society in the *Liber Apologeticus* into virgins, continent and married, she notes how Abbo is able to develop his claims for monastic privileges. She also examines, in a way comparable to that of R. I. Moore in his essay, the connection between property and celibacy and the central importance of chastity in preventing loss of land.

Like the earlier essays in this section, that by Michael Frassetto, based on the sermons of Ademar of Chabannes in the early eleventh century, considers the continuing importance of ritual purity in the minds of monks supporting reform in the church. Frassetto, however, is particularly interested in the role of the recently appearing heretics, about whom Ademar has so much to say, in generating ecclesiastical reform in reaction to their teachings. It is the asceticism of the heretics and their attacks on the material aspects of Christian observance which causes Ademar in his writings and the church leaders of Aquitaine in their ecclesiastical gatherings of the period to condemn their criticisms and reaffirm the sacraments, in particular the Eucharist. Also needed in response to the asceticism of the heretics was a reaffirmation of the purity of the clergy by a condemnation of clerical marriage. The heretics were charged to be false Christians, antichrists who only appeared to be holy, a theme Ademar develops at great length in the apocalyptic imagery in his sermons treating the years immediately before 1033 and the Last Days. In this context the heretics were a sure sign of the end.

David Van Meter's essay on the argument for clerical celibacy in Francia in the first half of the eleventh century nicely draws together many of the themes considered in the other essays of this section. Examining the central importance of the ternary division of society in the minds of many of the monks of the period, especially concentrating on Abbo of Fleury and the Cluniacs, he shows how the eschatological perspective on celibacy played a central role in the reform movement. Of particular importance in this respect was Gerard of Cambrai who was so active an opponent of the heretics of the time. The theme of a world about to be renewed is also reflected in the pivotal nature of this period, years so crucial for the ecclesiastical reform which will not be fully institutionalized until the papal revolution later in the century.

That revolution in many ways is the heart of this book and is examined in the third section by four noted scholars who have already written extensively about the central importance of the eleventh century. R. I. Moore's essay examines the relationship between clerical property and the support of the reformers for clerical celibacy. He is particularly interested in the connection between the growing amount of land under ecclesiastical control and the pressures place on the church by the rapidly increasing population, on which point he draws upon earlier work by himself and by such scholars as David Herlihy. As in the essays by Jestice and Van Meter, he is particularly interested in the connection between Cluny and celibacy, here utilizing the work of Barbara Rosenwein and Dominique Iogna-Prat. Reform for many monasteries, especially Cluny, becomes closely associated with the restoration of ecclesiastical property. This return of lands is also connected with the Peace of God, mentioned by Frassetto and Van Meter, which also promoted clerical celibacy and contributed to a restructuring of the lay society.

If R. I. Moore's essay focused primarily on monastic sponsorship of sexual purity in the eleventh century as a way of managing and maintaining property holdings, that by Megan McLaughlin examines the promotion of clerical celibacy by studying the image of the bishop as bridegroom. During the eleventh century the episcopal ring came to be seen as the symbol of the bishop's relationship with his church. From this sign would in substantial part spring the problem of lay investiture, with the emperor investing his bishops with ring and staff. Well treated is the development of the image of the bishop's ring in the polemical literature of the late eleventh century in which the conservatives were in strong opposition to the reformers' use of the image of the bishop or priest as bridegroom.

The essays by Professors Blumenthal and Cowdrey bring us to the central figure in the papal reform movement of the eleventh century, Pope Gregory VII. The pieces nicely complement each other. The Blumenthal piece is broader in scope than that of Cowdrey and devotes more attention to the antecedents and precedents for the prohibition of nicolaitism by Pope Gregory VII in 1075, especially the actions of Pope Leo IX and the legislation of 1059. She indicates that Gregory VII contributed nothing original to what later appeared in the legislation of Lateran II of 1139, which was later incorporated into Gratian's *Decretum*, but that it was the legislation of 1059 which acted as a guide on the matter throughout his papacy. H. E. J. Cowdrey's essay focuses much more sharply on the actions of the man Gregory VII with regard to the chastity of the clergy. One of the particular strengths of the piece is its drawing on Gregory's letters in order to concentrate on the period of 1074 to early 1076, a time before his energies had to be more fully expended in the controversy with Henry IV. The examination of the papal legates carrying the reform north of the Alps and the often negative reception is also of great value. Cowdrey is in agreement with Blumenthal on the lack of originality of Gregory VII on the issue of nicolaitism, but he does see this papacy as the turning point on the issue because of the pope's forcefulness and his emphasis on the necessity of a chaste clergy.

The final section of the book examines some medieval and modern consequences of the insistence on celibacy for the clergy. The four essays have very different orientations. Maureen Miller, extending her study of the church in northern Italy, which she began with her book on the diocese of Verona, 950-1150,[17] looks at the effect of reform at the local level and indicates that the ideal of celibacy for the clergy would be pursued if given adequate support from the regional church. Like that of Professor Moore, her essay is particularly interested in the connection between church land and the family strategies to provide for the progeny. She points to Ratherius of Verona as one who understood that financial support was necessary if the clergy were to be reformed. She also demonstrates the triumph of the eleventh-century reform by which the clergy would be supported by their churches through the integration of proprietary churches into the diocesan structure. The success of the reform was also seen in the increasing tendency for clerics to live together in community and thus give mutual support to one another in seeking to achieve celibacy.

Frank Gentry's study of Heinrich of Melk's views on clerical life examines the effects of the Gregorian Reform in Germany by looking at the popular piety of the twelfth century through the eyes of a lay critic. The essay indicates that the issue of clerical marriage was barely mentioned in German vernacular literature before Heinrich who attacked unworthy priests. What is especially important, as Gentry notes, is that the issues of celibacy and simony were no longer the sole concern of churchmen writing in Latin. He also draws an interesting parallel between the lay involvement in church reform in the twelfth century and that occurring in the Catholic Church today.

The study by Jane Tibbetts Schulenburg centers on another group who are having a great impact on the reconsideration of celibacy in the modern church–women. Examining how the ordering of space reflects a society, she considers the medieval church's attitude toward women polluting sacred space, a problem especially keen in reform periods focusing on celibacy. Through an examination of the hagiographical depiction of women during the Benedictine centuries, the period 800-

1200, with its roots in the misogyny of the desert fathers, she is able to show the severe warping of Christian values in this world without women.

The essays in this book study celibacy as the desired norm for clerics, celibacy as an essential part of a reform dynamic during the Benedictine centuries. In so many ways it was the monks as the intellectual leaders of the period who shaped the ideal of what a cleric should be. This was the ideal that became set in the program of the Gregorian reformers, a program which in numerous ways has remained normative for the Roman Catholic Church to this day. This was the program that guided the fathers at the Council of Trent in the sixteenth century in the creation of a fortress Catholicism, a church on the defensive.

Another council was called to reform the Catholic Church in 1959 by Pope John XXIII, a council summoned to bring the church into the late twentieth century, a council for *aggiornamento*. Its purpose was to open windows and permit the church to meet the needs of the modern world, to reform. Progressive churchmen like Karl Rahner, Hans Küng and Yves Congar played a central role in shaping its agenda and worked behind the scenes to help it achieve success. Père Congar in the introduction to the second edition of his master work *Vraie et fausse réforme dans l'église*, which appeared a few years after the conclusion of Vatican II, is suffused with the good cheer and enthusiasm of that period when the possibilities of *aggiornamento* seemed so wide and likely to succeed.[18]

Yet already the forces of reaction were gaining dominance, especially on the question of celibacy. As with the question of birth control, Pope Paul VI, who had succeeded John XXIII in 1963 and had presided over the latter part of the council, had taken the issue of celibacy off the conciliar agenda and was preparing a papal letter on the matter. In this encyclical of 1967, entitled *Sacerdotalis Caelibatus*, he proclaimed celibacy a jewel and required its continued observance for the clergy of the Roman Catholic Church.[19] He offers his historical perspective and some of his justification in the following passage: "From the beginning of the fourth century, the Church of the West strengthened, spread and confirmed the practice [clerical celibacy] by means of various provincial councils and through supreme pontiffs. More than anyone else, the supreme pastors and teachers of the Church of God, the guardians and interpreters of the patrimony of the faith and

of holy Christian practices, promoted, defended, and restored
ecclesiastical celibacy in successive eras of history, even when they met
opposition from the clergy itself and when the practices of a decadent
society did not favor the heroic demands of virtue."[20] One doubts that
Pope Gregory VII would have said it much differently. As Peter
Hebblethwaite notes in his excellent biography of Paul VI, the pope's
attempt to settle the issue only caused more difficulty and resulted in
great disappointment.[21] The numbers leaving the priesthood swelled and,
together with the unhappiness over his letter on birth control, resulted in
a deflating of the enthusiasm for reform resulting from Vatican II.[22]

This disillusionment has continued for many throughout the papacy
of John Paul II, who has strongly supported the tradition of celibacy and
rejected calls for change on the subject.[23] The historian George Williams
noted early in his papacy that John Paul was an advocate for a new
ascetical ideal for all Christians, one that emphasizes the sanctity of the
whole person and special emphasis on a Pauline celibacy for all priests.[24]
It is an observation that has become more true the longer this papacy has
lasted. His personal asceticism and strong emphasis on the necessity of
clerical celibacy and papal centralization clearly link him to such
eleventh-century reformers as Peter Damian and Pope Gregory VII.

But ultimately one must wonder how successful his efforts to stem
the tide of change will be. The winds that Pope John XXIII allowed to
enter the Roman Catholic Church continue to blow vigorously. The
role of the laity continues to increase, as they are forced to take on more
responsibilities in a church suffering so large a shortage of clergy.[25] As
more women recognize that they too are in the image of Christ and
should have a right to exercise their priesthood at the altar, one can
expect to hear them demand ever more insistently for what is their due.
As the Roman Catholic Church increasingly comes to recognize the
reality of its catholicity, one must expect the rapidly growing regional
churches in Latin America, Africa, and Asia to question Western
ecclesiastical customs that have little meaning for these areas. And as the
Roman Catholic Church in the new millennium reaches out to its
separated Christian brethren and to members of other religions on this
rapidly contracting planet, can it afford to cling to nonessential customs
that can only prove to be divisive? Will the Catholic Church of the new
millennium reform by following the Gregorian prescriptions on celibacy
and seek a more centrally unified Church, as Pope Paul VI and John
Paul II have preached? Or will the Catholic Church of the next

millennium follow a path of greater decentralization, one which might even make celibacy optional and dependent on the determination of the regional church? These are not questions that historians can answer but only ask. Whatever the answer, the issue of celibacy will remain of central importance for the foreseeable future, and a study of its evolution and practice requisite to an understanding of the history of the Roman Catholic Church and to its subsequent development.

NOTES

1. Y. Congar, *Fifty Years of Catholic Theology: Conversations with Yves Congar*, ed. B. Lauret and tr. J. Bowden (Philadelphia, 1988), 48.

2. It is clear that the problem of a shortage of priests is also found in the developing world, especially Latin America. See in general on the shortage of priests, R. A. Schoenherr and L. A. Young, *Full Pews and Empty Altars: Demographics of the Priest Shortage in the United States Catholic Dioceses* (Madison, Wisconsin, 1993), esp. 10-13 on the phenomenon as worldwide.

3. Schoenherr and Young, *Full Pews and Empty Altars*, 25.

4. Schoenherr and Young, *Full Pews and Empty Altars*, 25.

5. Schoenherr and Young, *Full Pews and Empty Altars*, preface, xvii.

6. See the comments on this point by T. Szulc, *Pope John Paul II: the Biography* (New York, 1995), 471.

7. On this point see in particular the useful survey by T. C. Fox, *Sexuality and Catholicism* (New York, 1995), especially chap. 10 entitled "Sex and Authority".

8. A. W. Sipe, *Sex, Priests and Power: Anatomy of a Crisis* (New York, 1995), chap. 7, "Priests and Men," esp. 136. See also Fox, *Sexuality and Catholicism*, ch. 5, "Homosexuality."

9. Sipe, *Sex, Priests and Power*, p. 75, claims that about six percent of U. S.

Catholic clergy have had sexual contact with minors. See also Fox, *Sexuality and Catholicism*, 189-197, who draws on Sipe's research.

10. D. R. Hoge, *The Future of Catholic Leadership: Responses to the Priest Shortage* (Kansas City, 1987), 122-29, esp. 126.

11. One of the best studies of the importance of the idea of reform in the history of the church, in particular as a study of the contributions of the Protestant theologians of the sixteenth century, remains Y. Congar, *Vraie et fausse réforme dans l'église*, 2nd ed. (Paris, 1968). Congar writes favorably, yet with a critical perspective, of the Protestant Reformation theme of *ecclesia semper reformata, semper reformanda*. See esp. 417-18. On the importance of Congar's study see Hans Küng, *The Council, Reform and Reunion*, trans. C. Hastings (New York, 1961), 53.

12. Küng, *Council, Reform and Reunion*, esp. 9, 12-37 and 51. Richard McBrien in his handbook *Catholicism* (San Francisco, 1994), 663 says of this work, "It was undoubtedly the single most influential book in the council's preparatory phase because it alerted so many people in the Catholic world to the possibilities for renewal and reform through the medium of Vatican II."

13. G. Ladner, *The Idea of Reform: Its Impact on Christian Thought and Action in the Age of the Fathers* (Cambridge, Mass., 1959). Of his other writings on reform and renewal particularly important are "Die mittelalterliche Reform-Idee," *Mitteilungen des Instituts für österreichische Geschichtsforschung*, 60 (1952), 31-59; "Gregory the Great and Gregory VII. A Comparison of their Concepts of Renewal," *Viator*, 4 (1973), 1-26; and "Terms and Ideas of Renewal," in *Renaissance and Renewal in the Twelfth Century*, eds. R. L. Benson and G. Constable (Cambridge, Mass., 1982), 1-33.

14. Gerd Tellenbach is surely correct in his recent book *The Church in Western Europe from the Tenth to the Early Twelfth Century*, trans. T. Reuter (Cambridge, 1993) to demand greater precision in the use of the word "reform" (p. 157) and to chastise scholars who find in the eleventh century late medieval or Protestant notions of *reformatio* or view the eleventh century as a reform period in opposition to the degenerate church of the tenth or early eleventh centuries (pp. 161-2). Anyone who has worked on the period between 900 and 1050 knows

how complex and vital so much of the ecclesiastical life of the period is. It is difficult to disagree with Tellenbach on p. 166 when he states, "One may thus say that the demand for clerical celibacy in the eleventh century was indeed a part of the ecclesiastical 'reform programme'; but it was neither new nor more easily enforced than in earlier periods."

15. In particular the essays in the second section of this book.

16. P. Jestice, p. 81.

17. Maureen Miller, *The Formation of a Medieval Church: Ecclesiastical Change in Verona, 950-1150* (Ithaca, NY, 1993).

18. Congar, *Vraie et fausse*, 7-14.

19. On this encyclical see the comments of Fox, *Sexuality and Catoblicism*, 181-82.

20. *The Papal Encyclicals 1958-1981*, ed. C. C. Ihm (Ann Arbor, 1990), CH. 36, P. 209.

21. P. Hebblethwaite, *Paul VI: The First Modern Pope* (New York, 1993), esp. 498.

22. On his letter on birth control, *Humanae Vitae*, see Fox, *Sexuality and Catholicism*, chap. 3, pp. 66-83.

23. Szulc, *Pope John Paul II*, 470-71.

24. G. H. Williams, *The Mind of John Paul II: Origins of His Thought and Action* (New York, 1981), 288-291.

25. Yet as Père Congar, *Fifty Years of Catholic Theology*, 48-50, states after commenting on the extraordinary way that the laity have helped to fill the vacuum created by the lack of priests, the fullness of Catholicism requires the presence of ordained priests.

Contributors

Paul Beaudette is an Assistant Professor in the Department of Religious Studies at Mount Saint Vincent University in Halifax, Nova Scotia. He received a B.A. from the University of Notre Dame in 1976, an M.Div. from the Toronto School of Theology in 1980, an M.Sc.Ed from Niagara University in 1986, and a Ph.D. from the Graduate Theological Union in Berkeley in 1994. He also served from 1982-1988 as an ordained priest.

Ute-Renate Blumenthal is Professor of history and Director of Medieval and Byzantine Studies at the Catholic University of America. She has written a number of articles on the papacy in the eleventh and twelfth centuries and is the author of *The Early Councils of Pope Paschal II, 1100-1110* and *The Investiture Controversy: Church and Monarchy from the Ninth to the Twelfth Century*. She also has edited the collection *Carolingian Essays* and is currently preparing a biography of Pope Gregory VII.

Daniel Callahan, Professor of history at the University of Delaware, received his Ph.D. in 1968 from the University of Wisconsin, Madison, where his major professor was David Herlihy. He has published articles on tenth- and eleventh-century spirituality, with a concentration on the writings of Ademar of Chabannes. His most recent pieces include, "The Manichaeans and the Antichrist in the Writings of Ademar of Chabannes: The Origins of Popular Heresy in the Medieval West and 'The Terrors of the Year 1000,'" *Studies in Medieval and Renaissance History* 15 (1995), 163-223 and "The Cult of St. Michael the Archangel and 'The Terrors of the Year 1000'" in *The Apocalyptic Year 1000:Religious Expectations and Social Change, ca. 950-1050*, eds. R. Landes and D. Van Meter, forthcoming. He is currently working on the book *The Making of a Millennial Pilgrim: Jerusalem and the Cross in the Life and Writings of Ademar of Chabannes*.

Herbert Edward John Cowdrey is Senior Research Fellow in Modern History, St. Edmund Hall, Oxford. He earned degrees at Trinity College, Oxford and has served as Fellow and Tutor in Modern History at St. Edmund Hall, Oxford. He is the author of numerous articles and reviews in learned journals and the author of *The Cluniacs and the Gregorian Reform*, *The Epistolae Vagantes of Pope Gregory VII*, and *The Age of Abbot Desiderius*. He is currently completing a full-length study of Pope Gregory VII.

Elizabeth Dachowski received her B.A. from Indiana University and her M.A. and Ph.D. in Medieval History from the University of Minnesota. She is currently revising her dissertation, on the political activities of Abbo of Fleury (d. 1004), for possible publication as a book. Her main area of interest is the intersection between religious institutions and the monarchy in tenth- and eleventh-century France. She is currently working on a study of the monasteries of northern Francia during the rise to power of the Robertian-Capetian dynasty, and is also pursuing research into the imitation of Porphyrian acrostic poetry in the early Middle Ages. Dachowski was a Fordham University Medieval Fellow for the 1996-97 academic year and currently holds a position teaching World and European history at Lock Haven University, in central Pennsylvania.

Michael Frassetto received a Fulbright-Hayes graduate fellowship to study in the German Democratic Republic in 1989-1990 and earned his Ph.D. from the University of Delaware in 1993. His dissertation addressed the sermons of Ademar of Chabannes and the origins of medieval heresy and his work continues to examine the sermons and their implications.

Francis G. Gentry is presently Professor of German at Penn State University. He has been Chair of the German department at the University of Wisconsin and Head of the German department at Penn State. He is a former president of the Medieval Association of the Midwest and is currently President of the Pennsylvania Chapter of the Alexander von Humboldt Association of America. He is the editor of numerous books and articles dealing with German literature with special concentration on Early Middle High German literature as well as the *Nibelungenlied*. Currently he is working on a book-length project dealing with the classical period of medieval German literature.

Phyllis G. Jestice (Ph.D. History and Humanities, Stanford University, 1989) is the author of *Wayward Monks and the Religious Revolution of the Eleventh Century* (Brill's Studies in Intellectual History, 1997). This work, as well as several articles, examine the changing roles of monks in society, especially the rise of new religious orders, to help understand the reform of Christian belief and practice in the eleventh century. She is currently working on a study of women regents in Ottonian Germany. She is Assistant Professor of history at the University of California, Davis.

Mayke de Jong (1950) was educated at the University of Amsterdam, and is presently Professor of Medieval History at Utrecht University. She has published on a range of early medieval topics, notably monasticism and political ritual. Recent publications include: In "Carolingian Monasticism: The Power of Prayer," in *The New Cambridge Medieval History* vol. II, ed. Rosamond McKitterick (Cambridge 1995), 622-53; *Samuel's Image: Child Oblation in the Early Medieval West* (Leiden/New York/Köln 1996); "What Was *Public* about Public Penance? *Paenitentia publica* and Justice in the Carolingian World," in *La Giustizia ne'll Alto Medioevo (secoli ix-xi)*, Settimane di Studio 44 (Spoleto 1997), 863-902.

Megan McLaughlin is Associate Professor of history and women's studies at the University of Illinois at Urbana-Champaign. She has written on the social and cultural significance of rituals for the dead, as well as on the history of women and gender in medieval Europe. The subject of her current research is the intersection of sexuality, gender, and authority in conflicts over church reform during the eleventh and early twelfth centuries.

Maureen C. Miller is Associate Professor of history at Hamilton College. A graduate of the American University, she received her M.A. degree from the Catholic University of America and her Ph.D. from Harvard University where she studied with the late David Herlihy. Her book, *The Formation of a Medieval Church: Ecclesiastical Change in Verona, 950-1150*, won the American Catholic Historical Association's John Gilmary Shea prize for the best book on Catholic history published in 1993. She is presently completing a new study entitled *The Bishop's Palace:*

Architecture, Episcopal Authority, and Clerical Culture in Medieval Italy.

R. I. Moore was educated at Oxford University, and has three children. He has taught medieval history at the Universities of Sheffield and Newcastle upon Tyne, where he is presently Professor of Medieval History, and was a visiting professor at the University of Chicago in 1989. His interest in popular heresy in the Middle Ages (*The Birth of Popular Heresy*, 1975; *The Origins of European Dissent*, 1977) has led him to reflect more broadly on the history of persecution (*The Formation of a Persecuting Society*, 1987) and latterly on comparative world history. He is currently working on a study of the transformation of European society in the eleventh century, and is Editor of the Blackwell History of the World.

Edward Peters is the Henry Charles Lea Professor of History at the University of Pennsylvania. His interests in ecclesiology focus chiefly on matters of ecclesiastical discipline and criminal law. His books, *Witchcraft in Europe, 1100-1700: A Documentary History* (with Alan C. Kors, 1972), *Heresy and Authority in Medieval Europe* (1980),and *Inquisition* (1988) reflect these interests.

Jane Tibbetts Schulenburg is Professor of History in the Department of Liberal Studies, Division of Continuing Studies, and Medieval Studies and Women's Studies at the University of Wisconsin-Madison. She has published several articles on women in medieval society and the Church. Her major study, *Forgetful of Their Sex: Female Sanctity and Society, ca. 500-1100* will be published fall 1997 by the University of Chicago Press. She is currently working on a book on medieval women and proscriptions of sacred space, 500-1200.

David C. Van Meter is a doctoral candidate at Boston University and is working on the religious history of northern France and Flanders in the eleventh and twelfth centuries. He has published several articles on that topic, most recently "Count Baldwin IV, Richard of Saint-Vanne, and the Inception of Monastic Reform in Eleventh-Century Flanders" in the *Revue bénédictine*. He is also the co-editor, with Richard Landes, of the forthcoming *The Apocalyptic Year 1000: Religious Expectations and Social Change in Western Europe, 968-1033*.

Index

DATE DUE

MAR 2 7 2000			
			Printed in USA

HIGHSMITH #45230